UPSSSC JE

Civil Engineering (Paper-2)

Latest Edition
Practice Kit

10 Tests
10 Mock Test

Based On Real Exam Pattern

✓ Thoroughly Revised and Updated

✓ Detailed Analysis of all MCQs

Title	: UPSSSC JE Civil Engineering (Paper-2)
Author Name	: Mr. Rohit Manglik
Published By	: EduGorilla Community Pvt. Ltd.
Publishers Address	: 12/651, First Floor Opp. Arvindo Park, Near Jama Masjid, Indira Nagar, Lucknow, Uttar Pradesh-226016, India

Copyright EduGorilla

ISBN : 978-93-90257-16-4

Second Edition

Disclaimer EduGorilla

ROHIT MANGLIK
CEO, EduGorilla

Dear Applicants,

People say *"Success comes to those who work hard."* But I've seen people working hard for their exams day in and day out for marginal success. While others succeed in their examinations by putting in just half the work. So are they God Gifted? No! I believe that it's because they work *smart* and not just *hard*. Similarly, for your exams, you should strategize your preparation so as to increase the likelihood of success. Well with EduGorilla get ready to increase your *chances of selection* in your exam by *16x*.

EduGorilla helps you in not only working *hard* but also working in a *smart and strategic* manner. With EduGorilla's preparation package, you get a chance to make your exam preparation easy, and a fun learning path towards selection. Finding the right path to your preparations can be difficult if you don't know in which direction to head. Don't worry, we have you covered! EduGorilla will be your guide to success in your journey. With our Preparation Package, you can prepare strategically and beat the exam in just one attempt.

EduGorilla's Preparation Package includes-

- **Test Series**
- **Books**

Our preparation package is handcrafted as per the latest changes, expert opinions, and students' discretion. Thus, enabling you to get through each stage of the selection process for your exam.

Our Books are designed by the teachers and experts of the respective exam with a combined 150+ years of experience; to provide you with easy, efficient, and effective learning. Our books are smart, in the sense that not only do they give you the answers to the questions but also provide similar questions for practice.

EduGorilla's competent Test Series gives you real-time experience and confidence through which you can clear your offline or online exam in just one attempt. We currently host 83,000+ mock tests for 1,440+ competitive and academic exams.

Thus, EduGorilla misses no chance to assist you in your preparation and covers all stages of the exam, so that you don't have to look anywhere else.

We provide complete preparation packages for defense, banking, teaching, and other National & State-Level exams. Hence, it doesn't matter which exam you aspire to because you will reach your success.

ALL THE BEST !

Let EduGorilla be your Guide to Success.

Rohit Manglik,
Founder and CEO, EduGorilla

INTRODUCTION

EduGorilla focuses on guiding students to succeed in their examinations. With that in mind, our book, titled "UPSSSC JE : Civil Engineering (Paper-2)", has been drafted through the collective efforts of our distinguished experts with 150+ years of combined experience. This book consists of questions that are created following the latest changes in the syllabus and exam pattern. We compiled the book on the basis of questions that are most likely to appear in the UPSSSC JE CE (Civil). Through EduGorilla's "UPSSSC JE : Civil Engineering (Paper-2)" your chances of success will increase 16x.

EduGorilla does this through our Complete Preparation Package. This package consists of well-conceptualized and structured content in the form of questions that are tailor-made according to your needs and will help you practice for exams in a smart way by pinpointing all the necessary information. It also provides hints and solutions, along with a smart answer sheet for your self-evaluation. You can assess your shortcomings and work accordingly on areas that may require more of your attention.

EduGorilla promises to help you succeed in your examination and accomplish your dream goals. We believe in our aspirants and see them at the top of the merit list. And the first step towards the top is to start preparing with us. EduGorilla's "UPSSSC JE : Civil Engineering (Paper-2)" includes the following attributes.

➤ Well-Researched Content

➤ Top-Notch Quality

➤ Detailed Answers and Analysis

➤ Smart Answer Sheet

➤ Exam Relevant Questions

Therefore, EduGorilla fortifies your preparation and makes it durable enough to help you stand tall and beat the examination.

UPSSSC JE CE (Civil)
Scan QR code for Eligibility, Exam Pattern, Syllabus and more.

Book ID: 0654

TABLE OF CONTENTS

Mock Test	1-152
Mock Test - 1	1-26
Mock Test - 2	27-43
Mock Test - 3	44-63
Mock Test - 4	64-77
Mock Test - 5	78-92
Mock Test - 6	93-104
Mock Test - 7	105-116
Mock Test - 8	117-127
Mock Test - 9	128-140
Mock Test - 10	141-152

Mock Test 01

Q.1 Which of the following effect of Fly ash on cement concrete is false?

A. Reduction in permeability of concrete
B. Reduces the amount of air-entraining agent
C. Increases the heat of hydration of cement
D. Slightly improves the resistance to sulphate attack

Q.2 A clay has an unconfined compressive strength of 240 kN/m^2 in an undisturbed state. The clay was then remolded and had unconfined compressive strength of 60 kN/m2. Based on the sensitivity of soil, it is classified as ______.

A. Little Sensitive
B. Sensitive
C. Extra sensitive
D. Quick

Q.3 The effective stress strength parameters of soil are c'= 10 kPa and ϕ = 30°, then shear strength on a plane within the saturated soil mass at a point where total normal stress is 300 KPa and pore water pressure is 150 KPa, will be ______.

A. 90.5 kPa
B. 96.6 kPa
C. 101.5 kPa
D. 105.5 kPa

Q.4 Most effective equipment for compacting granular soil such as sand, gravel, and crushed stone is ______.

A. Bull Dozers
B. Smooth wheel Rollers
C. Sheep-Foot Rollers
D. Pneumatic-tired Rollers

Q.5 The clay deposit of thickness 10 cm and void ratio 0.5 undergoes settlement and now its final void ratio is 0.2. The thickness (cm) of the settlement layer is ________.

A. 1
B. 1.5
C. 2
D. 2.5

Q.6 An excavation is made to the maximum possible depth in a clay soil having γt = 18 kN/m^3, C = 100 kN/m^2, Φ = 30°. The active earth pressure, according to Rankine's theory, at the base level of excavation is ____.

A. 115.47 kN/m^2
B. 54.36 kN/m^2
C. 27.18 kN/m^2
D. 13.25 kN/m^2

Q.7 Consider the following statements:
Ranking's theory and Coulomb's theory give the same value of coefficients of active and passive earth pressures when.

1. the retaining wall has a vertical back.

2. the backfill is cohesionless.

3. angle of slope of backfill is equal to the angle of friction.

4. angle of slope of backfill is 0°.

5. angle of wall friction is 0°.

6. angle of wall friction is equal to the angle of internal friction of soil.

Of these statements

A. 1, 2, 3 and 5 are correct
B. 1, 2, 4 and 5 are correct
C. 2, 3 and 6 are correct
D. 1, 4 and 6 are correct

Q.8 The coefficient of discharge of a venturimeter meter is ______.

A. lesser than nozzle meter
B. lesser than an orifice meter
C. greater than both the orifice meter and nozzle meter
D. lower than a nozzle meter but greater orifice meter

Q.9 Bernoulli's equation represents the total energy per unit of a certain quantity. That quantity is:

A. Energy per unit specific volume
B. Energy per unit mass
C. Energy per unit volume
D. Energy per unit weight

Q.10 At a sudden expansion,

A. The energy gradient line falls but the hydraulic gradient line rises
B. The energy gradient line is unaffected but the hydraulic gradient line falls
C. Both the energy gradient line and the hydraulic gradient line fall
D. The energy gradient line falls, but the hydraulic gradient line is unaffected

Q.11 A pitot tube is used to measure the velocity at a certain point in a water pipe. The differential pressure noted across pitot tapping is 1.962 kg/cm^2. The velocity of water in pipe is:

A. 1.962 m/sec
B. 19.62 m/sec
C. 9.81 m/sec
D. 4.905 m/sec

Q.12 Which one of the following is not a method of plane tabling?

A. Orientation
B. Radiation
C. Intersection
D. Resection

Q.13 For maximum transmission of power through a pipe with a total head, the total head loss due to friction hf is given by ______.

A. H/10
B. 2H/3
C. H/2
D. H/3

Q.14 When the water drawn from the central hole made in the wash hand basin, the type of flow of water is ____.

A. forced vortex
B. free vortex
C. tangential flow
D. transitional flow

Q.15 The value of the radial distance from the center line of the pipe at which the velocity would be equal to the average velocity of the laminar flow is.

A. 0.666 R
B. 0.696 R
C. 0.707 R
D. 0.727 R

Q.16 In an open channel flow, the discharge corresponding to critical depth is ______.

A. Minimum
B. Maximum

C. Zero **D.** Average

Q.17 What is a condition for a hydraulically efficient channel?
A. Minimum flow rate
B. Maximum wetted perimeter
C. Constant velocity
D. Minimum wetted perimeter

Q.18 For a given discharge in a horizontal frictionless channel, two depth may have the same specific energy. These two depths are known as ______.
A. alternate depths
B. conjugate depths
C. sequent depths
D. normal and critical depths

Q.19 Which of the following is the most accurate instrument for measuring stream velocity?
A. Twin float
B. Surface float
C. Partially submerged rod
D. Current meter

Q.20 The length of the hydraulic jump is.
A. 5 to 7 times the height of the jump
B. 3 times the height of the jump
C. more than 10 times the height of the jump
D. 12 times the height of the jump

Q.21 For a circular channel of diameter D, the depth of flow for maximum discharge is.
A. 0.70 D **B.** 0.61 D **C.** 0.95 D **D.** 0.81 D

Q.22 A rectangular open channel of width 5.0 m is carrying a discharge of 100 m³/s. The Froude number of the flow is 0.80. The depth of flow in the channel is.
A. 4 m **B.** 8 m **C.** 16 m **D.** 20 m

Q.23 A venturi flume is used to measure.
A. pressure of the liquid
B. discharge of liquid
C. pressure difference between two points in a channel
D. pressure difference between two points in a pipe

Q.24 The discharge over the rectangular weir is equal to:
A. $\frac{2}{3}Cd\sqrt{2gL}LH^{\frac{3}{2}}$ **B.** $\frac{3}{2}Cd\sqrt{2gL}LH^{\frac{3}{2}}$
C. $\frac{3}{2}Cd\sqrt{2gL}LH^{\frac{2}{3}}$ **D.** $\frac{2}{3}Cd\sqrt{2gL}LH^{\frac{2}{3}}$

Q.25 The specific speed of a turbine is the speed of an imaginary turbine, identical with the given turbine, which.
A. delivers unit discharge under unit head
B. delivers unit discharge under the unit speed
C. develops unit horsepower under unit head
D. develops unit horsepower under unit speed

Q.26 If the coefficient of discharge is 0.60 then the discharge over a right-angled notch is:
A. 0.417 H 5/2 **B.** 1.417 H 5/2
C. 4.171 H 5/2 **D.** 7.141 H 5/2

Q.27 A turbine generates the power of 150,000 kW while working at the speed of 300 rpm at the head of 100 m. What is the specific speed of the turbine?
A. 300 **B.** 340 **C.** 367 **D.** 452

Q.28 In the Sutro weir, the discharge of the weir is proportional to ___.
A. H¹ᐟ² **B.** H³ᐟ² **C.** H⁵ᐟ² **D.** H

Q.29 The turbine suitable for low heads and high flow rates is:
A. Pelton wheel **B.** Francis
C. Kaplan **D.** All of these

Q.30 Centrifugal pumps have which of the following advantages?
1. Low initial cost
2. Compact, occupying less floor space
3. Easy handling of highly viscous fluids
Select the correct answer using the options given below :
A. 1, 2 and 3 **B.** 1 and 2 only
C. 1 and 3 only **D.** 2 and 3 only

Q.31 The first watering which is given to a crop is called:
A. Base **B.** Duty **C.** Kor **D.** Delta

Q.32 Correct statement from the following is.
A. Crop period is slightly more than base period.
B. Base period is slightly more than crop period.
C. Crop period is equal to the base period.
D. Crop period and base period are expressed in hours.

Q.33 Given that the base period is 100 days and the duty of the canal is 1000 hectares per cumec, the depth of water will be:
A. 0.864 cm **B.** 8.64 cm
C. 86.4 cm **D.** 864 cm

Q.34 The field capacity of a soil is 25%, its permanent wilting point is 15% and specific dry unit weight is 1.5. If the depth of the root zone of a crop is 80 cm, the storage capacity of the soil is.
A. 8 cm **B.** 10 cm **C.** 12 cm **D.** 14 cm

Q.35 An identified source of irrigation water has ion concentrations of Na⁺, Ca⁺⁺ and Mg⁺⁺ as 28, 12 and 20 milli equivalents per litre, respectively. The SAR of this water is approximately:
A. 3 **B.** 4 **C.** 7 **D.** 9

Q.36 Outlet discharge for a particular crop is given by:
A. $\frac{Area}{Outlet\ factor}$ **B.** $\frac{Outlet\ factor}{Area}$
C. Area × outlet factor **D.** None of these

Q.37 Assertion (A): Duty of drip irrigation is very high.
Reason (R): Losses are least in drip irrigation.
A. Both Assertion (A) and Reason (R) are individually true and Reason (R) is the correct explanation of Assertion (A)
B. Both Assertion (A) and Reason (R) are individually true but Reason (R) is NOT the correct explanation of Assertion (A)
C. Assertion (A) is true but Reason (R) is false
D. Assertion (A) is false but Reason (R) is true

Q.38 In an irrigated field, the net irrigation requirement is 15 cm, the application efficiency is 80% and water conveyance efficiency is 60%. What is the gross irrigation requirement (in cm)?

A. 11.25　　　**B.** 18.75　　　**C.** 25　　　**D.** 31.25

Q.39 Because of large stream discharge, _______ irrigation is more suitable for permeable soil.

A. Free flooding　　　　　**B.** Check flooding
C. Check basin　　　　　　**D.** Furrow

Q.40 According to Lacey, the bed slope is given by _______.
f is silt factor and Q is discharge in m³.

A. $\dfrac{f^{\frac{4}{3}}}{3340Q^{\frac{1}{2}}}$　　**B.** $\dfrac{f^{\frac{2}{3}}}{3340Q^{\frac{1}{4}}}$　　**C.** $\dfrac{f^{\frac{5}{3}}}{3340Q^{\frac{1}{6}}}$　　**D.** $\dfrac{f^{\frac{1}{3}}}{3340Q^{\frac{5}{3}}}$

Q.41 Force considered for the analysis of an elementary profile of a gravity dam under empty reservoir condition are.

A. Uplift pressure　　　　　**B.** Water pressure
C. Self-weight　　　　　　　**D.** Wave pressure

Q.42 The maximum possible height of a safe dam having an elementary profile is _______.
f = allowable stress of dam material, G = specific gravity of dam material, and w = Unit weight of water

A. $\dfrac{f}{w\sqrt{G+1}}$　　**B.** $\dfrac{f}{w\sqrt{G}}$　　**C.** $\dfrac{f}{w(G+1)}$　　**D.** $\dfrac{f}{w\sqrt{G-1}}$

Q.43 An irrigation outlet is said to be proportional when its:

A. Sensitivity = 1　　　　　**B.** Flexibility = 1
C. Setting = 1　　　　　　　**D.** all of the above

Q.44 If the sensitivity of an irrigation module is 0.5 then what per cent variation in outlet discharge will be caused by a 50 % variation in canal water depth?

A. 100%　　　**B.** 50%　　　**C.** 25%　　　**D.** 12.5%

Q.45 The volume of water held by a natural stream channel is known as.

A. Bank storage　　　　　　**B.** Useful storage
C. Valley storage　　　　　**D.** Surcharge storage

Q.46 The lining of a canal is necessary:
A. To minimise the seepage losses in a canal
B. To prevent erosion of bed and slopes due to high velocity
C. To increase the discharge in canal section by an increment of velocity

A. Only A　　　　　　　　　**B.** Only B
C. A and C　　　　　　　　　**D.** A, B and C

Q.47 The normal annual precipitation at stations X, A, B, and C are 700 mm, 1000 mm, 900 mm and 800 mm respectively. If the storm precipitation at three station A, B and C were 100 mm, 90 mm and 80 mm respectively, then the storm precipitation for station X will be.

A. 70 mm　　　**B.** 80 mm　　　**C.** 90 mm　　　**D.** 105 mm

Q.48 The area between the isohyets 45 cm and 55 cm is 100 square km and between 55 cm and 65 cm is 150 square km. The average depth of annual precipitation over the above basin of 250 square km will be.

A. 50 cm　　　**B.** 55 cm　　　**C.** 56 cm　　　**D.** 60 cm

Q.49 If the seepage pressure is equal to the submerged weight of the mass of the soil, then the effective stress is _______.

A. Remains the same　　　　**B.** Becomes zero
C. Becomes unity　　　　　　**D.** Becomes maximum

Q.50 Meyer's formula is an empirical formula used to determine?

A. Transpiration
B. Evaporation losses
C. Infiltration capacities
D. None of the above

Q.51 If the catchment area is 100 Sq. km and the value of constant is 12.47, then the maximum flood discharge as per Dicken's formula is.

A. Q = 12.47 × 100²ᐟ³ 　　　**B.** Q = 100 × 12.47³ᐟ⁴
C. Q = 100 × 12.47²ᐟ³ 　　　**D.** Q = 12.47 × 100³ᐟ⁴

Q.52 If a structure with a useful life period N year is designed for a Tr year flood, then risk in the design is given by.

A. $\dfrac{1}{T_r}$　　　　　　　　**B.** $\left(\dfrac{1}{T_r}\right)^{N}$

C. $1-\left(1-\dfrac{1}{T_r}\right)^{N}$　　**D.** $\left(1-\dfrac{1}{T_r}\right)^{N}$

Q.53 A 4-hour rainfall in a catchment of 250 sq. km, produces rainfall depths of 6.2 cm and 5.0 cm in successive 2-hour unit period. Assuming the φ index of the soil to be 1.2 cm per hour, the runoff volume in hectare meter will be.

A. 16　　　**B.** 22　　　**C.** 1600　　　**D.** 2200

Q.54 A 8 hours unit hydrograph of catchment is triangular in shape with base width of 64 hours and peak ordinate of 20 m3/s. the equilibrium discharge of S-curve obtained by using this 8-hour unit hydrograph is.

A. 60 m³/s　　**B.** 80 m³/s　　**C.** 100 m³/s　　**D.** 800 m³/s

Q.55 Which of the following admixtures are called water reducers?

A. Plasticizer
B. Waterproofing agents
C. Retarders
D. Accelerators

Q.56 The main object of providing a camber is.

A. to make the road surface impervious
B. to make the road surface durable
C. to drain off rainwater from the road surface, as quickly as possible
D. all the above

Q.57 The ruling gradient in a hill road is 6% and a horizontal curve is provided for a radius of 75 meters. The compensated gradient of the road will be.

A. 3%　　　**B.** 4%　　　**C.** 5%　　　**D.** 6%

Q.58 A pavement of width 14 m on a horizontal curve of radius 250 m. If the longest wheelbase of vehicle expected on the road is 7.0 m, then the mechanical widening required for the curve will be.

A. 0.18 m   **B.** 0.25 m   **C.** 0.39 m   **D.** 0.51 m

Q.59 What will be the shift of the transition curve, if the length of the transition curve is 80 m and a radius of the curve is 300 m?

A. 0.011   **B.** 0.78   **C.** 0.89   **D.** 21.33

Q.60 Minimum desirable radius of curvature for horizontal curve at a design speed of 50 km/hour in urban areas is.

A. 60.0 m   **B.** 80.0 m   **C.** 100.0 m   **D.** 125.5 m

Q.61 If the length of the transition curve is 65 m, the radius is 300 m and the velocity is 80 kmph, then the rate of change radial acceleration of transition curve will be.

A. 80.0 cm/s^3 **B.** 56.2 cm/s^3
C. 41.3 cm/s^3 **D.** 40.2 cm/s^3

Q.62 If the vertical curve connects a 1% upgrade with 1.4% downgrade, and the rate of change of grade is to be 0.06% per 20 m stations, the length of a vertical curve is.

A. 133.3 m   **B.** 40 m   **C.** 400 m   **D.** 800 m

Q.63 Assuming the safe stopping sight distance to be 80 m on a flat highway section and with the radius of the negotiable horizontal curve is 125. What would be the required setback distance? (Take length of circular curve greater than safe stopping sight distance).

A. 5.12 m   **B.** 8.75 m   **C.** 7.56 m   **D.** 6.35 m

Q.64 The attrition test on stones is performed:

A. To determine the crushing strength of the stone
B. For assessing the resistance of stone to the sun, rain, wind etc.
C. To ascertain the stability of the stone when exposed to acid fumes
D. For determining the rate of wear of stone due to grinding action under traffic

Q.65 A first-class brick should not absorb more than _______ of its dry weight after 24 hours immersion in normal water.

A. 10%   **B.** 15%   **C.** 20%   **D.** 25%

Q.66 Fillet welds are designed to resist:

A. Tensile stress   **B.** Shear stress
C. Compressive stress   **D.** Torsional stress

Q.67 Which of the following is the reason for the decrease in the use of stones as building material?

A. Steel and R.C.C. are less bulky and more durable
B. Strength of stones cannot be rationally analyzed
C. Stones are not conveniently available in plains
D. All options are correct

Q.68 Which of the following is the main composition of granite?

A. Quartz, feldspar and mica
B. Quartz, and lime
C. Quartz, and silica
D. Silica, lime and alumina

Q.69 The average crushing and tensile strength of hand molded bricks in kN/m^2 is:

A. 60000 and 2000   **B.** 50000 and 1000
C. 55000 and 1500   **D.** 65000 and 2500

Q.70 The tension coefficient of a member indicates the:

A. Force per unit displacement
B. Force per unit length of the member
C. Force in a member
D. Shear in a member

Q.71 Which of the following tests are used for testing of tiles?

1. breaking strength test
2. impact test
3. transverse strength test
4. water absorption test

A. 1 and 3 only   **B.** 1, 2 and 3 only
C. 1, 2 and 4 only   **D.** 1, 2, 3 and 4

Q.72 Which of the following is softwood?

A. Deodar   **B.** Teak
C. Sal   **D.** Mahogany

Q.73 Which test represents the temperature at which the bitumen attains a particular degree of softening?

A. Flash and Fire Point Test
B. Spot Test
C. Softening Point Test
D. Float Test

Q.74 Consider the following statements with respect to defects of timber and identify the correct one:

A. Chip mark is the defect arises due to conversion of timber.
B. Brown rot is the defect arises due to conversion of timber.
C. Chip mark is the defect arises due to Fungi.
D. Bow is the type of defect arises due to Natural forces.

Q.75 In a hot bituminous plant, while liquid asphalt is combined with the aggregate for mixing, the temperature of the asphalt should be in the range of.

A. 300°F   **B.** 300°C   **C.** 500°F   **D.** 500°C

Q.76 The detachment of the paint film from the surface is known as _______.

A. Chalking   **B.** Cracking
C. Flaking   **D.** Wrinkling

Q.77 Percentage of free carbon in bitumen is.

A. more than that in tar   **B.** less than that in tar
C. equal to that in tar   **D.** none of the above

Q.78 Synthetic rubber paints are prepared from:

A. Resin   **B.** Rubber
C. Synthetic fibres   **D.** Polyvinyl Chloride

Q.79 The ingredient of paint which gives it, the binding property and helps to spread the paint evenly and uniformly on the surface is _______.

A. Base   **B.** Vehicle   **C.** Solvent   **D.** Filler

Q.80 Solution of natural or synthetic resin in a volatile solvent is known as:

A. Lacquer **B.** Enamel Paints
C. Driers **D.** Pigment

Q.81 What do you mean by 'Ware house pack' of cement?
A. full capacity of the warehouse
B. pressure exertion of the bags of upper layers
C. pressure compaction of the bags on lower layers
D. packing the ware house

Q.82 To obtain cement dry powder, limestones and shales or their slurry is burnt in a rotary kiln at a temperature between?
A. 1100° and 1200°C **B.** 1200° and 1300°C
C. 1300° and 1400°C **D.** 1400° and 1500°C

Q.83 The approximate composition of iron oxide in ordinary portland cement is about _____.
A. 3% to 8% **B.** less than 0.5%
C. less than 1.3% **D.** 0.5% to 6%

Q.84 Which of the below is not a property of ferro cement?
A. Impervious nature
B. Capacity to resist shock
C. No need of formwork
D. Strength per unit mass is low

Q.85 _______ is added to make white concrete.
A. Fly ash **B.** Metakaolin
C. Rise husk **D.** Pigments

Q.86 Pozzolana is essentially a siliceous material containing clay up to.
A. 20% **B.** 40% **C.** 60% **D.** 80%

Q.87 An excess of free lime in Portland cement
A. results in an increase in the strength
B. increases the initial setting time
C. causes unsoundness in the product
D. improves the quality of product

Q.88 For the repair of roads:
A. low-heat cement is used
B. rapid-hardening cement is used
C. high-alumina cement is used
D. sulphate-resisting cement is used

Q.89 If 1500 g of cement is required to have 1875 g cement paste of normal consistency, the percentage of water is _____.
A. 20% **B.** 25% **C.** 30% **D.** 35%

Q.90 An aggregate is said to be flaky if its least dimension is less than.
A. 1/5th of the mean dimension
B. 2/5th of the mean dimension
C. 3/5th of the mean dimension
D. 4/5th of the mean dimension

Q.91 Bulking of sand occurs in the moisture content of _____.
A. 3% **B.** 5% **C.** 10% **D.** 12%

Q.92 The concrete in which preliminary test are performed for designing the mix are called:

A. Rich concrete **B.** Controlled concrete
C. lean concrete **D.** Ordinary concrete

Q.93 Crushing strength test on aggregates used for highway is dealt by _____.
A. IS : 2386 (part 1) -1963
B. IS : 2386 (part 2) -1963
C. IS : 2386 (part 3) -1963
D. IS : 2386 (part 4) -1963

Q.94 The maximum total quantity of dry aggregate by mass per 50 kg of cement, to be taken as the sum of the individual masses of fine and coarse aggregates (kg), for M20 Grade of concrete, is.
A. 625 **B.** 480 **C.** 330 **D.** 225

Q.95 Which type of "Bogue compound" will control the sulphate attack?
A. C_4AF **B.** C_3A **C.** C_3S **D.** C_2S

Q.96 Generally, the ratio of different ingredients (Cement Sand and aggregate) in a concrete mix of grade M 20 is:
A. 1: 2: 5 **B.** 1: 1.5: 3 **C.** 1: 3: 6 **D.** 1: 1: 2

Q.97 Grading of sand causes great variation in?
A. workability of concrete
B. strength of concrete
C. durability of concrete
D. All option are correct

Q.98 A concrete sample with a compaction factor of 0.92 is classified as _______.
A. Flowing concrete having high workability
B. Plastic concrete having medium workability
C. Stiff plastic concrete having low workability
D. Stiff concrete having very low workability

Q.99 Which of the following handbook deals with the design and specification of different concrete mixes?
A. SP 16: 1980 **B.** SP 23: 1982
C. SP 24: 1983 **D.** SP 54: 1987

Q.100 In small works, concrete is transported using:
A. Conveyer belts **B.** Pumps
C. Pans **D.** Buckets

Q.101 Segregation in cement concrete is defined as _______.
A. separation of coarser particles from mix
B. appearance of cement and water slurry surface of finished concrete
C. formation of capillary pores in fresh cement concrete
D. none of above

Q.102 Which process comes after batching in manufacture process of concrete?
A. Transportation **B.** Placing
C. Mixing **D.** Compacting

Q.103 What percentage of the fine aggregate of fineness modulus 2.5 is to be combined with the coarse aggregate of fineness modulus 4.1 for obtaining a combined aggregate of fineness modulus 3.5?

A. 20 **B.** 30 **C.** 40 **D.** 60

Q.104 Match the following List – I (Concrete carrier) with List-II (Suitability) and select the correct option.

List -I (Concrete carrier)	List-II (Suitability)
A. Chute	1. Suitable for transporting concrete from ground level to multi-story building.
B. Transit Mixer	2. Suitable for conveying concrete for a shorter distance
C. Skip and Hoist	3. Suitable for conveying concrete for longer distance
D. Belt and Conveyors	4. Suitable for transporting concrete from ground level to lower level

A. A – 1, B – 2, C – 3, D – 4
B. A – 2, B – 3, C – 4, D – 2
C. A – 4, B – 3, C – 1, D – 2
D. A – 1, B – 2, C – 4, D – 3

Q.105 The difference in shrinkage between surface and interior of concrete results in:

A. Efflorescence **B.** Crazing
C. Segregation **D.** Bleeding

Q.106 Which of the following refers to the process of proper and accurate measurement of concrete ingredients for uniformity of proportion?

A. grading **B.** curing **C.** Mixing **D.** Batching

Q.107 How are concrete mixers specified?

A. by the number of cement bags used in a batch
B. by the nominal volume of concrete that can be mixed in a batch
C. by the volume of water used
D. by the volume of aggregate used

Q.108 The ultrasonic test for hardened concrete of good quality is indicated if the pulse velocity is:

A. Below 3.0 km/s
B. Between 3.0 to 3.5 km/s
C. Above 3.5 km/s
D. Above 4.5 km/s

Q.109 The process of removing the irregularities from the surface of concrete left after screeding is called?

A. floating **B.** curing
C. trowelling **D.** none of these

Q.110 Aerated concrete is produced by the addition of:

A. Zinc sulphate
B. Magnesium sulphate
C. Powdered aluminium
D. Sodium nitrate

Q.111 The light-weight aggregate concrete density can be as low as?

A. 200 kg/m³ **B.** 250 kg/m³
C. 300 kg/m³ **D.** 400 kg/m³

Q.112 Soil scientist collects unsaturated $200\ cm^3$ sample of soil having weight $220\ g$. if the dried weight of soil is $180\ g$. then, find the water content available in the soil.

A. 0.222 **B.** 0.176 **C.** 0.133 **D.** 0.166

Q.113 Density of No fines concrete is about ________.

A. 300 – 1200 kg/m³ **B.** 1600 – 2000 kg/m³
C. 2000 – 3200 kg/m³ **D.** 3200 – 4000 kg/m³

Q.114 The process of striking off the excess concrete to bring the top surface up to proper grade is known as:

A. Trowelling **B.** Floating
C. Screeding **D.** None of the above

Q.115 The addition of surfactants in the concrete mix results in:

(i). Increase in the water cement ratio

(ii). Decrease in the water cement ratio

(iii). Increase in the strength of concrete

(iv). Decrease in the curing duration

(v). Increase in the density of concrete

Which one of the following statements is correct?

A. iii, iv and v **B.** ii, iii and v
C. i, iii and iv **D.** i and iv only

Q.116 The fiber-reinforced concrete is mainly employed to increase the?

A. Compressive strength of the concrete
B. Tensile strength of the concrete
C. Dynamic modulus of elasticity
D. Permeability of the concrete

Q.117 The volume of aggregate in self-compacted concrete is?

A. 50 to 60% **B.** 40 to 50%
C. 60 to 70% **D.** 30 to 40%

Q.118 Plinth area should not include ______.

A. stair cover (mumty) **B.** area of porch
C. lift well **D.** balcony

Q.119 Contingency fund generally forms _____ of the estimated cost.

A. 1% to 3% **B.** 3% to 5%
C. 5% to 8% **D.** 8% to 10%

Q.120 For 2.5 cubic meter thick cement concrete (1: 2: 4) damp-proof-course, the number of stone chips required will be:

A. 2 m³ **B.** 2.2 m³ **C.** 2.5 m³ **D.** 2.8 m³

Q.121 Accuracy in measurement of the area should be _____.

A. 1 square centimetre
B. 10 square centimetre
C. 100 square centimetre
D. 1 square meter

Q.122 Cost of electrification is approximate _____ of the building cost.

A. 4% to 5% **B.** 5% to 7%
C. 7% to 9% **D.** 9% to 12%

Q.123 A cable-supported at two ends primarily resists external loads by:

A. Bending
B. Compression
C. Tension
D. Bending and compression

Q.124 Partition of specified thickness is measured in _____.

A. Numbers
B. running metres
C. square metres
D. cubic metres

Q.125 The brickwork is measured in a square meter, in case of?

A. Honeycomb brickwork
B. Brick flat soling
C. Half brick walls or the partition
D. All options are correct

// Smart Answer Sheet //

Correct — Percentage of students who answered correctly.　**Skipped** — Percentage of students who skipped.

Q.	Ans.	Correct / Skipped	Q.	Ans.	Correct / Skipped	Q.	Ans.	Correct / Skipped	Q.	Ans.	Correct / Skipped	Q.	Ans.	Correct / Skipped
1	C	39.76 % / 12.98 %	17	D	24.54 % / 32.66 %	33	C	26.77 % / 12.58 %	49	B	24.34 % / 38.74 %	65	C	49.7 % / 29.2 %
2	B	21.3 % / 30.83 %	18	A	7.3 % / 33.27 %	34	C	13.39 % / 36.31 %	50	B	19.88 % / 31.24 %	66	B	36.92 % / 30.42 %
3	B	17.65 % / 28.8 %	19	D	32.45 % / 14.2 %	35	C	18.66 % / 32.25 %	51	D	17.24 % / 27.99 %	67	D	49.09 % / 31.44 %
4	B	20.89 % / 30.43 %	20	A	26.57 % / 24.14 %	36	A	19.27 % / 26.57 %	52	C	27.38 % / 25.97 %	68	A	41.18 % / 31.84 %
5	C	12.17 % / 37.53 %	21	C	46.45 % / 18.05 %	37	A	28.8 % / 33.27 %	53	C	10.75 % / 40.37 %	69	A	16.43 % / 35.29 %
6	A	4.06 % / 34.48 %	22	A	6.49 % / 36.11 %	38	D	9.53 % / 35.5 %	54	B	8.72 % / 36.11 %	70	B	24.95 % / 32.25 %
7	B	12.98 % / 35.09 %	23	B	49.49 % / 10.35 %	39	B	16.23 % / 33.06 %	55	A	18.05 % / 26.98 %	71	D	38.13 % / 14.2 %
8	C	33.47 % / 31.03 %	24	A	40.37 % / 30.83 %	40	C	24.34 % / 33.27 %	56	C	31.24 % / 31.03 %	72	A	40.16 % / 22.72 %
9	D	25.96 % / 32.05 %	25	C	14.6 % / 35.91 %	41	C	40.16 % / 21.3 %	57	C	18.05 % / 36.31 %	73	C	34.48 % / 32.86 %
10	A	15.21 % / 31.65 %	26	B	20.08 % / 34.28 %	42	C	12.78 % / 33.67 %	58	C	11.16 % / 36.1 %	74	A	18.26 % / 32.86 %
11	B	14.4 % / 33.06 %	27	C	11.56 % / 23.73 %	43	B	12.37 % / 26.58 %	59	C	25.15 % / 31.44 %	75	A	12.17 % / 33.67 %
12	A	22.11 % / 34.89 %	28	D	16.23 % / 32.25 %	44	C	12.37 % / 36.11 %	60	D	10.75 % / 27.59 %	76	C	36.51 % / 27.99 %
13	D	25.56 % / 22.31 %	29	C	25.96 % / 21.1 %	45	C	22.52 % / 23.12 %	61	B	9.94 % / 39.35 %	77	B	27.38 % / 32.66 %
14	B	39.55 % / 30.23 %	30	A	20.08 % / 29.41 %	46	D	42.6 % / 30.63 %	62	D	7.71 % / 36.31 %	78	A	18.05 % / 31.04 %
15	C	33.47 % / 28.6 %	31	C	51.32 % / 25.96 %	47	A	12.37 % / 34.08 %	63	D	3.04 % / 35.5 %	79	B	34.89 % / 15.01 %
16	B	37.93 % / 26.37 %	32	A	28.8 % / 25.97 %	48	C	10.34 % / 38.75 %	64	D	37.32 % / 32.05 %	80	A	22.31 % / 24.95 %

Q.	Ans.	Correct / Skipped	Q.	Ans.	Correct / Skipped	Q.	Ans.	Correct / Skipped	Q.	Ans.	Correct / Skipped	Q.	Ans.	Correct / Skipped
81	C	26.17 % / 22.51 %	90	C	47.06 % / 31.24 %	99	B	11.36 % / 32.05 %	108	B	21.1 % / 34.28 %	117	A	24.95 % / 19.27 %
82	D	36.31 % / 28.6 %	91	B	46.45 % / 32.45 %	100	C	45.84 % / 26.17 %	109	A	34.69 % / 21.9 %	118	D	29.21 % / 29.41 %
83	D	26.98 % / 31.44 %	92	B	34.89 % / 32.86 %	101	A	49.7 % / 32.25 %	110	C	27.59 % / 31.44 %	119	B	45.84 % / 18.05 %
84	D	18.46 % / 29.61 %	93	D	7.71 % / 26.57 %	102	C	42.39 % / 31.65 %	111	C	15.21 % / 18.06 %	120	B	25.56 % / 27.58 %
85	B	23.94 % / 32.65 %	94	D	18.26 % / 34.28 %	103	D	13.79 % / 37.73 %	112	A	35.29 % / 30.63 %	121	C	27.18 % / 22.31 %
86	D	10.55 % / 31.44 %	95	B	20.89 % / 27.99 %	104	C	29.21 % / 30.63 %	113	B	29.41 % / 20.49 %	122	C	30.43 % / 31.44 %
87	C	39.35 % / 32.05 %	96	B	60.24 % / 27.39 %	105	B	30.83 % / 32.66 %	114	C	32.25 % / 30.83 %	123	C	29.82 % / 26.57 %
88	B	47.26 % / 31.04 %	97	D	50.91 % / 32.86 %	106	D	27.99 % / 31.85 %	115	B	21.7 % / 30.84 %	124	C	38.34 % / 33.47 %
89	B	29.21 % / 33.87 %	98	B	24.14 % / 31.84 %	107	B	40.77 % / 25.96 %	116	B	27.18 % / 31.44 %	125	D	46.45 % / 33.47 %

//Hints and Solutions//

1. The effect of fly ash on cement concrete is not that the heat of hydration of cement will increase. The effects of fly ash on cement concrete are as follows:

- Permeability of concrete reduces.
- Improves resistance of concrete to sulphate attack
- Reduces heat of hydration in concrete such that substitution of 30% fly ash results in the reduction of 50-60% of the heat of hydration.
- Reduces the amount of air-entraining agent
- Increases the initial setting time such that 30% substitution can increase setting time upto 2 hours.
- Coarser fly ashes having high carbon content are more liable to increase dry shrinkage than finer fly ashes having low carbon content.
- The modulus of elasticity of altered concrete is lower at early ages but higher at later ages.
- Lesser compressive strength at early ages but equal strength at later ages.

Hence, the correct option is (C).

2. The sensitivity of the soil is given by:

$$S = q_u / q_r$$

q_u = unconfined compressive strength of soil in undisturbed state

$$= 240 kN/m^2$$

qr = unconfined compressive strength of soil in remolded state =

$$60 kN/m^2$$
$$s = 240/60 = 4$$

Classification of Soil based on Sensitivity:

Sensitivity	Nature of oil
Less than 1	Insensitive
1 to 2	Little Sensitive
2 to 4	Moderately Sensitive
4 to 8	Sensitive
8 to 16	Extra sensitive
>16	Quick

∵ Sensitivity $(S) = 4$

∴ Soil is classified as Sensitive

3. Concept:
Terzaghi established that the normal stresses which control the shear strength of the soil are effective stresses. Therefore, the shear strength of the soil can be written as

Shear strength, $S = c' + \sigma^- \tan$

where c' = cohesion intercept in terms of effective stress

ϕ' = the angle of shearing resistance in terms of effective stress

σ^- = effective normal stress

Given:

$$c' = 10 kPa$$
$$\varphi = 30°$$

$$\sigma = 300 kPa$$
$$u = 150 kPa$$

Calculations:

$$\sigma^- = \sigma - u = 300 - 150 = 150 kPa$$
$$S = 10 + (150) \times \tan 30°$$
$$= 96.6 KPa$$

4. Smooth wheel Rollers: These are plain steel rollers, self-propelled type, weighing fro, 5 to 15 tonnes and are used for ordinary rolling work where deep compaction is not required. It is most suitable for compacting granular such as sand, gravel or crushed stones.

Sheep-Foot Roller: These consists of a hollow steel drum, and have projected feet or projections mounted on the surface. It is required for compacting earthwork in embankments and canals where compaction deep into the layer of Earth is required. It is suitable for cohesive and impervious soil.

Pneumatic-tired Roller: It is suited for compacting fine-grained and well-graded sand.

5. The void ratio is the ratio of the volume of voids to the volume of solids in a soil sample. It is denoted by 'e'.

The volume of solids remains the same in both the conditions

Therefore, $V_s = V/(1+e)$

Where V_s = volume of solids, V = volume of soil, e = void ratio

$V_s = V_1/(1+e_1) = V_2/(1+e_2)$

Also $H_1/(1+e_1) = H_2/(1+e_2)$ (Since V = A x H and taking Area as constant)

H_1 = 10 cm

H_2 = 10 cm × 1+0.2/1+0.5 = 8 cm

$\Delta H = H_1 - H_2 = 10 - 8 = 2$ cm

6. Concept:
Critical depth/Unsupported vertical cut (Hc): It is the depth up to which vertical excavation of cohesive soil can stand without any lateral support.

$$H_c = 4C / y\sqrt{k}a$$

Active earth pressure $\Rightarrow P_a = k_a \times \sigma_v - 2C\sqrt{k}_a$

Where:

Z_c = Tension crack depth

k_a = Rankine's coefficient of active earth pressure

$\sigma_v = y \times H_c$

C = Cohesion

Calculation:

$$k_a = (1 - \sin 30)/(1 + \sin 30) = 1/3$$
$$H_c = 4 \times 100/18 \times \sqrt{1}/3 = 38.49 m$$
$$= 115.47 kN/m^2$$

∴ The active earth pressure, according to Rankine's theory, at the base level of excavation is $115.47 kN/m^2$.

7. Assumptions made by Rankine for the derivation of Earth Pressure are as follows:

1. The soil mass is homogenous and semi-infinite.

2. The soil is dry and cohesionless.

3. The ground surface is a plane, which may be horizontal or vertical.

4. The back of the retaining wall is smooth and vertical.

5. The soil element is in a state of plastic equilibrium.

Assumptions made by Coulomb's for the determination of Earth Pressure are as follows:

1. The backfill is a dry, cohesionless, homogenous, isotropic and ideally plastic material.

2. The slip surface is plane surface which passes through the heel of the wall.

3. The wall surface is rough. The resultant earth pressure on the wall is inclined at an angle δ to the normal wall, where δ is the angle of the friction of the wall and the backfill.

4. The sliding wedge itself acts as a rigid body.

By observing the assumptions of the two theories, it can be fairly understood that Rankine's theory and Coulomb's Theory give same value of coefficients of active and passive earth pressures when the retaining wall has a vertical back, backfill is cohesionless, angle of slope of backfill is 0° and angle of wall friction is 0°.

8. Coefficient of discharge is the ratio of actual discharge to the theoretical discharge.

Coefficient of discharge

⇒ Venturimeter – 0.95 to 0.98

⇒ Orifice meter – 0.62 to 0.65

⇒ Nozzle meter – 0.93 to 0.98

∴ Coefficient of discharge for venturi meter lies is higher than the nozzle meter and orifice meter.

Confusion Point:

Although the maximum value of the coefficient of discharge of nozzle meter and venturi meter appears to be same, the average value of the coefficient of discharge of venturi meter is more than nozzle meter.

9. Bernoulli's principle can be derived from the principle of conservation of energy.

The Bernoulli's theorem states that, in a steady flow, the sum of all forms of energy in a fluid along a streamline is the same at all points on that streamline

Bernoulli equation represented in head form (the total energy per unit weight):

P/ρg + v2/2g + Z = Constant

Where,

p/ρg = pressure head

V2/ρg= velocity head

Z = datum head

10. Hydraulic gradient Line (H.G.L) – Line representing the sum of pressure head and datum head.

Total energy line (T.E.L) – Line representing the sum of pressure head, datum head, and velocity head.

At a sudden expansion,

Diameter at a section suddenly increases to a larger one, which leads to the reduction in the velocity and so there is a sudden rise in the pressure.

⇒ Velocity decreased → Velocity head reduces, Pressure increased → Pressure head rises.

∴ The energy gradient line falls but the hydraulic gradient line rises.

Hence, the correct option is (A).

11. A pitot tube is a right-angled glass tube, large enough for capillary effects to be negligible, is used for the purpose. One end of the tube faces the flow while the other end is open to the atmosphere.

Since the static pressure, under this situation, is equal to the hydrostatic pressure due to its depth below the free surface, the difference in level between the liquid in the glass tube and the free surface becomes the measure of dynamic pressure. Therefore, we can write, neglecting friction.

$$p_o - p = \frac{\rho V^2}{2} = h\rho g$$

$$V = \sqrt{2gh}$$

where p_0, p and V are the stagnation pressure, static pressure and velocity respectively at point.

Here given:

$$\frac{p_o - p}{g} = 1.962\,\frac{kg}{cm^2} = 1.962 \times 10^4\,\frac{kg}{m^2}$$

$$V = \sqrt{\frac{2(p_o - p)}{\rho}} = \sqrt{\frac{2(1.962 \times 10^4)g}{10^3}} = \sqrt{384.944} = 19.62\text{m/s}$$

12. Orientation is not a method of plane tabling.

Plane table surveying is the graphical method of surveying in which field observation and plotting are done simultaneously helping the surveyor to compare the plotted details with actual features of the ground. Method of plane table surveying are,

1. Radiation

2. Intersection

3. Resection

4. Traversing

Radiation and intersection are the methods used for plotting the position of objects on the drawings.

Traversing and Resection are the methods used for locating the position of the instrument station on the drawing.

Hence, the correct option is (A).

13. The efficiency of power transmission through pipe ⇒ η = H−h$_f$/H

Maximum efficiency that can be achieved in transmission through the pipe is 66.67%

∴0.66=H−h$_f$/H ⇒ 0.66H−H=−h$_f$ ⇒h$_f$ = 0.33 ⇒ h$_f$=H/3

14. Forced Vortex is defined as that type of vortex flow, in which some external torque is required to rotate the fluid mass. The fluid mass in this type of flow rotates at constant angular velocity.

Examples of the forced vortex are.

1. A vertical cylinder containing a liquid which is rotated about its central axis with a constant angular velocity.

2. The flow of liquid inside the impeller of a centrifugal pump.

3. The flow of water through the runner of a turbine.

Free vortex flow is defined as the vortex flow in which no external torque is required to rotate the fluid mass. Thus the liquid in case of a free vortex is rotating due to the rotation which is imparted to the fluid previously.

Examples of free vortex flow are.

1. The flow of liquid through a hole provided at the bottom of a container like in washbasin.

2. The flow of liquid around a circular bend in a pipe.

3. A whirlpool in a river.

4. The flow of fluid in a centrifugal pump casing.

15. For flow through a circular pipe, the velocity at any point is given as

$$u = u_{\max}(1 - r^2/R^2)$$

We know that, for laminar flow through a circular pipe

$$u_{\max}/u_{avg} = 2$$

$$\therefore u_{avg} \Rightarrow u_{\max}/2 = u_{\max} \times (1 - r^2/R^2) \Rightarrow /2 = 1 - r^2/R^2 \Rightarrow r = R/\sqrt{2} =$$

$$0.707R$$

16. Critical depth: It is the depth of flow corresponding to minimum specific energy at the section.

For the critical conditions:

(i) Froude Number is 1.

(ii) Energy is minimum for the given discharge of the section.

(iii) Discharge per unit width is maximum for the given energy and force.

(iv) Force per unit weight of water is minimum for the given discharge.

17. The hydraulically efficient channel is also the most economical section of the channel as the cost of construction is minimum.

Minimum wetted perimeter design for a given cross-sectional area gives the maximum discharge for the section and hence it is termed as the most efficient section.

∴ To design an efficient channel, the wetted perimeter for the given discharge, should be minimum.

18. Alternate depths: For a given discharge Q in a channel, there will be two depths for a given specific energy. These two depths are known as alternate depths.

Conjugate depths: The two depths corresponding to the depth of flow, before and after of hydraulic jump having same momentum flux are termed as conjugate depths.

Sequent depths is same as conjugate depth.

19. For measuring the discharge or velocity of a streamflow current meter is used.

In this, the stream channel cross-section is divided into numerous vertical subsections.

In each subsection, the area is obtained by measuring the width and depth of the subsection, and the water velocity is determined using a current meter. The discharge in each subsection is computed by multiplying the subsection area by the measured velocity. The total discharge is then computed by summing the discharge of each subsection.

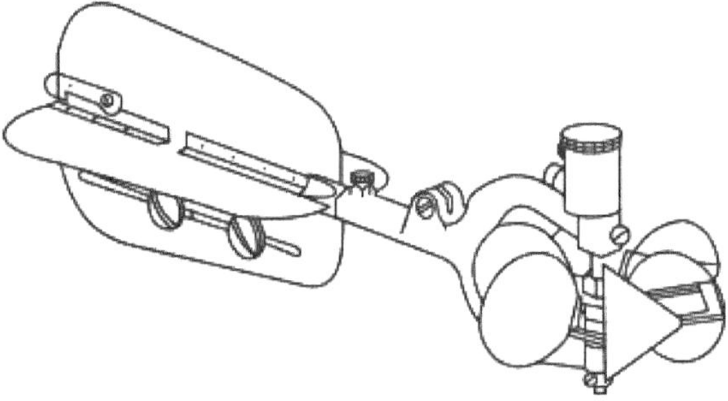

Hence, the correct option is (D).

20. Length of hydraulic Jump:

It is defined as the length between the two sections where one section is taken before the hydraulic jump and the second section is taken after the hydraulic jump.

For a rectangular channel, from experiment, length of hydraulic jump is found to be 5 to 7 times that of the height of the hydraulic jump.

Hence, the correct option is (A).

21. For a circular section (section which is converging on the top), hydraulic efficiency depends upon:

(i) Maximum Velocity

For maximum velocity case, R = 0.30 × d and y = 0.81 × d

(ii) Maximum discharge

For maximum discharge case, R = 0.29 × d and y = 0.95 × d

Where

d = diameter of the circular pipe

y = hydraulic depth

R = hydraulic radius

22. Froude number, $F_r = \dfrac{v}{\sqrt{gy}}$

where v = velocity, $y = depth$ of flow, g = acceleration due to gravity

Also, discharge, $Q = q \times B = v \times y \times B$ (since $q = v \times y$)

Therefore, $F_r^2 = \dfrac{q^2}{gy \times y^2} = \dfrac{q^2}{g \times y^3}$

$y^3 = \dfrac{q^2}{g \times Fr^2}$

$y^3 = \dfrac{(100/5)^2}{9.81 \times 0.80^2}$

$y^3 = \dfrac{400}{9.81 \times 0.64}$

$y^3 = 63.71 = 64$

$y = (64)^{\frac{1}{3}} = 4m$

23. A venturi flume is a critical-flow with a constricted flow which causes a drop in hydraulic grade line, creating critical depth. It is used in the flow measurement of very large flow rates, usually in millions of cubic units.

A venturi meter would normally measure in millimeters, whereas a venturi flume measure in meters.

24. Discharge over a rectangular weir:

$$Q = \frac{2}{3} C_d \cdot L \sqrt{2g}(H)^{\frac{3}{2}}$$

Where H: - still water head
Flow over a triangular weir (V-weir):

$$Q = \frac{8}{15} C_d \sqrt{2g} H^{\frac{5}{2}} \tan\left(\frac{\theta}{2}\right)$$

θ: Included angel of Notch.
Flow over a trapezoidal weir (or) Notch-

$$Q = \frac{2}{3} C_{d_1} \sqrt{2g} L H_1^{\frac{3}{2}} + \frac{8}{15} C_{d_2} \sqrt{2g} \cdot \tan\frac{\theta}{2} \cdot H^{\frac{5}{2}}$$

Where, $\left(\dfrac{\theta}{2}\right)$: weir angle of inclination with the vertical.

C_{d_1} = Coefficient of discharge for rectangular portion.

C_{d_2} = Coefficient of discharge for the triangular portion.

25. Specific speed is defined as the speed of the turbine which is similar in shape and geometric dimensions with actual turbine but of such a size that it should develop unit power (1 kilowatt) when working under the unit head at its maximum efficiency.

∵ Specific speed of the turbine is the speed at which unit power delivered at the unit head.

∴ The specific speed of a turbine is the speed of an imaginary turbine, identical with the given turbine, which develops unit horsepower under the unit head.

26. Discharge over a Traingular notch is given by:

$Q = 8/15\ C_d\ \sqrt{2g}\ \tan\theta/2\ H^{5/2}$

$C_d = 0.6$

For right angled notch, $\theta = 90°$

$Q = 8/15 \times 0.6 \times \sqrt{2 \times 9.81}\tan 90/2\ H^{5/2}$

$Q = 1.417\ H^{5/2}$

27. Specific speed: It is defined as the speed of a similar turbine working under a head of 1 m to produce a power output of 1 kW. The specific speed is useful to compare the performance of various type of turbines. The specific speed differs for different type of turbines and is same for the model and actual turbine.

Specific Speed of Turbine, $N_s = N \times \sqrt{P}/H^{5/4}$

Where N = speed of turbine, P = power generated, and H = head generated

$N_s = 300 \times \sqrt{150000}/100^{5/4} = 367.42 = 367$

28. The general form of head-discharge relationship for a weir can be expressed as $Q = kH^n$

Where k and n are the coefficients, of which n depends upon the weir shape and k depends upon the weir shape and its setting.

A type of weir for which the discharge varies linearly with head, known as Sutro Weir. It is used for flow measurement of small discharges and in automatic control of flow, sampling and dosing through float operated devices.

∴ For Sutro Weir ⇒ Q ∝ H

29. Classification of the turbine-based on the energy available at the inlet:

(i) Reaction Turbine: Turbine for which both pressure energy and kinetic energy is available at the inlet is a reaction turbine.

E.g. Francis Turbine, Kaplan Turbine and Propeller Turbine.

They are useful for low head and high discharge.

(ii) Impulse Turbine: Turbine for which only kinetic energy is available at the inlet is an impulse turbine.

E.g. Pelton Turbine and Turgo Impulse Turbine.

They are useful for high head and low discharge.

Confusion Point:

Francis Turbine cannot be a correct answer as it classified as Medium head Turbine.

∴ The most appropriate option is Kaplan Turbine.

30. The hydraulic machines which convert the mechanical energy into hydraulic energy are called pumps. If the mechanical energy is converted into pressure energy by means of the centrifugal force acting on the fluid, the hydraulic machine is called a centrifugal pump.

Centrifugal pumps	**Reciprocating pumps**
The discharge is continuous and smooth	The discharge is fluctuating and pulsating
It can handle a large quantity of liquid	It handles a small quantity of liquid only
It can be used for lifting**highly viscous liquids**	It is used only for lifting pure or less viscous liquids
It is used for large discharge through smaller heads	It is meant for a small discharge and high heads
cost of a centrifugal pump	cost of a reciprocating pump

is less as compared to reciprocating pump	is approximately four times the cost of a centrifugal pump
Centrifugal pump runs at high speed They can be coupled to an electric motor	It runs at low speed. Speed is limited due to consideration of separation and Cavitation
The operation of a centrifugal pump is smooth and without much noise.**The maintenance cost is low**	The operation of a reciprocating pump is complicated and with much noise. The maintenance cost is high.
It requires**a smaller floor area** and installation cost is low	It requires a larger floor area and installation cost is high
Efficiency is high	Efficiency is low

31. Kor watering: It is the first watering which is given to the crop when the crop is few centimetres high.

Paleo Irrigation: During the initial days of irrigation before the crop is sown, the soil is very dry. In such cases, the soil is moistened with water as it helps in ploughing and sowing the crops. It is the watering done prior to the sowing.

Duty: It is the number of hectares of land irrigated for full growth of a given crop by a supply of 1 cumec of water continuously during the entire base period of that crop.

Delta: The total water depth required by a crop to attain its full maturity in its base period.

32. Crop Period: The time period that elapsed for the instant of the sowing of the crop to the instant of its harvesting is called crop period.

Base Period: The time between the first watering of a crop at the time of its sowing to its last watering before the harvesting is called the base period or the base of the crop.

Crop period is slightly more than the base period, but for all practical consideration, they are taken as one and the same thing, and generally expressed in days.

33. Concept:

The relation between Delta (Δ), Duty (D) and Base period (B) is given by

Δ=864×B/D cm

Δ → depth of water required (cm)

D → Duty (hectares per cumec)

B → Base period (days)

Given:

D = 1000 hectares per cumec

B = 100 days

Calculations:

Δ=864 B/D

Δ=864×100/1000 = 86.4 cm

Hence, the depth of water will be 86.4 cm

34. Concept:

The storage capacity $=\gamma_d \times d \times (F.C - PWP)/\gamma_w$

Where:

FC = Field capacity

PWP = Permanent willing point

d = Depth of the root zone

γ_d = Dry Unit weight of soil

γ_w = Unit weight of water

Given:

Field capacity (F. C) = 25 % = 0.25

Permanent willing point (PWP) = 15 % = 0.15

Depth of the root zone (d) = 80 cm

Dry Unit weight of soil (γ_d) = 1.5 g /cc

Calculations:

The storage capacity $=\gamma_d \times d \times (F.C - PWP)/\gamma_w$

The storage capacity $=1.5 \times 80 \times (0.25 - 0.15)/1 = 12$ cm

Hence, the storage capacity of the soil is 12 cm.

35. $$SAR = \frac{Na^+}{\sqrt{\frac{Ca^{++}+Mg^{++}}{2}}} = \frac{28}{\sqrt{\frac{12+20}{2}}} = 7$$

36. The duty at the head water course is called as "outlet Discharge factor".

The ratio between the area of the crop irrigated and the quantity of water required during its entire period of growth is known as duty. Duty is measured in hectares per cumec.

Hence, Outlet factor $= \dfrac{\text{Area}}{\text{Outlet discharge}}$

37. Drip irrigation, also known as trickle irrigation, is an irrigation method that saves water and fertilizer by allowing water to drip slowly to the roots of plants, either onto the soil surface or directly onto the root zone.

Fertilizer and nutrient loss is minimized due to the localized application and reduced leaching. Soil erosion and Weed growth are lessened.

38. Gross Irrigation Requirement, GIR = $\dfrac{Net\ Irrigation\ Requirement\,(NIR)}{\eta_a \times \eta_c}$

Where η_a and η_c are the application and conveyance efficiency respectively.

GIR=15cm/0.8×0.6 = 31.25 cm

39. Check flooding:

Check flooding irrigation is more suitable for permeable soil due to large stream discharge, which are regulated with the help of low and flat levees.

Check flooding is similar to ordinary flooding except that the water is controlled by surrounding the check area with low and flat levees.

Furrow Irrigation:

In this type of irrigation, only one-fifth to one-half of the land surface is wetted by water. It, therefore, results in less evaporation, less pudding of soil and permits cultivation sooner after irrigation.

When crops like potatoes, corn, sorghum and sugar beets are grown, it is usually best to irrigate by the furrow method.

40. According to Lacey's, the design formulas to build canal is as follows:

(1) silt factor $\Rightarrow f = 1.76\sqrt{d_{mm}}$

(2) velocity of $flow \Rightarrow V = \left[\dfrac{Qf^2}{140}\right]^{\frac{1}{6}}$

(3) hydraulic mean depth $\Rightarrow R = \dfrac{5V^2}{2f}$

(4) wetted perimeter $\Rightarrow P = 4.75\sqrt{Q}$

(5) Bed slope $\Rightarrow S = \dfrac{f^{\frac{5}{3}}}{3340 \times Q^{\frac{1}{6}}}$

Hence, the correct relationship between the parameter given in the options as per Lacey's silt theory is the velocity of flow, $V = \left[\dfrac{Qf^2}{140}\right]^{\frac{1}{6}}$ i.e. between discharge, silt factor, and flow velocity.

41. Elementary profile dam:

Elementary profile of a gravity dam is triangular in shape as only three forces are assumed to be acting:

(a) Water Pressure, (b) Weight of the dam, and (c) Uplift pressure on the dam.

For reservoir empty condition i.e. no water

$\Rightarrow$ Water Pressure and Uplift pressure due to water would be zero.

$\therefore$ Only force to be considered for a elementary profile of a gravity dam is self-weight of the dam.

42. Elementary profile dam:

Elementary profile of a gravity dam is triangular in shape as only three forces are assumed to be acting:

(a) Water Pressure, (b) Weight of the dam, and (c) Uplift pressure on the dam.

For an elementary profile of gravity dam:

(i) Limiting height (h) is given by:

$h_c = f/w(G+1) \Rightarrow$ Uplift pressure not considered

$h_c = f/w \times (G-c+1) \Rightarrow$ Uplift pressure considered

Where, c = cohesion of the soil

43. Flexibility:

Flexibility is the ratio of the rate of change of discharge at an outlet to the rate of change of discharge of the distributary channel.

Depending on the value of Flexibility, the outlet can be classified as

(1) Proportional outlet (F = 1)

(2) Hyper Proportional outlet (F > 1)

(3) Sub Proportional outlet (F < 1)

Note:

Flexibility, F = $\dfrac{\left(\frac{dq}{q}\right)}{\left(\frac{dQ}{Q}\right)}$

Where,

q = discharge passing through the outlet = $C_1 y^n$

Q = flow rates in the distributary channels = $C_2 H^m$

y = depth of flow in the channel, H = Head on the outlet

m = outlet index, n = channel index

44. Sensitivity is the ratio of the rate of change of discharge through an outlet to the rate of change in the water surface level of distributary channel with respect to the normal depth of the flow in the channel.

Sensitivity, S = $\dfrac{\left(\frac{dq}{q}\right)}{\left(\frac{dy}{y}\right)}$

where q is the discharge through the outlet

y is the depth in the distributary canal.

Calculations:

$S = 0.5, dy/y = 50\%$

$\left(\dfrac{dq}{q}\right) = S \times \left(\dfrac{dy}{y}\right)$

$\left(\dfrac{dq}{q}\right) = 0.5 \times \dfrac{50}{100}$

$\left(\dfrac{dq}{q}\right) = 0.25$

$\left(\dfrac{dq}{q}\right) = 25\%$

45. (i) Bank Storage: When the reservoir is filled, a certain amount of water seeps into the permeable reservoir bank. This water comes out when the reservoir gets depleted. This volume of water is known as bank storage.

(ii) Useful storage: The volume of water stored in the reservoir between normal and minimum pool level is called useful storage.

(iii) Surcharge Storage: The volume of water stored between the maximum pool level and normal pool level is called surcharge storage.

(iv) Valley Storage: Before the construction of the dam, a variable amount of water is stored in the stream channel is called valley storage.

After construction of the dam, storage increases and there is a net increase in the storage is equal to the storage capacity of a reservoir minus natural valley storage.

Effective storage for flood mitigation = Useful Storage + Surcharge Storage–Valleys Storage

∴ The volume of water held by a natural stream channel is known as Valley Storage.

46. The laying of the impervious layer which protects the bed and sides of the canal is called canal lining. The lining of the canal is necessary for the following reasons:

(a) to minimise the seepage losses through the bed and sides of the canal.

(b) to prevent scouring and erosion of bed and sides of the canal due to the high velocity of flood water at the time of heavy rainfall.

(c) increase the discharge in the canal section by increasing the velocity.

(d) to prevent the growth of weeds along the bed and sides of the canal.

(e) to increase the command area.

47. Concept:
By Normal Ratio Method:

$$P_x = \frac{N_x}{N} \times \left[\frac{P_1}{N_1} + \frac{P_2}{N_2} + \cdots \ldots + \frac{P_n}{N_n} \right]$$

Where,
P_x = Storm precipitation for station x
N_x = Normal annual precipitation at station x
P_n = Storm precipitation for station n
n = number of adjacent stations

Calculation:

$$P_x = \frac{700}{3} \times \left[\frac{100}{1000} + \frac{90}{900} + \frac{80}{800} \right]$$

$$P_x = 70mm$$

48. Concept:
Isohyets: It is a line joining points of equal rainfall for a given interval. Isohyets are contours of equal precipitation analogous to contour lines on a topographic map. For the isohyetal method,

Mean precipitation for a catchment $\overline{p} =$

$$\frac{\text{Total volume of rainfall } (V)}{\text{Total area of catchment } (A)}$$

$$\overline{p} = \frac{\sum_{i=1}^{n} A_i \frac{(P_i + P_{i+1})}{2}}{A}$$

Calculation:

$$\overline{p} = \frac{\left(100 \times \left(\frac{45+55}{2} \right) + 150 \times \left(\frac{55+65}{2} \right) \right)}{250} = 56cm$$

49. If the leakage pressure is equal to the submerged weight of the mass of the soil, the effective stress becomes zero. In such a situation, the cohesive soil loses its shear strength and tends to flow with water. This phenomenon is known as the Bajan sand condition.

Hence, the correct option is (B).

50. Meyer's formula is the empirical equation used to determine the lakes evaporation (mm/day)

$E_L = k(e_w - e_a)[1 + u_9/16]$

E_L = lake evaporation (mm/day)

e_w = saturation vapour pressure at the water surface (mm of Hg)

e_a = actual vapour pressure of the overlying air at specified height (mm of Hg)

u_9 = monthly mean velocity (kmph) at a height of 9m above the ground

k = constant (0.36 for large deep water bodies and 0.50 for small shallow lakes)

51. Dicken's Method:
It was adopted for Northern India.

$$Q_P = C_D A^{\frac{3}{4}}$$

where
Q_P = Peak discharge in m^3/s
A = Area in km^2
C_D = coefficient applicable in the region.

Important Points:
Different empirical method for determining flood discharge are as follows:

Ryve's Method:

$$Q_P = C_R A^{\frac{2}{3}}$$

This formula is used only in Southern India.

Jarvi's Method:
This formula is applicable for Eastern India.

$$Q_P = C\sqrt{A}$$

Inglis Method:
This formula is used only in Maharashtra. Here three different cases are taken into consideration.

$$Q_P = \frac{124A}{\sqrt{A+10.4}} \cong 123\sqrt{A}$$

Calculation:

$$Q_P = C_D A^{\frac{3}{4}}$$

$$Q_p = 12.47 \times (100)^{\frac{3}{4}}$$

52. Concept:

Reliability:

Reliability is the probability that a particular flood never happens in the time span of n years.

Reliability = (1 - P)N

where,

P is the probability of a particular flood is equal or exceeded

P=1/T_r

Risk:

The Probability of a particular flood magnitude is equal or exceeded at least once in a time span of n years is called risk.

Risk = 1 - Reliability

Risk = 1 - (1 - P)^N

Risk = $1 - (1 - 1/T_r)^N$

53.

Time (hr)	0-2	2-4
Rainfall (cm)	6.2	5.0

$$\therefore \phi - index = \frac{P-R}{t}$$

where,

P = Rainfall depth

R = Runoff depth

t = Duration of rainfall

$$R = P - \phi_{index} \times t$$
$$R = (6.2 + 5.0) - 1.2 \times 4$$
$$R = 11.2 - 4.8$$
$$R = 6.4 cm$$

Runoff volume $= 6.4 \times 10^{-2} \times 250 \times 10^6$

Runoff volume $= 1600 \times 10^4 m^3$

Runoff volume $= 1600$ hectare - meter

(1 hectare $= 10^4 m^2$)

54. Let us assume the area of the catchment is A, then the area of triangle (from the shape of unit hydrograph) is equal to the volume of the water accumulated in the catchment area.

$$\frac{1}{2} \times Q_{Peak} \times \text{Base width} = \text{Area } (A) \times \text{depth of water}$$
$$\frac{1}{2} \times 20 \times 64 \times 3600 = A \times \frac{1}{100}$$
$$A = 230.4 \times 10^6 m^2 = 230.4 km^2$$

Therefore, the equilibrium discharge of S-curve obtained by using this 8-hour unit hydrograph will be

$$Q_s = 2.778 \frac{A}{T_0}$$

where A is in km^2 and T_0 is in hours

$$Q_s = 2.778 \times \frac{230.4}{8}$$
$$Q_s = 80 m^3/s$$

55. Plasticizers are called water reducers.

Plasticizers are those admixtures that reduce water requirements and increase the workability of concrete.

Example: Lignosulphonates, salts of sulphonates, hydrocarbons, polyglycol esters, carbohydrates, etc.

Hence, the correct option is (A).

56. Camber/Cant: It is the cross slope provided to raise the middle of the road surface in the transverse direction to drain off rainwater from the road surface.

The objectives of providing camber are as follows:

Surface protection especially for gravel and bituminous roads and hence making it more durable.

Sub-grade protection by proper drainage and hence to make the surface of pavement more impervious.

Quick-drying of pavement which in turn increases safety .

The main objective of providing camber will be to drain off rainwater from the road surface, as quickly as possible. As rest options are the ultimate result of the quick drainage of water from the pavement.

Important Points:

Camber to be provided for different types of pavement are as follows:

Type of pavement	Heavy Rain	Light Rain
Cement Concrete and high type bituminous surface	1 in 50	1 in 60
Thin Bituminous surface	1 in 40	1 in 50
WBM, gravel pavement	1 in 33	1 in 40
Earthen roads	1 in 25	1 in 33

57. Grade Compensation = minimum of $\left\{ \frac{75}{R}, \frac{30+R}{R} \right\}$

where,

R is the radius of the curve.

Grade Compensation = minimum of $\left\{ \frac{75}{75}, \frac{30+75}{75} \right\}$

Grade Compensation = minimum of {1.0, 1.4}

Grade Compensation = 1%

Therefore, compensated gradient = (6 − 1)% = 5%

You should know this point:

Grade compensation is not required for grades flatter than 4% because the loss of tractive force is negligible.

58. Concept:

Mechanical widening (Wm) on road is given by:

$W_m = nL^2/2R$

where

n = number of lanes

L = length of wheelbase

R = radius of the curve

Given:

As width of pavement = 14.0 m, this implies number of lanes are 4.

So, n = 4

L = length of the wheelbase = 7.0 m

R = radius of the curve = 250 m

Calculations:

$W_m = 4 \times 7^2/2 \times 250$

$W_m = 0.392$ m

Hence, the mechanical widening required for the curve will be 0.39 m.

59. A shift of the transition curve is given by:

$$S = \frac{L_s^2}{24R}$$

R = radius of the curve

L$_s$ = Length of the curve

S = 80²/24×300 = 0.89

60. Concept:

Minimum radius of curvature $(R_{\min})$ is given by:

$$R_{\min} = \frac{V^2}{g \times (e_{\max} + f_{\max})}$$

Where,

$V =$ velocity of vehicle in metres/sec

$g =$ acceleration due to gravity $(m/\sec^2)$

$f_{\max} =$ maximum value of coefficient of lateral friction $= 0.15$

$e_{\max} =$ maximum super elevation

As per IRC (Indian Road Congress)

Terrain/Location	$e_{\max}$
Urban	0.04
Plain \& Rolling	0.07
Hilly	0.1
Hilly and Snow Bound	0.07

Calculation:

$$V(m/s) = 50kmph \times 5/18 = 13.88$$

$$R_{\min} = \frac{13.88^2}{9.81 \times (0.04 + 0.15)} = 103.49m$$

∴ **The most appropriate answer is 125.50 meters as a minimum radius of 103.50 metres is required.**

61. Concept:

Length of transition curve is given by:

$$L_s = V^3/CR$$

where,

$V =$ speed of the vehicle, in m/s

Ls = Length of transition curve, in m

$R =$ Radius of circular curve, in m

$C =$ rate of change radial acceleration of transition curve

Calculations:

$$L_s = \frac{V^3}{CR}$$

$$C = \frac{V^3}{L_s R}$$

$$C = \frac{\left(80 \times \left(\frac{5}{18}\right)\right)^3}{65 \times 300}$$

$$C = 0.56 m/s^3$$

$$C = 56.27 cm/s^3$$

62. Deflection angle, N=1/N₁−1/N₂ = 0.01−(−0.014) = 0.024

Length of the vertical curve, L = $\dfrac{\frac{0.024}{0.0006}}{20}$ = 800 m

63. Concept:

The expression for Setback distance can be written as

$$\therefore M = R - (R)\cos\left(\frac{\alpha}{2}\right)$$

where,

$R =$ radius of the curve

$$\frac{\alpha}{2} = \frac{SSD}{2(R)} \times \frac{180°}{\pi}$$

Given:

Safe stopping sight distance $(SSD) = 80m$

Radius of the horizontal curve $= 125m$

Calculations:

$$\frac{\alpha}{2} = \frac{80}{2(125)} \times \frac{180°}{\pi}$$

$$\frac{\alpha}{2} = 18.33°$$

$$\therefore M = 125 - (125)\cos(18.33°)$$

$$M = 125 - (125)\cos(18.33°)$$

$$M = 6.35m$$

Hence, the required setback distance will be $6.35m$

64. An attrition test is a test which is carried out to measure the rate of wear of a granular material. One of the best examples of a material subjected to an attrition test are stones used in road construction, indicating the resistance of the material to being broken down under road traffic.

Percentage wear = Loss in weight /initial weight × 100%

65. First class bricks are good quality bricks compared to other classes. It should be:

Table moulded, uniform shape and Burnt in kilns.

Its surfaces and edges are sharp, square, smooth and straight.

It is used for important work which are permanent in nature.

It should be free from flaws, cracks, and stones.

In General, Quality of First-class brick should be such that:

It should produce clear metallic ringing sound when stuck with each other. (Soundness test)

The brick should possess sufficient hardness and does not show any impression over the surface when scratched with the finger nail. (Hardness Test)

Bricks, when immersed in water for 24 hours, should not absorb water by more than 20% in the case of First-class Brick. (Absorption Test)

66. Fillet welds are designed to resist shear stress.

Fillet Weld:

(i) This weld is required where members overlap each other or the connecting members are in different planes. in such cases, butt weld cannot be provided.

(ii) Fillet weld is predominantly subjected to shear stresses.

(iii) A fillet weld may be subjected to any general types of stress i.e. axial/direct stress (tensile or compressive), flexural stress (tension or compression), and shear stresses but the design of fillet weld is governed by shear stresses since a fillet weld always gets fail in shear.

Hence, the correct option is (B).

67. There are practical reasons of not using stone over brick, cement, concrete

1. Stone is not available everywhere, making it costlier
2. Stone wall would take more space than a normal brick wall
3. More building constructions are made with the use of brick walls and framed structures these days
4. Stone work is slow and difficult for masons while brick and concrete are faster and easiest
5. Steel and R.C.C. are less bulky and more durable
6. Strength of stones cannot be rationally analyzed

68. Granite:

1. Granite is hard, coarse-grained rocks of crystalline structure.
2. It is a type of igneous rocks (plutonic rocks).
3. Granites can be predominantly white, pink, or grey in colour, depending on their mineralogy.
4. These rocks mainly consist of feldspar, quartz, mica, and amphibole minerals.
5. It contains 20% and 60% quartz by volume, and at least 35% of the total feldspar.

69. The average crushing strength and tensile strength of hand molded bricks are 60,000 kN/m^2 and 2000 kN/m^2 respectively. The shearing strength of bricks is about one-tenth of the crushing strength

70. The tension coefficient of a member indicates the force per unit length of the member.

Tension Coefficient:

The tension coefficient for a member of a frame is defined as the pull or tension in that member divided by its length.

$$t = \frac{T}{L}$$

Where,

t = Tension coefficient

T = Pull or tension in member

L = Length of the member

Hence, the correct option is (B).

71. Various Test for Testing of tiles are:

(i) Moisture Expansion Test

(ii) Water Adsorption Test

(iii) Bond Strength Test

(iv) Transverse Strength Test

(v) Impact Test

(vi) Thermal Shock Resistance Test

(vii) Breaking Strength test

(viii) Chemical Resistance Test

(ix) Modulus of Rupture Test

(x) Surface Abrasion Test

(xi) Hardness Test

Hence, all the given test is required for the testing of tiles. The answer will be D.

72. Hardwood is generally obtained from Deciduous tree and softwood is obtained by Coniferous tree.

Examples of Hardwoods are

Oak, Sal, Teak, Babul, Mahogany, Shishum, etc.

Examples of Softwoods are

Chir, Deodar, Pine, Spruce, Kael (Botanical name - Pinus Wallachian), etc

Wood obtained from coniferous trees is soft, lightweight, weak and resinous. Hence is of limited engineering application.

Wood obtained from deciduous trees are hard, strong, heavyweight and not resinous. Hence it is suitable for engineering application.

73. Softening point test:

Softening point denotes the temperature at which the bitumen attains a particular degree of softening under the specifications of the test.

The test is conducted by using the Ring and Ball apparatus.

Float test/penetration test/ viscosity test

Normally the consistency or stiffness of bituminous material can be measured either by penetration test or viscosity test. But for a certain range of consistencies, these tests are not applicable and Float test is used.

Solubility test:

The bitumen content of a bituminous material is measured by means of its solubility in carbon disulfide and hence can be considered as purity test for bitumen.

Spot test:

A spot test is used to find out cracking in bitumen.

It is more sensitive than the Solubility test in terms of detection of cracking.

Flash Point:

The flash point of a material is the lowest temperature at which the vapour of a substance momentarily takes fire in the form of a flash under the specified condition of test.

Fire Point:

The fire point is the lowest temperature at which the material gets ignited and burns under the specified condition of test.

74. Defect arises due to conversion of timber:

Chip mark, Torn grain, Diagonal grain and wane.

Defect arises due to Fungi:

Heart rot, Brown rot, White rot, Dry rot, Wet rot, Sap stain and Blue stain.

Defects arises due to Natural forces:

Cup shakes, Ring shakes, Heart shakes, Star shake and radial shake.

Defects arises due to Seasoning:

Bow, warp, cup and Twist.

75. When liquid asphalt is combined with the aggregate for mixing, the temperature of the asphalt should be in the range of 300°F.

Drum and batch plants are the two most common plant types for hot-mixed asphalt. Therefore, both drum mix and batch plants have heating systems to keep the liquid asphalt at the required temperature.

If asphalt is delivered at a cooler temperature, the system must be capable of raising the temperature of the delivered asphalt cement.

The two methods commonly used for heating liquid asphalt are the direct fire and the hot oil processes.

76. Flaking: The paint film when subjected to chemical attack of atmosphere, sunlight and heat, all deteriorating it, flaking occurs on the painted surface. The most common causes of flaking paint are moisture underneath the coat and also paint applied over oil, dirt, grease or onto a poorly prepared, powdery surface. Flaking paint simply means it is the detachment of paint film (the breaking of coating system right from the primer to the top finishing coat) from the underlying surface in the form of flakes or scales. It is very important to check the surface before painting. Surface should be free from dust, grease, etc.

Chalking: The formation of a white, chalky powder on the surface paint film is known as "Chalking Paint".

Wrinkling: The surface of the paint which wrinkles and gathers together is called wrinkling paint. It forms a layer like undulating waves on the painted surface. The main reason behind an appearance of waves can be application of too much paint or the oil in the paint is more than required or drying at high temperature. Wrinkling paint is more noticeable with enamels and varnishes.

77. The bitumen has less affinity to water compared to tar. Tar have a chemical composition with more carbon content than bitumen. This result in tar to have higher viscosity, making it less workable compared to bitumen. The tar also possesses a higher susceptibility to temperature compared with bitumen.

78. Synthetic rubber paint is prepared from resins.

It can be used on those surfaces which are subject to a lot of wear and tear. This paint isn't just durable; it also offers a high chemical and urine resistance, making it ideal for agricultural and industrial use. It also offers protection against heavy rain, sunlight.

Hence, the correct option is (A).

79. Base: It is a solid substance in a fine state of division, and it determines the character of the paint and imparts durability to the surface which is painted. It reduces shrinkage cracks.

Vehicle: It is a liquid substance which holds the ingredients of paint in liquid suspension.

It has two important functions:

to make it possible to spread the paint evenly and uniformly on the surface in the form of a thin layer

to acts a binder for the ingredients of paint

to form an opaque layer to obscure the surface of the material to be painted

Solvent: It is used to make the paint thin so that it can be easily applied onto the surface.

Filler: It is a cheap, inert and special type of pigments used to increase the volume of paints.

80. Lacquer: It is a solution of natural or synthetic resin in a volatile solvent. It is obtained by dissolving resin and film forming nitro cellulose or shellac in a solvent.

Enamel Paints: Enamels consists of high-grade bases like zinc oxide or lead oxide ground in oil or varnish. They dry slowly leaving a hard tough and elastic film which is smooth and durable.

Enamel painted surfaces are washable and are not affected by acids, alkalis, grease or steam.

Driers: Driers are added to oil bound paints to accelerate drying process.

Pigment: Pigments are fine insoluble crystalline particles which give colour to the paint. They may be organic or inorganic compounds.

81. For numerous bags of cement stacked over and along with each other, it's recommended that bags should be removed from two or three layers in a stepwise manner so that the pile is stable and will not topple.

Otherwise, warehouse-pack or lump is developed due to pressure on the bottom layer of bags.

However, they can be easily removed by rolling the cement bags twice or thrice before using it to break the lumps if formed.

Note: The height of stack shall not be more than 10 bags to prevent the possibility of lumping up under pressure. The width of the stack shall not be more than four bags length or 3 meters.

∴ Warehouse pack of cement means the pressure compaction of the bags on lower layers

82. The raw materials used for cement production such as chalk, shale, limestone or clay are mixed either in dry condition or in wet condition.

The dry process of manufacturing of cement is the modern method of manufacturing of cement while the wet process is the oldest method of manufacturing of cement.

Dry process of manufacturing of cement is widely adopted because the blending of dry powders has now perfected and the wet process, which required much higher power consumption can be replaced with confidence.

In the wet process, to obtain cement dry powder, slurry formed of all raw materials are heated at 1400° to 1500°C.

83. Approximate oxide composition limits of ordinary portland cement are as follows:

Oxide	Percentage Content
CaO	$60 - 67$
SiO_2	$17 - 25$
Al_2O_3	$03 - 08$
Fe_2O_3	$0.5 - 6.0$
MgO	$0.1 - 4.0$
Alkalies (K_2O, Na_2O)	$0.4 - 1.3$
SO_3	$1.3 - 3.0$

84. Ferroecement developed by P.L. Nervi, an Italian architect, and engineer, in 1940. It consists of closely spaced wire meshes which are impregnated with rich cement mortar mix. The wire mesh is usually of 0.5 to 1.0 mm diameter wire at 5 mm to 10 mm spacing and cement mortar is of the cement-sand ratio of 1: 2 or 1: 3 with water/cement ratio of 0.4 to 0.45.

The ferrocement elements are usually of the order of 2 to 3 cm in thickness with 2 to 3 mm external cover to the reinforcement. The steel content varies between 300 kg to 500 kg per cubic meter of mortar.

The basic idea behind this material is that concrete can undergo large strains in the neighbourhood of the reinforcement and the magnitude of strains depends on the distribution and subdivision of reinforcement throughout the mass of concrete.

It is impervious in nature, has the capacity to resist shock and no formwork is required to gain initial strength.

The main advantages are the simplicity of its construction, a lesser dead weight of the elements due to their small thickness, its high tensile strength, fewer crack widths compared to conventional concrete, easy repairability, noncorrosive nature and easier mouldability to any required shape.

85. Metakaolin is a type of pozzolanic materials which enhances the strength, density, and durability of concrete. Metakaolin is refined kaolin clay that is fired (calcined) under carefully controlled conditions to create an amorphous aluminosilicate that is reactive in concrete.

It is very fine and highly reactive, gives fresh concrete a creamy, nonsticky texture that makes finishing easier.

It reduces efflorescence by consuming calcium hydroxide. Whiteness is a huge advantage over other pozzolans such as silica fume, which is a dark steel-grey or fly ash, which is a light greyish colour.

∴ Metakaolin is added to make white concrete.

86. Pozzolanic material is essentially a siliceous or aluminous material which while in itself does not cementitious properties. Which, in the presence of water and in finely divided form reacts with calcium hydroxide, liberated in the hydration process, at ordinary temperature.

This compounds formed from reaction possesses cementitious properties.

Pozzolana material may contain clay of up to 80%.

87. Soundness of cement is affected by the presence of excess lime (CaO) in the cement. This excess lime hydrates very slowly and forms slaked lime that occupies a larger volume than the original free calcium oxide.

The slow hydration process, therefore, affects the properties of hardened concrete. The difference in the rate of hydration of free lime and slaked lime leads to change in volume of hardened concrete. The cement which exhibits this type of volume changes is described as unsound cement.

88. Rapid hardening cement is similar to Ordinary Portland cement (OPC) but with higher tri-calcium silicate (C₃S) content and finer grinding. It gains strength more quickly than OPC, though the final strength is only slightly higher.

The one-day strength of this cement is equal to the three-day strength of OPC with the same water-cement ratio.

The rapid rate of development of strength is attributed to the higher fineness of grinding and higher C₃S and lower C₂S content.

A higher fineness of cement particles exposes a greater surface area for the action of water and a higher proportion of C₃S results in quicker hydration.

The use of rapid heading cement is recommended in the following situations:

(a) In pre-fabricated concrete construction.

(b) Where formwork is required to be removed early for re-use elsewhere.

(c) Road repair works

(d) In cold weather concrete where the rapid rate of development of strength reduces the vulnerability of concrete to the frost damage

89. Water content is defined as the ratio of the mass of water to the mass of solids.

w = M_w/M_s = 1875−1500/1500 = 375/1500 = 0.25

Percentage of water (% water) = Water content (w) × 100 = 25%

90. An aggregate is said to be flaky is its least dimension is less than 3/5 of the mean dimension and the aggregate is said to be elongated if its greatest dimension is greater than 1.8 times the mean dimension.

91. Bulking of sand: The increase in the volume of sand due to increase in moisture content is known as bulking of sand. A film of water is created around the sand particles which forces the particles to get aside from each other and thus the volume is increased.

Bulking of sand is maximum at 4.6 % moisture content.

∴ Maximum moisture content (in percentage) based in the sand is 5%.

Note: Five to eight percent of the increase in moisture in the sand can increase the volume of sand up to 20 to 40 percent.

92. Controlled concrete: A concrete mix which is designed on the basis of test of the strength conducted in the laboratory on the trial mixture of cement and aggregate to be actually used in the construction is termed as controlled concrete.

Ordinary concrete is designed by volume and is used as PCC and not for structural related works, while Controlled concrete is designed by weight and designed to get a controlled mix, strength and durability as per structural requirements.

93. Various Tests for Aggregates with IS codes:

Property of aggregate	Type of Test	Test Method
Crushing strength	Crushing test	IS: 2386 (part 4) -1963
Hardness	Los Angeles abrasion test	IS: 2386 (Part 5)-1963
Toughness	Aggregate impact test	IS: 2386 (Part 4)-1963
Durability	Soundness test- accelerated durability test	IS: 2386 (Part 5)-1963
Shape factors	Shape test	IS : 2386 (Part 1)-1963
Specific gravity and porosity	Specific gravity test and water absorption test	15: 2386 (Part 3)-1963
Adhesion to bitumen	Stripping value of aggregate	(S: $6241 - 1971$

94. Concept:

In an analysis of rates per cu m at first, a volume of 10 cu m has been considered in the calculations to avoid one place of decimal.

But it is difficult to assess exactly the amount of each material to produce 10 cu m of wet concrete when deposited in place. As the dry volume of materials is usually about 50% to 60% more than their wet volume.

Quantities of ingredients may closely be determined by a 'thumb rule' as given below:

To find the volume of cement, sand and coarse aggregate divide a numerical number 15.4 variable up to 15.7 according to the proportioning and 'Water cement ratio' by the summation of the proportions of the ingredients used and then multiply the result thus obtained by their respective strength of proportioning.

Calculation:

For M20 i.e. 1:1.5:3 proportion:

Summation of proportion = 1 + 1.5 + 3 = 5.5.

The numerical number should be 15.4 to obtain round of figure after dividing the number by 7.

Quantity of cement = 15.4/5.5 × V = 50 kg

∴ Total Volume (V) = 17.857

Quantity of aggregate = (15.4 × 4.5)/5.5 × V = 225 kg

95. Sulphate attack on concrete is a chemical breakdown mechanism where sulphate ions attack components of the cement paste.

The compounds responsible for sulphate attack on concrete are water-soluble sulphate-containing salts, such as alkali-earth (calcium, magnesium) and alkali (sodium, potassium) sulphates that are capable of chemically reacting with components of concrete.

C_3A controls the effect of sulphate in cement.

96. The nominal mixes of fixed cement-aggregate ratio (by volume) vary widely in strength and may result in under- or over-rich mixes. For this reason, the minimum compressive strength has been included in many specifications. These mixes are termed standard mixes.

IS 456-2000 has designated the concrete mixes into a number of grades as M10, M15, M20, M25, M30, M35, and M40. In this designation, the letter M refers to the mix and the number to the specified 28-day cube strength of mix in N/mm^2. The mixes of grades are as follows:

Strength	Nominal Mix Design
M10	1: 3.6
$M15$	$1 : 2 \cdot 4$
M20	**1: 1.5: 3**
$M25$	1: 1: 2

97. Grading of Aggregates: This will have maximum influence on workability. A well-graded aggregate is the one which has the least amount of voids in a given volume. If other factors are kept constant, and the total voids are less, an excess paste is available to give a better lubricating effect. With an excess amount of paste, the mixture becomes cohesive and fatty which prevents segregation of particles.

Aggregate particles will slide past each other with the least amount of compacting efforts. The better the grading, the less is the void content and the higher the workability.

Good gradation results in better interlocking, packaging, and densification of concrete resulting in its higher strength along with increasing its durability.

98. Compaction factor test: This test is generally used for the concrete which possesses very 'Low workability' for which slump test is not suitable.

The principle of this test is based upon determining the degree of compaction achieved by the concrete by the standard amount of work done when it is allowed to fall from standard height.

This test gives more precise results than the slump test.

Compactionfactor=Weight of partially compacted concrete/Weight of fully compacted concrete

Compaction Factor	Workability
0.95	Flowing concrete having high workability
0.92	**Plastic concrete having medium workability**
0.85	Stiff plastic concrete having low workability
0.75	Stiff concrete having very low workability

99. The Bureau for Indian standards has published numerous handbooks, which serve as useful supplements to the 1978 version of the IS code.

(i) SP 16: 1980 – Design Aids for reinforced concrete to IS 456:1978

(ii) SP 23: 1982 – Handbook on concrete mixes

(iii) SP 24: 1982 – Explanatory Handbook on IS 456: 1975

(iv) SP 34: 1987 – Handbook on concrete reinforcement and detailing

The following handbook are required to be updated in line with the revised (2000 version) of the code, but many of the provisions continue to be valid in regard to structural design provision.

100. Pans: Used for conveying concrete for very small work such concreting the sidelines of small-sized drains.

Belt Conveyors: It has very limited applications in construction as concrete tends to segregate on steep inclines, at transfer points, and at points where the belt passes over the rollers. Also, the concrete tends to dry and become stiff if carried over the longer distance. Therefore, it is suitable for conveying for shorter distance only.

Transit Mixer: It is one of the most popular equipments for transporting concrete over longer distance particularly in RMC. The capacity of each transit mixer is about 6 m3. Rotating speed of the drum is about 4 – 16 revolutions per minutes.

Chute: This is generally provided for transporting concrete from ground level to a lower level. The slope of the chute should not be flatter than 1 vertical to 2.5 horizontal.

Skip and Hoist: This is the most widely adopted technique for transporting at a higher level e.g. construction of the multi-story building, etc.

Buckets are never used to conveying concretes.

101. Crazing: Crazing in concrete is the development of a network of fine random cracks or fissures on the surface of concrete caused by shrinkage of the surface layer. These cracks are rarely more than 3 mm deep. They do not affect the structural integrity of concrete.

Poor or inadequate curing, Excessive laitance on surface and Sprinkling cement on the surface to dry up the bleed water are the common causes of crazing in concrete.

Efflorescence: Efflorescence is a crystalline deposit of salts that can form when salty water is present in or on brick, concrete, stone, stucco or other building surfaces. It has a white or greyish tint and consists of salt deposits left behind when water evaporates.

Bleeding: Bleeding is one form of segregation, where water comes out to the surface of the concrete, being the lowest specific gravity among all the ingredients of concrete. It seriously affects the durability and strength of concrete.

Segregation: Segregation of concrete is the separation of ingredients of concrete from each other. In the case of segregation, the heavy aggregate particles settle down leaving a sand cement mix on top affecting the quality adversely.

∴ Segregation in cement concrete is defined as the separation of coarser particles from the mix.

102. Batching is preferably done by weighing method and the correct sequence of operations involved in concrete production are:

(i) Batching

(ii) Mixing

(iii) Handling

(iv) Transportation

Batching is the process, in which the quantity or proportion of materials like cement, aggregates, water, etc. are measured on the basis of weight or volume to prepare the concrete mix.

Mixing is the process of mixing different ingredients of the concrete mix e.g. aggregates, binding materials, water, admixtures, etc.

103. Concept:

$R = \dfrac{p_2 - p}{p - p_1} \times 100$

where,

R = proportion of fine aggregate to the combined aggregate by weight

p_1 = fineness modulus of fine aggregate

p_2 = fineness modulus of coarse aggregate

p = desired fineness modulus for concrete mix

Calculation:

$p_1 = 2.5$

$p_2 = 4.1$

p = 3.5

Let x be the proportion of fine aggregate to the combined aggregate by weight

∴ $\dfrac{x}{1} = \dfrac{4.1 - 3.5}{3.5 - 2.5} \times 100 = 60\%$

104. Belt Conveyors: It has very limited applications in construction as concrete tends to segregate on steep inclines, at transfer points, and at points where the belt passes over the rollers. Also, the concrete tends to dry and become stiff if carried over the longer distance. Therefore, it is suitable for conveying for shorter distance only.

Transit Mixer: It is one of the most popular equipments for transporting concrete over longer distance particularly in RMC. The capacity of each transit mixer is about 6 m3. Rotating speed of the drum is about 4 – 16 revolutions per minutes.

Chute: This is generally provided for transporting concrete from ground level to a lower level. The slope of the chute should not be flatter than 1 vertical to 2.5 horizontal.

Skip and Hoist: This is the most widely adopted technique for transporting at a higher level e.g. construction of the multi-story building, etc.

105. Crazing: Crazing in concrete is the development of a network of fine random cracks or fissures on the surface of concrete caused by shrinkage of the surface layer. These cracks are rarely more than 3mm deep. They do not affect the structural integrity of concrete.

Poor or inadequate curing, Excessive laitance on surface and Sprinkling cement on the surface to dry up the bleed water are the common causes of crazing in concrete.

Efflorescence: Efflorescence is a crystalline deposit of salts that can form when salty water is present in or on brick, concrete, stone, stucco or other building surfaces. It has a white or greyish tint and consists of salt deposits left behind when water evaporates.

Bleeding: Bleeding is one form of segregation, where water comes out to the surface of the concrete, being lowest specific gravity among all the ingredients of concrete. It seriously affects the durability and strength of concrete.

Segregation: Segregation of concrete is separation of ingredients of concrete from each other. In case of segregation, the heavy aggregate particles settle down leaving a sand cement mix on top affecting the quality adversely.

106. Grading of the aggregates has a great effect on the workability, uniformity, and finishing qualities of concrete. Different grades of aggregate would lead to a significant reduction in void ratio resulting in more compact, dense and high strength concrete.

Curing: It is the process of hardening the concrete mixes by keeping its surface moist for a certain period, in order to enable the concrete to gain more strength.

Mixing is the process of mixing different ingredients of the concrete mix e.g. aggregates, binding materials, water, admixtures, etc.

Batching is the process, in which the quantity or proportion of materials like cement, aggregates, water, etc. are measured on the basis of weight or volume to prepare the concrete mix. It is preferably done by the weighing method so to avoid the problem of bulking of sand.

∴ Batching refers to the process of proper and accurate measurement of concrete ingredients for uniformity of proportion.

107. Concrete mixing is normally done by mechanical means called mixer.

The size of a mixer is designated by a number representing its nominal mix batch capacity in litres, i.e., the total volume of mixed concrete in litres which can be obtained from the mixer per batch.

The capacity of a mixer for a particular job should be such that the required volume of concrete per hour is obtained without speeding up the mixer or reducing the mixing time below the specified period and without overloading the mixer above its rated capacity.

108. Ultrasonic Pulse velocity method deals with the noting of time of travel of electronically generated mechanical pulse which is further used to analyse the velocity of pulse through the structure that represents its quality.

This test is used to establish uniformity of concrete, estimation of pulse modulus of elasticity, estimation of strength of concrete, determination of setting characteristics of concrete, estimation of crack depth, measurement of thickness of concrete pavement.

This test calculates dynamic modulus of elasticity of concrete.

Velocity of Pulse (km/sec)	Quality of concrete
> 4.5	Excellent
3.5 to 4.5	Very Good
3 to 3.5	Good
< 3	Doubtful

109. The finishing of concrete surface is finally achieved by the following operations:

1. Screeding: it is the levelling operation that removes humps and hollows and give a true and uniform concrete surface.

2. Floating: It is the process of removing the irregularities from the surface of concrete left after screeding.

3. Trowelling: It is the final operation of finishing the concrete surface. It is performed where smooth and dense surface is required.

4. Curing: It is the process of hardening the concrete mixes by keeping its surface moist for a certain period, in order to enable the concrete to gain more strength.

110. Aerated concrete is made by introducing air or gas into a slurry composed of Portland cement or lime and finely crushed siliceous filler so that when the mix sets and hardens, a uniformly cellular structure is formed.

Aerated concrete can be manufactured by:

1. By the formation of gas by chemical reaction within the mass during liquid or plastic state.

2. By mixing preformed stable foam with the slurry.

3. By using finely powdered metal (usually aluminium powder) with the slurry and made to react with the calcium hydroxide liberated during the hydration process, to give out large quantity of hydrogen gas.

111. Light-Weight Aggregate Concrete:

By using expanded perlite or vermiculite, a concrete of density as low as 300 Kg/m³ can be produced.

By the use of expanded slag, sintered fly ash, bloated clay etc., a concrete of density 1900 kg/m³ can be obtained.

The strength of the light-weight concrete may also vary from about 0.3 N/mm² to 40 N/mm².

A cement content of 200 kg/m³ to about 500 kg/m³ may be used.

112. It is given,

Weight of unsaturated sample $= 220\ g$

Weight of dried sample $=$ Weight of solids, $W_s = 180 gm$

Now, finding the weight of water, W_w

So, $W_w =$ Weight of unsaturated sample - Weight of dried sample

$$= 220 - 180 = 40\ g$$

So, Water content, $w = \dfrac{40}{180} = 0.222$

There is no use of sample volume in finding out the water content.

Hence, the correct option is (A).

113. The density of Low weight concrete is about 300 – 1200 kg/m³.

The density of No fines concrete is about 1600 – 2000 kg/m³.

The density of Conventional concrete is about 2400 kg/m³.

The density of Heavyweight concrete is about 3000 – 6000 kg/m³.

114. Screeding: It is the process of striking off the excess concrete to bring the top surface up to proper grade is known as screeding.

Floating: It is the process of removing the irregularities on the surface of the concrete which are left after screeding.

Trowelling: Trowelling is the final operation of finishing. It provides a smoother finish which is hard and abrasion resistant.

115. The introduction of suitable surfactants into the concrete mix results in the formation of fine and stable air bubbles. When the fresh mixture begins to cure, the bubbles within it become mineralized and become an integral part of it. In this way, an additional space is created inside the concrete structure inside which the freezing water expands.

This prevents an increase in internal pressure, which is responsible for the formation of cracks during low temperatures.

As the voids in concrete are reduced, so less water is required to lubricate the mix, thus water cement ratio will be decreased, and strength of concrete will be increased. Addition of surfactants will increase the density of concrete.

116. Plain concrete possesses a very low tensile strength, limited ductility and little resistance to cracking. Poor tensile strength is due to the propagation of such microcracks, eventually leading to brittle fracture of the concrete.

In order to increase the tensile strength of the concrete, the conventional reinforced steel concrete is practiced, but they do not increase the inherent tensile strength of the concrete.

Whereas by addition of small, closely spaced and uniformly dispersed fiber to concrete would act as a crack arrester and would substantially increase the static and dynamic tensile strength of the concrete.

Fiber reinforced concrete can be defined as the composite material consisting a mixture of cement, mortar, or concrete and uniformly dispersed suitable fibers.

Note:

Glass fiber used in making fiber concrete has very high tensile strength of 1020 – 4080 N/mm².

Carbon fiber used in making fiber concrete has also very high tensile strength of 2110 – 2185 N/mm².

Asbestos is also a mineral fiber used in making fiber concrete having tensile strength of 560 – 980 N/mm².

117. Indicative proportions of materials are shown below for self-compactible concrete:

1. Water/powder ratio by volume is to be 0.80 to 1.00
2. Total powder content to be 160 to 240 liters (400-600 kg) per m3
3. The sand content may be more than 38% of the mortar volume
4. Coarse aggregate content should normally be 28 to 35% volume of the mix
5. Water/cement ratio is selected based on the strength required
6. In any case, water content should not exceed 200 litres/m3
7. The volume of aggregates in total would form 50 to 60% of the volume of concrete

118. Plinth area is the covered built-up area measured at the floor level of any storey or at the floor level of the basement. Plinth area is also called a built-up area and is the entire area occupied by the building including internal and external walls. Plinth area is generally 10-20% more than the carpet area.

It includes:

(i) Stair cover (mumty), (ii) Internal shaft for sanitary installation, (iii) garbage chute, (iv) Lift well, (v) Machine room and (vi) area of porch than cantilevered.

It should not include:

(i) Area of loft, (ii) Balcony, (iii) Area of an architectural feature, band, cornice, etc., (iv) Area of vertical sun breaker, (v) Cantilevered Porch, (vi) Spiral staircase, (vii) Open platform, etc.

119. The term "contingencies" indicates the incidental expenses of a miscellaneous character which cannot be reasonably predicted during the preparation of estimate.

Contingency fund forms about 3% to 5% of the total estimate of the project is provided for any unforeseen expenditure. It is taken as 3% according to the practice of CPWD and 5% according to that of the PWD.

120. Concept:

In an analysis of rates per cu m at first, a volume of 10 cu m has been considered in the calculations to avoid one place of decimal.

But it is difficult to assess exactly the amount of each material to produce 10 cu m of wet concrete when deposited in place. As the dry volume of materials is usually about 50% to 60% more than their wet volume.

Quantities of ingredients may closely be determined by a 'thumb rule' as given below:

To find the volume of cement, sand and coarse aggregate divide a numerical number 15.4 variable up to 15.7 according to the proportioning and 'Water cement ratio' by the summation of the proportions of the ingredients used and then multiply the result thus obtained by their respective strength of proportioning.

Calculation:

For 1: 2: 4 proportion with stone chips:

Summation of proportion = 1 + 2 + 4 = 7. The numerical number should be 15.4 to obtain round of figure after dividing the number by 7.

∴ For 10 cu m of concrete

Quantity of cement = 15.4/7 = 2.2 cu m, sand = 2.2 × 2 = 4.4 cu m and stone chips = 2.2 × 4 = 8.8 cu m.

∴ Quantity of stone chips for 2.5 cu m = 8.8 × 2.5/10 = 2.2 cu m

Important Point:

In the case of brick ballast, the numerical number is variable from 15.7 to 16.0 as the void in brick ballast is higher than that of stone chips.

121. The thickness of slabs, partitions, etc and the sectional dimensions of columns, pillars, beams should be taken to the nearest half centimetre (0.005 m).

The dimension should be measured to the nearest one centimetre (0.01 m).

The area should be work out to the nearest 0.01 square metre (0.01 m^2) i.e. 0.01 × 10^4 = 100 cm^2.

The cubic content should be work out to the nearest 0.01 cubic metre (0.01 m^3).

122. Cost of electrical works depends upon the type of wiring, specification, and location of the service line from the main meter point.

For first-class work of C.T.S. wiring, an amount equivalent to 8% of the cost of the building structure is recommended.

∴ Electrification cost may be generally taken around 8% of the estimated cost of the building.

Sometimes to include the costs of fans, lights, etc., an additional 3% cost is provided and thus electrification cost may sum up to 11% of the building cost.

123. A cable-supported at two ends primarily resists external loads by tension.

The cable is defined as the structure in pure tension having the funicular shape of the load. The cables are considered to be perfectly flexible (no flexural stiffness) and inextensible. As they are flexible they do not resist shear force and bending moment. It is subjected to axial tension only and it is always acting tangential to the cable at any point along the length. If the weight of the cable is negligible as compared with the externally applied loads then its self-weight is neglected in the analysis of the cable.

Hence, the correct option is (C).

124. The principle of units of measurements normally consists of the following:

(a) Single units work like doors, windows, trusses, etc., are expressed in numbers.

(b) Works consists of linear measurements involve length like cornice, fencing, handrail, bands of specified width, etc., are expressed in running meters (m).

(c) Works consist of areal surface measurements involve area like plastering, whitewashing, partitions of specified thickness, etc., and are expressed in square meters (m^2)

(d) Works consists of cubical contents which involve volume like earthwork, cement concrete, Masonry, etc. are expressed in Cubic meters (m^3).

125. The brickwork is measured in square meters, in case of

Honeycomb Brickwork: The thickness of the wall and the pattern of honeycombing shall be stated in measurement. Honeycomb openings shall not be deducted.

Halfway brick wall with cement or lime mortar: Net measurement shall be taken after deduction of all openings. Bricks on the edge wall shall be calculated in square meters.

Brick Flat Soling: Measurement shall include the fillings between gaps such as sands between bricks.

∴ All of the options are correct.

Q.1 For construction of structures under water, the type of lime used is ____.
A. hydraulic lime
B. fat lime
C. quick lime
D. pure lime

Q.2 The compound of Portland cement which reacts immediately with water and also sets first is ____.
A. Tri-calcium silicate
B. Di-calcium silicate
C. Tri-calcium aluminate
D. Tetra calcium alumino ferrite

Q.3 Rapid hardening cement attains early strength due to ____.
A. larger proportion of lime grounded finer than normal cement
B. lesser proportion of lime grounded coarser than normal cement
C. lesser proportion of lime grounded finer than normal cement
D. larger proportion of lime grounded coarser than normal cement

Q.4 Generally, the normal consistency for OPC ranges from ____.
A. 5 % to 15%
B. 10% to 25%
C. 15% to 25%
D. 25% to 35%

Q.5 Soundness test of cement determines ____.
A. quantity of free lime
B. ultimate strength
C. durability
D. initial setting

Q.6 Bulking of sand is caused due to ____.
A. surface moisture
B. air voids
C. viscosity
D. clay contents

Q.7 For a 50 kg cement bag, water required is ____.
A. 16.5 liters
B. 18.5 liters
C. 20.5 liters
D. 22.5 liters

Q.8 Pick up the correct statement from the following Method of sawing timber ____.
A. tangentially to annual rings, is known as tangential method in four quarters such that each board cuts annual rings at
B. angles not less than 45 °, is known as quarter sawing method
C. cut out of quarter logs, parallel to the mudullary rays and perpendicular to annual rings is known as radial sawing
D. All options are correct

Q.9 For the manufacture of plywood, veneers are placed so that grains of adjacent veneers are ____.
A. at right angles
B. parallel
C. inclined at 45 °
D. inclined at 60 °

Q.10 The portion of the brick without a triangular corner equal to half the width and half the length is called ____.
A. closer
B. queen closer
C. king closer
D. squint brick

Q.11 The height of the sink of wash basin above floor level is kept ____.
A. 60 cm
B. 70 cm
C. 75 cm to 80 cm
D. 80 cm

Q.12 Pick up the correct statement from the following.
A. In order to check up the average depth of excavation, 'Dead mans' are left at the mid-widths of borrow pits
B. The earthwork calculation in excavation is made from the difference in levels obtained with a level
C. The earthwork done in excavation is to form the road embankment includes the formation of correct profiles and depositing the soil in layers
D. All options are correct

Q.13 If the formation level of a highway has a uniform gradient for a particular length and the ground is also having a longitudinal slope, the earthwork may be calculated by ____.
A. Mid-section formula
B. Trapezoidal formula
C. Prismoidal formula
D. All options are correct

Q.14 A cement concrete road is 1000 m long, 8 m wide and 15 cm thick over the sub-base of 10 cm thick gravel. The cubic content of concrete (1:2:4) for the road specified in is ____.
A. 300 m^3
B. 600 m^3
C. 900 m^3
D. 1200 m^3

Q.15 The cross-sectional area of the embankment of a canal fully in embankment, (refer the figure given below) is:-

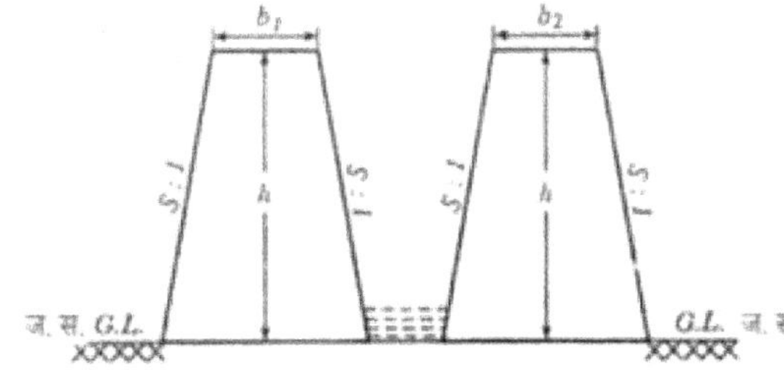

A. $1/2(b_1 + b_2)h$
B. $(b_1 + b_2)h + Sb^2$
C. $(b_1 + b_2)h + Sh^2$
D. $2[(b_1 + b_2)(b + Sh)]$

Q.16 The following item of earthwork is not measured separately ____.
A. Setting out of works
B. Site clearance
C. dead men
D. All options are correct

Q.17 Pick up the incorrect statement from the following ____.

A. No deduction is made for the volume occupied by reinforcement

B. No deduction is made for the openings up to 0.1 sq.m

C. No deduction is made for volumes occupied by pipes, not exceeding 100 sq. cm in cross- section

D. None of the these

Q.18 While estimating a reinforced cement structure the omitted cover of concrete is assumed ____.

A. at the end of reinforcing bar, not less than 25 mm or twice the diameter of the bar

B. in thin slabs, 12 mm minimum or diameter of the bar whichever is more

C. for reinforcing longitudinal bar in a beam 25 mm minimum or diameter of the largest bar which is more

D. All options are correct

Q.19 For 100 sq. m cement concrete (1:2:4) 4 cm thick floor, the quantity of cement required is ____.

A. 0.90 m³   **B.** 0.94 m³   **C.** 0.88 m³   **D.** 1.00 m³

Q.20 If h is the difference in height between end points of a chain of length the required slope correction is ____.

A. $h^2/(2l)$ **B.** $h/(2l)$ **C.** h^2/l **D.** $h^2/(4l)$

Q.21 Correction per chain length of 100 links along a slope of a radians is ____.

A. $100\ a^2$ **B.** $100\ a$

C. $100\ a^3$ **D.** $100\ a^{(-1)}$

Q.22 Check lines (or proof lines) in Chain Surveying are essentially required ____.

A. to plot the chain lines

B. to plot the offsets

C. to indicate the accuracy of the survey work

D. to increase the out-turn

Q.23 For taking offsets with an optical square on the right hand side of the chain line it is held ____.

A. by right hand upside down

B. by left hand upright

C. by right hand upright

D. by left hand upside down

Q.24 The conventional sign shown in the figure below represents a.

A. road bridge
C. canal bridge

B. railway bridge
D. aqua duct

Q.25 In an adjusted level when the bubble is central, the axis of the bubble tube becomes parallel to ____.

A. line of sight   **B.** line of collimation

C. axis of the telescope   **D.** None of the these

Q.26 An internal focusing type surveying telescope may be focused by the movement of ____.

A. objective glass of the telescope

B. convex-lens in the telescope

C. concave lens in the telescope

D. plano-convex lens in the telescope

Q.27 A dumpy level is set up with its eye-piece vertically over a peg A. The height from the top of peg A to the center of the eye-piece is 1.540 m and the reading on peg B is 0.705 m. The level is then setup over B. The height of the eye-piece above peg B is 1.490 m and a reading on A is 2.195 m. The difference in level between A and B is ____.

A. 2.900 m   **B.** 3.030 m   **C.** 0.770 m   **D.** 0.785 m

Q.28 The constant vertical distance between two adjacent contours is called ____.

A. horizontal interval

B. horizontal equivalent

C. vertical equivalent

D. contour interval

Q.29 The direction of steepest slope on a contour is ____.

A. along the contour

B. at an angle of 45 ° to the contour

C. at right angles to the contour

D. None of these

Q.30 Geologic cycle for the formation of soil, is ____.

A. Upheaval → transportation → deposition → weathering

B. Weathering → upheaval → transportation → deposition

C. Transportation → upheaval → weathering → deposition

D. weathering → transportation → deposition → upheaval

Q.31 Water content of a soil sample is the difference of the weight of the given sample at the given temperature and the weight determined after drying it for 24 hours at temperatures ranging from ____.

A. 80 ° to 90 ° C   **B.** 90 ° to 95 ° C

C. 95 ° to 100 ° C   **D.** 105 ° to 110 ° C

Q.32 Fundamental relationship between dry density (γd), bulk density (γ) and water content (ω) is ____.

A. γ = γ^d/(1+ω)   **B.** γd = γ/(1+ ω)

C. ω = γ/(1+γd)   **D.** ω = γ/(1-γd)

Q.33 Pick up the correct statement from the following ____.

A. The void ratio in soils is defined as the ratio of the volume of voids to the volume of solids

B. The porosity of a soil is defined as the ratio of the volume of voids to the gross volume of the soil

C. The bulk density of a soil is defined as the unit weight of the soil in natural state

D. All options are correct

Q.34 Alcohol is used in manometer, because ____.

A. its vapor pressure is low

B. it provides suitable meniscus for the inclined tube

C. its density is less

D. it provides longer length for a given pressure difference

Q.35 The property of fluid by virtue of which it offers resistance to shear is called ____.

A. surface tension   **B.** adhesion

C. cohesion   **D.** viscosity

Q.36 The unit of kinematic viscosity is ____.

A. m^2/sec   **B.** kg-sec/m^2

C. newton-sec/m^2 **D.** newton-sec^2/m

Q.37 The total pressure on the surface of a vertical sluice gate 2m x 1m with its top 2 m surface being 0.5 m below the water level will be ____.

A. 500 kg   **B.** 1000 kg   **C.** 1500 kg   **D.** 2000 kg

Q.38 Meta-centric height is given as the distance between ____.

A. the centre of gravity of the body and the meta-centre

B. the centre of gravity of the body and the centre of buoyancy

C. the centre of gravity of the body and the centre of pressure

D. centre of buoyancy and meta-centre

Q.39 The difference of pressure between the inside and outside of a liquid drop is ____.

A. p = T x r   **B.** p = T/r   **C.** p = T/2r   **D.** p = 2T/r

Q.40 The property by which a liquid opposes relative motion between its different layers is called ____.

A. surface tension

B. co-efficient of viscosity

C. viscosity

D. osmosis

Q.41 The atmospheric pressure with rise in altitude decreases ____.

A. linearly

B. first slowly then steeply

C. first steeply and then gradually

D. unpredictable

Q.42 Barometer is used to measure ____.

A. pressure in pipes, channels etc.

B. atmospheric pressure

C. very low pressure

D. difference of pressure between two points

Q.43 Flow meters based on obstruction principle like orifice plates can be used with Reynold's number upto approximately ____.

A. 500   **B.** 1000   **C.** 2000   **D.** 4000

Q.44 The state of the soil when plants fail to extract sufficient water for their requirements is ____.

A. maximum saturated point

B. permanent wilting point

C. ultimate utilization point

D. None of these

Q.45 The field capacity of a soil is 25%, its permanent wilting point is 15% and specific dry unit weight is 1.5. If the depth of root zone of a crop is 80 cm, the storage capacity of the soil is ____.

A. 8 cm   **B.** 10 cm   **C.** 12 cm   **D.** 14 cm

Q.46 According to the recommendations of Nagpur Conference the width formation of an ideal National Highway in hard rock cutting is ____.

A. 8.9 m   **B.** 7.9 m   **C.** 6.9 m   **D.** 6.5 m

Q.47 If L is the length of a rail and R is the radius of a curve, the versine h for the curve is ____.

A. a= L/4R   **B.** a= L^2/4R

C. h= L^2/8R   **D.** h= L^2/16R

Q.48 Pick up the incorrect statement from the following.

A. Manholes are provided in sewer pipes at suitable intervals

B. Catch basins are generally provided in sewers for carrying drainage discharge

C. Inlets are generally provided in all sewers

D. None of the these

Q.49 If q is the average sewage flow from a city of population P, the maximum sewage flow ____.

A. Q = [(4+√P)/(18+ √P)]q

B. Q = [(18 +P)/(4+ √P)]q

C. Q = [(18+√P)/(4 + √P)]q

D. Q = [(5+√P)/(15 + √P)]q

Q.50 A body is said to be in equilibrium if ____.

A. it moves horizontally

B. it moves vertically

C. it rotates about its C.G.

D. None of these

Q.51 The forces acting normally on the cross section of a bar shown in the figure given below.

A. Compressive stress   **B.** tensile stress

C. shear stress   **D.** None of these

Q.52 At yield point of a test piece, the material ____.

A. obeys Hooke's law

B. behaves in an elastic manner

C. regains its original shape on removal of the load

D. undergoes plastic deformation

Q.53 If a concrete column 200 x 200 mm in cross-section is reinforced with four steel bars of 1200 mm^2 total cross-

sectional area. What is the safe load for the column if permissible stress in concrete is 5 N/mm^2 and E_s =15 E_c?

A. 264 kN **B.** 274 kN **C.** 284 kN **D.** 294 kN

Q.54 A steel rod of sectional area 25 sq. mm connects two parallel walls 5 m apart. The nuts at the ends were tightened when the rod was heated at 100 ° C. If α_{steel} = 0.000012/C °, E_{steel} = 0.2 MN/mm2, the tensile stress developed at a temperature of 50 ° C is ____.

A. 80 N/mm^2
B. 100 N/mm^2
C. 120 N/mm^2
D. 150 N/mm^2

Q.55 The ratio of tangential and normal components of a stress on an inclined plane through θ ° to the direction of the force is ____.

A. sin θ **B.** cos θ **C.** tan θ **D.** Sin2θ

Q.56 Pick up the correct statement from the following.

A. For a uniformly distributed load, the shear force varies linearly

B. For a uniformly distributed load, bending moment curve is a parabola

C. For a load varying linearly, the shear force curve is a parabola

D. All options are correct

Q.57 At any point of a beam, the section modulus may be obtained by dividing the moment of inertia of the section by ____.

A. depth of the section

B. depth of the neutral axis

C. maximum tensile stress at the section

D. maximum compressive stress at the section

Q.58 The moment of inertia of a circular section about any diameter D, is ____.

A. $(\pi D^2)/64$
B. $(\pi D^4)/32$
C. $(\pi D^3)/64$
D. $(\pi D^4)/64$

Q.59 In case of principal axes of a section ____.

A. sum of moment of inertia is zero

B. difference of moment of inertia is zero

C. product moment of inertia is zero

D. None of these

Q.60 The locus of the moment of inertia about inclined axis to the principal axis is ____.

A. straight line **B.** parabola
C. circle **D.** ellipse

Q.61 The ratio of moments of inertia of a triangular section about its base and about a centroidal axis parallel to its base is ____.

A. 1 **B.** 1.5 **C.** 2 **D.** 3

Q.62 If aggregates completely pass through a sieve of size 75 mm and are retained on a sieve of size 60 mm, the particular aggregate will be flaky if its minimum dimension is less than ____.

A. 20.5 mm **B.** 30.5 mm **C.** 40.5 mm **D.** 50.5 mm

Q.63 For the construction of thin R.C.C. structures the type of cement to be avoided is ____.

A. ordinary Portland cement

B. rapid hardening cement

C. low heat cement

D. blast furnace slag cement

Q.64 Percentage of pozzolanic material containing clay upto 80% used for the manufacture of pozzolana cement is ____.

A. 30% **B.** 40% **C.** 50% **D.** 60%

Q.65 Pick up the incorrect statement applicable to the field test of good cement.

A. When one thrusts one's hand into a bag of cement, one should feel warm

B. The color of the cement is bluish

C. A handful of cement thrown into a bucket of water should not sink immediately

D. All options are incorrect

Q.66 Pick up the correct statement from the following.

A. The maximum size of a coarse aggregate is 80 mm and minimum is 4.75 mm

B. The maximum size of the fine aggregate is 4.75 mm and minimum 0.075 mm

C. The material having particles of size varying from 0.075 mm to 0.002 mm is known as silt

D. All options are correct

Q.67 Sand generally contains salt if it is obtained from ____.

A. nala beds

B. river beds

C. sea beds

D. All options are correct

Q.68 Pick up the correct statement from the following.

A. Bulking of sand is caused due to formation of a thin film of surface moisture

B. Fine sand bulks more than coarse sand

C. With 10% moisture content by weight the bulking of sand is increased by 50%

D. All options are correct

Q.69 If fineness modulus of sand is 2.5 it is graded as ____.

A. very fine sand **B.** fine sand
C. medium sand **D.** coarse sand

Q.70 An ordinary Portland cement when tested for its fineness, should not leave any residue on I.S. Sieve No.9, more than ____.

A. 5% **B.** 10% **C.** 15% **D.** 20%

Q.71 Pick up the correct statement from the following.

A. Insufficient quantity of water makes the concrete mix harsh

B. Insufficient quantity of water makes the concrete unworkable

C. Excess quantity of water makes the concrete segregated

D. All options are correct

Q.72 Pick up the incorrect statement from the following.

A. A rich mix of concrete possesses higher strength than that a lean mix of desired workability with excessive quantity of water

B. The strength of concrete decreases as the water cement ratio increases

C. If the water cement ratio is less than 0.45, the concrete is not workable and causes honey-combed structure

D. Good compaction by mechanical vibrations, increases the strength of concrete

Q.73 Pick up the correct statement from the following.

A. The concrete gains strength due to hydration of cement

B. 28-day strength decreases with increasing curing temperature.

C. The concrete does not set at freezing point

D. All options are correct

Q.74 Hardening of cement occurs at ____.

A. rapid rate during the first few days and afterwards it continues to increase at a decreased rate

B. slow rate during the first few days and afterwards it continues to increase at a rapid rate

C. uniform rate throughout its age

D. None of these

Q.75 Pick up the correct statement from the following.

A. Higher workability indicates unexpected increase in the moisture content

B. Higher workability indicates deficiency of sand

C. If the concrete mix is dry, the slump is zero

D. All options are correct

Q.76 The top diameter, bottom diameter and the height of a slump mould are ____.

A. 10 cm, 20 cm, 30 cm

B. 10 cm, 30 cm, 20 cm

C. 20 cm, 10 cm, 30 cm

D. 20 cm, 30 cm, 10 cm

Q.77 Pick up the correct statement from the following.

A. Segregation is necessary for a workable concrete

B. Consistency does not affect the workability of concrete

C. If the slump increases, workability decreases

D. None of these

Q.78 The grade of concrete M 150 means that compressive strength of a 15 cm cube after 28 days, is ____.

A. 100 kg/cm^2

B. 150 kg/cm^2

C. 200 kg/cm^2

D. 250 kg/cm^2

Q.79 The preliminary test is repeated if the difference compressive strength of three test specimens, exceeds ____.

A. 5 kg/cm^2

B. 8 kg/cm^2

C. 10 kg/cm^2

D. 15 kg/cm^2

Q.80 According to load factor method, the permissible load W on a short column reinforced with longitudinal bars and lateral stirrups is ____.

A. Stress in concrete x area of concrete

B. Stress in steel x area of steel

C. Stress in concrete x area of concrete + stress in steel x area of steel

D. None of these

Q.81 The length of the lap in a compression member is kept greater than [bar diameter x (Permissible stress in bar)/(Five times the bond stress)] or is ____.

A. 12 bar diameters

B. 18 bar diameters

C. 24 bar diameters

D. 30 bar diameters

Q.82 A short column 20 cm x 20 cm in section is reinforced with 4 bars whose area of cross section is 20 sq.cm. If permissible compressive stresses in concrete and steel are 40 kg/cm2 and 300 kg/cm2, the safe load on the column should not exceed ____.

A. 412 kg

B. 4120 kg

C. 412000 kg

D. None of these

Q.83 A column is regarded as long column if the ratio of its effective length and lateral dimension exceeds ____.

A. 10

B. 15

C. 20

D. None of these

Q.84 If the size of a column is reduced above the floor, the main bars of the columns ____.

A. continues up

B. bend inwards at the floor level

C. stops just below the floor level and separates lap bars provided

D. All options are correct

Q.85 The pitch of the main bars in a simply supported slab should not exceed its effective depth by ____.

A. three times

B. four times

C. five times

D. six times

Q.86 Distribution reinforcement in a simply supported slab is provided to distribute ____.

A. load

B. temperature stress

C. shrinkage stress

D. All options are correct

Q.87 In a simply supported slab the minimum spacing between two reinforcement bars should be at least equal to the maximum aggregate grain dimension with a margin of ___ mm

A. 2

B. 3

C. 4

D. 5

Q.88 The modular ratio 'm' of a concrete whose permissible compressive stress is 'C' may be obtained from the equation ____.

A. m = 700/3C

B. m = 140/3C

C. m = 280/3C

D. m = 350/3C

Q.89 For M 15 grade concrete (1 : 2 : 4) and steel grade Fe415, the moment of resistance factor is ____.

A. 0.87

B. 2.07

C. 2.7

D. 2.00

Q.90 If the thickness of a structural member is small as compared to its length and width, it is classified as ____.

A. one dimensional

B. two dimensional

C. three dimensional

D. None of these

Q.91 Design of a riveted joint assumes that ____.
A. the bending stress in rivets is accounted for
B. the riveted hole is to be filled by the rivet
C. the stress in the plate is not uniform
D. the friction between plates is considered

Q.92 Rolled steel T-sections are used ____.
A. as columns
B. with flat strips to connect plates in steel rectangular tanks
C. as built up sections to resist axial tension
D. None of these

Q.93 With a percentage increase of carbon in steel, decreases its ____.
A. strength
B. hardness
C. brittleness
D. ductility

Q.94 If P is the wind pressure in kg/cm², v is the velocity in km/hour and K is constant of proportionality then ____.
A. $P=K/v^2$
B. $v=K/P^2$
C. $P=Kv^2$
D. $P=Kv$

Q.95 Factor of safety is the ratio of ____.
A. yield stress to working stress
B. tensile stress to working stress
C. compressive stress to working stress
D. bearing stress to working stress

Q.96 The ratio of shearing stress to shearing strain within elastic limit, is known as ____.
A. modulus of elasticity
B. Shear modulus
C. bulk modulus of elasticity
D. tangent modulus of elasticity

Q.97 The rivets which are heated and then driven in the field are known ____.
A. power driven shop rivets
B. power driven field rivets
C. hand driven rivets
D. cold driven rivets

Q.98 The gross diameter of a rivet is the diameter of ____.
A. cold rivet before driving
B. rivet after driving
C. rivet hole + 1 mm
D. None of these

Q.99 Working shear stress on the gross area of a rivet as recommended by Indian Standards is ____.
A. 785 kg/cm²
B. 1025 kg/cm²
C. 2360 kg/cm²
D. None of the these

Q.100 The net force as per Navier stokes Equation is presented by.
A. $F_x = F_{Gravity} + F_{Pressure} + F_{Viscous} + F_{Turbulence} + F_{compressibility}$
B. $F_x = F_{Gravity} + F_{Pressure} + F_{Viscous} + F_{Turbulence}$
C. $F_x = F_{Gravity} + F_{Pressure} + F_{Viscous}$
D. $F_x = F_{Gravity} + F_{Pressure}$

Q.101 A water sample has concentration of OH^- ion measured on 0.17 mg/L at 25°C. What is the pH of the water sample?
A. 10
B. 9
C. 8
D. 7

Q.102 In an over-reinforced concrete beam?
A. Actual depth of neutral axis is more than the critical depth of neutral axis
B. Moment of resistance is more than that of balanced section
C. Both A and B
D. None of these

Q.103 A sample of soil with water content of 50%, void ratio of 1.25 and specific gravity of soil 2.5 will be said to be in a state of:
A. Full saturation
B. Partial saturation
C. Over saturation
D. Zero saturation

Q.104 Match the given water quality parameters in group I to the cause for rejection values in group II.

Group I
(P) Alkalinity
(Q) Chloride Content
(R) Iron
(S) Manganese

Group II
(1) 1 mg/L
(2) 0.5 mg/L
(3) 600 mg/L
(4) 1000 mg/L

A. P -4, Q-3, R-2, S-1
B. P -3, Q-4, R-1, S-2
C. P -4, Q-1, R-2, S-3
D. P -3, Q-2, R-1, S-4

Q.105 As per IS 456 – 2000, the dosage of retarders, plasticisers and superplasticisers shall be restricted to ____, ____ and ____ percent respectively by weight of cementitious materials ?
A. 1.0, 0.5 and 2.0
B. 0.5, 1.0 and 2.0
C. 1.0, 2.0 and 0.5
D. 0.5, 2.0 and 1.0

Q.106 As per IS 800 – 2007, in case of staggered pitch, pitch may be increased by ____ percent of values specified above provided gauge distance is less than ____ mm.
A. 33, 50
B. 25, 75
C. 33, 75
D. 50, 75

Q.107 For the cross-section given below, what is the distance between elastic neutral axis and plastic neutral axis.

A. 67.22 mm

B. 35 mm

C. 32.22 mm

D. 33.72 mm

Q.108 The rear driving wheels of a car are providing a tractive force of 400 N. The vehicle is negotiating a curve such that the turning angle stands at 8°. The curve resistance due to turning of vehicle will be.

A. 396.11 N

B. 3.89 N

C. 55.67 N

D. 344.33 N

Q.109 As per IRC 52 – 2001, for the purpose of measuring the stopping sight distance, the height of eye level of driver as _______ m and the height of the object as ______ m above the road surface is considered.

A. 1.2 , 0.15

B. 0.15 , 1.2

C. 1.2 , 0.5

D. 1.2 , 0.75

Q.110 Change points in levelling are?

A. the instrument stations that are changed from one position to another

B. the staff stations that are changed from point to point to obtain the reduced levels of the points

C. the staff stations of known elevations

D. the staff station where back sight and fore sight readings are taken

Q.111 For the matrix

$$\begin{matrix} 2 & -3 & 5 \\ 0 & 1 & 2 \\ 0 & 0 & 0 \end{matrix}$$

the Eigen values of A^{-1} are

A. 2, 1, 0

B. 1/2, 1, ∞

C. -2, -1, 0

D. does not exist

Q.112 The final value of $x(t) = [2 + e^{-3t}]u(t)$ is

A. 2

B. 3

C. e^{-2t}

D. 0

Q.113 The integral

$$\int \frac{\sin^2 x \cos^2 x}{(\sin^5 x + \cos^3 x \sin^2 x + x \cos^2 x + \cos^5 x)^2} dx \text{ is equal to:}$$

A. $\frac{1}{1+\cot^3 x} + C$

B. $\frac{-1}{1+\cot^3 x} + C$

C. $\frac{1}{3(1+\tan^3 x)} + C$

D. $\frac{-1}{3(1+\tan^3 x)} + C$

Q.114 A single bored pile 20m long, 500 mm diameter and adhesion coefficient (α) 0.4 is penetrated in the soil strata having properties as below :

Depth (m) 0 – 5 5 – 10 10 – 15 15 – 20

Undrained shear strength (kPa) 50 70 90 190

If $\varphi_u = 0$ is valid and $N_c = 9$ and factor of safety is 2.5, the safe load carrying capacity of the single bored pile is ?

A. 573.32 kN

B. 663.93 kN

C. 636.93 kN

D. 537.32 kN

Q.115 A cantilever beam of width 450 mm and effective depth 550 mm is laterally restrained at a distance L from the free end. The maximum value of 'L' to ensure proper stability is

A. 27 m

B. 13.5 m

C. 11.25 m

D. 36.82 m

Q.116 A tension test bar is found to taper uniformly from (D – a) cm diameter to (D + a) cm diameter. What is the error involved in using the mean diameter to calculate the young's modulus ?

A. $\frac{a^2}{D^2} percent$

B. $\left(\frac{10a}{D}\right)^2 percent$

C. $10.\frac{a^2}{D^2} percent$

D. $\frac{(10a)^2}{D} percent$

Q.117 A rigid wheel 1.25 m in diameter is to be provided with a thin steel tyre. If the stress in the steel type is not to exceed 140 MN/m^2, the minimum temperature to which the type is to be raised so that it can be fitted over the wheel is ____°C. Take E = 200 GN/m^2; ∝ = 12 × 10–6/°C.

A. 58.43 °C

B. 58.39 °C

C. 58.33 °C

D. 58.70 °C

Q.118 A spiral column of diameter 500 mm is subjected to an unfactored load of 1600 KN with longitudinal reinforcement 8-16 mmand effective length of column is 3.5 m. The column is provided with helical reinforcement of diameter 6 mm. The concrete used is M25 and reinforcement provided is FeClear cover used is 40 mm.

The pitch of the helical reinforcement satisfying the criteria as per IS456 – 2000 is ____ mm.

A. 30mm

B. 25mm

C. 15mm

D. 20mm

Q.119 A single angle section ISA 100 × 75, 8 mm is used to resist tensile load with connection as shown below. Use 20 mm shop bolts of grade 4.6 for the connection. The block shear strength of the connection is ______ kN.

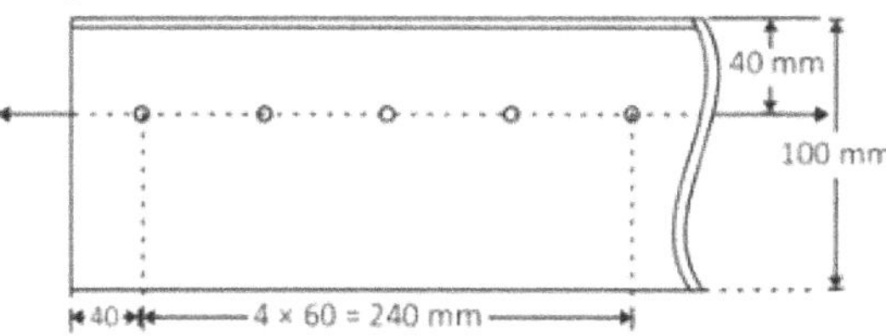

A. 355.88

B. 353.48

C. 359.85

D. 320.10

Q.120 A fast moving vehicle travelling a speed of 70 kmph is intending to overtake a slow-moving vehicle travelling with a speed of 40 kmph. To assess the overtaking opportunity the fast-moving vehicle travels a certain distance during the reaction time of 2 seconds. The distance at this moment between the two vehicles is 15 m. The overtaking vehicle then accelerates at the rate of 0.99 m/s^2 and overtake the slow-moving vehicle to a position such that at this instant, the distance between the two vehicles is 20m. For the case of two-way traffic, the overtaking sight distance is ______ m

A. 325.69

B. 350.47

C. 314.42

D. 320.56

Q.121 For the network shown below, the critical path is?

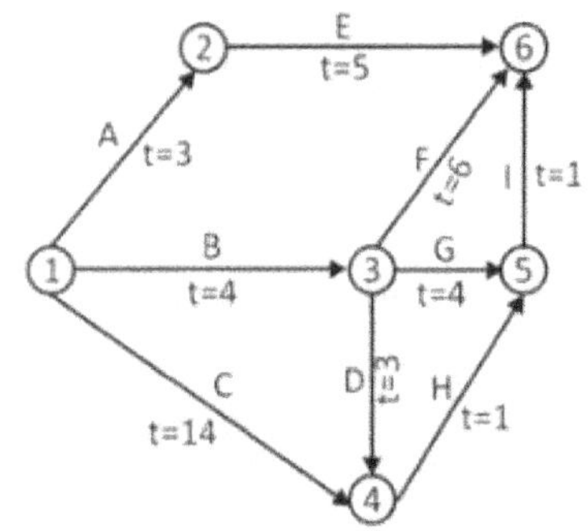

A. B-D-H-I   **B.** B-G-I   **C.** C-H-I   **D.** A-E

Q.122 Given below are the plots for various properties of a bitumen mix -

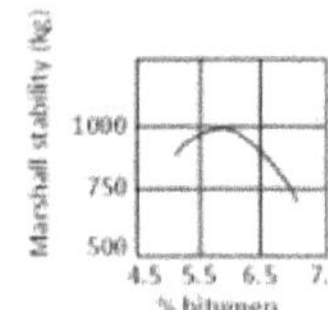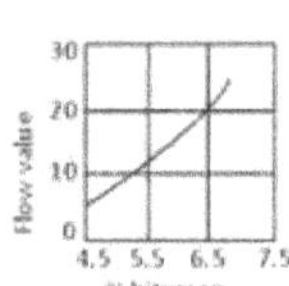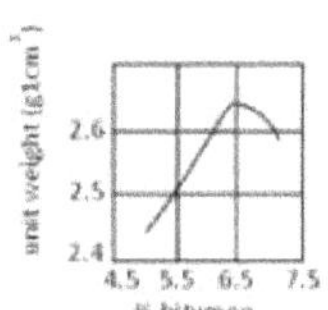

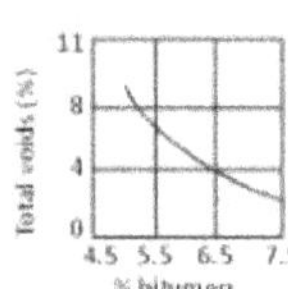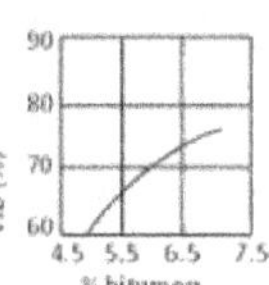

The optimum bitumen content of the mix is

A. 6.5 %   **B.** 6.17 %   **C.** 6.33 %   **D.** 6.0 %

Q.123 A solid waste sample has following composition:

Component	Percent by mass	Moisture%
Food wastes	15	70
Paper	45	6
Cardboard	10	5
Plastics	5	2
Garden Trimmings	4	60
Wood	10	20
Tin cans	6	3

What is the moisture content of the solid waste sample?

A. 18.38   **B.** 19.35   **C.** 20.42   **D.** 23.38

Q.124 For a function

$$f = 5x^2 y\hat{i} + 5x^2 y\hat{j} + 3yz^2\hat{k}$$ the divergence at (0.5, -2, 2) is.

A. -4   **B.** -10   **C.** -14.5   **D.** -32.75

Q.125 If f(1) = 1, f'(1) = 2, then

$$\lim_{x\to 1} \frac{\sqrt{f(x)}-1}{\sqrt{x}-1}$$ is ___.

A. 0   **B.** 1   **C.** 2   **D.** 3

// Smart Answer Sheet //

Correct Percentage of students who answered correctly. **Skipped** Percentage of students who skipped.

Q.	Ans.	Correct / Skipped	Q.	Ans.	Correct / Skipped	Q.	Ans.	Correct / Skipped	Q.	Ans.	Correct / Skipped	Q.	Ans.	Correct / Skipped
1	A	63.08 % / 9.23 %	17	D	44.62 % / 29.23 %	33	D	66.15 % / 26.16 %	49	C	24.62 % / 43.07 %	65	D	52.31 % / 27.69 %
2	C	66.15 % / 21.54 %	18	D	60.0 % / 30.77 %	34	A	40.0 % / 21.54 %	50	D	7.69 % / 30.77 %	66	D	56.92 % / 33.85 %
3	A	47.69 % / 27.69 %	19	C	35.38 % / 35.39 %	35	D	49.23 % / 26.15 %	51	A	64.62 % / 26.15 %	67	C	63.08 % / 26.15 %
4	D	27.69 % / 26.16 %	20	A	76.92 % / 15.39 %	36	A	50.77 % / 27.69 %	52	D	35.38 % / 27.7 %	68	D	58.46 % / 32.31 %
5	A	60.0 % / 27.69 %	21	B	26.15 % / 26.16 %	37	D	10.77 % / 41.54 %	53	C	15.38 % / 49.24 %	69	B	43.08 % / 30.77 %
6	A	61.54 % / 27.69 %	22	C	70.77 % / 21.54 %	38	A	41.54 % / 32.31 %	54	C	7.69 % / 61.54 %	70	B	55.38 % / 29.24 %
7	D	58.46 % / 26.16 %	23	B	32.31 % / 35.38 %	39	D	52.31 % / 29.23 %	55	C	47.69 % / 32.31 %	71	D	64.62 % / 26.15 %
8	D	58.46 % / 32.31 %	24	C	21.54 % / 18.46 %	40	C	60.0 % / 27.69 %	56	D	58.46 % / 27.69 %	72	A	30.77 % / 24.61 %
9	A	55.38 % / 26.16 %	25	A	33.85 % / 29.23 %	41	B	41.54 % / 29.23 %	57	B	40.0 % / 32.31 %	73	D	64.62 % / 26.15 %
10	C	46.15 % / 29.23 %	26	C	41.54 % / 32.31 %	42	B	67.69 % / 21.54 %	58	D	58.46 % / 29.23 %	74	A	47.69 % / 32.31 %
11	C	64.62 % / 27.69 %	27	C	27.69 % / 47.69 %	43	C	41.54 % / 33.84 %	59	C	20.0 % / 35.38 %	75	D	63.08 % / 26.15 %
12	D	64.62 % / 27.69 %	28	D	66.15 % / 21.54 %	44	B	56.92 % / 26.16 %	60	D	20.0 % / 40.0 %	76	A	58.46 % / 29.23 %
13	D	58.46 % / 32.31 %	29	C	38.46 % / 32.31 %	45	C	23.08 % / 49.23 %	61	D	36.92 % / 29.23 %	77	D	38.46 % / 27.69 %
14	D	18.46 % / 40.0 %	30	D	46.15 % / 21.54 %	46	B	41.54 % / 33.84 %	62	C	40.0 % / 43.08 %	78	B	67.69 % / 27.69 %
15	C	38.46 % / 35.39 %	31	D	64.62 % / 27.69 %	47	C	43.08 % / 33.84 %	63	D	23.08 % / 27.69 %	79	D	27.69 % / 32.31 %
16	D	64.62 % / 24.61 %	32	B	58.46 % / 26.16 %	48	C	20.0 % / 32.31 %	64	A	35.38 % / 30.77 %	80	C	47.69 % / 27.69 %

Q.	Ans.	Correct / Skipped	Q.	Ans.	Correct / Skipped	Q.	Ans.	Correct / Skipped	Q.	Ans.	Correct / Skipped	Q.	Ans.	Correct / Skipped
81	C	49.23 % / 33.85 %	90	B	36.92 % / 32.31 %	99	B	36.92 % / 33.85 %	108	B	9.23 % / 55.39 %	117	C	1.54 % / 61.54 %
82	D	18.46 % / 44.62 %	91	B	46.15 % / 30.77 %	100	C	26.15 % / 40.0 %	109	A	41.54 % / 30.77 %	118	B	6.15 % / 56.93 %
83	D	27.69 % / 27.69 %	92	B	32.31 % / 33.84 %	101	B	9.23 % / 49.23 %	110	D	53.85 % / 23.07 %	119	A	3.08 % / 61.54 %
84	D	46.15 % / 30.77 %	93	D	58.46 % / 29.23 %	102	C	50.77 % / 29.23 %	111	D	12.31 % / 56.92 %	120	C	1.54 % / 60.0 %
85	A	53.85 % / 26.15 %	94	C	50.77 % / 29.23 %	103	A	41.54 % / 36.92 %	112	A	6.15 % / 49.23 %	121	C	12.31 % / 43.07 %
86	D	53.85 % / 29.23 %	95	A	55.38 % / 29.24 %	104	B	30.77 % / 35.38 %	113	D	12.31 % / 55.38 %	122	C	7.69 % / 50.77 %
87	D	32.31 % / 35.38 %	96	B	40.0 % / 29.23 %	105	B	21.54 % / 40.0 %	114	C	1.54 % / 60.0 %	123	D	1.54 % / 58.46 %
88	C	60.0 % / 32.31 %	97	B	56.92 % / 29.23 %	106	D	6.15 % / 47.7 %	115	C	16.92 % / 52.31 %	124	D	9.23 % / 52.31 %
89	B	6.15 % / 35.39 %	98	B	32.31 % / 30.77 %	107	C	9.23 % / 55.39 %	116	B	13.85 % / 49.23 %	125	C	1.54 % / 56.92 %

//Hints and Solutions//

1. For construction of structures under water, hydraulic lime is used. Fat lime lime can not be used due to its poor setting in wet conditions.

2. Tri-calcium aluminate is the first bogus compound formed when water is added to the cement, this compound is formed with 24 hour and it produces the maximum heat of evolution.

3. Rapid hardening cement attains early strength due to larger proportion of lime grounded finer than normal cement. Finer grinding of cements leads to increase in heat of evolution, and attains the early strength.

4. The Standard or Normal consistency for Ordinary Portland cement varies between 25-35%.

5. Soundness test of cement determines the free lime content, lime is very prone to volume increase on reacting with water. If free lime content is more then soundness will be more which is a undesirable property for good cement.

6. Bulking of sand is caused due to thin film of surface moisture, when sand contains 4 to 6% of moisture content a thin layer of water surface form around the sand particle which increases the volume of sand, is known as bulking of sand.

7. For a 50 kg cement bag, water required is 22.5 liters for complete hydration of cement.

8.

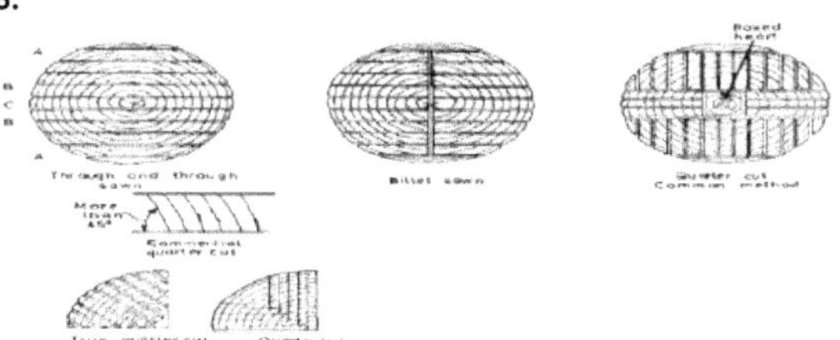

9. For the manufacture of plywood, veneers are placed so that grains of adjacent veneers are at right angles. on placing at right angles plywood equally strong in tension and compressions and not deflected in particular direction.

10. The portion of the brick without a triangular corner equal to half the width and half the length is called king closer, and with a triangular corner but having half of its original length and width is known as queen closer.

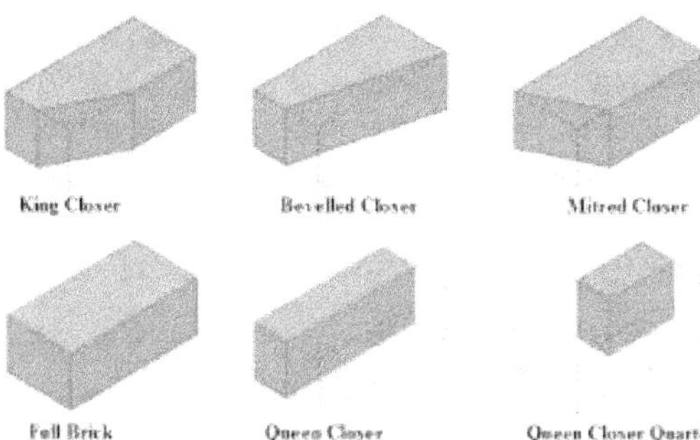

11. The height of the sink of wash basin above floor level is kept 75 to 80 cm for easy free vortex formation into the sink basin.

12. Excavation work does not include the top soiling and rest of the things are correct related to the excavation of average depth, excavation calculation, formation of correct profiles and depositing the soil in layers necessary for road embankment by excavation of earth.

13. If the formation level of a highway has a uniform gradient for a particular length and the ground is also having a longitudinal slope, the earthwork may be calculated by Mid-section formula, Trapezoidal formula, Prismoidal formula.

14. the sub-base of 10 cm thick gravel bed is not required the concrete so calculation only done for the lengh, width, and thickness of concrete pavement.

V=1000x8x0.15=1200m³

15. The cross-sectional area of the embankment of a canal fully in embankment is $(b_1 + b_2) + 2Sh^2$
Hint: $A1 = (2b1 + 2sh) \times h/2 = (b1 + sh)h$
Similarly, $A_2 = (b_2 + sh)h$
$A = A_1 + A_2 = (b_1 + b_2)h + 2sh^2$

16. All these earth work is measured simultaneously as Setting out of works, Site clearance, dead men.

17. No deduction is made for the volume occupied by reinforcement, No deduction is made for the openings up to 0.1 m², No deduction is made for volumes occupied by pipes, not exceeding 100 cm² in cross- section.

18. While estimating a reinforced cement structure the omitted cover of concrete is assumed, at the end of reinforcing bar, not less than 25 mm or twice the diameter of the bar, in thin slabs, 12 mm minimum or diameter of the bar whichever is more, for reinforcing longitudinal bar in a beam 25 mm minimum or diameter of the largest bar which is more.

19. Dry volume of concrete is 154% of wet volume of concrete

The volume of concrete (wet) = 100 x 0.04 = 4 m³

Dry volume will be = 4 x 1.54 = 6.16 m³

NOw, quantity of cement will be = volume of dry concrete x cement proportion into the concrete,

= 6.16 x (1/7) = 0.88 m³

20. If h is the difference in height between end points of a chain of length the required slope correction is $h^2/(2l)$. Slope correction negative in nature.

21. Correction per chain length of 100 links along a slope of a radians is 100 a.

Correction is applied to per chain link and a is the correction factor.

22. Check lines (or proof lines) in Chain Surveying are essentially required

to indicate the accuracy of the survey work.

23. For taking offsets with an optical square on the right hand side of the chain line it is held by left hand upright. While For taking offsets with an optical square on the left hand side of the chain line it is held by right hand upright.

24. The conventional sign is the canal bridge.

25. In an adjusted level when the bubble is central, the axis of the bubble tube becomes parallel to line of sight.

26. An internal focusing type surveying telescope may be focused by the movement of concave lens in the telescope. For removal of parallax in the setting operation.

27. This is the reciprocal leveling,

Dumpy level set up some where, the reading at A = h_A = 1.540m

The reading at B = h_B = 0.705m

And when dumpy level at B then reading at A = h'_A = 2.195m

And at B = h'_B = 1.490m

The difference in level between A and B is = [(h_A - h_B) + (h'_A - h'_B)]/2 = 0.770m

28. The constant vertical distance between two adjacent contours is defined as the counter interval. In interval is small it is steep gradient.

29. The direction of steepest slope on a contour is at right angles to the contour.

30. Geologic cycle for the formation of soil, is weathering → transportation → deposition → upheaval.

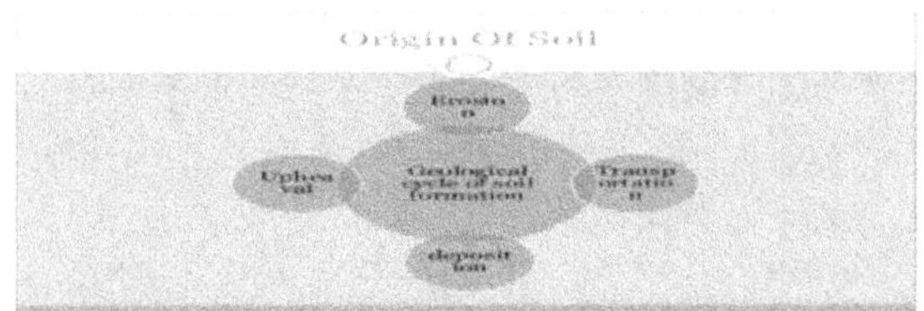

31. This is the oven dry method of determination of water content the temperatures ranging from 105 ° to 110 ° C specially in case of inorganic soil. For organic soil the temperature ranges from 80^0 to 85^0 C.

32. Fundamental relationship between dry density (γd), bulk density (γ) and water content (ω) is $\gamma d = \gamma/(1+\omega)$

33. The void ratio in soils is defined as the ratio of the volume of voids to the volume of solids(V_v/V_s), The porosity of a soil is defined as the ratio of the volume of voids to the gross volume of the soil(V_v/V), The bulk density of a soil is defined as the unit weight of the soil.

34. Alcohol is used in manometer, because its vapor pressure is low. In manometer low pressure fluid gives quite satisfactory result.

35. The property of fluid by virtue of which it offers resistance to shear is called viscosity.

As newton's law t= $\tau = \mu\left(d_u/d_y\right)$

τ = shear stress, μ = viscosity, $\left(d_u/d_y\right)$ = velocity gradients.

36. The unit of kinematic viscosity is m²/sec

kinematic viscosity =dynamic viscosity/density

37. The total pressure on sluice gate will be given by WxAxY = 2000 kg

W = density of water = 1000 kg/m³

A=area 2 x 1 = 2m²

Y = distance from water surface = 0.5 + (1/2) = 1 m

38. Meta-centric height is given as the distance between the centre of gravity of the body and the meta-centre.

39. The difference of pressure between the inside and outside of a liquid drop is 2T/r

40. The property by which a liquid opposes relative motion between its different layers is called viscosity.

41. The atmospheric pressure with rise in altitude decreases first slowly then steeply.

42. A barometer is a scientific instrument used in meteorology to measure atmospheric pressure. Pressure tendency can forecast short term changes in the weather. Many measurements of air pressure are used within surface weather analysis to help find surface troughs, high pressure systems and frontal boundaries.

43. Flow meters based on obstruction principle like orifice plates can be used with Reynold's number upto approximately 2000, above 2000 this flow shows transition and more than 4000 shows turbulent behabour.

44. Permanent wilting point is defined as when plant fails to extract sufficient water to growth of crop. And finally plant wiltup.

45. the storage capacity of the soil is = $[(y \times d) \times (FC - WP)]\gamma$ = 0.12 m = 12 cm

γ = 1.5, FC = 25% , WP = 15% , γw = 1

46. To discuss improving the condition of roads, the government convened a conference of chief engineers of provinces at Nagpur in 1943. The result of the conference is famous as the Nagpur plan.
A twenty-year development programme for the period (1943-1963) was finalized. It was the first attempt to prepare a co-ordinated road development programme in a planned manner.

According to the recommendations of Nagpur Conference, the width formation of an ideal National Highway in hard rock cutting is 7.9 m

47. If L is the length of a rail and R is the radius of a curve, the versine h for the curve is h= L²/8R

48. Inlets are not generally provided in all sewers, Manholes are provided in sewer pipes at suitable intervals, Catch basins are generally provided in sewers for carrying drainage discharge.

49. If q is the average sewage flow from a city of population P, the maximum sewage flow Q = [(18+ √P)/(4 + √P)]q

50. A body is said to be in equilibrium if it remain its position toward the original position.

51. The forces acting normally on the cross section of a bar shown in the figure given below compressive in nature.

52. At yield point of a test piece, the material undergoes plastic deformation. When material obeys hooks law it is the limit of proportionality, when material regains its original shape on removal of the load it is the elastic limit.

53. Permissible stress in steel/permissible stress in concrete = E_s/E_c. Permissible stress in steel = 5 ✕ $15E_c/E_c$ = 75 N/mm²

Now,

P = 5 x (200 x 200 - 1200) + (1200 x75) = 284000N = 284 kN

54. α_{steel} = 0.000012/C °, E_{steel} = 0.2 MN/mm², $\Delta T = (100 - 50) = 50$ ºC

now stress in rod = αsteel x ΔT x Esteel = 120 N/mm²

55. Tangential stress = - $-\sigma \sin\theta, \cos\theta$

Normal stress = $\sigma \cos^2\theta$

Then their ratio = -tan θ

56. dm/ds =shear force , ds/dx = loading.

For a uniformly distributed load, the shear force varies linearly, For a uniformly distributed load, bending moment curve is a parabola, For a load varying linearly, the shear force curve is a parabola

57. At any point of a beam, the section modulus may be obtained by dividing the moment of inertia of the section by depth of the neutral axis.

Z = section modulus = I/Y, I= moment of inertia, Y = depth from neutral axis.

58. The moment of inertia of a circular section about any diameter D, is $(\pi D^4)/64$.

59. In case of principal axes of a section I_{XY} = 0

60. The locus of the moment of inertia about inclined axis to the principal axis is ellipse.

61. Moment of inertia of triangle about its base = bh³/12,

And about its centroidal axis = bh³/36

Then their ratio about base to centroidal axis = 3.

62. If aggregates completely pass through a sieve of size 75 mm and are retained on a sieve of size 60 mm,

Avg Size = (75+60)/2 = 67.5mm

the particular aggregate will be flaky if its minimum dimension is less than 0.6 ✕67.5 = 40.5 mm

63. For the construction of thin R.C.C. structures the type of cement to be avoided is blast furnace slag cement, rate of gain of strength is quite low.

64. Percentage of pozzolanic material containing clay upto 80% used for the manufacture of pozzolana cement is 30%.

65. When one thrusts one's hand into a bag of cement, one should feel cool.

The color of the cement is greyish colour.

A handful of cement thrown into a bucket of water should sink immediately.

66. The maximum size of a coarse aggregate is 80 mm and minimum is 4.75 mm, The maximum size of the fine aggregate is 4.75 mm and minimum 0.075 mm, The material having particles of size varying from 0.075 mm to 0.002 mm is known as silt.

67. Sand generally contains salt if it is obtained from sea beds.

68. Bulking of sand is caused due to formation of a thin film of surface moisture.

Fine sand bulks more than coarse sand. With 10% moisture content by weight the bulking of sand is increased by 50%. So all options are correct.

69. If fineness modulus of sand is 2.5 it is graded as fine sand.

Fineness modulus 2.2 – 2.4 = very fine.

Fineness modulus 2.5 – 2.7 = fine

Fineness modulus 2.7 -2.9 = medium

Fineness modulus 2.9 – 3.2 = course.

70. An ordinary Portland cement when tested for its fineness, should not leave any residue on I.S. Sieve No.9, more than 10%.

71. Insufficient quantity of water makes the concrete mix harsh, Insufficient quantity of water makes the concrete unworkable, Excess quantity of water makes the concrete segregated

72. A rich mix of concrete possesses higher strength than that a lean mix of desired workability with excessive quantity of water this wrong statement this leads to higher shrinkage and chances of segregation of concrete.

73.

- The concrete gains strength due to the hydration of cement.

- The concrete does not set at freezing point.

- Excessive rates of heating and cooling should be avoided to prevent damaging volume changes. Temperatures in the enclosure surrounding the concrete should not be increased or decreased more than 22°C to 33°C (40°F to 60°F) per hour depending on the size and shape of the concrete element. For example, there is reduced drying shrinkage and creep as compared to concrete cured at 23°C (73°F) for 28 days.

- One-day strength increases with increasing curing temperature, but 28-day strength decreases with increasing curing temperature.

74. Hardening of cement depends on the fineness of cement, quantity of gypsum, and bogus compounds.

- Cement hardens when it comes into contact with water. This hardening is a process of crystallization. Crystals form (after a certain length of time which is known as the initial set time) and interlock with each other.

- Concrete is completely fluid before the cement sets, then progressively hardens.

- The rate at which concrete sets is independent of the rate at which it hardens. Rapid-hardening cement may have similar setting times to ordinary Portland cement.

- Rapid rate during the first few days and afterwards it continues to increase at a decreased rate

75. Higher workability indicates unexpected increase in the moisture content, Higher workability indicates deficiency of sand, If the concrete mix is dry, the slump is zero.

76. The top diameter, bottom diameter and the height of a slump mould are 10 cm, 20 cm, 30 cm.

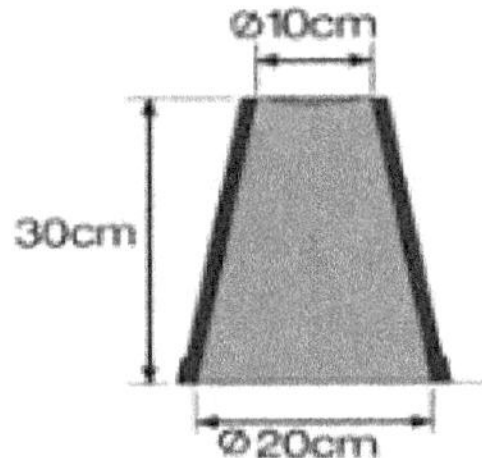

77. Segregation cause ill effect on the strength of concrete.

Consistency much more affect workability for a good workable mixture need 0.78p consistency.

As slump increase the workability also increases.

78. As per IS 456:2000

The grade of concrete M 150 means that compressive strength of a 15 cm cube after 28 days, is 150 kg/cm^2

79. The preliminary test is repeated if the difference compressive strength of three test specimens, exceeds 15 kg/cm^2.

80. According to load factor method, the permissible load W on a short column reinforced with longitudinal bars and lateral stirrups is Stress in concrete x area of concrete + stress in steel x area of steel

And for long column suitable reduction factor is used as $C_r = 1.25 - (L_{eff}/48B)$

81. As per IS 456:2000

The length of the lap in a compression member is kept greater than [bar diameter x (Permissible stress in bar)/(Five times the bond stress)] or is 24 bar diameters.

82. Permissible load on short column = Stress in concrete x area of concrete + stress in steel x area of steel

W = 40x(20x20 - 20) + 20x300 =21200kg.

83. A column is regarded as long column if the ratio of its effective length and lateral dimension exceeds 12.

84. If the size of a column is reduced above the floor, the main bars of the columns, continues up, bend inwards at the floor level, stops just below the floor level and separates lap bars provided.

85. Main reinforcement which is based on the maximum bending moment shall not be less than 0.15 percent of the gross sectional area. The pitch of the main bars shall not exceed the following:

1. Three times the effective depth of slab, and
2. 30 cm.

Distribution bars are running at right angles to the main reinforcement and the pitch shall not exceed

1. Five times the effective depth of slab, and
2. 45 cm.

The diameter of main bars may be from 8 mm to 14 mm. for distribution bars, steel 6 mm or 8 mm are generally used.

86. Distribution reinforcement in a simply supported slab is provided to distribute load, temperature stress, shrinkage stress.

87. As per IS 456:2000

In a simply supported slab the minimum spacing between two reinforcement bars should be at least equal to the maximum aggregate grain dimension with a margin of 5 mm

88. The modular ratio 'm' of a concrete whose permissible compressive stress is 'C' may be obtained from the equation m=280/3C.

89. Moment Resistance factor $\left(R_{ulim} \right)$

$$R_{ulim} = \frac{M_{ulim}}{bd^2} = 0.36 \frac{x_{umax}}{d} \left(1 - 0.42 \frac{x_{umax}}{d} \right) f_{ck}$$
$$R_{ulim} = 0.36 \frac{0.48d}{d} \left(1 - 0.42 \frac{0.48d}{d} \right) 15 = 2.07$$
$$\{ x_{umax} = 0.48d \text{ for } Fe415 \}$$

90. If the thickness of a structural member is small as compared to its length and width, it is classified as two dimensional structure.

91. Design of a riveted joint assumes that the riveted hole is to be filled by the rivet.

92. Rolled steel T-sections are used with flat strips to connect plates in steel rectangular tanks. Flanges in T-beam increases the moment carrying capacity of tank.

93. With a percentage increase of carbon in steel, decreases its ductility, steel become more brittle. Corbon content in steel the major deciding factor towards ductility.

94. If P is the wind pressure in kg/cm^2, v is the velocity in km/hour and K is constant of proportionality then P=Kv^2

95. Factor of safety is the ratio of yield stress to working stress.

96. The modulus of rigidity, also known as shear modulus, is defined as a material property with a value equal to the shear stress divided by the shear strain.

97. The rivets which are heated and then driven in the field are known power driven field rivets.

98. The gross diameter of a rivet is the diameter of rivet after driving.

Gross dia or nominal dia. is taken shank dia. + 1.5 , up 25 mm shank dia. And >25 add 2 in place of 1.5 .

99. Working shear stress on the gross area of a rivet as recommended by Indian Standards is 1025 kg/cm²

100. F_x = F Gravity + F Pressure + F Viscous + F Turbulence + F compressibility in Newton's equation

F_x = F Gravity + F Pressure + F Viscous + F Turbulence is Reynolds Equation,

F_x = F Gravity + F Pressure + F Viscous is Navier stokes Equation.

F_x = F Gravity + F Pressure is Euler equation.

101. $[OH^-] = 0.17mg/L$

Concentration in moles/L, $[OH^-] = \frac{0.17\times10^{-3}}{10} =$
1×10^{-5} moles $/L$
$pOH = -\log_{10}[OH^-] = -\log_{10}[1 \times 10^{-5}]$
$pOH = 5$
$pH + pOH = 14$
$pH = 14 - pOH = 9$
$pH = 9$

102. In an over reinforced section, the percentage of steel provided is more than that in balanced section.

Hence $x_a > x_c$ where x_c is the critical depth of neutral axis and MR > MR_{bal}.

103. Given, w = 50%; e = 1.25 ; G = 2.5

G w = se

$$S = \frac{Gw}{e}$$

$$S = \frac{2.5\times0.5}{1.25} = 1$$

Hence degree of saturation S = 1 or 100%

Hence soil sample is in a state of full saturation.

104. Alkalinity has cause for rejection value 600 mg/L.

Chloride content has cause for rejection value 1000 mg/L.

Iron has cause for rejection value of 1mg/L.

Manganese has cause for rejection value of 0.5 mg/L.

105. As per clause 10.3.3 of IS 456 – 2000, Dosages of retarders, plasticisers and superplasticisers shall be restricted to 0.5, 1.0 and 2.0 percent respectively by weight of cementations materials and unless a higher value is agreed upon between the manufacturer and the constructor based on performance test.

106. As per clause 10.2.3.4 of IS 800 – 2007, when fasteners are staggered at equal intervals and the gauge does not exceed 75 mm, the spacing specified between centres of fasteners may be increased by 50 percent of values specified above provided gauge distance is less than 75 mm.

107. Elastic neutral axis-

$$y_e = \frac{200\times10\times5+150\times10\times\left(10+\frac{150}{2}\right)+100\times10\times\left(10+150+\frac{10}{2}\right)}{200\times10+150\times10+100\times10}$$

$$y_e = 67.22mm$$

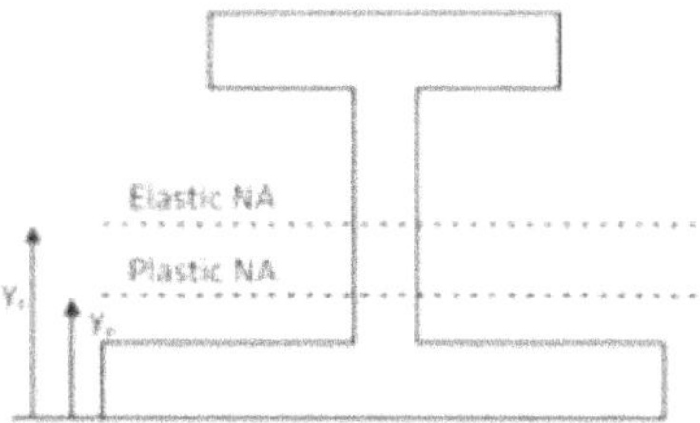

Plastic Neutral Axis -
Plastic NA divided the areas in two equal halves.
$200 \times 10 + 10\,(y_p - 10) = 10 \times (150 + 10 - y_p) + 100 \times 10$
$2000 + 10y_p - 100 = 1600 - 10y_p + 1000$
$20y_p = 700$
$Y_p = 35mm$

Hence distance between elastic NA (y e) and plastic

$NA(y_p) = Y_e - y_p = 67.22 - 35 = 32.22mm$

108. Curve resistance = T – Tcosα

Here T = 400 N ; α = 8°

∴ curve resistance = T (1 – cosα) = 400 × (1 – cos 8°) = 3.89 N

109. As per table 6 of $IRC52 - 2001,$
Criteria for measuring sight distance is as under -

	Driver eye height	Height of object
Safe SSD	1.2 m	0.15m
ISD	1.2 m	1.2 m

110. A change point, also known as turning point, is the point where both back sight and fore sight readings are made on a staff held at that point. By taking the fore sight, the elevation of the change point is determined and by taking back sight, the height of instrument is determined. Hence a change point is required before moving the level from one section to another.

111. for the given matrix A, 0 is an Eigen value of A.

∴ A is singular ∴A⁻¹ does not exist

∴ Eigen values of A⁻¹ do not exit.

112. The final value theorem

$$\lim_{x \to \infty} x(t) = [2 + e^{-3t}]u(t) = 2$$

113. $\int \dfrac{\sin^2 x\cos^2 x\,dx}{(\sin^5 x+\cos^3 x\sin^2 x+\sin^3 x\cos^2 x+\cos^5 x)^2}$

$\int \dfrac{\sin^2 x\cdot\cos^2 x\,dx}{\{(\sin^2 x(\sin^3 x+\cos^3 x)+\cos^2 x(\sin^3 x+\cos^3 x)\}^2}$

$$\int \frac{\sin^2 x \cdot \cos^2 x\, dx}{\{(\sin^2 x + \cos^2 x)(\sin^3 x + \cos^3 x)\}^2}$$

$$\int \frac{\sin^2 x \cos^2 x\, dx}{(\sin^3 x + \cos^3 x)^2}$$

Divide by $\cos^3 x$ in numerator and denominator we get $=$

$$\int \frac{\sec^2 x \cdot \tan^2 x}{(\tan^3 x + 1)^2}\, dx$$

Let $1 + \tan^3 x = t$

$$3\tan^2 x \sec^2 x\, dx = dt$$

$$= \frac{1}{3}\int \frac{dt}{t^2} = -\frac{1}{3}\frac{1}{t} + C$$

$$= -\frac{1}{3(1+\tan^3 x)} + C$$

Hence, the correct option is (D).

114. $Q_{up} = A_b \cdot q_b + A_s \cdot q_s$

$A_b = \frac{\pi}{4} \times 0.5^2 = 0.1963 m^2$

$A_s = \pi d L = \pi \times 0.5 \times 20 = 31.416 m^2$

$q_b = C N_c = 9c = 9 \times 190 = 1710 kN/m^2$

At the po int of bearing
the undrained shear
strength is $190 kPa$

$$\overline{C} = \frac{50\times5+70\times5+90\times5+190\times5}{20} = 100 kN/m^2$$

$q_5 = \alpha \overline{c} = 0.4 \times 100 = 40 kN/m^2$

$Q_{up} = 0.1963 \times 1710 + 31.416 \times 40 = 1592.313 kN$

$\therefore$ safe load $= \frac{Q_{up}}{Fos} = \frac{1592.313}{2.5} = 636.93 kN$

115. As per clause 23.3 of 15456: 2000

$L \leq \{$ or

$25b = 25 \times 450 = 11250 mm = 11.25 m$

or $\frac{100 b^2}{d} = \frac{100 \times 450^2}{550} = 36818.2 mm = 36.82 m\}$

Thus $L = 11.25 m$

116. Extension $\delta = \frac{4PL}{\pi d_1 d_2 E}$

$E = \frac{4PL}{\pi d_1 d_2 \delta}$

Here $d_1 = D + a$ and $d_2 = D - a$

$E = \frac{4PL}{\pi (D^2 - a^2)\delta}$

If mean diameter adopted, let E' be computed young's modulus

$E' = \frac{4PL}{\pi D^2 \delta}$

$\therefore$ Percentage error $=$

$\frac{E - E'}{E} \times 100\%$

$$= \frac{\frac{4PL}{\pi(D^2-a^2)\delta} - \frac{4PL}{\pi D^2 \delta}}{\frac{4PL}{\pi D^2 \delta}} \times 100\%$$

$$= \frac{\frac{1}{D^2-a^2} - \frac{1}{D^2}}{\frac{1}{D^2}} \times 100\% = \frac{a^2}{D^2} \times 100\% = \left(\frac{10a}{D}\right)^2$$

117. From 58.30 to 58.40

Let $D =$ Diameter of rigid wheel

$D =$ least diameter of steel tyre

Strain in tyre $= \frac{D-d}{d}$

Strain in tyre $= \left(\frac{D-d}{d}\right) E = \sigma$

$\therefore \frac{D}{d} - 1 = \frac{\sigma}{E}$

$\frac{D}{d} - 1 = \frac{140 \times 10^6}{200 \times 10^9} = 0.0007$

$\frac{D}{d} = 1.0007$

Let the steel be subjected to a temperature rise of $T°C$.

$\pi D = \pi d + \pi d \cdot \alpha T$

$\frac{\pi D}{\pi d} = 1 + \infty T$

$\frac{D}{d} = 1 + \infty T$

$1.0007 = 1 + \alpha T$

$T = \frac{0.0007}{12 \times 10^{-6}} = 58.33°C$

118. From 25 to 25

Range- $25 - 25$

Gross diameter $D_g = 500 mm$

Core diameter $D_C = D_g - 2 \times$ clear cover $= 500 - 2 \times 40 = 420 mm$

Helix diameter $D_H = D_C - \phi_h = 420 - 6 = 414 mm$

$\frac{V_h}{V_c} \geq 0.36 \frac{f_{ck}}{f_y}\left[\frac{A_g}{A_c} - 1\right]$

$\frac{\frac{1000}{p} \times \pi D_H \times \frac{\pi}{4}\phi_H^2}{\frac{\pi}{4}D_C^2 \times 1000} \geq 0.36 \frac{f_{ck}}{f_y}\left[\frac{\frac{\pi}{4}D_g^2}{\frac{\pi}{4}D_c^2} - 1\right]$

$\frac{\pi \times 414 \times 6^2}{420^2 \times p} \geq \frac{0.36 \times 25}{415}\left[\frac{500^2}{420^2} - 1\right]$

$p \leq 29.33 mm$

Check: (i) $p \leq 29.33 mm$ (ii)

$p \times 25 mm$

(iii)

$p \times 3\phi_s \cdot p \times 18 mm$

(iv)

$p > \frac{D_C}{6} = \frac{420}{6}$

$p \times 70 mm$

(v)

$p \times 75 mm$

Hence

$p = 25 mm$

119. From 355.50 to 356.00

$d = 20mm\, d_0 = 22mm$

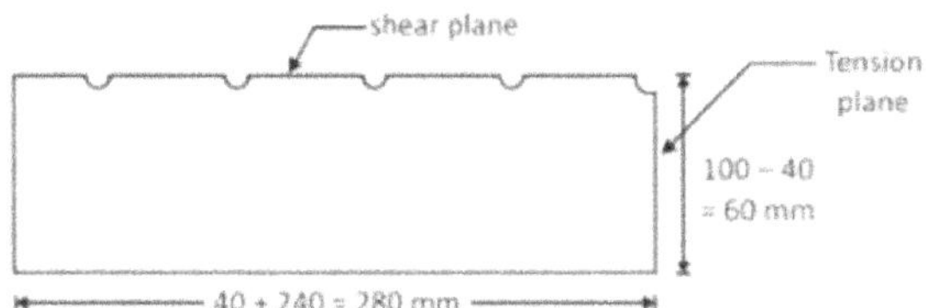

$A_{vg} = 280 \times 8 = 2240mm^2$; $A_{vn} = (280 - 4.5 \times 22) \times 8 = 1448mm^2$

$A_{tg} = 60 \times 8 = 480mm^2$; $A_{tn} = (60 - 0.5 \times 22) \times 8 = 392mm^2$

$T_{do_1} = A_{vg} \cdot \dfrac{f_y}{\sqrt{3} \times 1.1} + A_{tn} \cdot \dfrac{0.9 f_u}{1.25} = \dfrac{2240 \times 250}{\sqrt{3} \times 1.1} + \dfrac{392 \times 0.9 \times 410}{1.25} = 409642N$

$T_{db_d} = A_{vn} \cdot \dfrac{0.9 f_u}{\sqrt{3} \times 1.25} + A_{tg} \cdot \dfrac{f_y}{1.1} = \dfrac{1448 \times 0.9 \times 410}{\sqrt{3} \times 1.25} + \dfrac{480 \times 250}{1.1} = 355879N$

Hence block shear strength = Min. of

$T_{db_1} \& T_{db_2}$

$= 355.88 KN$

120. From 313 to 316

OSD for $2 -$ way traffic $= d_1 + d_2 + d_3$

$d_1 = 0.278 v_b t = 0.278 \times 40 \times 2 = 22.24m$

$d_2 = b + (s_1 + s_2)$ where $s_1 = 15m$; $s_2 = 20m$

$T = \sqrt{\dfrac{2(s_1 + s_2)}{a}}$

$T = \sqrt{\dfrac{2 \times (15 + 20)}{0.99}} = 8.41 seconds$

$d_2 = 0.278 v_b T + (s_1 + s_2) = 0.278 \times 40 \times 8.41 + 15 + 20 = 128.52m$

$d_3 = 0.278 \vee T = 0.278 \times 70 \times 8.41 = 163.66m$

Hence, OSD for $2 -$ way traffic $= d_1 + d_2 + d_3 = 22.24 + 128.52 + 163.66$

$050 = 314.42m$

121.

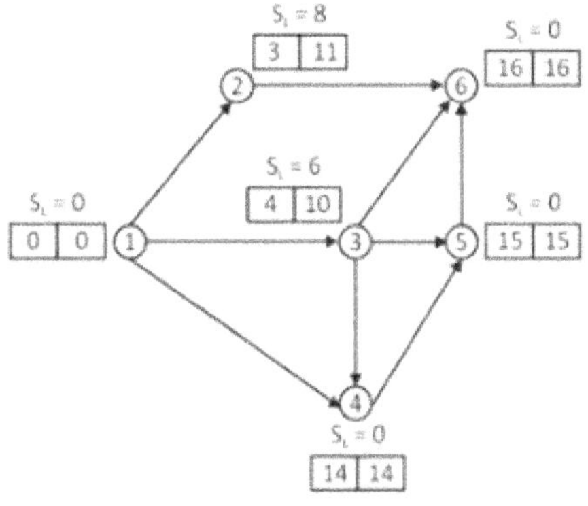

Hence critical path is C -H-I

122. The bitumen content corresponding to maximum stability = 6.0%

The bitumen content corresponding to maximum unit weight = 6.5 %

The bitumen content corresponding to 4% air voids = 6.5%

Hence the optimum bitumen content =

$\dfrac{6 + 6.5 + 6.5}{3} = 6.33\%$

123. If you add up the % by mass, it adds up to 95%. The balance 5% mass is comprised of moisture.

$= \left[\dfrac{15 \times 70 + 45 \times 6 + 10 \times 5 + 5 \times 2 + 4 \times 60 + 10 \times 20 + 6 \times 3 + 5 \times 100}{100} \right]$

$= 23.38\%$

Hence moisture content of solid waste sample is 23.38%

124. $div(f) = \dfrac{\partial f_1}{\partial x} + \dfrac{\partial f_2}{\partial y} + \dfrac{\partial f_3}{\partial z}$

$= 5\dfrac{\partial x^2 y}{\partial x} + 5\dfrac{\partial x^2 y}{\partial y} + 3\dfrac{\partial yz^2}{\partial z}$

$= 10xy + 5x^2 + 6yz$

$= -10 + 1.25 - 24 = -32.75$

125. Applying L' Hospital's rule

$\Rightarrow \lim_{x \to 1} \dfrac{\sqrt{f(x)} - 1}{\sqrt{x} - 1} = \lim_{x \to 1} \dfrac{\frac{1}{2}\frac{f'(x)}{\sqrt{f(x)}}}{\frac{1}{2}\frac{1}{\sqrt{x}}}$

$= \dfrac{f'(1)}{\sqrt{f(1)}} \sqrt{1} = 2$

Q.1 The most reliable estimate is

A. Plinth area estimate

B. Detailed eastimate

C. Prelimitnary estimate

D. Cube rate estimate

Q.2 The unit of measurement is per quintal for following

A. Collapsible gates with rails

B. Rolling shutters

C. Expanded metal wire netting

D. Reinforcement of R.C.C. works

Q.3 Floor Area Ratio (F.A.R.) means

A. Total floor areas of all floors- Area of ground / area of plot

B. Total floor areas of all floors- Area of ground / area of plinth

C. Total floor areas of all floors / area of plot

D. Total floor areas of all floors / area of plinth

Q.4 The quantity cement concrete damp-proofing course is measured in terms of ....

A. m

B. m^2

C. m^3

D. Lump-sum

Q.5 Hardness of rock can be teated in situ using

A. Amith's test

B. Schmidt Hammer

C. Acid test

D. Crystallization test

Q.6 Unit weight of brick work is about

A. 17 – 18kN/m^3

B. 18–19kN/m^3

C. 19–20kN/m^3

D. 20–21kN/m^3

Q.7 Which one of the following is the purest form of iron ?

A. Cast iron

B. Wrought iron

C. Mild steel

D. High carbon steel

Q.8 For R.C.C. construction, the maximum size of coarse aggregate is limited to

A. 10 mm

B. 15 mm

C. 20 mm

D. 25 mm

Q.9 Presence of oils in water for concreting

A. gives smooth surface

B. gives more slump

C. improves strength

D. reduces strength

Q.10 The volatile diluent added to a point is known as

A. drier

B. pigment

C. thinner

D. distemper

Q.11 If fore bearing of a line is N 30^0 E , the back bearing of the line is

A. N30^0 W

B. N30^0 E

C. S30^0 W

D. S30^0 E

Q.12 An anallatic lens is provided in a

A. Theodolite

B. Tacheometer

C. Dumpy level

D. Prismatic compass

Q.13 Which of the following methods of plane table surveying is used to locate the position of an inaccessible point ?

A. Radiation

B. Intersection

C. Traversing

D. Resection

Q.14 The multiplying constant of a theodolite is

A. $f + d$

B. $\frac{f}{d} + i$

C. $\frac{f}{i} + d$

D. $\frac{f}{i}$

Q.15 A building is an obstacle to

A. both chaining and ranging

B. chaining but not ranging

C. ranging but not chaining

D. neither chaining nor ranging

Q.16 The following bearings were observed while traversing with a compass. Which stations are affected by local attraction ?

Line	F.B.	B.B.
AB	104^{0}30′	284°30′
BC	48°15′	226°0′
CD	290°30′	115°15′
DA	180°15′	357^{0}15′

A. A and D

B. C and D

C. B and C

D. A and B

Q.17 The cross-seaction of a strip footing is shown below

G — L
300   375
150   500
150   625
750
150   100 thk PCC
(1 : 3 : 6)
75 th BFS
S

All dimensions are in mm.

The quantity of BFS under the footing per metre length is

A. 0.75 cu.m

B. 0.750 sq.m

C. 0.056 cu.m

D. 0.056 sq.m

Q.18 For a steel built-up column subjected to an axial force of 1200 kN, the lacing system is to be designed for resisting transverse shear of

A. 15 kN

B. 20 kN

C. 25 kN

D. 30 kN

Q.19 A soil has an average particle size of 0.2mm. It is prediominatly

A. gravel

B. silt

C. sand

D. clay

Q.20 The expression for the discharge (Q) through a flow net for isotropic soils is given by

A. $Q = K H \times \frac{N_F}{N_D}$

B. $Q = KH \sqrt{\frac{N_F}{N_D}}$

C. $Q = KH \left(\frac{N_F}{N_D}\right)^2$

D. $Q = KH \left(\frac{N_F}{N_D}\right)^3$

Q.21 The dimensions of surface tension are

A. $M^1 L^0 T^{-2}$

B. $M^1 L^{-1}$

C. $M^1 L^1 T^{-2}$

D. $F^1 T^{-2}$

Q.22 The height of hydraulic jump is equal to

A. sequent depth

B. difference in conjugate depths

C. difference in alternate depths

D. initial depth

Q.23 In a Newtonian fluid

A. the shear stress is directly proportional to the rate of fluid deformation

B. dynamic viscosity is directly proportional to the rate of fluid deformation

C. kinematic viscosity is directly proportional to the rate of fluid deformation

D. dynamic viscosity is zero

Q.24 Valid range for S, the degree of saturation soil, in percentage, is-

A. $S > 0$

B. $S \leq 0$

C. $0 \leq S \leq 100$

D. $0 < S < 100$

Q.25 A soil has a bulk density of 22kN/m^2 and water content 10%. The dry density of soil in kN/m^3 is

A. 18.6

B. 20.0

C. 22.0

D. 23.2

Q.26 A pycenometer is used to determine-

A. water content and void ratio

B. specific gravity and dry density

C. water content and specific gravity

D. void ratio and dry density

Q.27 Toughness index is defined as the ratio of

A. Plasticity index in Consistency index

B. Plasticity index to Flow index

C. Liquidity index to Flow index

D. Consistency index to Liquidity index

Q.28 The unit weight of a compeletly saturated soil is given by

Where, G= Specific gravity of solids

E= Void ratio

$\gamma \omega$ = Unit weight of water

A. $(G+e)\gamma \omega / (1+e)$

B. $\frac{(1+e)\gamma_w}{G+e}$

C. $\frac{(G-1)\gamma_w}{1+e}$

D. $\frac{(1-e)\gamma_w}{G+e}$

Q.29 Which of the following spilways is least suitable for an earthen dam ?

A. Chute spilway

B. Side channel spilway

C. Shaft spillway

D. Ogee spillway

Q.30 A floating body will remain in stable equilibrium if the metacentre is-

A. above the centre of buoyancy

B. above the centre of gravity

C. below the centre of gravity

D. below the centre of buoyancy

Q.31 The pressure of a liquid measured with the help of a piezometer tube is

A. atmospheric pressure

B. gauge pressure

C. absolute pressure

D. vaccum pressure

Q.32 A hydrometer is used to measure

A. velocity of fluids

B. velocity of gases

C. flow of fluids

D. specific gravity of liquids

Q.33 Continuity equation is based on the principle of conservation of

A. energy

B. mass

C. momentum

D. Both (A) and (B)

Q.34 The discharge over a broad-crested weir is maximum when the depth of flow is

A. H / 3

B. 2H / 3

C. H / 2

D. 2H / 5

Q.35 For the irrigation of a crop, the base period B (in days), depth of water Δ (in meters) are related to the duty D (in ha/cumec) at the field as

A. $D = 0.684B\Delta$

B. $D = 0.64B\Delta$

C. $D = 0.864B\Delta$

D. $D = 1.98B\Delta$

Q.36 In designing hydraulic structures in alluvial rivers, the equation that is used to calculate the normal depth of scour R for discharge intensity of q\,m^3/s/m is.

A. $R=1.35(q/f)^{2/3}$

B. $R=1.2(q^2/f)^{1/3}$

C. $R=1.35(q^2/f)^{1/3}$

D. $R=4.75(q)^{1/2}$

Q.37 An earthen channel has been desigened on Lacey formulae to carry a full supply discharge of 30 m^3/s . The median size of the soil is 0.3 mm. the mean velocity of flow at this discharge is

A. 0.98 m/s

B. 0.76 m/s

C. 2.2 m/s

D. 1.36 m/s

Q.38 The ratio between peak hourly water demand and maximum daily demand (per hour of course) is.

A. 1.5

B. 1.8

C. 2.0

D. 2.7

Q.39 The ozonation in drinking water helps to remove

A. colloidal particles

B. hardness

C. flocs

D. micro-organisms

Q.40 The total water consumption including domestic, commercial and industrial demands for average Indian people is.

A. 135 lpcd

B. 210 lpcd

C. 240 lpcd

D. 270 lpcd

Q.41 The curve provided at the change of gradient is called-

A. Horizontal curve   **B.** Transition curve

C. Reverse curve   **D.** Vertical curve

Q.42 To provide a cant in rails, wooden sleepers are cut to a slope at rail, which is known as-

A. coning   **B.** cutting   **C.** boxing   **D.** adzing

Q.43 If α is the angle of crossing, then the number of crossing 'N' according to centre line method is given by

A. 1/2 cot α/2   **B.** cot α/2

C. cot α **D.** 1/2 cosec α/2

Q.44 The recommended camber for water-bounding Macadam road is-

A. 1 in 40 to 1 in 50   **B.** 1 in 33 to 1 in 40

C. 1 in 25 to 1 in 33   **D.** 1 in 20 to 1 in 25

Q.45 Identify which of the following items is not considered while designing rigid pavements.

A. Centre of a panel

B. Edge of panel

C. Corner of a panel

D. Dowel bars between edges

Q.46 The ideal form of the curve for the summit curve is

A. spiral   **B.** parabola

C. circle   **D.** lemniscate

Q.47 Camber in the road is provided for

A. effective drainage

B. counteracting the centrifugal force

C. having proper sight distance

D. all the above

Q.48 The alum added as coagulant in water treatment functions better when the raw water is

A. acidic with high turbidity

B. alkaline with high turbidity

C. neutral with low turbidity

D. acidic with low turbidity

Q.49 The 'safe water' does not contain any

A. taste   **B.** colour   **C.** pathogen   **D.** odour

Q.50 Which of the following gases is responsible for acid rain?

A. VOC   **B.** NO_x **C.** CO   **D.** CH_4

Q.51 A town is required to treat 4.2 m³/min of raw water for daily domestic supply. Flocculating particles are to be produced by chemical coagulation. A column analysis indicated that an overflow rate of 0.2 mm/s will produce satisfactory particle removal in a settling basin at a depth of 3.5 m. The required surface area (in m²) for settling is :

A. 21   **B.** 350   **C.** 1728   **D.** 21000

Q.52 The bending stress on a prismatic beam is given by

A. My/Z   **B.** My/I   **C.** MZ/y   **D.** MI/y

Q.53 If the column ends are effectively held in position and restrained against rotation at both ends, then the effective length is

A. 2 L   **B.** L/2   **C.** 0.707 L   **D.** L

Q.54 The modulus of elasticity of steel is-

A. 2×10^4 M Pa   **B.** 1.2×10^5 M Pa

C. 2×10^5 M Pa   **D.** 2×10^6 M Pa

Q.55 Identify the eroneous statement.

Mild steel

A. has two yield points.

B. is a ductile material.

C. has small percent elongation at failure.

D. shows strain hardening.

Q.56 The maximum numerical value of poisson's ratio is

A. 0.0   **B.** 0.25   **C.** 0.5   **D.** 1.00

Q.57 The angle between the principal plane and the plane of maximum shear is

A. 135^0 **B.** 90^0 **C.** 45^0 **D.** 60^0

Q.58 For such element only under normal stresses, the radius of Mohr circle is

A. σ **B.** σ/2   **C.** 2σ **D.** 0.6 σ

Q.59 The modulus of elasticity of steel is more than that of concrete. It indicates that steel is

A. less elastic   **B.** more elastic

C. more plastic   **D.** less plastic

Q.60 Maximum shear stress produced on a solid circular shaft under torque is

A. $\frac{16T}{\pi D^4}$ **B.** $\frac{16T}{\pi D^3}$ **C.** $\frac{32T}{\pi D^4}$ **D.** $\frac{32T}{\pi D^3}$

Q.61 The working stress of a material is expected to be

A. equal to ultimate stress

B. equal to yield stress

C. less than yield stress

D. more than yield stress

Q.62 The relationship between Young's modulus, E, shear modulus, G, and Poisson's ratio v, is given by

A. $G = \frac{E}{2(1+V)}$ **B.** $E = \frac{G}{2(1+V)}$

C. $G = \frac{E}{2(1-V)}$ **D.** $E = \frac{G}{(1+V)}$

Q.63 The clay deposit of thickness 10 cm and void ratio 0.5 undergoes settlement and now its final void ratio is 0.2. The thickness (cm) of the settlement layer is _________.

A. 1   **B.** 1.5   **C.** 2   **D.** 2.5

Q.64 For the above cantilever beam, the absolute value of shear force at A is

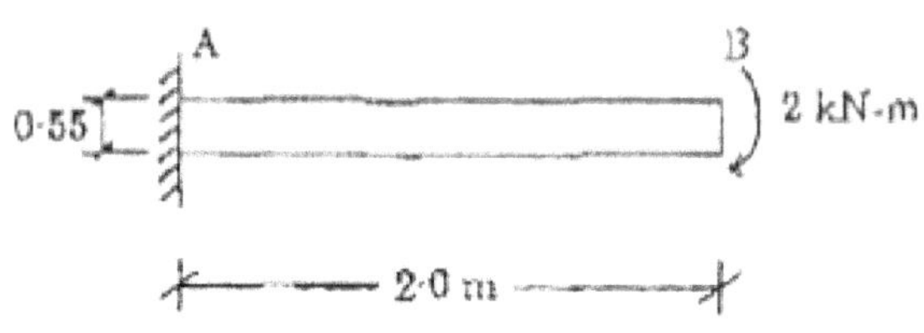

A. 1.0 kN   **B.** 4.0 kN   **C.** 0 kN   **D.** 2.0 kN

Q.65 According to IS : 383, the coarsest sand falls under grading zone
A. II   **B.** I   **C.** III   **D.** IV

Q.66 The initial setting time of fresh concrete should be
A. lower than 15 minutes
B. greater than 30 minutes
C. greater than 1 hours
D. not more than 10 hours

Q.67 Which apparatus we need to find soundness?
A. Le Chatelier   **B.** Vicat's apparatus
C. CTM   **D.** Pat test

Q.68 Find the odd entry among silica fume, rice husk ash, metakaolione and ground granulated blast furnace slag with respect to cement production.
A. Silica fume
B. Rice husk ash
C. Metakaoline
D. Ground granulated blast furnace slag

Q.69 To estimate 28 day crushing strength of concrete cubes from 7-day cube strength, we multiply the 7 day cube strength by
A. 3   **B.** 2.5   **C.** 1.5   **D.** 1.2

Q.70 The maximum deflection of tip of cantilever beam with concentrated load P at the free end is
A. $\frac{Pl^3}{3EI}$ **B.** $\frac{Pl^3}{8EI}$ **C.** $\frac{Pl^3}{12EI}$ **D.** $\frac{Pl^3}{24EI}$

Q.71 To obtain high compressive strength of cement at

(A) very slow rate $\left[1200°C \xrightarrow{30\ minutes} 500°C \xrightarrow{20\ minutes} \text{Ambient temperature}\right]$

(B) slow rate $\left[1200°C \xrightarrow{20\ minutes} 500°C \xrightarrow{15\ minutes} \text{Ambient temperature}\right]$

(C) moderate rate $\left[1200° \xrightarrow{15\ minutes} 500°C \xrightarrow{10\ minutes} \text{Ambient temperature}\right]$

(D) fast rate $\left[1200°C \xrightarrow{10\ minutes} 500°C \xrightarrow{5\ minutes} \text{Ambient temperature}\right]$

A. A   **B.** B   **C.** C   **D.** D

Q.72 Identify which grade of cement is not available in Indian market.
A. 23 grade   **B.** 33 grade   **C.** 43 grade   **D.** 53 grade

Q.73 Rapid setting cement contains relatively higher proportion of
A. $C_3 S$ **B.** $C_2 S$ **C.** $C_3 A$ **D.** $C_4 AF$

Q.74 Study the following statements:
I. For constant w/c ratio, finer sand decreases the workability.
II. Creep is the deformation of concrete under sustained loading.
The correct statement (s) is/are
A. Only I   **B.** Only II
C. Both I and II   **D.** None of these

Q.75 Peak of a flood hydrograph due to a six-hour storm is 470 m³/sec . The average depth of rainfall is 8.0 cms. Assume an infiltration loss of 0.25 cm/hour and a constant base flow of 15 m³/sec . The peak discharge of a 6 hour unit hydrograph for this catchment, will be :
A. 50 m³/sec   **B.** 60 m³/sec
C. 70 m³/sec   **D.** 90 m³/sec

Q.76 The thermal expansion coefficient of steel (α) is
A. $13×10^{-6}/°C$ and closely resembles to of α concentre
B. $11×10^{-6}/°C$ and differs wisely from of α concentre
C. $12×10^{-6}/°C$ and close to of α concentre
D. $14×10^{-6}/°C$ but nearly equal to of α concentre

Q.77 A water sample has a pH of 9.25. The concentration of hydroxyl ions in the water sample is :
A. $10^{-9.25}$ moles/l   **B.** $10^{-4.75}$ moles/l
C. 3.020 mg/l   **D.** 0.302 mg/l

Q.78 The tensile strength of concrete in flexure as per IS: 456, where fck is the characteristic strength of concrete.
A. $\sqrt{0.6}$ fck   **B.** $\sqrt{0.7}$ fck
C. $\sqrt{0.75}$ fck   **D.** $\sqrt{0.9}$ fck

Q.79 Low workability of concrete confroms to a slump of-
A. 25-50 mm   **B.** 50-100 mm
C. 75-100 mm   **D.** 100-150 mm

Q.80 Find mild and moderate exposures, if 20mm down coarse aggregates are used, minimum cement content per cubic meter of concrete must not be less than
A. 300 kg   **B.** 280 kg   **C.** 320 kg   **D.** 340 kg

Q.81 The bond strength of concrete increases with
A. the quantity of steel
B. the tensile strength of steel
C. the grade of concrete
D. the quantity of concrete

Q.82 The increased rate of strength gain of rapid hardening cement is achieved by
A. higher content of C_3S
B. higher content of C_3A
C. higher content of C_4AF

D. higher content of C_2S

Q.83 Bulking of sand is maximum if the percentage of moisture content is of the order of

A. 5 **B.** 8 **C.** 10 **D.** 15

Q.84 If a beam fails in bond then its bond strength can be increased most economically by

A. increasing the depth of beam
B. using thinner bars but more in number
C. using thicker bars but less in number
D. providing vertical stirrups

Q.85 The minimum cover in a slab should neither be less than the diameter of bar nor less than for mild reinforcement-

A. 10 mm **B.** 13 mm **C.** 20 mm **D.** 25 mm

Q.86 Total pressure on the vertical face of retaining wall of height h, per unit run exerted by the retained earth weighing ω per unit volume and angle of repose is φ given by

A. $\omega h \frac{1-\sin\phi}{1+\sin\phi}$
B. $\omega h^2 \frac{1-\sin\phi}{1+\sin\phi}$
C. $\frac{\omega h^2}{2}\left[\frac{1-\sin\phi}{1+\sin\phi}\right]$
D. $\frac{\omega h^2}{3}\left[\frac{1-\sin\phi}{1+\sin\phi}\right]$

Q.87 Maximum spacing of side face reinforcement of beams having depth of web more than 750 mm is

A. 300 mm
B. width of web of the beam
C. smaller of A and B
D. greater of A and B

Q.88 The modulus of rupture of concrete gives

A. the direct tensile strenght of the concrete
B. the direct compressive strength of the concrete
C. the tensile strength of concrete under bending
D. the characteristic strength of concrete

Q.89 Flat slab is supported on

A. beams
B. columns
C. walls
D. columns monolithically built with slab

Q.90 According to IS: 456 - 2000, side-face reinforcement should be provided when depth of web of a beam exceeds

A. 650 mm **B.** 700 mm **C.** 725 mm **D.** 750 mm

Q.91 The outstand of web stiffeners in terms of the thickness of flat 't' should be

A. 6 t **B.** 8 t **C.** 10 t **D.** 12 t

Q.92 When two plates are placed end-to-end and are joined by two cover plates, the joint is known as

A. lap joint
B. but joint
C. chain rivetted lap joint
D. double cover butt joint

Q.93 As per codal provisions, the effective buckling length of a cantilever steel column of length L is given by

A. 0.5 L **B.** 1.3 L **C.** 2 L **D.** 3 L

Q.94 Gross Diameter of a rivet hole should be greater than the nominal diameter of rivet by about

A. 4 to 5 mm **B.** 2.5 to 4 mm
C. 1.5 to 2 mm **D.** 0 to 1.5 mm

Q.95 Bearing stiffeners in plate girder are provided at

A. mid span **B.** equal interval
C. end supports **D.** neutral axis

Q.96 At a certain location of a plate grider of webe size 1000mm x 10mm a pair of bearing stiffeners 100mm x 5 mm is welded. The effective area of bearing stiffeners is

A. 1000 mm^2 **B.** 2000 mm^2
C. 3000 mm^2 **D.** 5000 mm^2

Q.97 According to IS : the permissible stress in axial tension in steel is

If f_y = Minimum yeild stress of strain

A. 0.56 f_y **B.** 0.66 f_y **C.** 0.70 f_y **D.** 0.6 f_y

Q.98 The gross diamter of rivet (hole) for a rivet with nominal diameter of 27mm is

A. 28 mm **B.** 28.5 mm **C.** 29 mm **D.** 29.5 mm

Q.99 The maximum permissible stress in shear for power driven shop rivet is

A. 80 N/mm^2 **B.** 90 N/mm^2
C. 100 N/mm^2 **D.** 250 N/mm^2

Q.100 As per IS: 800-1984, the lacings of compression member shall be proportioned to resist a total transverse shear 'S' equal to at least

A. 1.0% of axial load **B.** 2.0% of axial load
C. 2.5% of axial load **D.** 3.0% of axial load

Q.101 A strut is a

A. flexible member
B. compression member
C. torsion member
D. tension member

Q.102 Strength based classification of brick is made on the basis of

A. IS : 3101 **B.** IS : 3102 **C.** IS : 3495 **D.** IS : 3496

Q.103 Quartzite and marble are by nature

A. volcanic **B.** plutonic
C. sedimentary **D.** metamorphic

Q.104 Which of the following is the hardest wood?

A. Babul **B.** Chir **C.** Teak **D.** Shisham

Q.105 Commonly used lime in white washing is

A. quick lime **B.** fat lime
C. lean lime **D.** hydraulic lime

Q.106 28 day compressive strength of cement is tested on 70.7 mm size cubes of mortar having cement to sand proportion of

A. 1 : 5 **B.** 1 : 6 **C.** 1 : 3 **D.** 1 : 4

Q.107 The amount of water used in performing setting time test of cement is (assuming p = standard consistency of cement)

A. 0.60 p   **B.** 0.65 p   **C.** 0.80 p   **D.** 0.85 p

Q.108 As the cement sets and hardens, it generates heat. This is called as

A. heat of hydration   **B.** latent heat
C. heat of vaporization   **D.** sensible heat

Q.109 For one cubic metre of concrete (1 : 2 : 4), the number of cement bags required is

A. 4.5   **B.** 5.0   **C.** 5.3   **D.** 6.3

Q.110 The correct relation between theoretical oxygen demand (TOD), Biochemical oxygen demand (BOD) and Chemical oxygen demand (COD) is given by

A. TOD>BOD>COD   **B.** TOD> COD> BOD
C. BOD>COD>TOD   **D.** COD>BOD>TOD

Q.111 The grade of concrete M20 means that characteristic compressive strength of 15 cm cubes after 28 days is not less than

A. 10 N/mm²   **B.** 15 N/mm²
C. 20 N/mm²   **D.** 25 N/mm²

Q.112 The concrete cubes are prepared, cured and tested according to Indian Standard code:

A. IS : 515   **B.** IS : 516   **C.** IS : 517   **D.** IS : 518

Q.113 To prevent sulphate attack in concrete, for preparing concrete mix, water pH must be within

A. 7 – 10   **B.** 4 – 6   **C.** 5 – 7   **D.** 6 – 9

Q.114 The increase in the strength of concrete with time is :

A. linear   **B.** non-linear
C. asymptotic   **D.** all of the above

Q.115 The permanent deformation of concrete with time under steady load is called

A. visco-elasticity   **B.** vicidity
C. creep   **D.** relaxation

Q.116 Mild steel used in RCC structures conforms to

A. IS : 432   **B.** IS : 1566   **C.** IS : 1786   **D.** IS : 2062

Q.117 Which of the following has least carbon content?

A. Wrought iron   **B.** Cast iron
C. Mild steel   **D.** Pig iron

Q.118 Steel corrodes in exposure of air and moisture and forms rust which has :

A. 2.5 times the volume of steel
B. 0.5 times the volume of steel
C. equal volume compared to amount of steel rusted
D. twice the volume of steel

Q.119 The number of bricks (conventional size) required for one square metre of brick on edge soling is

A. 54   **B.** 64   **C.** 34   **D.** 44

Q.120 In a detailed estimate the provision for contingencies is usually.

A. 1%   **B.** 3 to 5%
C. 10%   **D.** 12% to 20%

Q.121 Most accurate method of estimation is based on

A. Building cost index estimate
B. Plinth area estimate
C. Detailed estimate
D. Cube rate estimate

Q.122 Volume by Trapezoidal Formula Method is determined by the formula

A. $D\left\{\frac{A_0+A_n}{2} + A_2 + A_4 + A_6 \dots A_{n-1}\right\}$

B. $D\left\{\frac{A_1+A_n}{2} + A_0 + A_1 + A_3 \dots A_{n-1}\right\}$

C. $D\left\{\frac{A_0+A_1}{2} + A_1 + A_3 + A_5 \dots A_{n-1}\right\}$

D. $D\left\{\frac{A_0+A_n}{2} + A_1 + A_2 + A_3 + A_4 \dots A_{n-1}\right\}$

Q.123 The quantity of wood for the shutters of doors and windows is calculated in

A. m³   **B.** lump-sum
C. m   **D.** m²

Q.124 If 'i' is the rate of interest expressed in decimal and 'n' is the number of years, then coefficient of annual sinking fund factor, I_c is

A. $I_c = \frac{[(1+i)^n - 1]}{(1+i)^n - 1}$ **B.** $I_c = \frac{i}{(1+i)^n - 1}$

C. $I_c = \frac{i}{(1-i)^n + 1}$ **D.** $I_c = \frac{i}{(1+i)^n + 1}$

Q.125 If R and T are rise and tread of a stair spanning horizontally and steps are supported by wall on the side and by stringer beam on the otherside, the steps are designed as beam of width:

A. $\frac{(R+T)}{2}$ **B.** $R + T$

C. $T - R$ **D.** $\sqrt{R^2 + T^2}$

// Smart Answer Sheet //

Correct — Percentage of students who answered correctly. **Skipped** — Percentage of students who skipped.

Q.	Ans.	Correct / Skipped
1	B	67.39 % / 6.52 %
2	D	56.52 % / 19.57 %
3	C	56.52 % / 21.74 %
4	B	34.78 % / 17.39 %
5	B	63.04 % / 19.57 %
6	B	19.57 % / 26.08 %
7	B	69.57 % / 17.39 %
8	C	60.87 % / 19.56 %
9	D	63.04 % / 19.57 %
10	C	47.83 % / 26.08 %
11	C	69.57 % / 19.56 %
12	B	60.87 % / 19.56 %
13	B	58.7 % / 17.39 %
14	D	67.39 % / 17.39 %
15	A	60.87 % / 19.56 %
16	B	36.96 % / 21.74 %
17	D	4.35 % / 19.56 %
18	D	30.43 % / 36.96 %
19	C	34.78 % / 17.39 %
20	A	50.0 % / 17.39 %
21	A	52.17 % / 21.74 %
22	B	50.0 % / 23.91 %
23	A	63.04 % / 19.57 %
24	D	2.17 % / 13.05 %
25	B	67.39 % / 17.39 %
26	C	71.74 % / 19.56 %
27	B	69.57 % / 19.56 %
28	A	50.0 % / 17.39 %
29	B	10.87 % / 32.61 %
30	B	67.39 % / 19.57 %
31	B	63.04 % / 17.39 %
32	D	41.3 % / 17.4 %
33	B	69.57 % / 17.39 %
34	B	47.83 % / 21.74 %
35	C	67.39 % / 21.74 %
36	C	50.0 % / 23.91 %
37	B	6.52 % / 41.31 %
38	A	23.91 % / 21.74 %
39	D	52.17 % / 17.4 %
40	A	15.22 % / 21.74 %
41	D	36.96 % / 19.56 %
42	D	34.78 % / 19.57 %
43	A	17.39 % / 28.26 %
44	B	28.26 % / 19.57 %
45	B	4.35 % / 23.91 %
46	B	52.17 % / 19.57 %
47	A	69.57 % / 17.39 %
48	B	60.87 % / 21.74 %
49	C	65.22 % / 17.39 %
50	B	63.04 % / 19.57 %
51	B	8.7 % / 43.47 %
52	B	65.22 % / 19.56 %
53	B	36.96 % / 19.56 %
54	C	58.7 % / 19.56 %
55	C	30.43 % / 19.57 %
56	C	71.74 % / 19.56 %
57	C	39.13 % / 21.74 %
58	A	8.7 % / 30.43 %
59	B	58.7 % / 19.56 %
60	B	41.3 % / 19.57 %
61	C	32.61 % / 19.56 %
62	A	41.3 % / 23.92 %
63	C	23.91 % / 43.48 %
64	C	28.26 % / 34.78 %
65	B	30.43 % / 28.27 %
66	B	73.91 % / 21.74 %
67	A	45.65 % / 17.39 %
68	D	17.39 % / 23.91 %
69	C	54.35 % / 19.56 %
70	A	45.65 % / 26.09 %
71	C	26.09 % / 32.61 %
72	A	65.22 % / 17.39 %
73	A	30.43 % / 17.4 %
74	C	45.65 % / 28.26 %
75	C	4.35 % / 45.65 %
76	C	69.57 % / 23.91 %
77	D	2.17 % / 28.26 %
78	B	69.57 % / 21.73 %
79	A	58.7 % / 17.39 %
80	A	30.43 % / 23.92 %

Q.	Ans.	Correct / Skipped	Q.	Ans.	Correct / Skipped	Q.	Ans.	Correct / Skipped	Q.	Ans.	Correct / Skipped	Q.	Ans.	Correct / Skipped
81	A	2.17 % / 19.57 %	90	D	67.39 % / 21.74 %	99	C	50.0 % / 19.57 %	108	A	78.26 % / 17.39 %	117	A	45.65 % / 19.57 %
82	A	50.0 % / 17.39 %	91	D	32.61 % / 26.09 %	100	C	65.22 % / 19.56 %	109	D	58.7 % / 21.73 %	118	A	19.57 % / 19.56 %
83	A	69.57 % / 17.39 %	92	D	63.04 % / 19.57 %	101	B	71.74 % / 17.39 %	110	B	28.26 % / 21.74 %	119	A	39.13 % / 21.74 %
84	B	60.87 % / 21.74 %	93	C	45.65 % / 28.26 %	102	C	10.87 % / 23.91 %	111	C	78.26 % / 17.39 %	120	B	71.74 % / 17.39 %
85	C	28.26 % / 19.57 %	94	C	76.09 % / 17.39 %	103	D	73.91 % / 17.39 %	112	B	54.35 % / 26.08 %	121	C	71.74 % / 19.56 %
86	C	60.87 % / 23.91 %	95	C	43.48 % / 26.09 %	104	D	50.0 % / 19.57 %	113	D	63.04 % / 23.92 %	122	D	63.04 % / 19.57 %
87	A	13.04 % / 23.92 %	96	A	4.35 % / 39.13 %	105	B	67.39 % / 17.39 %	114	B	26.09 % / 19.56 %	123	D	69.57 % / 19.56 %
88	C	17.39 % / 23.91 %	97	D	43.48 % / 17.39 %	106	C	69.57 % / 19.56 %	115	C	69.57 % / 19.56 %	124	B	63.04 % / 19.57 %
89	B	15.22 % / 17.39 %	98	C	65.22 % / 19.56 %	107	D	69.57 % / 17.39 %	116	A	54.35 % / 21.74 %	125	D	54.35 % / 28.26 %

//Hints and Solutions//

1. A detailed cost estimate is prepared when competent administrative authority approved the preliminary estimates. This is a very accurate and reliable type of estimate. Quantities of items of work are measured and the cost of each item of work is calculated separately.

The rates of different items are provided according to the current workable rates and the total estimated cost is calculated. 3 to 5 % of the estimated cost is added to this for contingencies as miscellaneous expenditure.

The detailed Estimated should consist of following details and documents.

• Report

• General Specifications

• Detailed Specifications

• Drawings/plans – layout plans, elevation, sectional views, detailed drawings etc.

• Designs and calculations – In the case of buildings design of foundations, beams, slab etc.

2. Collapsible gates with rails = Square meter

Rolling shutter = Square meter

Expanded metal wire netting = Sqaure meter

Reinforcement of R.C.C. works = per quintal

3. It is the relationship between the total amount of usable floor area that a building has, or has been permitted for the building, and the total area of the lot on which the building stands. This ratio is determined by dividing the total, or gross, floor area of the building by the gross area of the lot.

4. Units of measurement for damp proof course is meter i.e m^2(m square)

Damp proofing in construction is a type of moisture control applied to building walls and floors to prevent moisture from passing into the interior spaces.

Hence, the correct option is (B).

5. The Schmidt hammer rebound test was developed to determine the compressive strength of concrete, and has been used to determine the hardness and compressive strength of rock material. This equipment is portable, easy to use, and can be applied both in die laboratory and in the field.

6. Unit weight of brick is $18-19kN/m^3$

Unit Weight is also known as Specific weight. Unit weight is the weight of the material per unit volume. As we know that the volume is quantified in terms of litres or m^3 and weight is measured in terms of Kg or KN. The Unit weight of materials is the weight of material/unit volume which means the Unit weight is expressed in Kg/L or KG/ m^3 or KN/ m^3.

7. Wrought iron is an iron alloy with a very low carbon content in contrast to cast iron. It is a semi-fused mass of iron with fibrous slag inclusions, which gives it a "grain" resembling wood that is visible when it is etched or bent to the point of failure.

A tough malleable form of iron suitable for forging or rolling rather than casting, obtained by puddling pig iron while molten. It is nearly pure but contains some slag in the form of filaments.

8. • The nominal maximum size of coarse aggregate should be as large as possible within the limits specified but

• In no case greater than 1/4th of the minimum thickness of the member, provided that the concrete can be placed without difficulty so as to surround all reinforcement thoroughly and fill the corners of the form.

• For most work, 20mm aggregate is suitable. Where there is no restriction to the flow of concrete into sections, 40mm or larger size may be permitted.

• When reinforcements are closely spaced or small cover, consideration should be given to the use of 10mm nominal size.

9. Presence of oil such as linseed oil, vegetable oil or mineral oil in water above 2% reduces the strength of concrete up to 25%.

10. A solvent is a substance that dissolves a solute (a chemically distinct liquid, solid or gas), resulting in a solution. A solvent is usually a liquid but can also be a solid, a gas, or a supercritical fluid. The quantity of solute that can dissolve in a specific volume of solvent varies with temperature. Common uses for organic solvents are in dry cleaning, as paint thinners (e.g. toluene, turpentine), as nail polish removers and glue solvents (acetone, methyl acetate, ethyl acetate), in spot removers (e.g. hexane, petrol ether), in detergents (citrus terpenes) and in perfumes (ethanol). Water is a solvent for polar molecules and the most common solvent used by living things; all the ions and proteins in a cell are dissolved in water within a cell. Solvents find various applications in chemical, pharmaceutical, oil, and gas industries, including in chemical syntheses and purification processes.

11. In quadrant circle bearing for changing Fore Bearing to Back Bearing and vice-versa only the NE changes to SW and angle remains same.

12. It is a special convex lens, fitted in between the object glass and eyepiece, at a fixed distance from the object glass, inside the telescope of a tachometer. The function of the analectic lens is to reduce the stadia constant to zero.

13. i. Radiation

In this method, plane table is located at one point "o" as shown in fig. and perform the whole from that point. From point O, sight the points A, B, C, D and E using alidade, locate and plot the points as a, b, c, d and e in the drawing sheet.

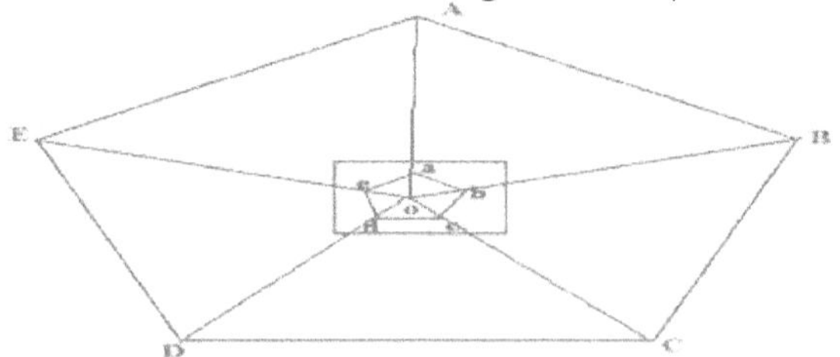

ii. Intersection

In this method we can locate the point by plotting two rays from two known stations. As shown in figure, P and Q are the known station. First the equipment is placed on P and plot the lines by sighting the stations A, B and Q. then shift the equipment to station Q and plot the lines by sighting stations A, B and P. Finally, the intersection of A and B rays is the required location of point of intersection.

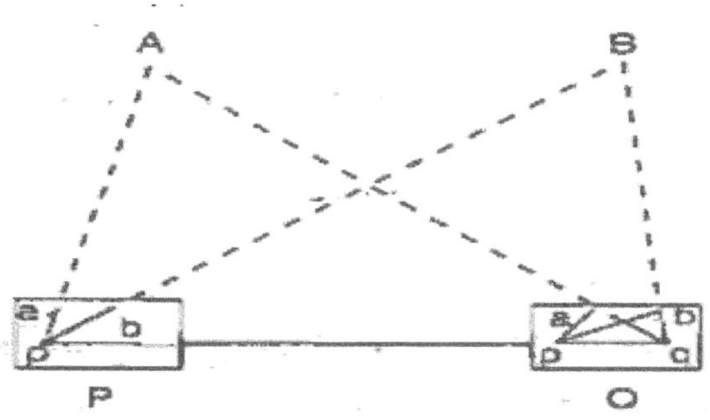

iii. Traversing

Traversing is the connection of series of straight lines. In case of traversing, plane table is located at one point for suppose A as shown below. From that point sight towards B and measure the distance AB. Then shift the plane table to point B and sight towards A and measure BA. Average distance of AB and Ba are plotted to scale in drawing sheet. Then Sight the point C from B and measure BC and repeat the same procedure until last point. Conduct some checks at some points. Finally traverse lines are plotted on the drawing sheet.

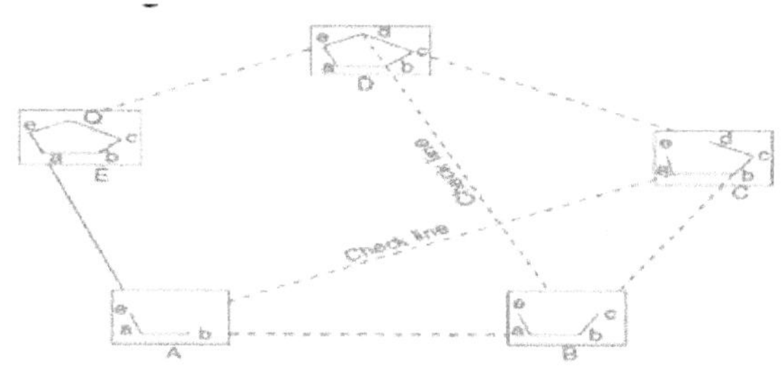

iv. Resection

Resection is a method of plane table surveying in which location of plane table is unknown and it is determined by sighting it to known points or plotted points. It is also called method of orientation and it can be conducted by two field conditions as follows.

• The three-point problem

• The two-point problem

14. Multiplying constant is $\left(\dfrac{f}{i}\right)$ and additive constant is $\dfrac{f}{i} + d$

15. The three main obstacles in chaining of a line are of the following types:

i. Chaining Free, Vision Obstructed

ii. Chaining Obstructed, Vision Free

iii. Chaining and Vision Both Obstructed.

It sometimes happens that a survey line passes through some object such as a pond, a building, a river, a hedge etc. which prevents the direct measurement of that part of the line which the object intersects. The interfering object in such a case is called on obstacle.

Due to building both vision and measurement are obstructed hence both chaining and ranging are not possible when building come across chaining and ranging.

It is necessary to overcome obstacles so that chaining may be continued in a straight line. Special methods are, therefore, employed in measuring distances across the obstacles.

16. If the difference of the FB and BB of a line is , both stations are free from local attraction.

Line	F.B.	B.B.	Difference
AB	$104°30'$	$284°30'$	180
BC	$48°15'$	$226°0$	$177°45'$
CD	$290°30'$	$115°15'$	$175°15'$
DA	$180°15$	$357°15'$	$177°$

17. The quantity of BSF under the footing per metre length is

$0.075 × 0.75 = 0.056$ sq.m

18. The lacing system in a column is designed to resist transverse shear of 2.5% of axial load

Pd = 2.5% of Axial Load

= 2.5% of 1200

= 30 kN

19.

very coarse soil	Boulder size		more than 300 mm
very coarse soil	Cobble size		80 to 300 mm
Coarse Soil mm	Gravel size (G)	Coarse	20 to 80
Coarse Soil mm	Gravel size (G)	Fine	4.75 to 20
Coarse Soil mm	Sand size (S)	Coarse	2 to 4.75
Coarse Soil	Sand size (S)	Medium	0.425 to 2 mm
Coarse Soil mm	Sand size (S)	Fine	0.075 to 0.425
Fine Soil mm	Silt size (M)		0.002 to 0.075
Fine soil mm	Clay size (C)		less than 0.002
Fine sand	diameter		0.2-0.02mm

Hence, the correct option is (C).

20.

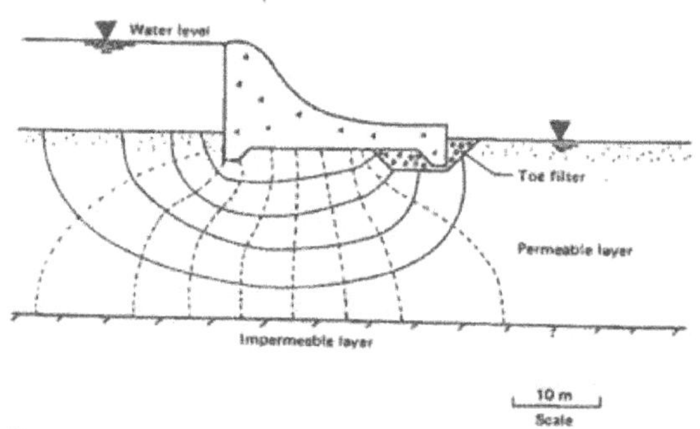

$$Q = KH \frac{N_F}{N_D}$$

is the expression for the discharge (Q) through a flow net for isotropic soils.

ND = total number of potential drops in the entire flow net;

NF = the total number of flow channels in the flow net.

21.

$$\text{Surface tension} = \frac{\text{force}}{\text{Length}}$$

$$= \frac{M^1 L^1 T^{-2}}{L^1} = M^1 L^0 T^{-2}$$

22. A hydraulic jump occurs when the upstream flow is supercritical (F>1). To have a jump, there must be a flow impediment downstream. The downstream impediment could be a weir, a bridge abutment, a dam, or simply channel friction. Water depth increases during a hydraulic jump and energy is dissipated as turbulence.

In Hydraulic jump there is discontinuity in the surface characterized by a steep upward slope of the profile accompanied by lot of turbulence and eddies.

The eddies cause energy loss.

The depth before and after the hydraulic jump are known as conjugate depths.

23. The shear stress is directly proportional to the rate of fluid deformation

$$t = \mu \frac{du}{dy}$$

24. Degree of saturation represents the portion of volume of voids which is filled with water i.e.

$$S = \frac{V_w}{V_v} \times 100$$

For a fully saturated soil, $V_w = V_v$

$$\therefore S = 100$$

For a dry soil, $V_w = 0$ $\therefore S = 0$

$$0 \leq S \leq 100$$

Hence, the correct option is (D).

25. $\gamma d = \dfrac{\gamma}{1+w} = \dfrac{22}{1+0.1} = 20.0$

26. pycnometer also called pyknometer or specific gravity bottle, is a device used to determine the density of a liquid. A pycnometer is usually made of glass, with a close-fitting ground glass stopper with a capillary tube through it, so that air bubbles may escape from the apparatus. This device enables a liquid's density to be measured accurately by reference to an appropriate working fluid, such as water or mercury, using an analytical balance.

27. It is ratio of Plasticity Index and Flow Index of a soil sample. This gives us an idea of shear strength of soil at its plastic limit. When toughness index is less than 1, the soil is said to be friable, which means it can be easily crushed at plastic limit.

28. $\gamma = \dfrac{(G+Se)\gamma_w}{(1+e)}$

here $S = 1$

29. >Seepage through embankments in the earthen dam is controlled by drain trenches.

>Seepage through foundation in an earthen dam is controlled by providing impervious cut-off.

>The flow of water after spilling over the weir crest in chute spillway and side channel spillway respectively are at right angle and parallel to weir crest.

>The discharge passing over an Ogee spillway is given by C L H$^{3/2}$ where, L is the effective length of spillway crest and H is the total head over the spillway crest including velocity head.

>Co-efficient of discharge of an Ogee spillway depends on depth of approach and upstream slop and also on downstream apron interference and downstream submergence.

>Ogee spillway is least suitable for earthen dams as compared to chute spillway, side channel spillway and shaft spillway.

30. If M lies above G, then it is in stable equilibrium,

If M lies below G, then unstable equilibrium,

If M coincides with G, then neutral

31. The pressure of a liquid measured with the help of a piezometer tube is Gauge pressure. A piezometer is either a device used to measure liquid pressure in a system by measuring the height to which a column of the liquid rises against gravity, or a device which measures the pressure (more precisely, the piezometric head) of groundwater [1] at a specific point. A piezometer is designed to measure static pressures, and thus differs from a pitot tube by not being pointed into the fluid flow.

32. A hydrometer is an instrument used for measuring the relative density of liquids based on the concept of buoyancy. They are typically calibrated and graduated with one or more scales such as specific gravity.

A hydrometer usually consists of a sealed hollow glass tube with a wider bottom portion for buoyancy, a ballast such as lead or mercury for stability, and a narrow stem with graduations for measuring. The liquid to test is poured into a tall container, often a graduated cylinder, and the hydrometer is gently lowered into the liquid until it floats freely. The point at which the surface of the liquid touches the stem of the hydrometer correlates to relative density. Hydrometers can contain any number of scales along the stem corresponding to properties correlating to the density.

33. A continuity equation in physics is an equation that describes the transport of some quantity. It is particularly simple and powerful when applied to a conserved quantity, but it can be generalized to apply to any extensive quantity. Since mass, energy, momentum, electric charge and other natural quantities are conserved under their respective appropriate conditions, a variety of physical phenomena may be described using continuity equations.

The continuity equation reflects the fact that mass is conserved in any non-nuclear continuum mechanics analysis. The equation is developed by adding up the rate at which mass is flowing in and out of a control volume, and setting the net in-flow equal to the rate of change of mass within it.

34. The discharge over the broad-crested weir is given by,

$$Q = C_d L_\omega \times h\sqrt{2h(h-h)}$$

In order to measure the discharge over the broad-crested weir, two heads (i.e. H and h) need to be measured. However, experiments have shown that the flow adjusts itself to have maximum discharge for the available head. The downstream head over the weir can be computed mathematically by differentiating equation (1) with respect to and equating it to zero i.e.

$$dQ \quad \frac{dQ}{dh} = C_d \times L_\omega \times \sqrt{2g}\left[\sqrt{H-h} - \frac{h}{2\sqrt{H-h}}\right]$$

=0

This value of h is known as depth of flow.

35. Delta (Δ):

Some quantity of water is required for any crop to come to its maturity. The total quantity of water required for any crop during its base period(B) for its full-fledged nourishment when expressed in depth of water (i.e. in 'cm' or in 'inches') is called its Delta

Duty (D):

Duty of a water simply expresses the number of hectares of land that can be irrigated for the full growth of the given crop by supplying 1 cumec water continuously during the entire base period of that crop.

D=0.864BΔ

Where, B = Base Period in days

36. As regards scour estimation around bridge piers, two codal provisions are available in India, both of which depend on the Lacey–Inglis method with slight variation. The Indian Railway Standards (1985), IRC: 5 (1998) and IRC: 78 (2000) stipulate that in channels with alluvial beds where the width of effective linear waterway provided is not less than Lacey's width (equation (2)), Lacey's depth be calculated using (1). In case where, due to

constriction of waterway, the width is less than Lacey's width, or where it is narrow and deep as in the case of incised rivers, Lacey's depth be calculated using the equation:

R=1.35(q²/f)^(1/3)

37. $V = \left(\frac{Qf^2}{140}\right)^{\frac{1}{6}}$

$f = 1.76\sqrt{d}$

$f = 1.76\sqrt{0.3} = 0.964$

$V = \left(\frac{30\times 0.964^2}{140}\right)^{\frac{1}{6}} = 0.76 m/s$

38. Peak hourly demand = maximum daily demand /24

39. Ozonation is used for disinfection

40. Water Consumption for Various Purposes:

Sr. No.	Type of Consumption	Normal Range (Lit/Capita/Day)	Average	Percentage
1	Domestic Consumption	65 - 300	160	35
2	Industrial and commercial consumption	45 – 450	135	30
3	Public uses along with Fire demand	20 – 90	45	10
4	Losses and waste	45 – 150	62	25

41. A vertical curve provides a transition between two sloped roadways, allowing a vehicle to negotiate the elevation rate change at a gradual rate rather than a sharp cut. The design of the curve is dependent on the intended design speed for the roadway, as well as other factors including drainage, slope, acceptable rate of change, and friction. These curves are parabolic and are assigned stationing based on a horizontal axis.

42. In order to obtain an inward slope of 1 in 20 for the rail, the sleeper are cut to form a table. The Process of cutting the wooden sleeper or casting the concrete sleeper accordingly is known as Adzing of sleepers.

43. A crossing is designated either by the angle the gauge faces make with each other or, more commonly, by the number of the crossing, represented by N. There are three methods of measuring the number of a crossing, and the value of N also depends upon the method adopted.

Method of measuring the number of crossing

Centerline Method

N =1/2 cot α/2

Right Angle Method

N=cot α

Isosceles triangle Method

N= 1/2 cot α/2

44. Camber or Cant is the cross slope provided to raise middle of the road surface in the transverse direction to drain off rain water from road surface. The objectives of providing camber are:

Surface protection especially for gravel and bituminous roads

Sub-grade protection by proper drainage

Quick drying of pavement which in turn increases safety

Too steep slope is undesirable for it will erode the surface. Camber is measured in 1 in n or n% and the value depends on the type of pavement surface. The values suggested by IRC for various categories of pavement is given in Table 1. The common types of camber are parabolic, straight, or combination of them

IRC Value for Camber

Surface Type	Heavy Rain	Light Rain
Concrete/ Bituminous	2%	1.7%
Gravel/WBM	3%	2.5%
Earthen	4%	3.0%

Hence, the correct option is (B).

45. Edge of panel is not considered while designing rigid pavements due to following aspcts:

i. The design of rigid pavement is based on providing Its structural strength by the pavement slab itself by its beam action.

ii. Flexural strength of concrete is a major factor for design.

iii. It distributes load over a wide area of subgrade because of its rigidity and high modulus of elasticity.

46. Many curve forms can be used with satisfactory results, the common practice has been to use parabolic curve in summit curve. This Primarily because of the ease with it can be laid out as well as allowing a comfortable transition from one gradient to another. Although circular curve offers equal sight distance at every point on the curve, for very small deviation angle a circular curve and parabolic curves are almost congruent. Furthermore, the use parabolic curve was found to give excellent riding comfort.

47. We have seen almost all highways being raised in the middle portion of the road surface with respect to the edges. This cross slope in the transverse direction is called as the Camber (or Cant). It is generally provided with the sole purpose of draining the rain water from the road surface towards the edges.

Other objectives of providing camber are:

i. Protection of the road surface, especially for gravel and bituminous roads by draining the unwanted water as quickly as possible.

ii. Protection of the subgrade by providing good drainage conditions.

iii. For safety considerations, as wet pavement conditions are quite undesirable from safe driving point of view.

48. One of the first of the several steps that municipal water suppliers use to prepare water for distribution is getting it as clear and as particulate-free as possible. To accomplish this, the water is treated with aluminum sulfate, commonly called alum, which serves as a flocculant.   Raw water often holds tiny suspended particles that are very difficult for a filter to catch. Alum causes them to clump together so that they can settle out of the water or be easily trapped by a filter.

Alum added as coagulant in water treatment functions better when the raw water is alkaline with high turbidity.

49. Safe water doesn't contain any pathogen. According to the World Health Organization's 2017 report, safe drinking-water is water that "does not represent any significant risk to health over a lifetime of consumption, including different sensitivities that may occur between life stages".

50. Acid rain, or acid deposition, is a broad term that includes any form of precipitation with acidic components, such as sulfuric or nitric acid that fall to the ground from the atmosphere in wet or dry forms. This can include rain, snow, fog, hail or even dust that is acidic.

Acid rain results when sulfur dioxide (SO_2) and nitrogen oxides (NO_x) are emitted into the atmosphere and transported by wind and air currents. The SO_2 and NO_x react with water, oxygen and other chemicals to form sulfuric and nitric acids. These then mix with water and other materials before falling to the ground.

51. Q = 4.2 m³/min = 0.07 m³/s

Vo = 0.2 mm/s = 0.2×10⁻³ m/s

$$V_o = \frac{Q}{A}$$

$$A = \frac{Q}{V_o}$$

$$= = \frac{0.07}{.2 \times 10^{-3}} = 350 m^2$$

52. When a member is being loaded similar to that in figure one bending stress (or flexure stress) will result. Bending stress is a more specific type of normal stress. When a beam experiences load like that shown in figure one the top fibers of the beam undergo a normal compressive stress. The stress at the horizontal plane of the neutral is zero. The bottom fibers of the beam undergo a normal tensile stress. It can be concluded therefore that the value of the bending stress will vary linearly with distance from the neutral axis.

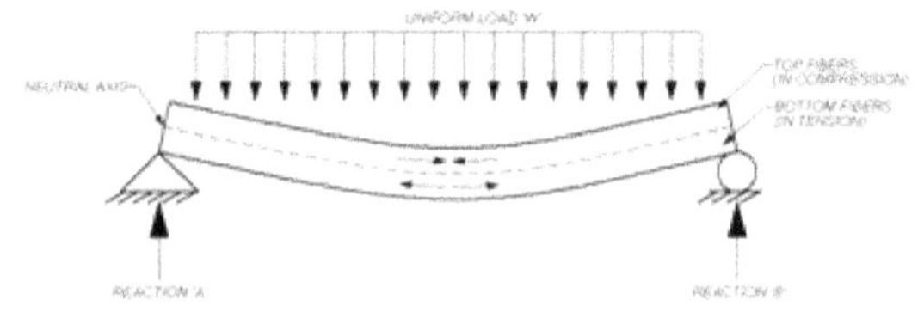

σb =My/I

Where

σ_b – Bending Stress

M – Bending moment due to applied load

y – Vertical distance away from N.A

I – Moment Inertia about N.A

53.

Boundary Condition	Theory	Code Value
Both ends pin code	1.0L	1.0L
Both ends fixed	0.5L	0.65L
One end fixed and the other end pinned	0.7L	0.8L
One end fixed and the other free to sway	1.2L	1.2L
One end fixed and the other end free	2.0L	2.0L

Effectively held in position at both end and restrain against rotation is equivalent to Both end fixed hence according to thermotical value effective length should be L/2

54. The modulus of elasticity of steel is 2×10^5 M Pa

55. From below graph it has seen that mild steel an sustain large amount of deformation before failure.

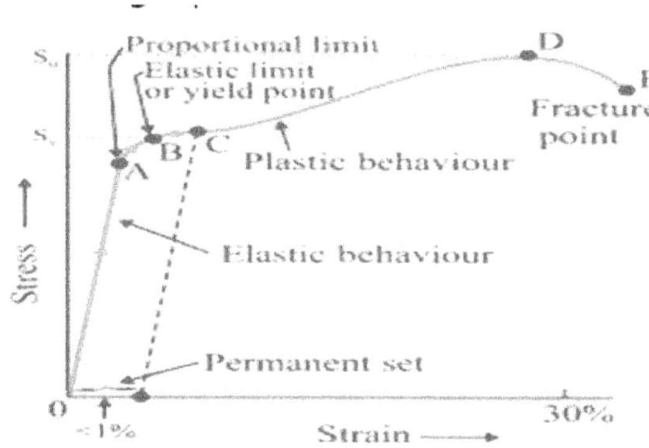

56. The Poisson's ratio of a stable, isotropic, linear elastic material must be between −1.0 and +0.5 because of the requirement for Young's modulus, the shear modulus and bulk modulus to have positive values. Most materials have Poisson's ratio values ranging between 0.0 and 0.5.

57. Important point on Mohr' Theory

1. Principal stresses occur on mutually perpendicular planes.

2. Shear stresses are zero on principal

planes.

3. Planes of maximum shear stress occur at 45° to the principal planes.

4. The maximum shear stress is equal to one half the difference of the principal stresses.

58. Radius of Mohr's circle t $t = \dfrac{v_1 + \sigma_2}{2} - \dfrac{\sigma - (-a)}{2} = \sigma$

59. An elastic modulus (also known as modulus of elasticity) is a quantity that measures an object or substance's resistance to being deformed elastically (i.e., non-permanently) when a stress is applied to it. The elastic modulus of an object is defined as the slope of its stress–strain curve in the elastic deformation region.

60. $t = \dfrac{T_y}{I_p} = \dfrac{T \times \frac{d}{2}}{\frac{\pi d^4}{32}} = \dfrac{16T}{\pi D^3}$

61. Safe working stress is known as the maximum allowable stress that a material or object will be subjected to when in service. This stress is always lower than the Yield stress. If working stress is more than yield stress, then material will fail.

62. Relation between Young Modulus and Shear Modulus

E = 2G (1 + v)

Relation between Young Modulus and Bulk Modulus

E= 3K(1+2v)

Relation between Young Modulus, Bulk Modulus and Shear modulusRelation between Young Modulus and Shear Modulus

E = 2G (1 + v)

Relation between Young Modulus and Bulk Modulus

E = 3K (1 + 3V)

Relation between Young Modulus, Bulk Modulus and Shear modulus

$$E = \frac{9GK}{3K+G}$$

63. The void ratio is the ratio of the volume of voids to the volume of solids in a soil sample. It is denoted by 'e'.

The volume of solids remains the same in both the conditions

Therefore, V_s = V/(1+e)

Where V_s = volume of solids, V = volume of soil, e = void ratio

V_s = V_1/(1+e_1) = V_2/(1+e_2)

Also H_1/(1+e_1) = H_2/(1+e_2) (Since V = A x H and taking Area as constant)

H_1 = 10 cm

H_2 = 10 cm × 1+0.2/1+0.5 = 8 cm

ΔH = H_1–H_2 = 10 – 8 = 2 cm

64. BMD for AB cantilever,

$$Also \ \frac{dM}{DA} = S$$

and $\frac{Dm}{dx}$ for BMD is zero

65.

Sieve Size	Percentage of Passing For			
	Grading Zone-I	Grading Zone-II	Grading Zone-III	Grading Zone-IV
10 mm	100	100	100	100
4.75 mm	90 – 100	90 – 100	90 – 100	95 – 100
2.36 mm	60 – 95	75 – 100	35 – 100	95 – 100
1.18 mm	30 – 70	55 – 90	75 – 100	90 – 1000
600 micron	15 – 34	35 – 59	60 – 79	80 – 100
300 micron	5 – 20	8 – 30	12 – 40	15 – 50
150 micron	0 – 10	0 – 10	0 – 10	0 – 15

Zone-I represents the coarse sand and zone-IV represents the finer sand in all the four zones.

66. The time to reach this stage is termed as setting time. The time at which cement paste loses its plasticity is called initial setting time. Final setting time is the time when the paste completely loses its plasticity. It is the time taken for the cement paste or cement concrete to harden sufficiently and attain the shape of the mould in which it is cast

Initial setting time= 30 minutes

Final Setting time = 600 minutes

67. This test is performed with the help of Le Chatelier apparatus as shown in figure below. It consists of a brass mould of diameter 30 mm and height 30 mm.

Hence, the correct option is (A).

68. GGBFS confirming IS 12089 chemical requirements can be used as an mineral admixture as part replacement to cement, whereas other three are used as cementituous material.

69. Compressive strength of different grades of concrete at 7 and 28 days

Grade of Concrete	Min. Compressive strength N/mm2 at 7 days	Specified Compressive strength N/mm2 at 7 days
M15	10	15
M20	13.5	20
M25	17	25
M30	20	30
M35	23.5	35
M40	27	40
M45	30	45

From above value it has seen crushing strength of 28 days are 1.5 times crushing strength of 7 days.

70. In order to solve this problem, consider any x- section, x-x located at a distance x from the left end or the reference, and write down the expression for the sheer force and the bending moment

S.F|x–x = –W

B.M|x–x = –W.x

therefore, M|x–x = –W.x

the governing equation M/EI = d2y/dx2

Substitution the value of M in terms of x then integrating the equation one get

$$\frac{M}{EI} = \frac{d^2y}{dx^2}$$

$$\frac{d^2y}{dx^2} = -\frac{Wx}{EI}$$

$$\int \frac{d^2y}{dx^2} = \int -\frac{Wx}{EI} dx$$

$$\frac{dy}{dx} = \frac{Wx^2}{2EI} + A$$

Integrating once more,

$$\int \frac{dy}{dx} = \int -\frac{Wx^2}{6EI} + Ax + B$$

$$y = -\frac{Wx^3}{6EI} + Ax + B$$

The constants A and B are required to be found out by utilizing the boundary conditions as defined below-

i.e at x = L; y=0................(i)

at x = L; dy/dx = 0.............(ii)

Utilizing the second condition, the value of constant A is obtained as

A = Wl2/2EI

While employing the first condition yields,

$$y = -\frac{WL^3}{6EI} + AL + B$$

$$B = \frac{WL^3}{6EI} - AL$$

$$= \frac{WL^3}{6WI} - \frac{WL^3}{2EI}$$

$$\frac{WL^3 - 3WL^3}{6EI} = -\frac{2WL^3}{6EI}$$

$$B = \frac{WL^3}{3EI}$$

Substituting the value of A and B we get

$$y = \frac{1}{EI}\left[-\frac{Wx^3}{6EI} + \frac{WL^2x}{2EI} - \frac{WL^3}{3EI}\right]$$

The slope, as well as the defined, would be maximum at the free

and hence putting $x = 0$ we get $y_{max} = -\frac{WL^3}{3EI}$

$$(slope)_{max} m = +\frac{WL^2}{2EI}$$

71. In moderate colling condtion temperature of clinker is brought down to in 15 min and in further 10 min the temperature is brought, down to atmospheric.

72. Ordinary Portland Cement (OPC) is graded according to their strength. The grade indicates the compression strength (mpa) of the cement that will attain after 28 days of setting. There are 3 types of ordinary Portland cements which are available in India they are 33 grade,43 grade and 53 grades. 23 grade cement is not available in Indian market.

73. These compounds contribute to the properties of cement in different ways

• Tricalcium aluminate, C_3A : -

It liberates a lot of heat during the early stages of hydration, but has little strength contribution. Gypsum slows down the hydration rate of C_3A . Cement low in C_3A is sulfate resistant.

• Tricalcium silicate, C_3S : -

This compound hydrates and hardens rapidly. It is largely responsible for Portland cement's initial set and early strength gain.

• Dicalcium silicate, C_2S :

C_2S hydrates and hardens slowly. It is largely responsible for strength gain after one week.

• Ferrite, C_4AF :

This is a fluxing agent which reduces the melting temperature of the raw materials in the kiln (from 3,000o F to 2,600o F). It hydrates rapidly, but does not contribute much to strength of the cement paste.

By mixing these compounds appropriately, manufacturers can produce different types of cement to suit several construction environments.

Tetracalcium aluminoferrite (C_4AF) is responsible for early setting of cement and It is also related to heat of hydration. This compound is formed within 24 hours. Generally high quantity of this compound is avoided as it leads to cracking.

74. For a constant water/cementious material ratio, an increase in the aggregate/cementious material ratio will decrease workability, also, more cementious material is needed when finer aggregate gradings are used. A fine aggregate deficiency results in a mixture that is harsh, prone to segregation, and difficult to finish. On the contary, an excess of fine aggregate will lead to some extent more permeable and less economical concrete, although the mixture will be easily workable.

75. Peak discharge of flood hydrograph = 470 m³/sec

Base flow = 15 m³/sec

Peak discharge of surface run-off hydrograph = 470 – 15 = 455 m³/sec

Rainfall Excess = 8.0 – 0.25 × 6 = 6.5 cm

Peak discharge of unit hydrograph

= 455/6.5 = 70 m³/sec.

76. Thermal expansion is the tendency of matter to change its shape, area, and volume in response to a change in temperature.

Temperature is a monotonic function of the average molecular kinetic energy of a substance. When a substance is heated, the kinetic energy of its molecules increases. Thus, the molecules begin vibrating/moving more and usually maintain a greater average separation. Materials which contract with increasing temperature are unusual; this effect is limited in size, and only occurs within limited temperature ranges (see examples below). The relative expansion (also called strain) divided by the change in temperature is called the material's coefficient of thermal expansion and generally varies with temperature

Material	Thermal Expansion Coefficient
Concrete	$12 \times 10^{\,6}/^{\circ}C$
Steel	$11 \times 10^{\,6}/^{\circ}C$ to $13 \times 10^{\,6}/^{\circ}C$

77. $pH = -\log[H+]$
$9.25 = -\log[H+]$
$[H^+] = 10^{-9.25} mol/l$
$[H^+][OH^-] = 10^{-14}$

$$[OH^-] = \frac{10^{-14}}{10^{-9.25}} = 10^{-4.75} mol/l$$
$$= 10^{-4.75} \times 17 \times 1000$$
$$= 0.302 mg/l$$

78. The flexural and splitting tensile strengths shall be obtained as described in IS: 516 and IS: 5816 respectively. When the designer wishes to use an estimate of the tensile strength from the compressive strength, the following formula may be used:

Flexural strength, fer = $\sqrt{0.7}$ fck; N/ mm^2 where fck, is the characteristic cube compressive strength of concrete in N/ mm^2

79. Workability of concrete is defined as the ease and homogeneity with which a freshly mixed concrete or mortar can be mixed, placed, compacted and finished. Strictly, it is the amount of useful internal work necessary to produce 100% compaction.

Workability of concrete (comparison of Slump test, Compacting Factor Test and Vee-Bee Test)

Degree of Workability	Slump (mm)	Compacting Factor	Vee- Bee Test (Sec)	Suitability
Very Low	0-25	0.78	20-10	Road where mechanical vibrator used
Low	25 – 50	0.85	10 – 5	Roads where compaction is done manually. Mass concrete foundations without vibration. Lightly reinforced sections with vibration.
Medium	50 – 100	0.92	5 – 2	Manually compacted flat slabs. Manually compacted normal reinforced concrete. Heavily reinforced sections with vibration.
High	100 – 175	0.95	2 – 0	Section with congested reinforcement without vibration

80.

Exposure	Plain Concrete	Reinforced Concrete
	Minimum Cement (kg/m3)	Minimum Cement (kg/m3)
Mild	220	300
Moderate	240	300
Severe	250	320
Very Severe	260	340
Extreme	280	360

81. The bond strength is the measure of the effectiveness of the grip between concrete and steel and has no standard quantitative definition. In pull out tests on plain bars, the maximum load generally represents the bond strength that can be developed between concrete and steel. With plain bars the maximum load is not very different from the load at the first visible slip, but in the case of deformed bar, the maximum load may correspond to a large slip which may not be obtained in practice before other types of failure occur.

It is preferable therefore when comparing plain and deformed bars to determine not only the maximum load but also the load at the arbitrary amount of slip and also plot the complete load slip curves for the plain and deformed bars under comparison. One such basis of comparison is the load at a relative movement (slip) between steel and concrete of 0.125 mm at the free end of the bar in a pull-out test.

82. These compounds contribute to the properties of cement in different ways

• Tricalcium aluminate, C_3A : -

It liberates a lot of heat during the early stages of hydration, but has little strength contribution. Gypsum slows down the hydration rate of C_3A . Cement low in C_3A is sulfate resistant.

• Tricalcium silicate, C_3S : -

This compound hydrates and hardens rapidly. It is largely responsible for Portland cement's initial set and early strength gain.

• Dicalcium silicate, C_2S :

C_2S hydrates and hardens slowly. It is largely responsible for strength gain after one week.

• Ferrite, C_4AF :

This is a fluxing agent which reduces the melting temperature of the raw materials in the kiln (from 3,000o F to 2,600o F). It hydrates rapidly, but does not contribute much to strength of the cement paste.

By mixing these compounds appropriately, manufacturers can produce different types of cement to suit several construction environments.

Tetracalcium aluminoferrite (C_4AF) is responsible for early setting of cement and It is also related to heat of hydration. This compound is formed within 24 hours. Generally high quantity of this compound is avoided as it leads to cracking.

83. For bulking of sand, water content is 4-6%

84. Bond Strength of Concrete: The force that resists to separation of mortar and concrete from reinforcing steel (or other materials with which it is in contact) such as adhesion, friction due to shrinkage and longitudinal shear in the concrete engaged by bar deformation.

It depends much on concrete mix design, although it also depends on the reinforcement surface condition. The addition of latex to the concrete/mortar mix is known to increase the bond strength between cement and aggregate, between cement and reinforcement, and between old mortar and new mortar, due to the latex interfacial layer. When number of the bars increase adhesive force is increase and ultimately the bond strength increases.

85. Minimum cover in slab depends upon the durability condition

Exposure Condition	Nominal Concrete Cover
Mild	20 mm
Moderate	30 mm
Severe	45 mm
Very Severe	50 mm
Extreme	75 mm

86. Total earth pressure is given by,

$(h2γKa)/2$

here γ = $ω$ and Ka = $(1-\sinφ)/(1+\sinφ)$

87. Where the depth of the web in a beam exceeds750mm, side face reinforcement shall be provided along the two faces. The total area of such reinforcement shall be not less than 0.1 percent of the web area and shall be distributed equally on two faces at a spacing not exceeding 300 111m or web thickness whichever is less.

88. The modulus of rupture of concrete gives the tensile strength of concrete under bending.

Modulus of rupture is a measure of the tensile strength of concrete beams or slabs. Flexural strength identifies the amount of stress and force an unreinforced concrete slab, beam or other structure can withstand such that it resists any bending failures.

Modulus of Rupture is also known as flexural strength, or bend strength, or transverse rupture strength is a material property, defined as the stress in a material just before it yields in a flexure test. The transverse bending test is most frequently employed, in which a specimen having either a circular or rectangular cross-section is bent until fracture or yielding using a three point flexural test technique. The flexural strength represents the highest stress experienced within the material at its moment of yield.

89. A flat slab is a two-way reinforced concrete slab that usually does not have beams and girders, and the loads are transferred directly to the supporting concrete columns.

• Advantage of Flat Slab

1. Flexibility of layout

2. Easy placement of Reinforcement

3. Ease of Frame work

4. Less Construction times

5. Pre-fabricated Welded Mesh

90. Where the depth of the web in a beam exceeds750mm, side face reinforcement shall be provided along the two faces. The total area of such reinforcement shall be not less than 0.1 percent of the web area and shall be distributed equally on two faces at a spacing not exceeding 300 111m or web thickness whichever is less

91. For tension field action to develop in the end panels, adequate anchorage should be provided all around the end panel.

The end panel, when designed for tension field will impose additional loads on end post; hence, it will become stout (Fig 8.2 of the code). For a simple design, it may be assumed that the capacity of the end panel is restricted to Vcr, so that no tension field develops in it (Fig 8.1 of the code). In this case, end panel acts as a beam spanning between the flanges to resist shear and moment caused by Hq and produced by tension field of penultimate panel.

92. Butt joint are joint where two pieces of metal to be joined are in the same plane. These types of joint require only some kind of preparation and are used with thin sheet metals that can be welded with a single pass.

Type of the Joint

1. Single Butt Joint

2. Double Butt Joint

Lap Joint:

Lap welding joints are used most often to joint two pieces with differing thicknesses together. Also considered a fillet type, the weld can be made on one or both sides. A Lap Joint is formed when 2 pieces are placed in an over lapping pattern on top of each other.

93. Effective length of compression members

Boundary Condition	Theory	Code Value
Both ends pin code	1.0L	1.0L
Both ends fixed	0.5L	0.65L
One end fixed and the other end pinned	0.7L	0.8L
One end fixed and the other free to sway	1.2L	1.2L
One end fixed and the other end free	2.0L	2.0L

94. In engineering practice, it is often required that two sheets or plates are joined together and carry the load in such ways that the joint is loaded. Many times, such joints are required to be leak proof so that gas contained inside is not allowed to escape. A riveted joint is easily conceived between two plates overlapping at edges, making holes through thickness of both, passing the stem of rivet through holes and creating the head at the end of the stem on the other side.

The diameter of the hole is slightly greater than the diameter of the rivet shank. As the rivet is heated and driven, the rivet fills the hole fully. The gross or effective diameter of a rivet means the diameter of the hole or closed rivet. Strengths of rivet are based on gross diameter.

Gross Diameter = Nominal Diameter + 1.5

95. Bearing stiffeners are the additional stiffeners required at the point of concentrated loads for the purpose of protecting the web from compressive loads and they provide vertical stiffness which are provided at the points of application of loads and at the end reactions.

The bearing stiffeners are provided to prevent the web from crushing and buckling side way, under the action of concentrated load.

96. 1000 mm^2

web size 1000 mm $\times$ 10 mm

Size of bearing stiffeness

is welded in pair.=100 $\times$5 mm is welded in pair

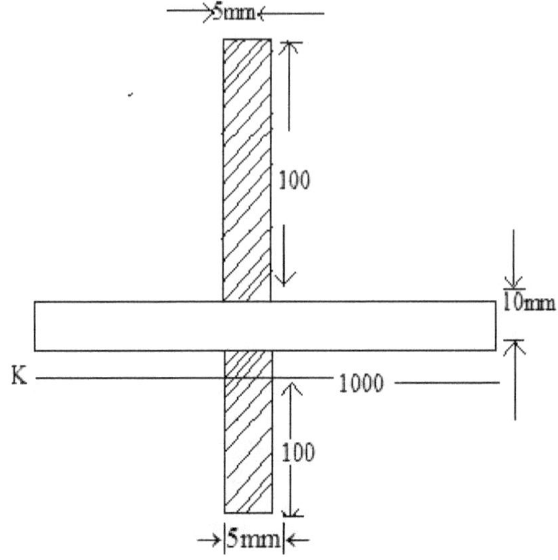

Bearing area = Area of stiffeners

(100\times5)+(100\times5)

=1000 mm^2

97. It is related to the guaranteed minimum yield point of steel with an appropriate factor of safety. Most of the codes assume a factor of safety of 1.67.

The direct stress in axial tension according to IS should not exceed σ_{al} given by the equation,

σ_{al} = 0.6 σ_y

Where, σ_y minimum yield stress of steel in N/ m m^2 (MPa).

98. If 27 ≥ 25mm The gross diameter is (27+2) mm.

99.

Type of rivet	Axial Tension (MPa)		
Power Driven	100	100	300
Hand Driven	80	80	250

For field rivets, the permissible stresses are reduced by 10%

Bearing Stresses of rivet should not exceed by value of fy and 1.2fy for hand driven and power-driven rivets respectively.

100. The design considerations of lacing are as follows. That is one is means in clause 5.7.2.1, it is told that the lacing of compression members shall be proportion to resist a total transverse shear V at any point in the length of the member equal to at least 2.5 percent of the axial force in the member which shear shall be considered as divided equally among all transverse lacing systems in parallel planes. This will be clear when we will go through the example and when we will derive the equations, it will be clear. So, what we have seen that the transverse shear V at any point will be equal to 2.5 percent of the axial force in the member which shear shall be considered as divided equally among all transverse lacing systems in parallel planes. So, this we have to maintain.

101. A strut is a structural component commonly found in engineering, aeronautics, architecture and anatomy. Struts generally work by resisting longitudinal compression, but they may also serve in tension.

102. Strength based classification of brick is made on the basis of IS : 3495.

103. Both quartzite and marble are metamorphic rocks, meaning that although they undergo change via pressure and heat they don't melt. Marble comes from dolostone (limestone with dolomite) or limestone. Quartzite comes from quartz sandstone when the quartz grains of the sandstone are fused due to pressure and heat.

104. Shisham is the hardest wood .

105. Commonly used lime in white washing is fat lime.

106. 28 day compressive strength of cement is tested on 70.7 mm size cubes of mortar having cement to sand proportion of 1 : 3.

107. The amount of water used in performing setting time test of cement is (assuming p = standard consistency of cement) 0.85 p.

108. The heat produced by concrete during curing is called heat of hydration. This exothermic reaction occurs when water and cement react.

109. 1 m^3 of wet concrete with 1 part cement,
2 parts fine aggregate,
4 parts coarse aggregate.
Volume of dry concrete $= 1.52 m^3$
Quantity of cement $= 1 \times \left(\frac{1.52}{1+2+4} \right) = 0.217 m^3$
Density of cement $= 1440 kg/m^3$
So quantity in $kg = 0.217 \times 1440 = 312.48 kg$
1 bag of cement $= -50 kg$
No. of bags $= \frac{312.48}{50} = 6.3$ bags

110. The correct relation between theoretical oxygen demand (TOD), Biochemical oxygen demand (BOD) and Chemical oxygen demand (COD) is given by TOD > BOD > COD.

111. The grade of concrete M20 means that characteristic compressive strength of 15 cm cubes after 28 days is not less than 20 N/mm^2

112. The concrete cubes are prepared, cured and tested according to IS 516 Indian Standard code.

113. To prevent sulphate attack in concrete, for preparing concrete mix, water pH must be within 6 – 9.

114. The increase in the strength of concrete with time is non-linear.

115. The permanent deformation of concrete with time under steady load is called creep.

116. Mild steel used in RCC structures conforms to IS : 432.

117. Wrought iron has least carbon content.

118. corrosion of structural steel is an electrochemical process that requires the simultaneous presence of moisture and oxygen.

Hence, the correct option is (A).

119. For edge soling,

No. of bricks required $= \dfrac{1 \times 1}{0.250 \times 0.075} = 54$

120. In a detailed estimate the provision for contingencies is usually 3 to 5%.

121. Most accurate method of estimation is based on Detailed estimate.

122. Volume by Trapezoidal Formula Method is determined by the formula

$$D \left\{ \frac{A_0 + A_n}{2} + A_1 + A_2 + A_3 + A_4 \dots A_{n-1} \right\}$$

123. The quantity of wood for the shutters of doors and windows is calculated in m^2

124. $I_c = \dfrac{i}{(1+i)^n - 1}$

Hence option b is correct.

125. If R and T are rise and tread of a stair spanning horizontally and steps are supported by wall on the side and by stringer beam on the otherside, the steps are designed as beam of width $\sqrt{R^2 + T^2}$

Q.1 Permissible compressive strength of M200 concrete grade is-

A. 100 kg/cm² **B.** 150 kg/cm²
C. 200 kg/cm² **D.** 250 kg/cm²

Q.2 The shrinkage of concrete-

A. Is proportional to water content in the mix
B. Is proportional to cement concrete
C. Increase with age of concrete
D. All the above

Q.3 If d and n are the effective depth and depth of neutral axis respectively of a singly reinforced beam, the lever arm of the beam is-

A. d **B.** n **C.** d + n/3 **D.** d - n/3

Q.4 The length of the straight portion of a bar beyond the end of the hook should be at least-

A. Twice of the diameter
B. Thrice the diameter
C. Four times the diameter
D. Seven times the diameter

Q.5 Water cement ratio is generally experessed volume of water required per-

A. 10 kg cement **B.** 20 kg cement
C. 50 kg cement **D.** 40 kg cmement

Q.6 ISI has specified the full strength the full strength of concrete after-

A. 7 days **B.** 14 days **C.** 21 days **D.** 28 days

Q.7 The concrete mix which causes difficulty is obtaining a smooth finish is known to possess.

A. Segregation **B.** Internal fraction
C. Hardness **D.** Bleeding

Q.8 The flaky aggregate is said to be elongated if its length is-

A. Equal to the mean size
B. Twice the mean size
C. Thrice the mean size
D. Four times the mean size

Q.9 Consider the following statement: A simplysupported beam is subjected to a couple somewhere in the span. It would produce.

1. A rectangular SF diagram
2. Parabolic BM diagrams
3. both + ve and –ve BMs

which are maximum at the point of application of the couple of these statement-

A. 1, 2 and 3 are correct
B. 1 and 2 are correct
C. 2 and 3 are correct

D. 1 and 3 are correct

Q.10 A beam simply supported at both the ends of length 'L' carries two equal unlike couple 'M' at two ends, if the flexure rigidity EI is constant. Then the centeral deflection of the beam is given by-

A. $\frac{ML^2}{4EI}$ **B.** $\frac{ML^2}{16EI}$ **C.** $\frac{ML^2}{64EI}$ **D.** $\frac{ML^2}{8EI}$

Q.11 The pH value of fresh sewage is usually-

A. Less than 7 **B.** More than 7
C. Euqal to 7 **D.** Equal to zero

Q.12 A sptic tank is:

A. Setting tank **B.** A digestion tank
C. both **D.** None of these

Q.13 The ratio between stress and strain is called as-

A. Modulus of elasticity
B. Modulus of rigidity
C. Bulk modulus
D. None of the above

Q.14 Bernoulli's equation represents total energy per unit of certain quantity. That quantity is:

A. Energy per unit specific volume
B. Energy per unit mass
C. Energy per unit volume
D. Energy per unit weight

Q.15 A sand deposit has a porosity of 1/3 and its specific gravity is 2.5. The critical hydraulic gradient to cause sand boiling in the stratum will be-

A. 1.5 **B.** 1.25 **C.** 1.0 **D.** 0.75

Q.16 The % of chlorine in fresh blaching powder os about.

A. 10 to 20 **B.** 20 to 25 **C.** 30 to 35 **D.** 40 to 50

Q.17 Sewage treatment units are normally designed for:

A. 5 – 10 years. **B.** 15 – 20 years
C. 30 – 40 years **D.** 40 – 50 years

Q.18 According to IS : 456-2000, the maximum reinforcement in a column is-

A. 4% **B.** 2% **C.** 6% **D.** 8%

Q.19 The modular ratio M is given by:

A. $\frac{280}{\sigma_{dx}}$ **B.** $\frac{280}{2\sigma_{dx}}$
C. $\frac{280}{3\sigma_{dx}}$ **D.** None of the above

Q.20 The load factors for live load and dead load are-

A. 1.8 and 2.2 **B.** 2.2 and 1.5
C. 1.8 and 1.8 **D.** 2.2 and 2.2

Q.21 Moment of inertia is a concept application in case of :

A. A rotating body

B. A body moving in straight line
C. A body at rest
D. Both (A) and (B)

Q.22 When slenderness ratio in column lies between 32 to 120, it is known as-
A. Long column
B. Short column
C. Medium column
D. Stocky column

Q.23 In the construction industry, the contractor's profit is included in _____.
A. Unit rate of items
B. Specifications
C. Work charged establishments
D. Contingencies

Q.24 The % of elongation of the piece under tension indicates its:
A. Brittleness
B. Malleability
C. Stiffness
D. Ductility

Q.25 In a cantilever beam with u.d.l, the shear force varies as:
A. Linearly
B. Parabolically
C. Both A and B
D. None of the above

Q.26 The bending equation is written as:
A. $M/I = \sigma_b/Y = E/R$
B. $I/M = \sigma_b/Y = E/R$
C. $M/I = \sigma_b/Y = R/E$
D. $M/I = Y/\sigma_b = E/R$

Q.27 The heaviest I-section for the same depth is-
A. ISLB
B. ISMB
C. ISHB
D. ISWB

Q.28 Lap length in compression shall not be less than-
A. 15 φ
B. 20 φ
C. 24 φ
D. 30 φ

Q.29 Minimum thickness of load bearing RCC wall should be-
A. 50 cm
B. 100 cm
C. 150 cm
D. 200 cm

Q.30 For the deflection of simply supported beam to be within permissible limits, the ratio of its span to effective depth should not exceed-
A. 7
B. 20
C. 26
D. 13 mm

Q.31 If a uniform bar is supported at one end in a vertical direction and loaded at the bottom end by a load equal to the weight of the bar, the strain by a load equal to the weight of the bar, the strain energy as compared to that due to self weight will be-
A. Same
B. Half
C. Twice
D. Thrice

Q.32 Disinfection of drinking water is done to remove-
A. Turbidity
B. Odour
C. Colour
D. Bacteria

Q.33 A mild steel wire is 10 mm in diameter and 1 mm long. If wire is subjected to an axial tensile load 10 kN, find extension of the road (Take E = 200×10^9)-
A. 0.55
B. 0.10
C. 0.64
D. 0.75

Q.34 Permanent hardness of water can be removed by-
A. Adding alum
B. Adding lime
C. Adding chloride
D. Zeolite process

Q.35 The minimum diameter of an opeining of a manhole should be-
A. 25 cm
B. 50 cm
C. 75 cm
D. 100 cm

Q.36 To the calculated area of cover plates of build up beam, an allowance for rivet hole to be added is-
A. 10%
B. 13%
C. 15%
D. 18%

Q.37 The web plate is called unstiffened if the ratio of the depth and thickness is less than-
A. 35
B. 50
C. 60
D. 85

Q.38 According to IS 800 – 1962 the permissible bending stress in steel slab plate is-
A. 1500 kg/cm^2
B. 1420 kg/cm^2
C. 2125 kg/cm^2
D. 1890 kg/cm^2

Q.39 The method of design of steel framework for greatest rigitity and economy in wight is knwon as-
A. Simple deign
B. Semi rigid design
C. Fully rigid design
D. None of these

Q.40 According to IS 456 - 1978 the thickness of reinforced concrete footing on piles at its edge is kept less than-
A. 5 cm
B. 10 cm
C. 15 cm
D. 20 cm

Q.41 Snowcrete is one of the patent forms of-
A. Distemper
B. Water proof cement paint
C. Enamel paint
D. Cellulose paint

Q.42 The limiting length of an offset does not depend upon-
A. Accuracy of the work
B. Method of setting out perpendiculars
C. Scale of plotting
D. Indefinite feature to be surreyed

Q.43 The construction of optical square is based on the principle of optical-
A. Reflection
B. Refraction
C. Double refraction
D. Double reflection

Q.44 The effective span of simply supported slab is-
A. Distance between the centre of the bearing
B. Clear distance between the inner face of the wall plus twice the thickness of the wall
C. Clear span plus effective dpeh of the slab
D. None of these

Q.45 For a continuous floor slab supported on bea, the ratio of the end span of length and intermediate span length is-
A. 0.6
B. 0.7
C. 0.8
D. 0.9

Q.46 Autoclave test is sensitive to:
A. Unsoundness due to lime
B. Unsoundness due to magnesia
C. Unsoundness due to lime & magnesia
D. Unsoundness due to Sulphur trioxide & lime

Q.47 For a number of column constructed in a row, the type of foundation provided is

A. Footing   **B.** Raft   **C.** Strap   **D.** Strip

Q.48 Minimum spacing between horizontal parallel rainforcement of different size should not be less than-

A. One diameter of thinner bar
B. One diameter of thicker bar
C. Sum of diameter of thinner bar and thicker bars
D. Twice the diametet of thinner bar

Q.49 Column may be made of plan concrete if their unsupported length does not exceed their least, lateral diameter by-

A. Two times   **B.** Three times
C. Four times   **D.** Five times

Q.50 Abrasion test is conducted to find:

A. Hardness of aggregates
B. Strength of aggregates
C. Toughness of aggregates
D. Durability of aggregates

Q.51 Characteristic strength of conrete is measured at-

A. 14 days   **B.** 28 days   **C.** 91 days   **D.** 7 days

Q.52 Which of the following pairs is matched properly?

A. Class A – Concrete work
B. Class B – Mortar
C. Class C – Masonry work
D. Class D – White washing

Q.53 The minimum grade of reinforced concrete in sea water per IS 456 : 2000 is-

A. M15   **B.** M20   **C.** M30   **D.** M40

Q.54 Section modulus for a rectangular section is given as-

A. $\frac{bd^2}{36}$ **B.** $\frac{bd^2}{6}$ **C.** $\frac{bd^2}{2}$ **D.** $\frac{bd^2}{12}$

Q.55 Which one of the following is used as a carrier in paint?

A. Almond oil   **B.** Linseed oil
C. Mustard oil   **D.** Olive oil

Q.56 The value of ultimate creep coefficient for concrete-

A. Increases with age of loading
B. Decreases with age of loading
C. Remains constant
D. Is taken as 0.0003

Q.57 Slump test is used for-

A. Strength   **B.** Durability
C. Workability   **D.** Consistency

Q.58 The limit to Poisson's ratio is-

A. 0.25   **B.** 0.15   **C.** 0.50   **D.** 0.65

Q.59 Shrinkage in concrete can be reduced by using-

A. Low water cement ratio
B. Less cement in the concrete
C. Proper concrete mix

D. All the above

Q.60 In a cantilever reratining wall, the design moment is :

A. $\frac{K_a}{2}\gamma h^2$ **B.** $K_a\gamma h$
C. $M = \frac{K_a}{6}\gamma h^3$ **D.** $\frac{K_a}{12}\gamma h^3$

Q.61 Shear reinforcemnt is provided in the form of-

A. Vertical bars
B. Inclined bars
C. Combination of vertical & inclined bars
D. Any one of the above

Q.62 Minimum pitch of rivets should not be less than how many times of gross diameter of river?

A. 2 times   **B.** 2.5 times   **C.** 3 times   **D.** 4 times

Q.63 Effective throat thickness (t) and size of weld (S) are connected as-

A. t = kS²   **B.** t = S³
C. t = kS   **D.** $t = k\sqrt{S}$

Q.64 Bolts are most suitable to carry-

A. Shear   **B.** Bending
C. Axial tension   **D.** Shear and bending

Q.65 The total water consumption including domestc, commercial and industrial demands for average Indian people is:

A. 135 lpcd   **B.** 210 lpced
C. 240 lpced   **D.** 270 lpced

Q.66 For a rivet of 36 mm diameter, the diameter of rivet hole shall be taken as

A. 37.5 mm   **B.** 36.0 mm   **C.** 38.0 mm   **D.** 38.5 mm

Q.67 The operation of removing humps and hollows of uniform concrete surface is known as-

A. Floating   **B.** Screeding
C. Trowelling   **D.** Finishing

Q.68 What should be multiplied with permissible bearing stress to find out strength of rivet in bearing?

A. (p –d)t   **B.** $\frac{\pi}{4}d^2$ **C.** $\frac{\pi}{2}d^2$ **D.** dt²

Q.69 The minimum head room over a stair must be-

A. 200 cm   **B.** 205 cm   **C.** 210 cm   **D.** 220 cm

Q.70 Bulking of sand is-

A. Less in fine sand
B. More in coarse sand
C. More in medium sand
D. More in fine sand

Q.71 Pick the wrongly written assumption taken in analysis of riveted joints-

A. Friction in plate is negligible
B. Uniform stress is distribution in plates is not considered
C. Bending moment is not taken into considered
D. Total load on the joint is equally shared by all rivets

Q.72 Partial safety factors for concrete and steel respectively may be taken as-
A. 1.5 and 1.15   B. 1.5 and 1.78
C. 3 and 1.78   D. 3 and 1.2

Q.73 The shear stress distribution over a beam of solid circular section is such that-
A. $q_{max} = 2q_{mean}$ B. $q_{max} = 1.5q_{mean}$
C. $q_{max} = 1.33q_{mean}$ D. $q_{max} = 1.25q_{mean}$

Q.74 According to IS : 456 – 2000, the maximum reinforcement in a column is:
A. 4%   B. 2%   C. 6%   D. 8%

Q.75 A column is a compression member, the effective length of which exceeds three times of its least lateral dimension. This is applicable to-
A. Rectangular and circular sections
B. I section and circular sections
C. Rectangular, circular and I section sections
D. All the shapes of sections

Q.76 $EI\dfrac{d^3y}{dx^3} = shear$ for a beam represent:
A. Deflection   B. Slope
C. Moment   D. Shear

Q.77 For a fixed support in a plane structure, total number of reactions is:
A. 1   B. 2   C. 3   D. 4

Q.78 Standard loads are given in-
A. IS 885   B. IS 1375   C. IS 675   D. IS 875

Q.79 The characteristic strength of concrete is defined as that strength below which not more than —— of the test results are expected to fall-
A. 10%   B. 5%   C. 15%   D. 20%

Q.80 Minimum thickness of main steel members, not exposed to weather is-
A. 4.5 mm   B. 6.0 mm   C. 8.0 mm   D. 8.5 mm

Q.81 A rivetedjoint can fail in-
A. Tearing of plate only
B. Shearing of rivet only
C. Bearing of plate of rivet only
D. Any of the above

Q.82 Euler's formula is valid for-
A. Short column only
B. Long column only
C. Both short and long columns
D. None of the above

Q.83 Maximum value of slenderness ratio of lacing flats in a steel column is-
A. 120   B. 145   C. 18   D. 32

Q.84 A simply supported beam is considered as a deep beam if the ratio of effective span to overall depth is less than-
A. 1   B. 4   C. 3   D. 2

Q.85 The minimum thickness of a reinforced concrete wall should be-
A. 7.5 cm   B. 10 cm   C. 15 cm   D. 12.5 cm

Q.86 The type of weld used to connect two plates at a lap joint is called-
A. Butt weld   B. Slot weld
C. Plug weld   D. Fillet weld

Q.87 Water required grade bag of cement is-
A. 7 kg   B. 14 kg   C. 28 kg   D. 35 kg

Q.88 The minimum grade of reinforced concrete in sea water as per IS 456 : 2000 is :
A. M 15   B. M 20   C. M 30   D. M 40

Q.89 Ductility of which of the following is the maximum?
A. Mild steel   B. Cost iron
C. Wrought iron   D. Pig iron

Q.90 For a beam, the term M/EI is-
A. Stress   B. Rigidity
C. Curvature   D. Shear force

Q.91 If lines of action of forces in a system of force meet at a point then these forces are called as:
A. Parallel forces
B. Non-concurrent forces
C. Concurrent forces
D. Resultant forces

Q.92 Addition cover thickness in reinforced cement concrete members totally immersed in sea water is-
A. 25 mm   B. 30 mm   C. 35 mm   D. 40 mm

Q.93 A reinforced concrete beam, supported on columns at ends has a clear span 5 m and 0.5 , effective depth. It carries a total uniformly distribution load 100 kN/m. The design shear force for the beam is-
A. 250 kN   B. 200 kN   C. 175 kN   D. 150 KN

Q.94 Tension bars in a cantilever beam must be enclosed in the support up to-
A. L_d B. $\dfrac{L_d}{3}$ C. 12ϕ D. d

Q.95 Strain energy stored in a solid is given as:
A. $\sigma \times \varepsilon \times$ volume
B. $\sigma \times \varepsilon \times$ area of cross section
C. $0.5 \times \sigma \times \varepsilon \times l$
D. $0.5 \times \sigma \times \varepsilon \times$ Volume

Q.96 Relation between Young's modulus (E) and modulus of rigidity (N) is given as:
A. $E = 3N(1 + \mu)$ B. $E = 2N(1 - \mu)$
C. $E = 2N(1 + \mu)$ D. $E = 3N(1 - 2\mu)$

Q.97 The characterstic strength of concrete in the actual structure is taken as:
A. f_{ck} B. $0.85\,f_{ck}$ C. $0.67\,f_{ck}$ D. $0.447\,f_{ck}$

Q.98 In ordinary Portland cement, the first one react with water is-

A. C_3A **B.** C_2S **C.** C_3S **D.** C_4AF

Q.99 The purpose of lateral ties in short concrete columns is-

A. To avoid buckling of longitidioan bars
B. To facilitate construction
C. To facilitate compaction of concrete
D. To increase the load carrying capacity

Q.100 Pozzolans are rich in-

A. Silica
B. Silica and alumina
C. Silica alumina and alkali
D. Silica, aluminia alkali and iron

Q.101 The fixed point whose elevationis known, is called as

A. benchmark   **B.** change point
C. reduced level   **D.** station

Q.102 Which of the following statements in respect of a map A having scale 1 : 1000 and another map B having scale 1 : 5000 is true ?

A. Map A is a large scale map compared to map B
B. Map B is a large scale map compared to map A
C. Map B is a more detailed map compared to map A
D. None of the above

Q.103 The type of surveying which requires least office work is (least calculation) :

A. Theodolite surveying
B. Tacheometry
C. Trignometrical levelling
D. Plane table surveying

Q.104 Detailed plotting in plane table surveying is generally done by

A. Resection   **B.** Traversing
C. Both {A} and {B}   **D.** Radiation

Q.105 The fore bearing of line CD is 324^0 45' . The back bearing of the line is

A. 144^0 45'   **B.** 54^0 45'   **C.** 234^0 45'   **D.** 35^0 45'

Q.106 Radiation, intersection and resection are

A. Compass Surveying Techniques
B. Chain surveyign techniques
C. Levelling techniqures
D. Plane table surveying techniques

Q.107 The most accurate instrument for measuring horizontal and vertical angles is :

A. Theodolite   **B.** Dumpy level
C. Compass   **D.** Tape and chain

Q.108 The correction for slope in chaining is proportional to

A. $\sqrt{h}$ **B.** h   **C.** h^2 **D.** h^3

Q.109 A level line is a

A. line parallel to the mean spheroidal surface of the earth

B. line passing through centre of cross hairs and centre of eye-piece
C. line passing through objective lens and the eye-piece
D. horizontal line

Q.110 A staff reading taken on a point whose elevation is to be determined as a change point is called

A. foresight reading   **B.** backsight reading
C. intermediate sight   **D.** long sight

Q.111 The length of the tangent of a curve whose radius is R and the angle of deflection is

A. $R \tan \frac{\Delta}{2}$ **B.** $2R \sin \frac{\Delta}{2}$
C. $2R \tan \frac{\Delta}{2}$ **D.** $R \sin \frac{\Delta}{2}$

Q.112 Relative density of a compacted dense sand is approximately equal to

A. 0.4   **B.** 0.6   **C.** 0.95   **D.** 1.20

Q.113 Relationship between dry density γ_d, percentage air voids n_a, water content ω and specific gravity G of any soil is

A. $\gamma_d = \frac{(1+n_a)G\gamma_u}{1+uG}$ **B.** $\gamma_d = \frac{(1+n_a)G\gamma_w}{1-uG}$
C. $\gamma_a = \frac{(1-n_a)G_u}{1+uG}$ **D.** $\gamma_d = \frac{(1-n_a)Gr_w}{1-uG}$

Q.114 Match List-I with List-II and select the correct answer using the codes given below the lists:

List - I (Name of person)	List - II (Field of contribution)
A. Stoke	1. Flow-through capillary
B. Darcy	2. Classification of soils
C. Poiseuille	3. Consistency limits
D. Atterberg	4. Flow of water through a soil mass
	5. Velocity of setling particle

	A	B	C	D			A	B	C	D
A.	5	4	1	3		**B.**	4	1	5	2
C.	1	5	4	2		**D.**	3	2	1	5

Q.115 Water content of soil can

A. be less than 0%
B. be greater than 100%
C. never bthan e greater 100%
D. take values only from 0% to 100%

Q.116 If the volume of voids is equal to the volume of solids in a soil mass, than the values of porosity and voids ratio respectively are

A. 1.0 and 0.0   **B.** 0.0 and 1.0
C. 0.5 and 1.0   **D.** 1.0 and 0.5

Q.117 Gravel and sand belongs to the following category of soils

A. alluvial   **B.** cohesive
C. expansive   **D.** marine

Q.118 The coefficient of active earth pressure for a loose sand having an angle of internal friction ϕ is

A. $\dfrac{1-\sin\frac{\phi}{2}}{1+\sin\frac{\phi}{2}}$ B. $\dfrac{1+\sin\frac{\phi}{2}}{1-\sin\frac{\phi}{2}}$ C. $\dfrac{1-\sin\phi}{1+\sin\phi}$ D. $\dfrac{1+\sin\phi}{1-\sin\phi}$

Q.119 A retaining wall of trapezoidal section having base width 'b' retains earth at its back. For no tension to be developed at base, the resultant force will intersect the base from centre line of the base, within

A. b/3   **B.** b/4   **C.** b/5   **D.** b/6

Q.120 A plate load test is useful to estimate

A.   Both bearing capacity and settlement of foundation
B.   Consolidation of soil
C.   Bearing capacity of foundation
D.   Settlement of foundation

Q.121 The characteristic of an ideal fluid is

A.   one which satisfies continuity equation
B.   one which flows with least friction
C.   one which obeys Newton's law of Viscosity
D.   frictionless and incompressible

Q.122 The ratio of specific weight of a liquid to the specific weight of pure water at a standard temperature is called

A.   Compressibility of liquid
B.   Surface tension of liquid
C.   Density of liquid
D.   Specific gravity of liquid

Q.123 Pressure in terms of metres of oil (specific gravity = 0.9) equivalent to 4.5 m of water is

A. 4.05   **B.** 5.0   **C.** 3.6   **D.** 0.298

Q.124 Venturimeter is used to

A.   measure the velocity of a flowing liquid
B.   measure the pressure of a flowing liquid
C.   measure the discharge of liquid flowing through a pipe
D.   measure the pressure difference of liquid flowing between two points in a pipe line

Q.125 The length of a pipe is 1000 m and its diameter is 20 cm. If the diameter of an equivalent pipe is 40 cm, then its length is

A. 4000 m   **B.** 32000 m   **C.** 20000 m   **D.** 8000 m

// Smart Answer Sheet //

Correct — Percentage of students who answered correctly. **Skipped** — Percentage of students who skipped.

Q.	Ans.	Correct / Skipped
1	C	80.62 % / 10.63 %
2	D	66.25 % / 13.13 %
3	D	63.75 % / 18.75 %
4	C	50.0 % / 16.25 %
5	C	63.12 % / 22.51 %
6	D	73.75 % / 23.13 %
7	C	21.25 % / 20.0 %
8	B	22.5 % / 23.13 %
9	D	20.62 % / 23.76 %
10	D	27.5 % / 26.25 %
11	B	52.5 % / 18.75 %
12	C	63.75 % / 16.25 %
13	A	58.75 % / 21.25 %
14	B	30.0 % / 14.38 %
15	C	32.5 % / 21.88 %
16	C	44.38 % / 16.87 %
17	B	53.12 % / 16.25 %
18	C	56.25 % / 23.13 %
19	C	72.5 % / 20.0 %
20	B	50.62 % / 7.5 %
21	A	23.75 % / 15.63 %
22	C	66.88 % / 13.12 %
23	A	26.25 % / 20.0 %
24	D	56.25 % / 10.0 %
25	A	44.38 % / 22.5 %
26	A	60.62 % / 23.76 %
27	C	58.13 % / 19.99 %
28	C	67.5 % / 12.5 %
29	B	44.38 % / 23.75 %
30	B	60.0 % / 13.12 %
31	C	16.88 % / 23.12 %
32	D	70.62 % / 16.26 %
33	C	26.88 % / 21.24 %
34	D	63.75 % / 10.63 %
35	B	43.12 % / 20.63 %
36	B	23.75 % / 18.75 %
37	D	41.88 % / 17.5 %
38	D	36.88 % / 25.62 %
39	C	28.75 % / 21.25 %
40	C	41.88 % / 23.74 %
41	B	41.88 % / 21.24 %
42	D	45.62 % / 14.38 %
43	D	47.5 % / 21.25 %
44	A	21.88 % / 15.0 %
45	D	20.0 % / 25.63 %
46	C	29.38 % / 16.87 %
47	D	26.88 % / 21.24 %
48	B	31.87 % / 18.13 %
49	C	11.25 % / 22.5 %
50	A	47.5 % / 23.75 %
51	B	75.0 % / 19.38 %
52	B	10.62 % / 20.63 %
53	C	61.25 % / 15.0 %
54	B	40.62 % / 23.76 %
55	B	31.25 % / 20.0 %
56	B	34.38 % / 18.12 %
57	C	67.5 % / 22.5 %
58	C	54.37 % / 23.13 %
59	D	64.38 % / 18.74 %
60	C	45.62 % / 19.38 %
61	D	42.5 % / 15.0 %
62	B	61.88 % / 23.12 %
63	C	53.12 % / 20.0 %
64	C	43.75 % / 18.13 %
65	D	46.25 % / 23.12 %
66	C	59.38 % / 21.24 %
67	B	38.75 % / 19.37 %
68	A	47.5 % / 23.12 %
69	B	15.62 % / 23.13 %
70	D	52.5 % / 23.12 %
71	B	30.63 % / 24.99 %
72	A	68.75 % / 10.63 %
73	C	55.62 % / 15.63 %
74	C	56.88 % / 23.12 %
75	A	16.88 % / 21.87 %
76	D	29.38 % / 23.74 %
77	C	56.25 % / 18.13 %
78	D	50.62 % / 23.76 %
79	B	64.38 % / 20.62 %
80	C	39.38 % / 12.5 %

Q.	Ans.	Correct / Skipped	Q.	Ans.	Correct / Skipped	Q.	Ans.	Correct / Skipped	Q.	Ans.	Correct / Skipped	Q.	Ans.	Correct / Skipped
81	D	61.88 % / 16.24 %	90	C	41.88 % / 23.12 %	99	A	55.62 % / 21.26 %	108	C	59.38 % / 15.62 %	117	A	51.25 % / 21.87 %
82	B	49.38 % / 13.12 %	91	C	48.12 % / 21.88 %	100	B	30.0 % / 18.75 %	109	A	43.12 % / 23.13 %	118	C	66.88 % / 12.5 %
83	B	59.38 % / 19.37 %	92	A	25.0 % / 23.12 %	101	A	75.62 % / 16.26 %	110	B	30.63 % / 13.75 %	119	D	31.87 % / 22.51 %
84	D	35.62 % / 25.0 %	93	A	29.38 % / 26.24 %	102	A	51.25 % / 23.13 %	111	A	48.75 % / 21.25 %	120	A	63.12 % / 12.5 %
85	B	53.12 % / 17.5 %	94	A	45.0 % / 15.62 %	103	D	64.38 % / 21.25 %	112	C	61.88 % / 11.87 %	121	D	51.25 % / 15.0 %
86	D	44.38 % / 23.12 %	95	D	40.0 % / 23.12 %	104	D	28.12 % / 23.76 %	113	C	46.88 % / 22.49 %	122	D	66.88 % / 15.0 %
87	C	31.25 % / 21.25 %	96	C	43.12 % / 17.5 %	105	A	56.25 % / 18.13 %	114	A	50.62 % / 13.13 %	123	B	29.38 % / 25.62 %
88	C	58.75 % / 23.13 %	97	C	49.38 % / 17.5 %	106	D	66.88 % / 23.12 %	115	B	44.38 % / 21.24 %	124	C	55.62 % / 15.63 %
89	C	30.0 % / 21.25 %	98	A	58.75 % / 23.13 %	107	A	71.25 % / 21.25 %	116	C	50.62 % / 17.51 %	125	B	30.63 % / 26.87 %

//Hints and Solutions//

1. Permissible compressive strength of M200 concrete grade is 200 kg/cm².

2. The shrinkage of concrete is proportional to water content in the mix. It is also proportional to cement concrete and increase with age of concrete.

3. Lever arm of the beam (LA) = (d − n/3)

4.

A +1 B +4 F +1 G +3 J +1 K

A +2 C +3 F +4 J +5 O +6 U

M +3 P +1 Q +2 S +1 T +2 V

A +3 D +2 F +2 H +2 J +2 L

The length of the straight portion of a bar beyond the end of the hook curve should be at least four times the diameter.

5. Water cemen ratio is generally expressed volume of water required per 50 kg cement.

6. ISI has specified per 50 kg cement.

It has a gain of strength beyonf 28 days.

The quantum of increase depends upon the grade and type of cement curing and enviromental conditions , etc. The design should be based on 28 days characterstic strength of concrete unless there is a evidence to justidy a higer strength for is a evidence to justify a higher strength for a particular due to age.

7. The concrete mix which causes difficulty is obtaining a smooth finish is known to possess hardness.

8. The flaky aggregate is said to be elondated if its length is twice the mean size.Flaky aggregateThe aggragate is said to be flaky when its least dimension is less than 3/5 th (or 60%) of its mean dimension.Elongated aggregateThe aggregate is said to be elongated when its length is greater than 180% of its mean dimesnin.

9.

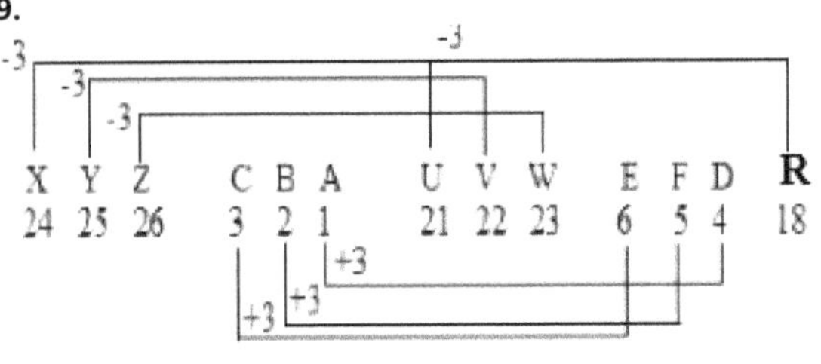

$\sum F_y = 0$

$R_A . R_B = 0$

$\sum M_B = 0$

$R_A L - M = 0$

$R_A = M/L$ and $R_B = -\dfrac{M}{L}$

Consider a section XX at a Distance x from end B

Shear force $S_{A-B} = M/L$

Bending moment $M_x = W_x$

Hence correct answer will be (d)

10. A ebam simply supported at both the ends carried two equal unllike couples at both ends.

Slope at both ends will be equal

$\theta_A = \theta_B$

$$\dfrac{ML}{2EI}$$

Deflection will be maximum at center

$\triangle_{max} = \triangle_{center}$

$$\dfrac{ML^2}{8EI}$$

11. The pH of the fresh sewage is slightly more than the water supplied to the community.

The majority of average sewage systems will be around 7.5-8.5 and will run alkaline as long as the sewage remains fresh and doesn't go septic.

12. A sptic tank is stroge tank and a digestion tank .

13. The ratio of normal stress to normal strain up to elastic limit is called modulus of elasticity

$$E = \dfrac{Normal\ stress}{Normal\ strain} = \dfrac{\sigma}{\varepsilon}$$

14. The correct answer that comes in place of quantity is mass. Explanation: The given equation is used for the case of determining the volume of fluids in terms of pressure velocity and elevation. Bernoulli's equation is per unit mass Representation energy.

Hence, the correct option is (B).

15. The critical hydraulic gradient for sand boiling condition is:

$$i_c = \dfrac{G-1}{1+e}$$

e = void ratio = $\dfrac{\eta}{1+\eta}$

η = porosity = 1/3

G = specific gravity = 2.5

Putting the values,

e = 0.5

i_c = 1.

16. The bleading powder is a white powder and it contains about 30 to 35 per cent of available chloride.

17. Sewage tretment units are normally d esigned for 15-20 years.

18. As per IS-456 2000, the maximum reinforcement used in column is 6%.

Hence, the correct option is (C).

19. The modular ratio m has the value

$$\frac{280}{3\sigma_{dx}}$$

20. The load factors for live load and dead load are 2.2 and 1.5 respectively. The load factor for the dead load will always be less than the load factor for the live load.

Hence, the correct option is (B).

21. Moment of inertia is a physical property that combines the mass and distribution of the particles around the rotation axis.

22. The columns which have their lengths varying form 8 times their diameter to 30 times their respective diameters or their slenderness ratio lying between 32 and 120 is classified under medium column.

23. In the construction industry, the contractor's profit is included in the unit rate of items.

Unit rate estimating is a method that can be used to calculate building costs. In unit rate estimating the prices of items on the bill of quantities are each calculated separately. The unit rate of items includes the contractor's profit.

Hence, the correct option is (A).

24. Ductility is a solid material's ability to deform under tensile stress this is often characterized by the material's ability to be strectched into a wire.

25. Shear force diagram is one degree higher than loading diagram.

As load is acting uniformly, therefore the shear force varies linearly and bending moment varies parabolically

26. Bending equation

M/I = σb/Y = E/R

27. ISHB is the heviest I-section for the same depth.

28. The lap length in compression shall be equal to the development length in compression, but not less than 24 φ .

29. The minimum thickness of walls shall be 100 mm.

30. Basic values of span to effective depth ratios * For spans up to 10 m

- Cantilever 7

- Simply supported 20

- Continuous 26

* For spans above 10 m , the values may be multiplied by 10/span in meters; except for cantiliver in which case deflection calculations should be made.

31. Strain energy (U) = $\frac{1}{2}W\Delta$

Now, axil deformation due to load W is given by

$\triangle_1$ = WL/AE

axial deformation due to self weight W is given by

$\triangle_2$ = WL/2AE

Now $\triangle_1$ = 2$\triangle_2$

and U ∞ $\triangle$

Hence strain energy due to load W is given by

$$U_1 = \frac{1}{2}W\,\Delta_1$$

U₁ = 2U₂

Hence strain energy as compared to that due to self weight will be double.

32. Distribution of drinking water is done to remove bacteria.

33. Elongation $= \dfrac{PL}{AE}$

$= \dfrac{100\times100\times1}{A\times200\times10^9}m$

$A = \dfrac{\pi}{4}d^2 = \dfrac{\pi}{4}\times(10\times10^{-3})^2 m^2$

$= 7.85\times10^{-5}m^2$

Elongation $= \dfrac{10\times1000\times1}{7.85\times10^{-5}\times200\times10^9}$

$= 6.369\times10^{-4}m$

$= 0.64nm$

34. Permanent hardness of water can be removed by Zeolite process.

35. The minimum diameter of an opening of a mamhole should be 50 cm.

36. To the calculated area of cover plates of a build up beam an allowance for rivet holes to be added is 13%

37. A web plate is kept unstiffened if the ratio of clear depth and thickness is less than 85.

38. According to IS 800 – 1962 the permissible bending stress in steel salb plate is 1890 kg/cm²

39. The method of design of steel framework for greatest rigidity and economy in weight is known as fully rigid design.

40. In reinforced concrete footing, the thickness at the edge shall not be less than 150 mm for footings on soils, nor less than 300 mm above the tops of piles for flooding on piles.

41. Snowcrete is one of the patent forms of water proof cement paint.

42. Offests is the lateral distance of an object or ground feature measured from a survey line. the limiting length of an offset depends upon accuracy of the work method of setting out perpendiculars, Scale of plotting etc. It does not depend upon Indefinite feature to be surveyed.

43. The construction of optical square is based on the principle of optical Double refleciton.

44. The effective span of simply supported slab is distance between the centre of the bearing.

45. For a continuous floor slab supported on beam, the ratio of the end span of length and intermediate span length is 0.9.

46. Autoclave test is sensitive to unsoundness due to lime & magnesia.

- Expansion of cement is measured/computed by soundness test.

- Soundness means the ability to resist volume expansion and it is an indication of durability.

- The unsoundness in cement is due to the presence of an excess of free lime, magnesia that could be combined with acidic oxide at the kiln.

- The soundness of cement may be determined by two methods, namely the Le-Chatelier method, and the autoclave method.

Hence, the correct option is (C).

47. For a number of column constructed in a row, the type of foundation provided is strip footing.

48. Minimum spacing between horizontal parallel reinforcement of different size should not be less than one diameter of thicker bar.

49. Column may be made of plain concrete if their unsupported length does not exceed their least lateral diameter by of the slab.

50. Abrasion Test is carried out to test the hardness property of aggregates and to decide whether they are suitable for different pavement construction works.

Hence, the correct option is (A).

51. In the designation of concrete mix M refer to the mix and the number to the specified compressive strength of 150 mm size cube at 28 days, expressed in N/mm^2 .

52. Based on the percentage of CaCO3 in limestone, lime is classified into 3 – Class A, B & C.Class A is used for masonry work, Class C is used for whitewashing and there is no class D.

Hence, the correct option is (B).

53. Concrete in Sea-water

Concrete in sea-water of exposed directly along the sea-coast shall be at least M20 grade in the case of plain concrete and M30 in case of reinforced concrete. The use iof slag or possolana cement is advantageous under such condition.

54. Let rectangular section of width b and depth d then.

Section modulus, $Z = \dfrac{1}{Y_{max}}$

where $I = \dfrac{bd^3}{12}$ & $y_{max} = \dfrac{d}{2}$

Now Z $Z = \dfrac{\frac{bd^3}{12}}{\frac{d}{2}} = \dfrac{bd^2}{6}$

55. Linseed oil is used as a carrier in paint.

Carrier:

- It is an oily liquid in which the base and pigment are soluble. It facilitates the paint to be conveniently spread evenly over the surface by means of a brush. It acts as a binder for the base and causes it to stick to the surface.

- Oils most commonly used as vehicles are Linseed oil, Poppy oil. Nut oil and Tung oil.

Hence, the correct option is (B).

56. The value of ultimate creep coefficient for concrete decreases with age of loading.

Age of loading	Creep coefficient
7 days	2.2
28 days	1.6
1 year	1.1

57. Slump test, Compacting factor test and Vee-Bee consistometer method is used for the measurement of workability.

58. Limiting values of Poisson's ratio are 0 and 0.5

59. Shrinkage can be reduced by using the maximum practical amount of aggregate in the mixture. The lowest water-to-cement ratio is important to avoid this type of shrinkage.

60. Cantilever retaining wall is always designed for earth pressure,

Design moment = Total earth pressure force x Liver arm

$$M = \frac{K_a}{6}\gamma h^3$$

61. Shear reinforcement is provided to resist shear and diagonal tension.

Shear reinforcement is usually provided in the form of stirrups to hold the longitudinal reinforcement and also to take the shear to which the structure is subjected to.

It is usually provided in the form of:

(i) Vertical stirrups

(ii) Inclined bars

(iii) Combination of Vertical stirrups and inclined bars

62. As per IS 800:1984, the minimum pitch of rivets should not be less than 2.5 times nominal diameter of rivet.

63. Effective throat thickness (t) and size of weld (S) are connected as t = kS.

64. bolts are most suitable to carry axial tension.

65.   Use   Demand

(A) Domestic use   200

(B) Industrial use   50

(C) Commercial use   20

Total 270 per capita demand

66. Diameter of rivet hole is given by:

D = diameter of rivet (mm) + 1.5 mm (For rivet diameter less than equal to 25 mm)

D = diameter of rivet (mm) + 2 mm (For rivet diameter greater than 25 mm)

Hence option C is correct.

67. The operation of removing humps and hollows of uniform concrete surface is known as Scredding.

68. Strength of rivet in bearing $\sigma_b.d.t$

This is applicable for single riveted joint. If however there are n rows of rivets per pitch length, we have strength of rivet in bearing $=(p-d)t\sigma_b$

And strength of rivet in shearing

$$= n.\frac{\pi}{4}d^2\sigma_3 \text{ for single shear}$$

$$= 2n.\frac{\pi}{4}d^2\sigma_3 \text{ for double shear}$$

69. Headroom

A problem is rarely solved without one section of stair passing beneath another or under a landing. In those cases, one must be certain to provide stairs will not bump his or her head. The minimum headroom of all parts of a stairway must not be less than 80 inches (203.2 cm). It is measured vertically from a tread nosing, floor surface, or landing.

70. Bulking: The increase in the volume of a given mass of fine aggregate caused by the presence of water is known as bulking.

The extent of bulking depends upon the percentage of moisture present in sand and its fineness. Bulking of sand is more in fine sand.

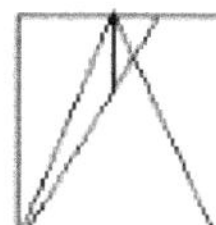

71. Assumption in Riveted connection

1. Friction between in the plates is neglected.

2. Initial tensile stress in the rivet is neglected.

3. The plates are rigid.

4. The rivet fills the hole completely.

5. Deformation of the the plates under the load is neglected.

6. Shearing deformation in the rivet is assumed proportional to the shearing stress.

7. Shearing stress in the rivet is assumed to be uniformly distributed over the rivet crossing section.

8. Unit shearing stress in all the rivets of a joint is uniform.

9. Tensile stress concentration due to rivet holes in the plates is neglected.

10. Bearing stress between rivets and plates is assumed to be uniformly distributed over the nominal contact surface between the rivets and plates.

11. Bending of rivets is neglected.

72. Partial safety factor for concrete = 1.5

Partial safety factor for steel = 1.15

73. Maximum shear stress is 1.33 times to average shear stress for circular beam i.e.

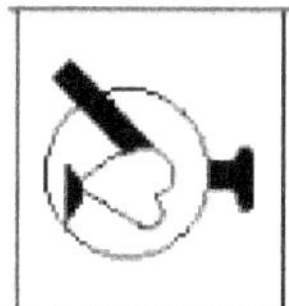

74. As per IS 456:2000, the maximum percentage of reinforcement in column is:

Asc (Max) = 6 % (If reinforcement is not lapped)

Asc(Max) = 4% (If reinforcement is lapped)

75. Rectangular and circular sections.

Hence option A is correct.

76. $EI\frac{dy}{dx} = slope$

$EI\frac{d^2y}{dx^2} = moment$

$EI\frac{d^3y}{dx^3} = shear$

77. Fixed support in a plane structure, total number of reactions is three.

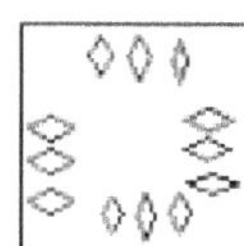

78. IS 875-1964: Code of practice for Structural Safety of Buildings; Loading Standards

79. The characteristic strength is defined as the material below which not more than 5 percent of the test results are expected to fall.

80. Steelwork Directly Exposed to Weather Where the steel is directly exposed to weather and is fully accessible for cleaning and repainting. The thickness shall be not less than 6 mm.

Where the steel is directly exposed to weather and is n ot accessible for cleaning and repainting, the thickness shall be not less than 8 mm. These provisions do not apply to the webs of indian standard rolled steel joists and channels or to packings.

Steelwork not Directly Exposed to Weather .The thickness of steel in main members not directly exposed to weather shall be not less than 6 mm.

The thickness of steel in secondary members not directly exposed to weather shall be not less than 4-5 mm.

81. A riveted joint may fail in the following ways

1. Tension failure in the plates

2. Shearing failure across one or more planes and shearing failure of the rivet

3. Bring failure between the plates and the rivets.

82. Euler's formula is valid for lng column only.

83. As per IS 800:1984, the slenderness ratio of the lacing bars should not be exceed 145.

Lacing is generally preferred in case of load is eccentric.

84. As per clause 29.1 of IS 456:2000, A beam shall be deemed to be a deep beam when the ratio of effective span to overall depth is less than:

(i) 2.0 for simply supported beam

(ii) 2.5 for continuous beam

85. The minimum thickness of walls shall be 10 cm.

86. When the lapped plates are to be jointed, fillet welds are used.

87. Normal range for amount of water used to mix each 50 kg bag of cement is between 20 liters and 30 liters.

88. Concrete in sea-water or exposed directly along the sea-coast shall be at least M 20 Grade in the case of plain concrete and M 30 in case of reinforced concrete.

89. Material Approx. Carbon
Content in \%age
Pig iron $3.5 - 4.5$
Cast iron $1.7 - 4.5$
Wrought iron $0.05 - 0.15$
Steel $0.25 - 1.5$

90. The curvature of a beam a section is M/EI.

91. In a concurrent force system, all forces pass through a common point.

92. actual cover in mild exposure-20mm for completely immresed-45 additional-45-20=25 mm

Hence, the correct option is (A).

93. The design shear force for the beam supported on column at ends is:

$V_d = \omega L/2$

w = uniformly distributed load acting over the span

L = span of the beam

$$V_d = \frac{100x5}{2} = 250kN$$

94. L_d

Hence option A is correct.

95. Strain energy stored in a solid

$$U = \frac{1}{2} \times stress \times strain \times volume$$

$$= 0.5 \times \sigma \times \varepsilon \times volume$$

96. Relation between Young's Modulus of elasticity, Modulus of rigidity (N) and Poisson's ratio (μ) is given by:

E = 2N(1 + μ)

97. For design purposes, the compressive strength of concrete in the structure shall be assumed to be 0.67 times the characteristic strength. The partial safety factor = 1.5 shall be applied in addition to this.

98. Ttricalcium aluminate $(C_3A) = 3CaO.Al_2O_3$

It contains

5-11% of cement.

it rapidly react with water

High heat of hydration

Responsible for flash set

99. The purpose of lateral ties in short concrete columns is to avoid buckling of longitudinal bars.

100. Puzzolanas are rich in silica and alumina and contain only a small quantity of alkalis.

101. The fixed point whose elevationis known, is called as benchmark.

102. Map A is a large scale map compared to map B

This statements in respect of a map A having scale 1 : 1000 and another map B having scale 1 : 5000 is true .

103. The type of surveying which requires least office work is (least calculation) plane table surveying.

104. Detailed plotting in plane table surveying is generally done by radiation.

105.
$$\text{Line} \quad CDF.B. = 324°45'$$
$$B.B \cdot = 324°45 - 180°00'$$
$$= 144°45'$$

106. Radiation, intersection and resection are plane table surveying techniques.

107. The most accurate instrument for measuring horizontal and vertical angles is theodolite .

108. The correction for slope in chaining is proportional to h^2 .

109. A level line is a line parallel to the mean spheroidal surface of the earth.

110. A staff reading taken on a point whose elevation is to be determined as a change point is called backsight reading.

111. The length of the tangent of a curve whose radius is R and the angle of deflection is $R \tan \dfrac{\Delta}{2}$

112. Relative density of a compacted dense sand is approximately equal to 0.95.

113. $Y_d = \dfrac{(1-n_a)GY_w}{1+uG}$

114. A - Velocity of selling particle

B - Flow of water through a soil mass

C - Flow through capillary

D - Consistency limits

115. Water content of soil can be greater than 100%.

116. Volume of void (V_v) = Volume of solids (V_s)

Void ratio, $e = \dfrac{V_v}{V_s} = 1$

Porosity, $n = \dfrac{V_v}{V} \times 100$

Where V is total volume of soil

$V = V_v + V_s = 2V_v$

So $n = 0.5$

117. Gravel and sand belongs to the alluvial category of soils.

118. The coefficient of active earth pressure for a loose sand having an angle of internal friction φ is

$\dfrac{1-\sin\phi}{1+\sin\phi}$

119. A retaining wall of trapezoidal section having base width 'b' retains earth at its back. For no tension to be developed at base, the resultant force will intersect the base from centre line of the base, within b/6.

120. A plate load test is useful to estimate bearing capacity and settlement of foundation.

121. The characteristic of an ideal fluid is frictionless and incompressible.

122. The ratio of specific weight of a liquid to the specific weight of pure water at a standard temperature is called specific gravity of liquid.

123. Pressure is terms of metres of oil

$= \dfrac{4.5}{0.9} = 5m$

124. Venturimeter is used to measure the discharge of liquid flowing through a pipe.

125. For pipe to be equivalent, head loss should be equal

$\therefore \quad h_f = \dfrac{fLV^2}{2gD^5} = \dfrac{fLQ^2}{2gD^5}$

or, $\quad \dfrac{L_1}{D_1^5} = \dfrac{L_2}{D_2^5}$

or, $\quad L_2 = 1000 \times \left(\dfrac{40}{20}\right)^5 = 32000m$

Q.1 Material following Hooke's Law have : -

A.   Linear Stress-Strain Curve

B.   Curve-Linear Stress-Strain Curve

C.   Parabolic Stress-Strain Curve

D.   (A) & (B) Both

Q.2 Malleability is the property by which material can

A.   be stretched

B.   cannot be stretched

C.   be uniformly extended in a direction without rupture

D.   absorb energy without fracture

Q.3 Moment of inertia of a rectangular section, having 'b' width and depth 'd', about its vertical centroidal axis is-

A. $db^3/12$ **B.** $db^3/3$ **C.** $bd^3/12$ **D.** $bd^3/3$

Q.4 Pick up the correct statement:

A.   Crippling stress depends only the geometry and Young's Modulus of a column

B.   Crippling stress varies parabolically with its slenderness ratio

C.   Crippling stress does not depend upon yield strain

D.   All of the above

Q.5 High content of Tricalcium in rapid hardening cement imparts-

A.   maximum heat generation

B.   quick setting

C.   early high strength

D.   expansive properties

Q.6 The effective slenderness ratio of a column fixed at both ends is:

A. 0.5 L/r   **B.** L/r   **C.** 0.65 L/r   **D.** 2 L/r

Q.7 The beam shown in figure is:

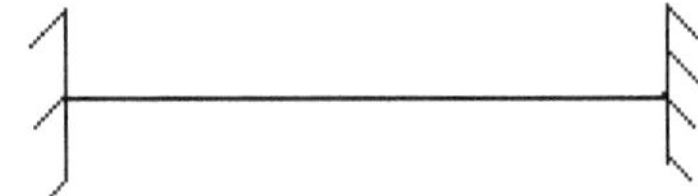

A.   determine and unstable

B.   indeterminate and stable

C.   extremely unstable

D.   determinate and stable

Q.8 If the area of tension reinforcement provided is greater than required for a balanced reaction, then the RCC beam is called:

A.   over-reinforced section

B.   balanced section

C.   over weight section

D.   none of the above

Q.9 The workability of a rounded aggregates for a given water content is a good because : -

A.   rounded aggregates require more cement paste for a given lubrication

B.   rounded aggregates require less cement paste for a given lubrication

C.   rounded aggregates have more voids

D.   rounded aggregates have greater surface area

Q.10 For constructing dams and foundation, the type of cement generally used is:

A.   portland blast furnace cement

B.   rapid hardening cement

C.   ordinary Potland cement

D.   high alumina content

Q.11 If normal shear stress is less than design shear strength of concrete, then

A.   minimum shear reinfocement is to be provided

B.   section to be designed for shear

C.   shear reinforcement is not required

D.   the section is unsafe

Q.12 The maximum strain in the tension reinforcement in the section at failure shall not be less than:

A. $\frac{f_y}{1.15E_s} + 0.002$ **B.** $\frac{f_y}{E_s} + 0.002$

C. $\frac{f_y}{E_s} - 0.002$ **D.** $\frac{f_y}{E_s} - 0.003$

Q.13 The limiting depth of neutral axis for a section of effective depth 50mm, using Fe 415 Grade of Steel

A. 300 mm   **B.** 350 mm   **C.** 324 mm   **D.** 264 mm

Q.14 Acid rain is caused due to which of the following ?

A. H_2SO_4 **B.** HNO_3

C. CH_4 **D.** (A) and (B) both

Q.15 A crop requires 19 cm of water in 14 days, then the duty of the crop is

A. 266 hec/cum   **B.** 637 hec/cum

C. 1173 hec/cum   **D.** 864 hec/cum

Q.16 The method of irrigation adopted at places where there exists acute scarcity of irrigation water is :-

A.   Sprinkler irrigation method

B.   Furrow irrigation method

C.   Trickle irrigation method

D.   Basin flooding

Q.17 If C, is the allowable rate of change of the centrifugal acceleration then length of transition curve is given by,

A. $L_s = \frac{v^3}{CR}$ **B.** $L_s = \frac{v^2}{CR}$

C. $L_s = \frac{vC}{R}$ **D.** $L_s = \frac{v^2R}{C}$

Q.18

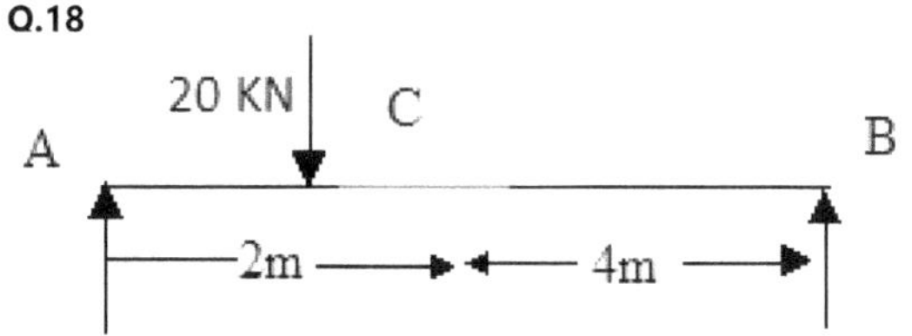

For the beam shown in figure the magnitude of the vertical reaction at 'A' is

A. 13.3 kN   **B.** 6.7kN   **C.** 7 kN   **D.** 14 kN

Q.19 Dissolved oxygen in streams is :
A. Maximum at noon
B. Minimum at noon
C. Maximum at midnight
D. same throughout the day

Q.20 The relation between
K = Bulk Modulus
E = Young's Modulus and
G = Modulus of rigidity is given by

A. $\dfrac{5KG}{3K+G}$ **B.** $\dfrac{9KG}{3K+G}$ **C.** $\dfrac{3KG}{5K+G}$ **D.** $\dfrac{3KG}{K+G}$

Q.21 The value of Poission's ratio of concrete is
A. 0.2   **B.** 0.2   **C.** 0.3   **D.** 0.5

Q.22 A mild steel wire is 10 mm in diameter and 1mm long. If wire is subjected to an axial tensile load 10 kN, find extension of the road (Take E = 200×10^9)
A. 0.55   **B.** 0.10   **C.** 0.64   **D.** 0.75

Q.23 The maximum shear force in cantilever beam with uniformly distributed load W per unit length, over the whole length L, is
A. At the centre
B. At the free and
C. At the fixed end
D. Can't free

Q.24 For unstiffened webs of girders, the thickness of web shall not be less than
A. $D_1/50$ **B.** $D_1/85$ **C.** $D_1/100$ **D.** $D_1/150$

Q.25 As per IS : 456 in a two-way slab, the width of the middle strip along each span should be
A. 3/8 of the width of span in that direction
B. 3/8 of the width of the right angles
C. 3/4 of the shortest side of the slab
D. 3/4 of the width of the span in that direction

Q.26 A column is a compression member, the effective length of which exceeds
A. two times the least lateral dimension
B. three times the least lateral dimension
C. 2.5 times the least lateral dimension
D. 1.5 times the least lateral dimension

Q.27 The minimum clear cover (in mm) for footing, according to IS 456 : 2000, shall be
A. 20   **B.** 25   **C.** 40   **D.** 50

Q.28 In beams the maximum area of the reinforcement in tension reinforcement shall not exceed
A. 0.04 bD   **B.** 0.02 bD   **C.** 0.03 bD   **D.** 0.01 bD

Q.29 The effective span, of cantilever slab at the end of a continuous slab is,
A. Clear span + effective depth of the slab
B. Clear span + half of the effecitve depth of the slab
C. Length upto the centre of the support
D. Length up to the face of the support + half of the effective depth

Q.30 A RC column 4 m long and 400 mm in dia is reinforced by 8 bar of the 20 mm dia, find the safe load, the column can carry

σ_{cc} = 4 N/mm², σ_{se} = 130 N/mm²

A. 800 kN   **B.** 810 kN
C. 819.33 kN   **D.** 810.55 kN

Q.31 The maximum permissible stress for hand driven rivet in shear is : -
A. 100 N/mm²   **B.** 80 N/mm²
C. 250 N/mm²   **D.** 300 N/mm²

Q.32 The nominal diameter of a rivet is 20 mm. The strength of rivet in single shear if permissible shear stress in rivet is 100N /mm², , is,
A. 36.3 kN   **B.** 20.0 kN   **C.** 21.5 kN   **D.** 34.4 kN

Q.33 Grit is a
A. beam
B. short column
C. stiffness
D. long column

Q.34 The variation in declination due to magnetic storms is called
A. Diurnal   **B.** Annual   **C.** Secular   **D.** Irregular

Q.35 A metallic tape is made of
A. Steel
B. Invar
C. Linen
D. Cloth and Wires

Q.36 The survey done to locate boundaries of a field and to determine its area is called
A. Traverse survey
B. Cross-staff survey
C. Plane Table survey
D. Tacheometric survey

Q.37 Which of the following statements in respect of a map A having scale 1 : 2000 and anothe map B having scale 1 : 10000 is true ?
A. Map A is a large scale map compared to Map B
B. Map B is a large scale compared to Map A
C. Map B is more detailed map compared to Map A
D. None of these

Q.38 The length of a curve whose radius is R and the angle of deflection Δ is
A. $R \tan \frac{\Delta}{2}$ **B.** $2R \sin \frac{\Delta}{2}$
C. $2R \tan \frac{\Delta}{2}$ **D.** $R \sin \frac{\Delta}{2}$

Q.39 Levellling, centering and Orientation are work operation of

A. Compass Surveying Technique
B. Chain Suryeying Technique
C. Levelling Technique
D. Plane Table Surveying Technique

Q.40 Broadly spaced contour lines on a map shows that the area is

A. Flat
B. Steeply-Sloped
C. Vertical cliff
D. Overhang Cliff

Q.41 The quadratic bearing of a line is $S30^0 0'0''W$, its value in whole circle bearing is

A. 30^0
B. 40^0
C. 100^0
D. 210^0

Q.42 The ratio (water content - plastic)/plastic index for a soil mass is called

A. Liquidity index
B. Shrinkage ratio
C. Consistency index
D. Toughness index

Q.43 Coarse soil generally

A. cohesive
B. impermeable
C. having large particle size
D. none of the above

Q.44 Tri calcium aluminate (C_3A)

A. hydrates rapidly
B. generates less heat of hydration
C. increases
D. has loss rsistance to sulphate attack

Q.45 Velocity distribution in a turbulent boundary layer follows:

A. Logarithmic law
B. Parabolic law
C. Linear law
D. Cubic law

Q.46 The resistance of an aggregate to impact is known as

A. toughness
B. abrasion resistance
C. shear resistacne
D. crushing resistance

Q.47 If fineness modulus of a sand is 2.7, it is gared as,

A. very fine sand
B. fine sand
C. medium sand
D. coarse sand

Q.48 IRC has spefified the maximum value of stripping value of bitumen not be exceed

A. 2%
B. 3%
C. 4%
D. 5%

Q.49 Surge is an example of

A. Steady ripidly varied flow
B. Unsteady rapidly varied flow
C. Steady gradually varied flow
D. Unsteady Gradually varied flow

Q.50 The volume of voids to volume of solids is known as

A. Porosity
B. Void ratio
C. Air ratio
D. Air content

Q.51 Aneroid Baromete is a device used for meauring

A. Velocity
B. Pressure
C. Density
D. Discharge

Q.52 Viscosity is due to

I. Surface tension
II. Cohesion
III. Intermolecular attraction
IV. Vapour pressure

A. II,III
B. III
C. I
D. III, IV

Q.53 Euler's equation represents

A. Energy per unit eight
B. Unsteady flow equation
C. Momentum equation
D. Specific energy

Q.54 The dimension for vorticity is

A. T^2
B. T^{-1}
C. T^1
D. T^{-2}

Q.55 Resultant pressure of the liquid in case of an immersed body acts through which of the following?

A. Centre of gravity
B. Center of pressure
C. Metacentre
D. Centre of buoyancy

Q.56 The head loss in turbulent flow in pipe varies

A. Directly as the velocity
B. Inversely as the square of the velocity
C. Inversely as the square of the diameter
D. Approximately as the square of the velocity

Q.57 A hydraulic jump occurs in channel

A. Whenever the flow is supercritical
B. If the flow is controlled by a slucie gate
C. If the bed slope changes from mild to steep
D. If the bed slope changes from steep to mild

Q.58 The saturated unit weight of a fully saturated soil having void ratio is 0.67 and specific gravity is 2.67, is

A. $18.62 \ kN/m^3$
B. $19.00 \ kN/m^3$
C. $19.62 \ kN/m^3$
D. $20.05 \ kN/m^3$

Q.59 In long and short wall method of estimation, the length of long wall is the centre distance between the walls and

A. Breadth of the wall
B. Half breath of wall on each wall
C. One fourth breadh of wall on each side
D. None of the above

Q.60 The plan of a building is in the form of a rectangular with centre dimensions of the outer walls as 10.3 and 17.3m. The thickness of the walls in superstructure is 0.3m. Then its carpet area is

A. $150 \ m^2$
B. $157.59 \ m^2$
C. $165.36 \ m^2$
D. $170 \ m^2$

Q.61 The value of the property realized when it become absolutely useless except for sale as junk is known as

A. Slavage value
B. Scrap value
C. Book value
D. Junk value

Q.62 While estimating for plastering, usually no deduction is made for:

A. End of beams

B. Small opening upto 0.5 sq.m.

C. End of rafters

D. All of the above

Q.63 Estimate expected to be least accurate is:

A. Supplementary estimate

B. Plinth area estimate

C. Detailed estimate

D. Revised estimate

Q.64 Original cost of property minus depreciation is

A. Book value   **B.** Salvage value

C. Reliable value   **D.** Obsolence value

Q.65 Outer projection of a "Tread " is called

A. Nosing   **B.** Treader   **C.** Step   **D.** Going

Q.66 The part of the wall on which the arch rests, is called

A. Intrados   **B.** Extrados

C. Abutment   **D.** Span

Q.67 Pick up the incorrect statement:

A. Negative skin friction occurs when the soil layer surrounding a portion of the pile shaft settles more than the pile

B. Negative skin friction develops when a dence soil surrounding the pile settles after the pile has been installed

C. Negative skin friction occurs in the soil zone which moves downward relative to the pile

D. Negative skin friction imposes an extra downward load on the pile

Q.68 Accodring to Dicken's formula, the flood discharge Q in cumes is given by

A. $C A^{2/9}$ **B.** $C A^{3/4}$ **C.** $C A^{5/6}$ **D.** $C A^{7/8}$

Q.69 A 60% index of wetness means

A. Rain excess of 40%

B. Rain deficiency of 40%

C. Rain deficiency of 60%

D. None of the above

Q.70 The diameter of rivet hole in tension members using rivet of diameter more than 24 mm will be equal to

A. Rivet diameter + 3 mm

B. Rivet diameter + 2 mm

C. Rivet diameter + 1.5 mm

D. Rivet diameter

Q.71 Which one of the following will be preferred for a column?

A. ISLB   **B.** ISMB   **C.** ISWB   **D.** ISHB

Q.72 In case of tension member consisting of two angles back to back of same side of gussest plate, what is K equal to?

Where, A_1 – Area of connected leg

A_2 – Area of outstanding leg

A. $\frac{3A_1}{3A_1+A_2}$ **B.** $\frac{3A_1}{A_1+3A_2}$ **C.** $\frac{5A_1}{A_1+5A_2}$ **D.** $\frac{5A_1}{5A_1+A_2}$

Q.73 According to IS 456–2000, minimum slenderness ratio for a short column is

A. Less than 12   **B.** Less than 18

C. Between 18 & 24   **D.** More than 24

Q.74 Which one of the following is categorized as a long term of pre-stress in a pre-stressed concrete member?

A. Loss then to elsatic shortening

B. Loss due to friction

C. Loss due to relaxiation of strands

D. Loss due to anchorage slip

Q.75 A RCC beam of 200 mm which and 300 mm effective depth is reinforced with Fe 415 grade steel. The grade of concrete used is M20. The limiting moment carrying capcity of this beam is

A. 47.88 kNm   **B.** 53.28 kNm

C. 49.67 kNm   **D.** None of the above

Q.76 A two hinged arch is statically indeterminate by

A. 0 degree   **B.** 1 degree   **C.** 2 degree   **D.** 3 degree

Q.77 Flexibility method is also known as

A. Force method

B. Displacement method

C. Compatibility method

D. None of the above

Q.78 Which of the following material has a Poisson's ration more then 1?

A. Cork   **B.** Wood   **C.** Plastic   **D.** None

Q.79 The shape of the bending moment diagram for a uniformly distributed load is:

A. Cubic   **B.** Linear

C. Straight line   **D.** Parabolic

Q.80 A meterial has identical properties in all direction is said to be

A. Homogeneous   **B.** Isotropic

C. Elastic   **D.** Orthotropic

Q.81 The operation of levelling across any river is termed as

A. Profile levelling   **B.** Reciprocal leveling

C. Fly levelling   **D.** Simple levelling

Q.82 When lower values are inside the loop of a contour plot it indicates

A. High ground   **B.** Level ground

C. A depession   **D.** Sloping ground

Q.83 The reaitionship between tropical ground and sidereal year

A. TY – SY   **B.** TY < SY   **C.** TY = SY   **D.** None

Q.84 Which of the following is not a retarding admicture?

A. Tartaric acid   **B.** Sugar

C. Gypsum   **D.** Sodium silicate

Q.85 Pick the correct statement:

A. Angular of flaky particles reduce the workability and demand more cement and water to give the spcefied strength of concrete mix

B. Angular of flaky particules produce smoother mix for a given water/cement ratio

C. Angular or flaky particles do not affect the workability of concrete

D. Angular of flaky particles produce a good mix insted of rounded particles

Q.86 Bulking:

A. Decreases with fineness f aggregates

B. Increases with fineness of aggregates

C. Is not related to fineess of aggregates

D. Is higher for coarse aggregates

Q.87 The degree of workability is medium when the value of slump in mm is:

A. 25 – 50

B. 0 – 50

C. 50 – 100

D. 100 – 175

Q.88 Torsion resisting capacity of a given RC section

A. Decreases with decreas in stirrup spacing

B. Decreases with increases in longitudinal bars

C. Does not depend upon stirrup and longitudinal steels

D. Increases with the increases in stirrup and longitudional steel

Q.89 As per IS code, concrete should be cured at

A. 5^0C

B. 10^0C

C. 27^0C

D. 40^0C

Q.90 To form still water pocket in front of the canal head, the following is constructed:

A. Fish ladder

B. Dvivide wall

C. Dam

D. None of these

Q.91 When an irrigation canal passes over a river, the structure constructed is called

A. Cross drainage

B. Aqueduct

C. Super passage

D. Level crossing

Q.92 Garret diagram, for the design of irrigation channels, is bases on

A. Kennedy's theory

B. Lacey's theory

C. Kutter's formula

D. Manning's formula

Q.93 The maximum permissible shear stress given in BIS 456-1978 is based on

A. Diagonal tension failure

B. Diagonal compression failure

C. Flexural tension failure

D. Flexural compression failure

Q.94 From design point of view, spherical pressure vessels are preferred over cylindrical pressure vessels because they

A. Are cost effective in fabrication

B. Have uniform higher circumferential stress

C. Uniform lower circumferential stress

D. Have a large volume for the same quantity

Q.95 Acidity in water is caused due to

A. Mineral acids

B. Free CO_2

C. Iron sulphate and aluminium sulphate

D. All of the above

Q.96 The minimum value of camber provided for thin bituminous surface hill roads, is

A. 2.2%

B. 2.5%

C. 3.0%

D. 3.5%

Q.97 The wall constucted for the stability of an excavated protion of a road on the hill side, is known as

A. Retaining wall

B. Breast wall

C. Parapet wall

D. None of these

Q.98 Which type of fall can be generally used for moderate discharge of 40-60 cumes and low fall heights of 1m to 1.5 m?

A. Vertical drop fall

B. Ogee fall

C. Glacis fall

D. Baffle fall

Q.99 The yield of a well depends upon

A. Permeability of soil

B. Area of aquifer opening into the wells

C. Actual flow velocity

D. All of the above

Q.100 In reciprocal levelling, the error which is not completely eliminated , is to

A. Eath's curvature

B. Non-adjustment of line of collimation

C. Refraction

D. Non adjustment of the bubble tube

Q.101 Darcy-Weisbach equation to calculate the head loss due to friction for flow through pipes is applicable when the flow through the pipe can be

A. laminar only

B. turbulent only

C. both laminar and turbulent

D. subcritical flow

Q.102 When the flow in an open channel is gradually varied, the flow is said to be

A. steady uniform flow

B. steady non-uniform flow

C. unsteady uniform flow

D. unsteady non-uniform flow

Q.103 The relationship between atmospheric pressure (P_{atm}), gauge pressure (P_{gauge}) and absolute pressure (P_{abs}) is given by:

A. $P_{atm} = P_{abs} + P_{gauge}$

B. $P_{abs} = P_{atm} + P_{gauge}$

C. $P_{abs} = P_{atm} + P_{gauge}$

D. $P_{atm} = P_{abs} + P_{gauge}$

Q.104 Flow of water through a passage under atmospheric pressure is called

A. Pipe flow

B. Uniform flow

C. Open channel flow

D. Non-uniform flow

Q.105 Typically, a hydroelectric plant will have following hydraulic machine :

A. Hydraulic Turbine   **B.** Hydraulic Pump
C. Electric Motor   **D.** None of the above

Q.106 The discharge capacity required at the outlet to irrigate 2600 ha of sugarcane having a kor depth of 17 cm and a kor period of 30 days is

A. 2.3 m³/s   **B.** 1.71 m³/s
C. 14.7 m³/s   **D.** 0.18 m³/s

Q.107 The approximate cost of the complete labour as a percentage of the total cost of the building is

A. 10%   **B.** 25%   **C.** 40%   **D.** 5%

Q.108 The ratio of the quantity of water stored in the root zone of the crops to the quantity of water actually delivered in the field is known as

A. water use efficiency
B. water conveyance efficiency
C. water application efficiency
D. water storage efficiency

Q.109 The total cost of construction including cost of land is termed as

A. Market value   **B.** Capital cost
C. Book value   **D.** Rateable value

Q.110 The ruling minimum radius of the curve for ruling design speed V m/sec, coefficient of friction f, acceleration due to gravity g m/sec² and superelevation e is given by

A. $V^2 / (e\text{-}f)g$ **B.** $V^2 / (f\text{-}e)g$
C. $V^2 / (e\text{+}f)g$ **D.** $V / (e\text{+}f)g$

Q.111 Which of the following is a non-recording raingauge

A. Symon's raingauge
B. Tipping bucket type raingauge
C. Weighing type raingauge
D. Floating type raingauge

Q.112 The centrifugal force on a car moving on a horizontal circular curve is proportional to:

A. $Wv^2/(gR)$ **B.** $Wv/(gR)$
C. $Wv^2/(gR^2)$ **D.** $Wv/(gR^2)$

Q.113 Los Angles test for aggregates is done to determine the

A. Abrasion resistance   **B.** Water absorption
C. Crushing strength   **D.** Impact strength

Q.114 The resistance of an aggregate to wear is known as

A. Impact value   **B.** Abrasion resistance
C. Shear resistance   **D.** Crushing resistance

Q.115 For constructing road pavements, the type of cement generally used is

A. ordinary Portland cement
B. rapid hardening cement
C. low heat cement
D. blast furnace slag cement

Q.116 The population of a town as per census records were 2,00,000;2,10,000 and 2,30,000 for the year 1981, 1991 and 2001 respectively. Find the population of the town in the year 2011 using arithmetic mean method.

A. 250000   **B.** 255000   **C.** 240000   **D.** 245000

Q.117 Hardness of water is caused by the presence of the following in water:

A. Chlorides and sulphate
B. Calcium and magnesium
C. Nitrites and nitrates
D. Sodium and potassium

Q.118 Which one of the following sequences is the most suitable for treating raw surface water to make it suitable for drinking purpose?

A. Screening -> filtration -> sedimentation -> disinfection
B. Screening -> disinfection -> sedimentation -> filtration
C. Screening -> sedimentation -> disinfection -> filtration
D. Screening -> sedimentation -> filtration -> disinfection

Q.119 The correct graphical representation of BOD(Y) and time (t) is given by

A.

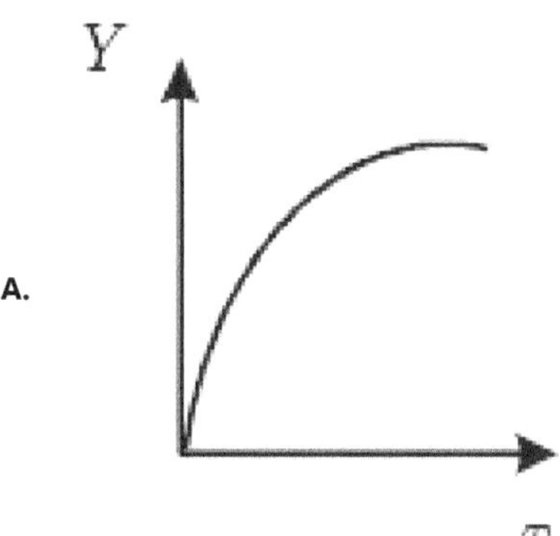

B.

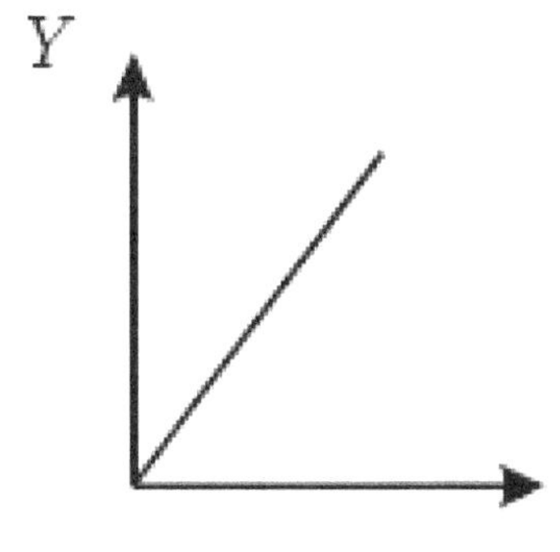

C.

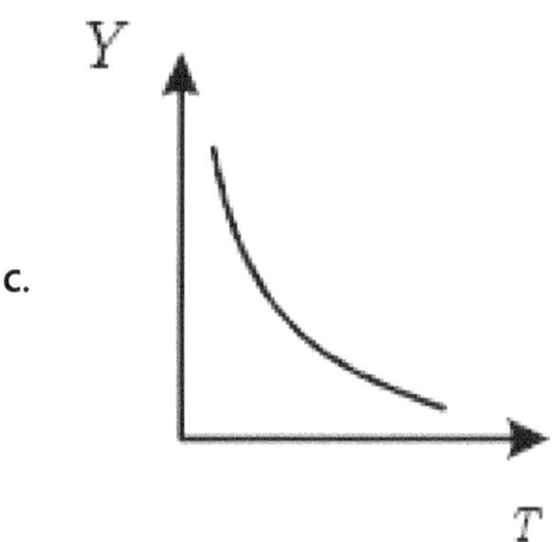

D. None of these

Q.120 The minimum dissolved oxygen which should always be present in water in order to save the aquatic life is

A. 1 ppm **B.** 4 ppm **C.** 10 ppm **D.** 40 ppm

Q.121 The global warming is caused mainly by

A. NO_x **B.** SO_x **C.** CO_2 **D.** O_2

Q.122 A material is called ductile if it

A. has little plastic elongation range

B. has long plastic elongation range

C. could be hammered into a very thin sheet

D. shows large elastic strain

Q.123 Strain energy per unit volume of a solid circular shaft under axial tension is

A. $\dfrac{\sigma^2}{8E}$ **B.** $\dfrac{\sigma^2}{16E}$ **C.** $\dfrac{\sigma^2}{2E}$ **D.** $\dfrac{\sigma^2}{4E}$

Q.124 The maximum shear force in a simply supported beam of span L, subjected to a central point load, W is given by the following expression :

A. W/2 **B.** WL **C.** `WL²/2 **D.** WL²/4

Q.125 For a cantilever beam of length L carrying a triangular load of intensity at the support and zero at the free end, the slope of the free end is given by

A. $\dfrac{WL^3}{24EI}$ **B.** $\dfrac{WL^3}{48EI}$ **C.** $\dfrac{WL^3}{8EI}$ **D.** $\dfrac{WL^3}{12EI}$

// Smart Answer Sheet //

Correct — Percentage of students who answered correctly.   **Skipped** — Percentage of students who skipped.

Q.	Ans.	Correct	Skipped
1	A	52.94 %	5.88 %
2	C	55.88 %	17.65 %
3	A	41.18 %	20.58 %
4	D	73.53 %	17.65 %
5	C	38.24 %	32.35 %
6	C	23.53 %	26.47 %
7	B	41.18 %	20.58 %
8	A	55.88 %	29.41 %
9	B	44.12 %	26.47 %
10	A	35.29 %	26.47 %
11	C	14.71 %	20.58 %
12	A	70.59 %	14.7 %
13	D	26.47 %	41.18 %
14	D	58.82 %	14.71 %
15	B	52.94 %	29.41 %
16	C	35.29 %	14.71 %
17	A	41.18 %	14.7 %
18	A	41.18 %	38.23 %
19	B	8.82 %	26.47 %
20	B	79.41 %	8.83 %
21	A	14.71 %	14.7 %
22	C	35.29 %	35.3 %
23	C	47.06 %	29.41 %
24	B	58.82 %	17.65 %
25	D	5.88 %	38.24 %
26	C	8.82 %	26.47 %
27	D	38.24 %	26.47 %
28	A	79.41 %	11.77 %
29	A	32.35 %	29.41 %
30	C	26.47 %	38.24 %
31	B	55.88 %	17.65 %
32	A	20.59 %	32.35 %
33	A	26.47 %	29.41 %
34	D	32.35 %	20.59 %
35	D	58.82 %	26.47 %
36	B	17.65 %	17.64 %
37	A	70.59 %	14.7 %
38	D	5.88 %	29.41 %
39	D	67.65 %	20.59 %
40	A	38.24 %	32.35 %
41	D	67.65 %	26.47 %
42	A	55.88 %	14.71 %
43	C	58.82 %	26.47 %
44	D	17.65 %	14.7 %
45	A	44.12 %	26.47 %
46	A	70.59 %	14.7 %
47	C	58.82 %	26.47 %
48	A	17.65 %	17.64 %
49	B	23.53 %	38.23 %
50	B	58.82 %	26.47 %
51	B	64.71 %	23.53 %
52	A	55.88 %	14.71 %
53	C	35.29 %	17.65 %
54	B	35.29 %	41.18 %
55	D	26.47 %	17.65 %
56	D	29.41 %	17.65 %
57	B	23.53 %	32.35 %
58	C	29.41 %	38.24 %
59	B	64.71 %	23.53 %
60	D	61.76 %	20.59 %
61	B	32.35 %	14.71 %
62	D	61.76 %	29.42 %
63	B	32.35 %	23.53 %
64	A	38.24 %	20.58 %
65	A	47.06 %	32.35 %
66	C	55.88 %	26.47 %
67	B	14.71 %	35.29 %
68	B	67.65 %	29.41 %
69	B	58.82 %	29.42 %
70	C	35.29 %	29.42 %
71	D	44.12 %	32.35 %
72	A	11.76 %	14.71 %
73	A	85.29 %	14.71 %
74	C	20.59 %	32.35 %
75	C	17.65 %	47.06 %
76	B	29.41 %	32.35 %
77	A	23.53 %	23.53 %
78	D	44.12 %	26.47 %
79	D	67.65 %	20.59 %
80	B	61.76 %	11.77 %

Q.	Ans.	Correct / Skipped		Q.	Ans.	Correct / Skipped		Q.	Ans.	Correct / Skipped		Q.	Ans.	Correct / Skipped		Q.	Ans.	Correct / Skipped
81	B	50.0 % / 14.71 %		90	B	32.35 % / 35.3 %		99	A	2.94 % / 23.53 %		108	C	64.71 % / 14.7 %		117	B	47.06 % / 26.47 %
82	C	58.82 % / 14.71 %		91	B	38.24 % / 26.47 %		100	C	52.94 % / 17.65 %		109	D	8.82 % / 32.36 %		118	D	55.88 % / 14.71 %
83	B	38.24 % / 29.41 %		92	A	50.0 % / 26.47 %		101	C	38.24 % / 14.7 %		110	C	73.53 % / 14.71 %		119	A	38.24 % / 23.52 %
84	D	29.41 % / 26.47 %		93	B	11.76 % / 35.3 %		102	B	47.06 % / 29.41 %		111	A	52.94 % / 20.59 %		120	B	73.53 % / 11.76 %
85	A	55.88 % / 20.59 %		94	D	11.76 % / 23.53 %		103	B	41.18 % / 26.47 %		112	A	67.65 % / 20.59 %		121	C	73.53 % / 14.71 %
86	B	58.82 % / 26.47 %		95	D	50.0 % / 26.47 %		104	C	52.94 % / 26.47 %		113	A	73.53 % / 26.47 %		122	B	35.29 % / 14.71 %
87	C	50.0 % / 20.59 %		96	B	58.82 % / 14.71 %		105	A	55.88 % / 20.59 %		114	B	79.41 % / 11.77 %		123	C	35.29 % / 35.3 %
88	D	35.29 % / 38.24 %		97	B	47.06 % / 20.59 %		106	B	23.53 % / 44.12 %		115	B	44.12 % / 29.41 %		124	A	50.0 % / 14.71 %
89	C	70.59 % / 26.47 %		98	C	8.82 % / 44.12 %		107	B	41.18 % / 29.41 %		116	D	50.0 % / 23.53 %		125	A	17.65 % / 32.35 %

//Hints and Solutions//

1. Hooke's law states that within elastic limit stress for most of the materials is proportional to the strain.

2. The property by which a metrial can be uniformly extended in a direction wihout reputure is malleability . A malleable material posses a high degree of plasticity.

3. If b and d is the width and depth of the rectangular beam, then the Moment of inertia of the rectangular section about vertical centroidal axis will be:

$$I_{Y-Y} = \frac{db^3}{12}$$

4. Euler's crippling stress is given by:

$$\sigma_{cr} = \frac{\pi^2 EI}{l^2{}_{eef}}$$

Where,

λ = slenderness ratio

E = Young's modulus of elasticity

Hence,

Crippling stress depends only upon the geometry and Young's Modulus of a column

Crippling stress varies parabolically with its slenderness ratio

Crippling stress does not depend upon yield strain

5. C_3S hydrates quickly and contributes more early strength . Rapid hardening cement contains more C_3S and less C_2S.

6. The effective length of fixed column, i.e., effectively held in position and restrained against rotation at both ends is 0.65 L/r.

7. Here r_e = 6

D_{se} = 6-3 = 3

The beam shown in figure is: indeterminate and stable

8. If the area of reinforcement provided is greater than the area of steel required for a balanced section, then the RCC beam is called as Over reinforcement section.

If the area of reinforcement provided is lesser than the area of steel required for a balanced section, then the RCC beam is called as Under reinforcement section.

9. For a given water content round and cubical shape aggregates are more workability than rough, , angular or flaky aggregates because the former type of aggregates requires less cement paste for lubrication as these less surface area and lesser voids.

10. Portland Blast Furnace Cement is a special blended cement with low heat of hydration characteristics for mass concreting. It is Used in ready mix concrete plants, used for structures meant for water retaining such as retaining wall, rivers, ports, tunnels for improvement in impermeability, used in mass concreting works such as dams, foundations which require low heat of hydration and in the places susceptible to chloride and sulphate attacks such as sub-structure, bored piles, pre-case piles and marine structures.

11. t_v — nominal shear stress, t_C — design shear strength of conrete and $t_{c,\max}$ -maximum design shear strength

If normal shear stress is less than design shear strength of concrete, then shear reinforcement is not required.

12. The maximum strain in the tension reinforcement in the section at failure shall not be less than:

$f_y/1.15E_s + 0.002$

Fy = characteristic strength of steel

Es = Modulus of elasticity of steel

1.15 = Factor of safety for steel strength

0.002 = Linear strain/Elastic strain

13. For Fe 415

$X_{4,lim}/d$ = 0.48

$X_{4,lim}$ = 0.48×550=264 mm

14. Acid rain is caused by a chemical reaction that begins when compounds like sulphur dioxide and nitrogen oxides are released into the air. These substances can rise very high into the atmosphere, where they mix and react with water, oxygen, and other chemicals to form more acidic pollutants, known as acid rain.

15. $D = \dfrac{864}{\Delta} = \dfrac{864 \times 14}{19} = 637\ hec/cum$

16. In this method, water is slowly and directly applied to the root zone of plants thereby minimizing the losses by evaporation and percolation.

17. It is usually a horizontal curve in plan provided to allow transition from a straight alignment to a circular curve gradually.

In General, it is a curve which connects a with infinite radius and radius R.

Transition curves are usually provided between a straight and curved track or roads.

Length of Transition curve is given by:

$L_s = V^3/CR$

18. $R_A + R_B$ = 20kN

$\sum M_A = 0$

$M_A = R_B \times 6 - 20 \times 2 = 0$

$6R_B = 40$

R_B =6.7kN and R_A = 13.3kN

19. Plants give oxygen during the day time, much more than what they require, activity being maximum at mid noon, due to sun's effects on photosynthesis.

20. The relation between Bulk modulus (K), Shear Modulus (G) and Young's Modulus (E) is given by:

E = 9KG/(3K+G)

21. Poisson's ratio is the ratio of lateral strain to longitudinal strain. The Poisson's ratio of a stable, isotropic, linear elastic material lies between −1.0 and +0.5.

For concrete, it is 0.2.

22. Elongation $= \dfrac{PL}{AE}$
$= \dfrac{100 \times 100 \times 1}{A \times 200 \times 10^9} m$
$A = \dfrac{\pi}{4} d^2 = \dfrac{\pi}{4} \times (10 \times 10^{-3})^2 m^2$
$= 7.85 \times 10^{-5} m^2$
Elongation $= \dfrac{10 \times 1000 \times 1}{7.85 \times 10^{-5} \times 200 \times 10^9}$
$= 6.369 \times 10^{-4} m$
$= 0.64 mm$

23.

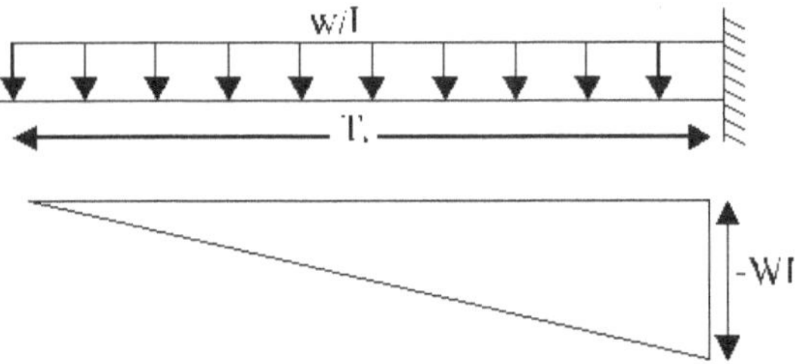

The maximum shear force in a cantilever beam with uniformly distributed load W per unit length, over the whole length L, is at the fixed end.

24. For the unstiffened web of the stiffener, the thickness of the web shall not be less than:

D₁/85

This implies no stiffener is required.

25. As per IS 456:2000, for Two way RC slab,

The width of the middle strip and end strip along each span should be 3/4 and 1/4 of the width of the span in that direction respectively.

26. A column is a compression member, the effective length of 2.5 times the least lateral dimension exceeds.

27. The minimum clear cover (in mm) for footing, according to IS 456 : 2000, shall be 50 mm.

28. In beams the maximum area of the reinforcement in tension reinforcement shall not exceed 0.04 bD.

29. The effective span, of cantilever slab at the end of a continuous slab is Clear span + effective depth of the slab.

30. $A_{sc} = 8 \times \dfrac{\pi}{4} \times 20^2 = 2513.23 mm^2$
$A_c = \dfrac{\pi}{4} \times 400^2 - 2513.27 = 123150.43 mm^2$
$P = \sigma_{sc} A_c + \sigma_{sc} A_{sc} = 4 \times A_c = 130 A_{sc}$
$P = 4 \times 123150.43 + 130 \times 2513.27$
$P = 819.33 kN$

31. The maximum permissible for rivets in shear will be:

τ = 100 MPa (Power driven shop rivets)

τ = 80 MPa (Hand driven rivets)

32. Strength of the rivet i single shear
$= \dfrac{\pi}{4} d^2 t_{vf}$
Gross diameter, $d = 20 + 1.5 = 21.5 mm$
Strength of rivet in single shear
$= \dfrac{\pi}{4} \times (21.5)^2 \times 100 \times 10^{-3} = 36.05 kN$

33. Grit is a beam.

34. The variation in declination due to magnetic storms is called Irregular.

35. METALLIC TAPE: A metallic tape is made of varnished strip of water proof linen interwoven with small brass, copper or bronze wires. Due to this tape does not stretch easily as a cloth tape. Metallic tapes are light in weight and flexible and are not easily broken.

36. Cross-staff survey: It is used to locate the boundaries of the given field and its area.

Instruments required in this survey are:

1. Cross-staff

2. Arrows

3. Ranging rods

4. Offsets rods

37. Large scale maps show great details .

Large scale maps means less reduction and a map covering a small area.

38. The length of the curve for its radius "R" and angle of deflection Δ is given by:

$$R \sin\dfrac{\Delta}{2}$$

39. The plane table surveying is one of the fastest and easiest methods of surveying. Plotting of plans and field observations can be done at the same time in plane table surveying.

Temporary adjustment of plane table surveying are:

1. Levelling

2. Centering

3. Orientation

40. Broadly spaced contours with equal spacing represent that area is Flat.

When contour lines are closer to each other, then the slope is called steep slope.

Contour lines generally do not meet or intersect each other.

If contour lines are meeting in some portion, it shows existence of a vertical cliff

41. When QSB, Sθ' W

Then WSB, θ = 180+30 = 210^0

42. Liquidity index is defined as the ratio of difference of natural water content and plastic limit of the soil to its plasticity index.

$I_L = (w_n - w_p)/I_p$

It represents the behaviour of the insitu fine grained saturated soil.

43. Coarse soil is generally have large particle size as compared to fine soil. These type of soil is highly permeable. These type of soils have very less cohesiveness.

44. Tri-calcium aluminate (C_3A) is mostly related to the heat of hydration. It releases large amount of heat during the first few days of hardening which generally results in early age cracking.

Cements with high content of C_3A are not suitable for mass concreting and are better to be mixed with fly ash.

C_3A has very less resistance to sulphate attack because alumina reacts with sulphate to form Alumino sulphate.

45. In turbulent boundary layer velocity distribution follows (1/7)th power law i.e., longithmic law.

46. Aggregates in the pavements are also subjected to impact due to moving wheel loads. The resistance to this impact is known as Toughness.

The relative measure of resistance to crushing under gradually applied compressive load is known as crushing resistance.

47. If fineness modulus of a sand is 2.7, it is gared as medium sand.

48. The stripping value of aggregates is determined as the ratio of the uncovered area observed visually to the total area of aggregates, expressed as a percentage.

IRC has specified maximum stripping value of aggregates should not exceed 2%.

49. Surge is an example of unsteayd rapidly varied flow. It occurs wherver there is a sudden change in the discharge or depth or both.

50. Void ratio is defined as the ratio of the volume of voids to the volume of solids present in a soil mass.

Porosity is defined as the ratio of volume of voids to the volume of soil.

51. Aneroid Barometer is a device used to measure the atmospheric pressure.

It is Invented in 1844 by French scientist Lucien Vidi, the aneroid barometer uses a small, flexible metal box called an aneroid cell (capsule), which is made from an alloy of beryllium and copper.

52. Viscosity is the resistance to the flow of fluid particles relative to one other.

Due to strong cohesive forces between the molecules, any layer in a moving fluid tries to drag the adjacent layer to move with an equal speed and thus produces the effect of viscosity.

It is also due to intermolecular attraction between the particles that keep them held together and the resistance of their movement relative to each other causes viscosity.

53. Euler's equation represents momentum equation in a 2-D, inviscid steady flow.

54. Vorticity is the curl of velocity field and a measure of local rotation of fluid i.e tendency of a fluid particle to rotate or circulate at a particular point.

Its dimension is per unit time (T^{-1})

55. When a body is immersed in a fluid it experience a upthrust which is equal to weight of the volume of water displaced. The line of action of this buoyant force on the object is called the center of buoyancy.

When a body floats the centre of buoyancy of body and centre of gravity lie on the same vertical line, called the central line. But if the body is tilted slightly the center of buoyancy shifts. The vertical line passing through the new center of buoyancy intersects the central line at a point called the meta centre.

56. The head loss in turbulent flow in a pipe varies. inversely as the square of the velocity. directly as the velocity. approximately as the square of the velocity.

57. A hydraulic jump occurs in channel if the flow is controlled by a slucie gate.

58.
$$\gamma_{sat} = \frac{G_1 e}{1+e} \gamma_W$$
$$\gamma_W = 9.81 kN/m^3$$
$$\Gamma_{sat} = \frac{2.67+0.67}{1+0.67} \times 9.81$$
$$= 19.62 kN/m^3$$

59. In long and short wall method, the wall along the length of room is considered to be long wall while the wall perpendicular to long wall is said to be short wall.

To get the length of long wall or short wall, First calculate the centre line lengths of individual walls. Then the length of long wall, (outer to outer) may be calculated after adding half width at each end to its centre line length.

60. Crapet area = (10.3−0.3)×(17.3−0.3) = 170 m²

61. Scrap Value: It is also called as Junk Value or Breakup Value of Demolition Value. It will represent the value of old materials in a building less cost of demolition.

Book Value: It shows the original investment of a Company on its assets, including properties and machinery less depreciation for the period passed.

Salvage Value: Value of Machinery realised on sales when its useful span of life is over but still it has not become useless.

62. While estimate for plastering, no deduction is made for:

(i) End of beams, posts, rafters etc.

(ii) For small opening up to 0.5 square meter

63. Plinth area Estimate: Plinth area is the covered built-up area measured at the floor level of any storey. Plinth area is generally

10-20% more than carpet area. The estimate prepared on the plinth area basis of the building by using suitable plinth area rates is called the plinth area estimate.

It is basically a rough cost estimate.

Detailed estimate is based on the plans and sections of the building so it is the most accurate estimate.

64. Book value: The book value of a property at a particular year is the original cost minus the amount of depreciation allowed per year and will be gradually reduced year to year and at the end of the utility period of the property, the book value will be only scrap value.

Book value is the amount shown in the account book after allowing necessary depreciations.

Salvage value: Salvage value is the estimated resale value of an asset at the end of its useful life.

65. The outer projection of a tread is known as nosing. An edge part of the tread protudes over the riser beneath.

66. The part of the wall on which the arch rests, is called abutment.

The clear horizontal distance between two supports of an arch, is called span.

The irrer curved surface of the arch is called extrados.

67. Negative skin f riction develops when a soft or loose soil surrounding the pile settles after the pile has been installed.

68. C A$^{3/4}$

Where C = Dicken's coefficient

A = Area of the basin in sq. km.

69. Index of wentnes, gives idea of the wethness of the year, and hence it indicates the deficiency after the pile has been installed.

A 60% index of wetness means rain deficiency of 40%.

70. The diameter of the rivets when hot is equal to the diameter of the hole and is called gross diameter.

Gross diameter = nominal diameter

+1.5mm,φ25mm

71. Generally rolled ISHB sections with additional intermediate support in the weak direciton are used as column sections.

72. If two angles are placed back to back and connected to both sides of the gusset plate, then

A_{net} = A_1+kA_2

A_1 =Area of connected leg

A_2 =Area of unconnected leg

$$K = \frac{3A_1}{3A_1 + A_2}$$

73. According to IS 456–2000, minimum slenderness ratio for a short column is less than 12.

74. Long term losses:
(i) Creep and shrinkage of concrete
(ii) Loss due to relaxation of strands
Immediate losses:
(i) Elastic shortening of concrete
(ii) Slip at anchorages

75. $X_{u,lim} = 0.48d = 0.48 \times 300 = 144 mm$
$M_{u,lim} = 0.36 f_{ck} X_{u,lim} b \left(d - 0.42 X_{u,lim} \right)$
$= 0.36 \times 20 \times 144 \times 200 (300 - 0.42 \times 144) \times 10_{-6}$
$= 49.67 kNm$

76. For two hinge arch, Degree of static indeterminacy is given by:

Ds=R-r

R = number of unknowns = 4

R = No of equilibrium equations available = 3

Ds = 4-3 = 1

77. Force method of analysis is also known as flexibility method of analysis, method of consistent deformation, flexibility matrix method.

In this method, member forces are taken as unknowns.

While Displacement method is known as stiffness method. In this method displacements are taken as unknowns.

78. In this question these is none materil has a Posisson's ration more then 1.

79. The shape of the bending moment diagram for a uniformly distributed load is parabolic.

80. A meterial has identical properties in all direction is said to be Isotropic.

81. The operation of levelling across any river is termed as reciprocal leveling.

82. A loop of a conrour plot indicates a prticular level, when plots of loop values goes on decreading inside it indicates   a fall in level , which is generally categorized as a depression.

83. Tropical year = 365.2422 days

Sidereal year = 365.2564 days

The reaitionship between tropical ground is TY < SY.

84. Sodium silicate is not a retarding admicture .

85. The correct statement is :-

Angular of flaky particles reduce the workability and demand more cement and water to give the spcefied strength of concrete mix.

86. Bulking Increases with finesses of aggregates and is neglible case of corase aggregates, It has great importance in case of fine aggregates or sand.

87. The degree of workability is medium when the value of slump in mm is 50 – 100 mm.

88. As the area of longitudinal and transverse reinforcement increases and hence the torsion resistance capacity of the section increases. To resist torsion section reinforcement must consist of closely spaced stirrups and longitudinal bars.

89. Curing is the process of preventing the loss of moisture from the concrete while maintaining a satisfactory temperature regime.

As per IS 456:2000, the concrete should be cured at 27 degrees Celsius

90. The divide wall is the long wall constructed at right angle to the weir or barrage. The functions of the divide wall are as follows:

1. To form a still water pocket in front of the canal head so that the suspended silt can be settled down which then later can be cleared through the scouring sluices from time to time.

2. It controls the eddy current or cross current in front of the canal head.

A fish ladder is a structure that allows migrating fish passage over or around an obstacle on a river.

91. An Aqueduct is an hydraulic structure which carries a canal across and above the drainage.

While super passage is completely reverse of aqueduct.

A syphon aqueduct is constructed where the water surface level of the drain at high flood is higher than the canal bed.

92. Garret's diagram is the graphical method of designing the channel dimensions based on Kennedy's theory.The theory says that, the silt carried by flowing water in a channel is kept in suspension by the eddy current rising to the surface.

93. The diagonal compression failure is a failure due to the crushing of concrete at the web in the diagonal direction prior to the yielding of stirrups. Normally it occurs in beams which are reinforced against heavy shear.

The maximum permissible shear stress as given in IS 456:1978 is based on diagonal compression failure.

94. As hoop stress in the cylindrical pressure vessels are twice as that of hoop stress in spherical pressure vessels, that's' why more thickness of section is required to resist the same load, therefore we preferred spherical section for pressure vessels.

95. Acidic water is water with a potential hydrogen (pH) of less than 7. Acidic water could contain metal ions such as iron, manganese, copper, lead, and zinc, mineral acids, Free CO_2, Iron sulphate and aluminium sulphate.

96. Minimum camber for type of road surface are:

1. Thin Bituminous surface = 2.5%

2. Cement concrete = 2.0 %

3. Water bound macadam = 3.0%

97. Breast wall: A wall built to sustain the face of a natural bank of earth is known as Breast wall.

While Retaining wall is used to sustain the earth behind.

Breast walls are constructed on hill side and retaining walls are constructed on valley side of road.

98. Glacis fall: It is a type of modern fall which is provided after a raised crest. It is suitable for a discharge upto 60 cumecs and 1.5 m drop.

99. For a well in an Unconfined and confined aquifer, the yield of a well depends upon:

1. Permeability of soil.

2. Drowdown in a well

3. Radius of influence of a well

100. In reciprocal levelling, the error which is not completely eliminated , is to refraction.

101. Darcy-Weisbach equation to calculate the head loss due to friction for flow through pipes is applicable when the flow through the pipe can be laminar and turbulent.

102. When the flow in an open channel is gradually varied, the flow is said to be steady non-uniform flow.

103. The relationship between atmospheric pressure (Patm), gauge pressure (Pgauge) and absolute pressure (Pabs) is given by

$P_{abs} = P_{atm} + P_{gauge}$

104. Flow of water through a passage under atmospheric pressure is called open channel flow.

105. Typically, a hydroelectric plant will have hydraulic machine.

106.
$$\Delta = 8.64 \frac{B}{D}$$
$$D = \frac{8.64B}{\Delta} = \frac{8.64 \times 30}{0.17}$$
$= 1524.7$ hectare/cumec
Discharge capacity required
$$= \frac{2600}{1524.7} = 1.71 m^3/s$$

107. The approximate cost of the complete labour as a percentage of the total cost of the building is 25%.

108. The ratio of the quantity of water stored in the root zone of the crops to the quantity of water actually delivered in the field is known as water application efficiency.

109. The total cost of construction including cost of land is termed as rateable value.

110. The ruling minimum radius of the curve for ruling design speed V m/sec, coefficient of friction f, acceleration due to gravity g m/sec^2 and superelevation e is given by V^2 / (e+f)g .

111. Symon's raingauge is a non-recording raingauge.

112. The centrifugal force on a car moving on a horizontal circular curve is proportional to Wv^2/(gR) .

113. Los Angles test for aggregates is done to determine the Abrasion resistance.

114. The resistance of an aggregate to wear is known as abrasion resistance.

115. For constructing road pavements, the type of cement generally used is rapid hardening cement.

116.

Year	Population	Increment
1981	200000	—
1991	210000	10000
2001	230000	20000

$$\text{Average increment} = \frac{10000 + 20000}{2} = 15000$$

Population in $2011 = 230000 + 15000 = 245000$

117. Hardness of water is caused by the presence of calcium and magnesium in water.

118. Screening -> sedimentation -> filtration -> disinfection

this sequences is the most suitable for treating raw surface water to make it suitable for drinking purpose.

119. The correct graphical representation of BOD(Y) and time (t) is given by

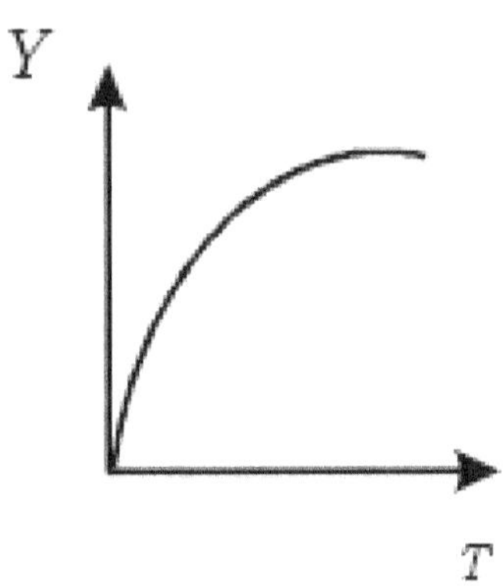

120. The minimum dissolved oxygen which should always be present in water in order to save the aquatic life is 4 ppm.

121. The global warming is caused mainly by CO_2.

122. A material is called ductile if it has long plastic elongation range.

123. $S.E = \dfrac{1}{2} \dfrac{\sigma^2}{E} \times Volume$

124. The maximum shear force in a simply supported beam of span L, subjected to a central point load, W is given by the W/2.

125. For a cantilever beam of length L carrying a triangular load of intensity at the support and zero at the free end, the slope of the free end is given by $\dfrac{WL^3}{24EI}$

Mock Test 06

Q.1 Dynamic viscosity has the dimensions as

A. MLT^{-2} **B.** $ML^{-1}T^{-1}$

C. $ML^{-1}T^{-2}$ **D.** $M^{-1}L^{-1}T^{-1}$

Q.2 The capillary rise or fall of a liquid is given by

A. $h = \dfrac{\sigma cos\theta}{4\rho gd}$ **B.** $h = \dfrac{4\sigma cos\theta}{\rho gd}$

C. $h = \dfrac{8\sigma cos\theta}{\rho gd}$ **D.** None of the above

Q.3 For a floating body, if the meta centre coincides with the centre of gravity, the equilibrium is called

A. stable **B.** unstable

C. neutral **D.** None of the above

Q.4 The velocity components in x and y directions in terms of stream function ψ are

A. $u = \dfrac{\partial\psi}{\partial x}$, $v = \dfrac{\partial\psi}{\partial y}$

B. $u = -\dfrac{\partial\psi}{\partial x}$, $v = \dfrac{\partial\psi}{\partial y}$

C. $u = \dfrac{\partial\psi}{\partial y}$, $v = \dfrac{\partial\psi}{\partial x}$

D. $u = -\dfrac{\partial\psi}{\partial y}$, $v = \dfrac{\partial\psi}{\partial x}$

Q.5 If the velocity, pressure, density etc, change at a point with respect to time, the flow is called

A. uniform **B.** compressible

C. unsteady **D.** incompressible

Q.6 The co-efficient of discharge (C_d)

A. for an orifice is more than that for a mouthpiece

B. for internal mouthpiece is more than that external mouthpiece

C. for a mouthpiece is more than that for an orifice

D. None of these

Q.7 The discharge through a trapezoidal notch is given as where $\theta/2$ = Slope of the side of the trapezoidal notch.

A. $Q = 2/3C_{d1} \times L \times H^{3/2} + 8/15C_{\alpha 2} \times \tan \theta/2 \times \sqrt{2g}H^{3/2}$

B. $Q = 2/3C_{d1} \times L \times H^{5/2} + 8/15C_{d2} \times \tan \theta/2 \times \sqrt{2g}H^{3/2}$

C. $Q = 2/3C_{dl} \times L \times H^{3/2} + 8/15C_{\alpha 2} \times \tan \theta/2 \times \sqrt{2g}H^{5/2}$

D. none of the above

Q.8 The error in discharge due to the error in the measurement of head over a rectangular notch is given by.

A. $\dfrac{dQ}{Q} = \dfrac{5}{2}\dfrac{dH}{H}$ **B.** $\dfrac{dQ}{Q} = \dfrac{3}{2}\dfrac{dH}{H}$

C. $\dfrac{dQ}{Q} = \dfrac{7}{2}\dfrac{dH}{H}$ **D.** $\dfrac{dQ}{Q} = \dfrac{1}{2}\dfrac{dH}{H}$

Q.9 Power transmitted through pipes will be maximum when

A. Head lost due to friction = 1/2 total head at inlet of the pipe

B. Head lost due to friction = 1/4 total head at inlet of the pipe

C. Head lost due to friction = total head at the inlet of the pipe

D. Head lost due to friction = 1/3 total head at the inlet of the pipe.

Q.10 The valve closure is said to be gradual if the time required to close the valve.

A. $t = \dfrac{2L}{C}$ **B.** $t \le \dfrac{2L}{C}$ **C.** $t < \dfrac{4L}{C}$ **D.** $t > \dfrac{2L}{C}$

Q.11 The C.G. of solid hemisphere lies on the central radius at a distance.

A. 3r/4 from the plane base

B. 3r/8 from the plane base

C. 8r/3 from the plane base

D. None of the above

Q.12 The C.G. of a semi-circular lamina lies on the central radius at a distance of

A. from base diameter $4r/3\pi$

B. 3r/8 from base diameter

C. 8r/3 from base diameter

D. None of the above

Q.13 The angle between the two principal planes is

A. 45^0 **B.** 90^0 **C.** 30^0 **D.** 60^0

Q.14 A simply supported beam is subjected to a uniformly varying load with zero intensity at the two ends increasing to w/m at the centre. The maximum B.M. will be equal to

A. wl²/12 **B.** wl²/24 **C.** wl²/6 **D.** wl²/8

Q.15 A cantilever is subjected to a concentrated load W at the mid-point of the span. The slope at the free end will be

A. WL²/6EI **B.** WL²/2EI

C. WL²/3EI **D.** WL²/8EI

Q.16 When a member is subjected to a twisting moment, the material will be subjected to

A. axial tension

B. shear stresses

C. bending stresses

D. axial compressive stress

Q.17 The maximum shear stress produced in a shaft is 5 N/mm². The shaft is of 40 mm diameter. The value of twisting moment is

A. 628 Nm **B.** 62.8 Nm

C. 125.6 Nm **D.** 1256 Nm

Q.18 The volumetric strain in a thin spherical shell will be.

A. $\dfrac{3\sigma d}{4tE}\left(1 - \dfrac{1}{m}\right)$ **B.** $\dfrac{4\sigma d}{3tE}\left(1 - \dfrac{1}{m}\right)$

C. $\dfrac{3\sigma d}{4tE}\left(1 + \dfrac{1}{m}\right)$ **D.** $\dfrac{3\sigma d}{4tE}\left(1 - \dfrac{2}{m}\right)$

Q.19 The Euler crippling load for a column with one end fixed and the other hinged is

A. $\frac{\pi^2 EI}{L^2}$ **B.** $\frac{4\pi^2 EI}{L^2}$ **C.** $\frac{\pi^2 EI}{4L^2}$ **D.** $\frac{2\pi^2 EI}{L^2}$

Q.20 The strain energy stored in a member due to shear stress is

A. $\frac{\tau^2}{2N} \times$ volume   **B.** $\frac{\tau^2}{2E} \times$ volume

C. $\frac{\tau^2 \times \text{area}}{2E}$ **D.** $\frac{\tau^2}{2N}$

Q.21 An isohyet is a line joining points of

A. equal rainfall intensity
B. equal rainfall depth
C. equal evaporation
D. equal humidity

Q.22 Intensity of rainfall means

A. total rainfall during a storm
B. rainfall per unit area
C. the rate at which the rainfall depth is accumulating
D. volume of rain water per unit area

Q.23 The snow fall is generally measured in terms of

A. weight of snow per unit area
B. equivalent depth of water
C. depth of snow fallen
D. any of the above

Q.24 The evaporation through plants and from the surrounding soil together is called

A. hydration   **B.** vapourisation
C. transpiration   **D.** evapotranspiration

Q.25 The unit of measurement is per quintal for

A. Collapsible gates with rails
B. Rolling shutters
C. Expanded metal wire netting
D. Reinforcement of R.C.C. works

Q.26 Floor Area Ratio (F.A.R.) means

A. $Total\ floor\ area\ of\ all\ floors\ -\ \frac{Area\ of\ ground\ floor}{Area\ of\ plot}$

B. $Total\ floor\ area\ of\ all\ floors\ -\ \frac{Area\ of\ ground\ floor}{Area\ of\ plinth}$

C. $\frac{Total\ floor\ area\ of\ all\ floors}{Area\ of\ plot}$

D. $\frac{Total\ floor\ area\ of\ all\ floors}{Area\ of\ plinth}$

Q.27 The damp proof course is measured in

A. length   **B.** area   **C.** volume   **D.** weight

Q.28 The most reliable estimate is

A. Plinth area estimate
B. Detailed estimate
C. Preliminary estimate
D. Cube rate estimate

Q.29 The cross-section of a strip footing is shown below

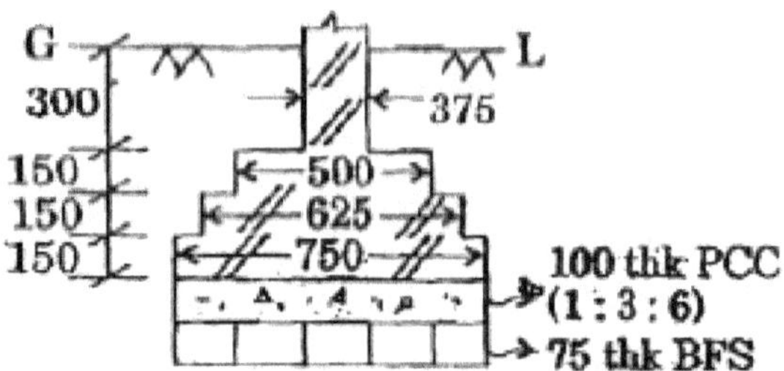

All dimensions are in mm.

The quantity of BFS under the footing per metre length is

A. 0.750 cu.m   **B.** 0.750 sq.m
C. 0.056 cu.m   **D.** 0.056 sq.m

Q.30 The measurement is NOT made in square metres in case of

A. Damp proof course   **B.** Form works
C. Concrete Jaffries   **D.** R.C. Chhajja

Q.31 For one sq.m. single brick flat soling (conventional size), the number of brick required is

A. 54   **B.** 62   **C.** 32   **D.** 44

Q.32 Coloured waters may affect the following water treatment unit

A. plain sedimenation
B. sedimentation aided by coagulation
C. filtration
D. chlorination

Q.33 The standard unit of turbidity is produced when

A. 1 mg of silicon dioxide is dissolved in 1 litre of distilled water
B. 1 mg of platinum is dissolved in 1 litre of distilled water
C. 1 mg of sodium chloride dissolved in llitre of distilled water
D. 1 mg of cobalt being dissolved in 1 litre of distilled water

Q.34 A water sample is termed turbid when it

A. fails to transmit light through it
B. is rich in suspended solids
C. is rich in both suspended and colloidal solids
D. is rich in total solids

Q.35 A minimum amount of..........mg/l of alkalinity is desirable in any water.

A. 10   **B.** 20   **C.** 50   **D.** 100

Q.36 A waste water sample of 5 ml is made upto 300 ml with distilled water. The sample had an initial D.O. of 8.0 mg/l and after 5 days the D.O. is O. BOD of the sample

A. 8 mg/l   **B.** 472 mg/l
C. 480 mg/l   **D.** test is invalid

Q.37 Presence of the following indicates recent pollution

A. ammonical nitrogen
B. albuminoidal nitrogen
C. nitrites
D. nitrates

Q.38 "Dental Caries" will be absent where the following is present

A. mottled enamel of teeth

B. itai-itai

C. methamoglobinemia

D. cancer

Q.39 Due to improper storing of water the following disease spreads.

A. tuberculosis

B. filarial

C. methemoglobinemia

D. fluorosis

Q.40 A deep well

A. easily gets dried up during summer

B. may yield constant discharge

C. is not deeper than a shallow well

D. is formed by just tapping the nearest aquifer to the ground

Q.41 If Q = quantity of water to be treated per day, V = volume of sedimentation basin then detention period in hours is

A. 24V/Q **B.** 24Q/V **C.** Q/24V **D.** V/24Q

Q.42 Loess is

A. over consolidated clay

B. fine sand

C. wind borne soil

D. marine soil

Q.43 In the unit phase diagram for a soil mass

A. total volume is taken as unit

B. volume of water is taken as unity

C. volume of soil solids is taken as unity

D. none of the above

Q.44 The principle involved in the relation $\gamma_{sub} = \gamma_{sat} - \gamma_w$ is.

A. Stoke's law

B. Archimedes principle

C. Darcy's law

D. All the above

Q.45 The composite correction to be applied for in a hydrometer reading is

A. $C = C_t - C_m \pm C_d$

B. $C = C_t \pm C_m - C_d$

C. $C = C_m - C_d \pm C_t$

D. None of these

Q.46 Stoke's law is applicable when the effective diameter of the particles is less than

A. 0.0002 mm **B.** 0.002 mm

C. 0.02 mm **D.** 0.2 mm

Q.47 A soil has a bulk density of 2.4g/cm³ and water content of 20%. What is its dry density?

A. 2 g/cm³ **B.** 1.2 g/cm³

C. 1.4 g/cm³ **D.** 1.6 g/cm³

Q.48 The groove which is cut for the determination of liquid limit has to flow a distance of

A. 10 mm **B.** 11 mm **C.** 12 mm **D.** 13 mm

Q.49 Two soils A and B are tested in the lab. For the consistency limits. The results are

	A	B
Liquid limit	40%	60%
Plastic limit	20%	25%

Which soil is more plastic?

A. A **B.** B

C. Both **D.** None of these

Q.50 The slope of the flow curve obtained in liquid limit test is called

A. liquidity index **B.** plasticity index

C. toughness index **D.** flow index

Q.51 The relationship between the time factor T_v coefficient of consolidation C_v the length of drainage path d, and time t is given by

A. $T_v = \frac{C_v \cdot d^2}{t}$ **B.** $T_v = \frac{C_v \cdot t^2}{d}$

C. $T_v = \frac{C_v \cdot t}{d^2}$ **D.** $T_v = \frac{C_v \cdot t^2}{d^2}$

Q.52 Grade compensation on curves is a maximum of

A. 56/R **B.** 76/R **C.** 100/R **D.** 156/R

Q.53 Super elevation + lateral friction should not be greater than

A. $V^2/127R$ **B.** $V^2/225R$

C. $V^2/7.4R$ **D.** $V^2/14.28R$

Q.54 In plains the minimum length of transition curve is

A. V^2/R **B.** $V^2/1.5R$ **C.** $2.7V^2/R$ **D.** $V^2/24R$

Q.55 for sight distance calculation Time of perception and reaction depends on

A. speed of the vehicle **B.** gradient of road

C. alertness of driver **D.** nature of pavement

Q.56 PUC equivalent for a bus is

A. 1.00 **B.** 1.75 **C.** 2.25 **D.** 6.00

Q.57 Yellow colour of a Coloured light traffic signal indicates

A. go **B.** stop

C. be ready to go **D.** clearance time

Q.58 Standard Gauge is

A. 1676 mm **B.** 1524 mm

C. 1435 mm **D.** 1000 mm

Q.59 The standard length of rail for BG is

A. 10 m **B.** 13 m **C.** 15 m **D.** 20 m

Q.60 The max. value of super elevation provided on Indian Railways is

A. 165 mm **B.** 140 mm **C.** 90 mm **D.** 65 mm

Q.61 Mountainous railways are those which have a grade steeper than

A. 1%   **B.** 3%   **C.** 6%   **D.** 8%

Q.62 Quartzite is a

A. sandy rock
B. silicious rock
C. organic rock
D. calcareous rock

Q.63 The quick lime as it comes from kilns is called

A. milk lime
B. hydraulic lime
C. lump lime
D. hydrated lime

Q.64 The initial setting time of ordinary Portland cement should not be less than

A. 15 minutes
B. 30 minutes
C. 45 minutes
D. One hour

Q.65 Snowcem is

A. mixture of lime and pigment
B. chalk powder
C. coloured cement
D. none of the above

Q.66 Compaction factor for good workability of concrete is

A. 0.   **B.** 0.80   **C.** 4.8   **D.** 0.95

Q.67 Slump test facilitates

A. Controlling of water cement ratio of concrete during construction
B. the determination of initial and final setting times of cement
C. the determination of workability of concrete
D. None of the above

Q.68 Creosote oil is used to preserve the wood from

A. rot and white ant
B. fire hazards
C. cracking
D. none of the above

Q.69 Timber can be made reasonably fire resistant

A. by soaking it in ammonium sulphate
B. by applying tar paint
C. by pumping creosote oil into timber under high pressure
D. none of the above

Q.70 Plywood is identified by

A. volume
B. weight
C. thickness
D. area

Q.71 The ingredient which gives the desired colour to a paint is called

A. base   **B.** pigment   **C.** vehicle   **D.** solvent

Q.72 The ingredient which accounts for the least in cement is

A. silica
B. iron oxide
C. lime
D. aluminium

Q.73 The separation of water on the fresh concrete is known as

A. segregation
B. hydration
C. bleeding
D. None of the above

Q.74 A pin jointed plane frame with j number of joints and n number of members will be internally redundant, if

A. n > (2j-3)
B. n < (2j-3)
C. n = (2j-3)
D. n > (2j+3)

Q.75 In a pin jointed frame it is sufficient if the forces in all the members meeting at a joint are

A. co-planer
B. co-planer and concurrent
C. equal in magnitude
D. none of the above

Q.76 The maximum strain in the tension reinforcement ant failure shall not be less than

A. $\frac{f_y}{1.15E_s} - 0.002$
B. $\frac{f_y}{1.15E_s} + 0.002$
C. $\frac{1.15E_s}{f_y} - 0.002$
D. $\frac{1.15E_s}{f_y} + 0.002$

Q.77 The depths to N.A. in a singly reinforced section is given by

A. $\frac{x_u}{d} = \frac{700}{1100+0.87f_y}$
B. $\frac{x_u}{d} = \frac{1100+0.87f_y}{700}$
C. $\frac{x_4}{d} = \frac{700}{1100-0.87f_y}$
D. $\frac{x_4}{d} = \frac{1100-0.87f_y}{700}$

Q.78 The maximum diameter of the reinforcement bars in RCC slabs is

A. 20 mm
B. 16 mm
C. span/100
D. thickness of slab/8

Q.79 The maximum diameter of the reinforcement bars in RCC beams is limited to

A. 28 mm
B. 40 mm
C. one-eighth of the least dimension of the beams
D. one-tenth of the depth of beams

Q.80 The effective width of flange in RCC T-beams should be restricted to

A. $\frac{l_0}{6} + b_w + 6D_f$
B. $\frac{l_0}{12} + b_w + 3D_f$
C. $l_0/3$
D. centre to centre distance of the beams

Q.81 The minimum distance over which a bar should be extended (curtailment) beyond which it is no longer needed for bending in RCC beams is

A. Effective depth of beam or 12 times the diameter of the bar whichever is greater
B. 48 times the diameter of the bar
C. 1.5 times the depth or 24 times the diameter of the bar whichever is greater
D. $\frac{\phi\sigma_s}{4\tau_{bd}}$

Q.82 The minimum amount of bottom reinforcemenmnt that should be continued over the entire length of the beam in RCC continuous beam is

A. 50%   **B.** 40%   **C.** $33\frac{1}{3}\%$ **D.** 25%

Q.83 The deflection including the effects of temperature, creep and shrinkage occurring after erection of partitions and the application of finishes should not normally exceed

A. span/250 or 20mm whichever is less

B. span/250

C. span/350 or 20mm whichever is less

D. span/350

Q.84 For cantilever beams and slabs, the basic value of span to effective depth ratio is

A. 7   **B.** 10   **C.** 20   **D.** 26

Q.85 A compression member is considered as short when both the slenderness ratio l_{ex}/D and l_{ey}/b are less than

A. 12   **B.** 1   **C.** 8   **D.** 16

Q.86 The size of the fillet weld is given by

A. smaller side of the triangle

B. throat of the fillet

C. smaller size of the plate welded

D. hypotenuse of the triangle supporting staff

Q.87 The minimum size of the fillet weld that can be used is

A. 1 mm   **B.** 2 mm   **C.** 3 mm   **D.** 5 mm

Q.88 Transverse spacing of the side fillet welds should not be less than

A. 16 times the thickness of the thinner part connected

B. 12 times the thickness of the thinner part connected

C. 20 times the thickness of the thinner part connected

D. 4 times the size of the weld or 40 mm whichever is greater

Q.89 The maximum permissible slenderness ratio of steel ties is

A. 180   **B.** 250   **C.** 350   **D.** no limit

Q.90 The maximum permissible slenderness ratio of steel ties likely to be subjected to possible reversal of stress due to wind or seismic forces is

A. 180   **B.** 250   **C.** 350   **D.** no limit

Q.91 The maximum slenderness ratio of steel members acting as wind bracings should be

A. 180   **B.** 250   **C.** 350   **D.** 400

Q.92 The maximum deflection allowed in steel columns should be {where L is the actual length of the column}

A. L/250   **B.** L/300   **C.** L/400   **D.** L/350

Q.93 A 30m chain after measuring a distance of 6000m was found to be 10 cm more than the designated length. If the chain was standardized before the commencement of survey then the true length is

A. 6020 m   **B.** 6010 m   **C.** 5990 m   **D.** 5980 m

Q.94 The magnetic bearing of a line is N 88⁰E . its true bearing is S 89⁰E . therefore its magnetic declination is

A. 2⁰W   **B.** 3⁰W   **C.** 3⁰E   **D.** 91⁰

Q.95 Isogonics lines are the lines having the same

A. elevation   **B.** bearing

C. declination   **D.** dip

Q.96 The very first reading taken is called

A. back sight   **B.** fore sight

C. intermediate sight   **D.** invert

Q.97 A change point is

A. the very first station

B. the last station

C. the intermediate station where F.S. and B.S. are taken

D. the station after which the instrument is shifted

Q.98 The following readings were taken on a uniformly sloping ground

0.500, 1.000, 1.500, 2.000, 1.2000, 1.700, 2.200, 2.700.

Hence difference in elevation between the first and last station is

A. 1.700 (fall)   **B.** 2.200 (fall)

C. 2.800   **D.** 3.000 (fall)

Q.99 Reciprocal levelling eliminates

A. collimation error

B. collimation, curvature and refraction error

C. curvature and refraction error

D. collimation and curvature error fully and refraction error partly

Q.100 Contour lines

A. end abruptly

B. cross each other

C. are uniformly spaced

D. close somewhere

Q.101 The property which makes the material suitable to be shaped easily by hammering, bending, rolling etc. without cracks or fracture is termed as

A. ductility   **B.** malleability

C. dilatability   **D.** none of these

Q.102 The impact test assess the property of material such as its

A. hardness   **B.** strength

C. toughness   **D.** brittleness

Q.103 The relationship between the Bulk modulus of elasticity 'K' and Young's Modulus of Elasticity 'E' is given in terms of Poisson's ratio (μ) as

A. $K = 3E(1 - 2\mu)$ **B.** $E = 2K(1 + \mu)$

C. $E = 3K(1 - 2\mu)$ **D.** $K = 2E(1 - 2\mu)$

Q.104 A simply supported beam of length L, carrying a load W concentrated at the centre of span will have a maximum bending moment of

A. WL/2   **B.** WL/4   **C.** WL/8   **D.** WL/16

Q.105 In a simply supported beam of length l carrying a uniformly increasing load from zero at right support (B) to W at left support (A). The shear force at B is equal to

A. Wl/6   **B.** Wl/3   **C.** Wl   **D.** $2\frac{Wl}{3}$

Q.106 In Newmark's influence chart for stress distribution there one 10 concentric circles and ten radial lines. The influence factor of the chart is

A. 0.1   **B.** 0.01   **C.** 0.001   **D.** 0.0001

Q.107 The shape of precast concrete pile is generally

A. Square

B. Round

C. Square or octangonal

D. Square or circular

Q.108 Consider the following statements related to triaxial test:

1.Failure occurs along predetermined plane

2.Intermediate and minor principal stresses are equal

3.Field conditions can be simulated

4.Field conditions can not be simulated

of these statements

A. 1, 2 and 3 are correct

B. 1, 2 and 4 are correct

C. 1, 3 and 4 are correct

D. 2, 3 and 4 are correct

Q.109 A soil sample has been found to have natural moisture content of 30%, liquid limit 60% and plastic limit of 28 %. It can therefore be said to possess

A. Very soft consistency

B. Soft consistency

C. Stiff consistency

D. Medium consistency

Q.110 Which one of the following correctly defines the 'Activity' of clays?

A. Plasticity index / Percentage of clay

B. Plastic limit / Liquidity index

C. Unconfined compression strength / Cohesion

D. Unconfined compression strength of remoulded sample / Unconfined compression strength of undisturbed sample

Q.111 What is the area of influence line diagram for the reaction at the hinged end of a uniform propped cantilever beam of span L?

A. L/8   **B.** L/2   **C.** L/4   **D.** 3L/8

Q.112 The maximum bending stress induced in a steel wire of modulus of elasticity 200 kN/mm^2 and diameter 1 m is approximately equal to

A. 50 N/mm^2 **B.** 100 N/mm^2

C. 200 N/mm^2 **D.** 400 N/mm^2

Q.113 For a RCC column effectively held in position and restrained against rotation at one end and at the other restrained against rotations but not held in position, the effective length is

A. 1.20   **B.** 0.80   **C.** 1.00   **D.** 1.50

Q.114 The pitch of bars of distribution steel in solid slab should not exceed ....times the effective depth of slab

A. 3 d   **B.** 2 d   **C.** 5 d   **D.** 6 d

Q.115 The behaviour of concrete under instantaneous loads is

A. elastic   **B.** plastic

C. anelastic   **D.** visco-elastic

Q.116 The lower water cement ratio in concrete introduces

A. improved frost resistance

B. greater wear resistance

C. smaller creep and shrinkage

D. all of the above

Q.117 In R.C.C., steel is used because it can provide good

A. tensile strength

B. compressive strength

C. bond strength

D. shear strength

Q.118 The width of an RCC beam is limited to

A. span/10   **B.** span/60

C. span/96+0.2m   **D.** span/112+0.1m

Q.119 The range of effective depth of a T-beam for heavy loads and light loads is taken as

A. span/10   **B.** span/15 to span/20

C. span/20 to span/25   **D.** span/20 to span/30

Q.120 Slope of line joining the surface of road and corner is

A. Cross fall

B. Cross slope

C. Camber

D. Any one of the above

Q.121 Average water depth (delta) required for sugarcane is

A. 145 cm   **B.** 160 cm   **C.** 175 cm   **D.** 190 cm

Q.122 Gradient of road in hilly area is kept as

A. Less than 10% to 20% in comparison to ruling gradient

B. less than 20% to 25% in comparison to ruling gradient

C. More than 10% to 20% in comparison to ruling gradient

D. less than 20% to 25% in comparison to ruling gradient

Q.123 Which of the following in most suitable for rotary

A. place of maximum traffic low

B. place of pedestrian

C. place of crowd

D. If at a place more roads are intersecting

Q.124 Maximum range of super elevation for broad gauge is

A. 7.62 cm   **B.** 8.32 cm

C. 10.16 cm   **D.** 16.76 cm

Q.125 Permissible compressive strength of M200 concrete grade is-

A. 100 kg/cm^2 **B.** 150 kg/cm^2

C. 200 kg/cm^2 **D.** 250 kg/cm^2

// Smart Answer Sheet //

Correct — Percentage of students who answered correctly. **Skipped** — Percentage of students who skipped.

Q.	Ans.	Correct / Skipped	Q.	Ans.	Correct / Skipped	Q.	Ans.	Correct / Skipped	Q.	Ans.	Correct / Skipped	Q.	Ans.	Correct / Skipped
1	B	28.57 % / 10.72 %	17	B	35.71 % / 35.72 %	33	D	14.29 % / 25.0 %	49	B	46.43 % / 39.28 %	65	C	50.0 % / 32.14 %
2	B	78.57 % / 14.29 %	18	A	17.86 % / 35.71 %	34	A	32.14 % / 21.43 %	50	D	32.14 % / 35.72 %	66	D	60.71 % / 32.15 %
3	C	64.29 % / 21.42 %	19	D	53.57 % / 28.57 %	35	B	32.14 % / 35.72 %	51	C	42.86 % / 25.0 %	67	A	7.14 % / 21.43 %
4	D	25.0 % / 32.14 %	20	A	14.29 % / 14.28 %	36	D	7.14 % / 42.86 %	52	B	57.14 % / 17.86 %	68	A	46.43 % / 35.71 %
5	C	28.57 % / 35.72 %	21	B	32.14 % / 21.43 %	37	A	21.43 % / 25.0 %	53	A	57.14 % / 17.86 %	69	A	50.0 % / 28.57 %
6	C	17.86 % / 42.85 %	22	C	35.71 % / 14.29 %	38	A	46.43 % / 35.71 %	54	C	39.29 % / 35.71 %	70	C	42.86 % / 32.14 %
7	C	53.57 % / 25.0 %	23	B	14.29 % / 32.14 %	39	B	28.57 % / 35.72 %	55	C	21.43 % / 25.0 %	71	B	64.29 % / 28.57 %
8	B	39.29 % / 35.71 %	24	D	53.57 % / 14.29 %	40	B	39.29 % / 35.71 %	56	C	32.14 % / 35.72 %	72	B	82.14 % / 14.29 %
9	D	42.86 % / 32.14 %	25	D	60.71 % / 28.58 %	41	A	17.86 % / 42.85 %	57	D	25.0 % / 28.57 %	73	C	71.43 % / 17.86 %
10	D	17.86 % / 39.28 %	26	C	50.0 % / 35.71 %	42	C	60.71 % / 17.86 %	58	C	21.43 % / 32.14 %	74	A	25.0 % / 35.71 %
11	B	39.29 % / 28.57 %	27	B	75.0 % / 25.0 %	43	B	25.0 % / 35.71 %	59	B	71.43 % / 28.57 %	75	B	46.43 % / 28.57 %
12	A	57.14 % / 25.0 %	28	B	57.14 % / 14.29 %	44	B	42.86 % / 21.43 %	60	A	32.14 % / 21.43 %	76	B	53.57 % / 32.14 %
13	B	35.71 % / 25.0 %	29	C	28.57 % / 39.29 %	45	C	32.14 % / 42.86 %	61	B	42.86 % / 21.43 %	77	A	53.57 % / 32.14 %
14	A	21.43 % / 32.14 %	30	D	57.14 % / 17.86 %	46	A	42.86 % / 17.85 %	62	B	57.14 % / 32.15 %	78	D	64.29 % / 32.14 %
15	D	14.29 % / 32.14 %	31	A	50.0 % / 21.43 %	47	A	57.14 % / 32.15 %	63	C	35.71 % / 25.0 %	79	C	60.71 % / 25.0 %
16	B	39.29 % / 17.85 %	32	D	28.57 % / 32.14 %	48	C	50.0 % / 17.86 %	64	B	82.14 % / 17.86 %	80	A	71.43 % / 17.86 %

Q.	Ans.	Correct		Q.	Ans.	Correct		Q.	Ans.	Correct		Q.	Ans.	Correct		Q.	Ans.	Correct
		Skipped				Skipped				Skipped				Skipped				Skipped
81	A	17.86 %		90	C	21.43 %		99	D	21.43 %		108	D	17.86 %		117	A	42.86 %
		42.85 %				50.0 %				25.0 %				39.28 %				28.57 %
82	D	32.14 %		91	C	14.29 %		100	D	35.71 %		109	C	14.29 %		118	B	32.14 %
		25.0 %				28.57 %				17.86 %				53.57 %				14.29 %
83	C	39.29 %		92	D	25.0 %		101	C	14.29 %		110	A	39.29 %		119	B	50.0 %
		25.0 %				35.71 %				25.0 %				21.42 %				32.14 %
84	A	57.14 %		93	A	28.57 %		102	B	14.29 %		111	C	3.57 %		120	B	28.57 %
		32.15 %				46.43 %				32.14 %				39.29 %				17.86 %
85	A	67.86 %		94	C	32.14 %		103	C	57.14 %		112	C	53.57 %		121	D	42.86 %
		28.57 %				28.57 %				28.57 %				28.57 %				21.43 %
86	A	17.86 %		95	C	32.14 %		104	B	42.86 %		113	A	32.14 %		122	B	21.43 %
		32.14 %				28.57 %				42.85 %				39.29 %				21.43 %
87	C	46.43 %		96	A	75.0 %		105	A	42.86 %		114	C	46.43 %		123	A	14.29 %
		32.14 %				17.86 %				28.57 %				21.43 %				42.85 %
88	A	17.86 %		97	C	50.0 %		106	C	21.43 %		115	A	25.0 %		124	D	28.57 %
		42.85 %				21.43 %				46.43 %				28.57 %				21.43 %
89	D	7.14 %		98	D	7.14 %		107	D	32.14 %		116	D	67.86 %		125	C	67.86 %
		28.57 %				46.43 %				28.57 %				17.85 %				32.14 %

//Hints and Solutions//

1. Dynamic viscosity has the dimensions as $ML^{-1}T^{-1}$

2. The capillary rise or fall of a liquid is given by $h = \dfrac{4\sigma\cos\theta}{\rho g d}$

3. For a floating body, if the meta centre coincides with the centre of gravity, the equilibrium is called neutral.

4. The velocity components in x and y directions in terms of stream function ψ are

$$u = -\frac{\partial\psi}{\partial y} \ , \ v = \frac{\partial\psi}{\partial x}$$

5. If the velocity, pressure, density etc, change at a point with respect to time, the flow is called unsteady.

6. The co-efficient of discharge (Cd) for a mouthpiece is more than that for an orifice.

7. The discharge through a trapezoidal notch is
$$Q = 2/3C_{d1} \times L \times H^{3/2} + 8/15C_{d2} \times \tan\theta/2 \times \sqrt{2g}H^{5/2}$$

8. The error in discharge due to the error in the measurement of head over a rectangular notch is $\dfrac{dQ}{Q} = \dfrac{3}{2}\dfrac{dH}{H}$

9. Power transmitted through pipes will be maximum when

Head lost due to friction = 1/3 total head at the inlet of the pipe.

10. The valve closure is said to be gradual if the time required to close the valve.

$$t > \frac{2L}{C}$$

11. The C.G. of solid hemisphere lies on the central radius at a distance 3r/8 from the plane base.

12. The C.G. of a semi-circular lamina lies on the central radius at a distance of base diameter $4r/3\pi$

13. The angle between the two principal planes is 90⁰.

14.

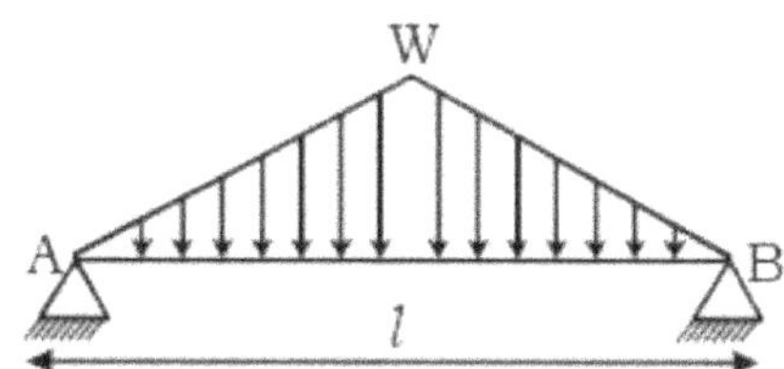

Total load on the beam
$$= \frac{1}{2} \times l \times w = \frac{wl}{2}$$
Due to symmetrical
$$R_a = R_b = \frac{wl}{4}$$
Maximum B.M will be at the distance of $1/2$
$$\text{Maximum B.M.} = \frac{wl}{4} \times \frac{l}{2} - \frac{w}{3l} \times \frac{l^3}{8} = \frac{wl^2}{12}$$

15. A cantilever is subjected to a concentrated load W at the mid-point of the span. The slope at the free end will be.

$$\text{Slope} = \frac{w\left(\frac{l}{2}\right)^2}{2EI} = \frac{wl^2}{8EI}$$

16. When a member is subjected to a twisting moment, the material will be subjected to shear stresses.

17. $\tau = 5N/mm^2 \quad D = 40mm$
$$\frac{T}{J} = \frac{\tau}{r} = \frac{C\theta}{L}$$
$$T = \frac{\tau J}{r}$$
$$= \frac{\frac{\pi}{32}(40)^4 \times 5}{20} = 62831.85Nmm$$
$$= 62.83Nm$$

18. The volumetric strain in a thin spherical shell will be.

$$\frac{3\sigma d}{4tE}\left(1 - \frac{1}{m}\right)$$

19. The Euler crippling load for a column with one end fixed and the other hinged is $\dfrac{2\pi^2 EI}{L^2}$

20. The strain energy stored in a member due to shear stress is.

$$\frac{\tau^2}{2N} \times \text{volume}$$

21. An isohyet is a line joining points of equal rainfall depth.

22. Intensity of rainfall means the rate at which the rainfall depth is accumulating.

23. The snow fall is generally measured in terms of equivalent depth of water.

24. The evaporation through plants and from the surrounding soil together is called evapotranspiration.

25. Particulars of item Units
(a) Damp proof course m^2
(b) Reinforcement of Qnintal
R.C.C. works
(c) Concrite : RCC, m^3
PCC, precast
(d) Rolling shutter m^2

26. Floor Area Ratio (F.A.R.)
means $\dfrac{Total\ floor\ area\ of\ all\ floors}{Area\ of\ plot}$

27. The damp proof course is measured in area.

28. The most reliable estimate is Detailed estimate.

29. The anantity of BFC (Brick flat soling) under the footing per meter length
$$= 1m \times 0.75m \times 0.075m$$
$$= 0.05625cum$$

30. Damp proof course $-m^2$
Form works $-m^2$

Concrete leffries, jail work $-m^2$

R.C.C. ehajja $\qquad -m^3$

31. No. of bricks required in single BFS = 32

No. of brick required in 1m' of brick on edge soling = 54

32. Coloured waters may affect the chlorination water treatment unit

33. The standard unit of turbidity is produced when 1 mg of cobalt being dissolved in 1 litre of distilled water.

34. A water sample is termed turbid when it fails to transmit light through.

35. A minimum amount of 20 mg/l of alkalinity is desirable in any water.

36. A waste water sample of 5 ml is made upto 300 ml with distilled water. The sample had an initial D.O. of 8.0 mg/l and after 5 days the D.O. is O. BOD of the sample

Test is invalid

37. Presence of the ammonical nitrogen indicates recent pollution.

38. "Dental Caries" will be absent where mottled enamel of teeth is present.

39. Due to improper storing of water the filaria Idisease spreads.

40. A deep well may yield constant discharge.

41. If Q = quantity of water to be treated per day, V = volume of sedimentation basin then detention period in hours is 24V/Q.

42. Loess is wind borne soil.

43. In the unit phase diagram for a soil mass, volume of water is taken as unity.

44. The principle involved in the relation $\gamma_{sub} = \gamma_{sat} - \gamma_w$ is Archimedes principle.

45. The composite correction to be applied for in a hydrometer reading is $C = C_m - C_d \pm C_t$

46. Stoke's law is applicable when the effective diameter of the particles is less than 0.0002 mm.

47. A soil has a bulk density of 2.4g/cm3 and water content of 20%. its dry density is 2 g/cm³.

48. The groove which is cut for the determination of liquid limit has to flow a distance of 12 mm.

49. More plastic index results more plasticity

$$\text{Soil } A \quad PI = 40 - 20 = 20$$
$$\text{Soil } B \quad PI = 60 - 25 = 35$$

Means soil B is more plastic

50. The slope of the flow curve obtained in liquid limit test is called flow index.

51. The relationship between the time factor Tv coefficient of consolidation Cv the length of drainage path d, and time t is given by $T_v = \dfrac{C_v.t}{d^2}$

52. Grade compensation on curves is a maximum of 76/R.

53. Super elevation + lateral friction should not be greater than V²/127R

54. In plains the minimum length of transition curve is 2.7V²/R.

55. For sight distance calculation Time of perception and reaction depends on alertness of driver.

56. PUC equivalent for a bus is 2.25.

57. Yellow colour of a Coloured light traffic signal indicates clearance time.

58. Standard Gauge is 1435 mm.

59. The standard length of rail for BG is 13 m.

60. The max. value of super elevation provided on Indian Railways is 165 mm.

61. Mountainous railways are those which have a grade steeper than 3%.

62. Quartzite is a silicious rock.

63. The quick lime as it comes from kilns is called lump lime.

64. The initial setting time of ordinary Portland cement should not be less than 30 minutes.

65. Snowcem is coloured cement.

66. Compaction factor for good workability of concrete is 0.95.

67. Slump test facilitates controlling of water cement ratio of concrete during construction.

68. Creosote oil is used to preserve the wood from rot and white ant.

69. Timber can be made reasonably fire resistant by soaking it in ammonium sulphate.

70. Plywood is identified by thickness.

71. The ingredient which gives the desired colour to a paint is called pigment.

72. The ingredient which accounts for the least in cement is iron oxide.

73. The separation of water on the fresh concrete is known as bleeding.

74. A pin jointed plane frame with j number of joints and n number of members will be internally redundant, if n > (2j-3).

75. In a pin jointed frame it is sufficient if the forces in all the members meeting at a joint are co-planer and concurrent.

76. The maximum strain in the tension reinforcement ant failure shall not be less than

$$\frac{f_y}{1.15E_s} + 0.002$$

77. The depths to N.A. in a singly reinforced section is given by.

$$\frac{x_u}{d} = \frac{700}{1100 + 0.87 f_y}$$

78. The maximum diameter of the reinforcement bars in RCC slabs is thickness of slab/8.

79. The maximum diameter of the reinforcement bars in RCC beams is limited to one-eighth of the least dimension of the beams.

80. The effective width of flange in RCC T-beams should be restricted to

$$\frac{l_0}{6} + b_w + 6D_f$$

81. The minimum distance over which a bar should be extended (curtailment) beyond which it is no longer needed for bending in RCC beams is effective depth of beam or 12 times the diameter of the bar whichever is greater.

82. The minimum amount of bottom reinformenemnt that should be continued over the entire length of the beam in RCC continuous beam is 25%.

83. The deflection including the effects of temperature, creep and shrinkage occurring after erection of partitions and the application of finishes should not normally exceed span/350 or 20mm whichever is less.

84. For cantilever beams and slabs, the basic value of span to effective depth ratio is

$$\frac{\text{span}}{\text{Effective depth}} \text{ for}$$

(i) cantilever $= 7$

(ii) simply supported $= 20$

(iii) continous $= 26$

85. A compression member is considered as short when both the slenderness ratio l_{ex}/D and l_{ey}/b are less than 12.

86. The size of the fillet weld is given by smaller side of the triangle.

87. The minimum size of the fillet weld that can be used is 3 mm.

88. Transverse spacing of the side fillet welds should not be less than 16 times the thickness of the thinner part connected.

89. The maximum permissible slenderness ratio of steel ties is no limit.

90. 350 is the right answer because table 3 of is 800 2007 states that "A member normally acting as a tie or bracing not considered effective when subjected to a possible reversal of stress into compression from the action of wind or earthquake forces".

91. The maximum slenderness ratio of steel members acting as wind bracings should be 350.

92. The maximum deflection allowed in steel columns should be {where L is the actual length of the column} L/350.

93. $True\ length = \dfrac{30.1 \times 6000}{30} = 6020m$

94. Magnetic Bearing $= N88°E = 88°$

True Bearing $= S89°E = 180° - 89° = 91°$

True Bearing = magnetic Bearing $\pm$ declination

Declination $= 91° - 88° = 3°E$

(East because value is positive)

95. Isogonics lines are the lines having the same declination.

96. The very first reading taken is called back sight.

97. A change point is the intermediate station where F.S. and B.S. are taken.

98.

B.S.	I.S.	F.S.	Rise	Fall
0.50				
	1.00			0.5
	1.50			0.5
1.20		2.00		0.5
	1.70			0.5
	2.20			0.5
		2.70		0.5

Σ fall = 3.0

99. Reciprocal levelling eliminates collimation and curvature error fully and refraction error partly.

100. Contour lines close somewhere.

101. The property which makes the material suitable to be shaped easily by hammering, bending, rolling etc. without cracks or fracture is termed as dilatability.

102. The impact test assess the property of material such as its strength.

103. The relationship between the Bulk modulus of elasticity 'K' and Young's Modulus of Elasticity 'E' is given in terms of Poisson's ratio (μ) as $E = 3K(1 - 2\mu)$

104. A simply supported beam of length L, carrying a load W concentrated at the centre of span will have a maximum bending moment of WL/4.

105. In a simply supported beam of length l carrying a uniformly increasing load from zero at right support (B) to W at left support (A). The shear force at B is equal to Wl/6.

106. In Newmark's influence chart for stress distribution there one 10 concentric circles and ten radial lines. The influence factor of the chart is 0.001.

107. The shape of precast concrete pile is generally square or circular.

108. The Correct statement is:-

Intermediate and minor principal stresses are equal

Field conditions can be simulated

Field conditions can not be simulated

109. A soil sample has been found to have natural moisture content of 30%, liquid limit 60% and plastic limit of 28 %. It can therefore be said to possess stiff consistency.

110. Plasticity index / Percentage of clay correctly defines the 'Activity' of clays.

111. L/4 is the area of influence line diagram for the reaction at the hinged end of a uniform propped cantilever beam of span L.

112. The maximum bending stress induced in a steel wire of modulus of elasticity 200 kN/mm2 and diameter 1 m is approximately equal to 200 N/mm^2.

113. For a RCC column effectively held in position and restrained against rotation at one end and at the other restrained against rotations but not held in position, the effective length is 1.20.

114. The pitch of bars of distribution steel in solid slab should not exceed 5d times the effective depth of slab.

115. The behaviour of concrete under instantaneous loads is elastic.

116. The lower water cement ratio in concrete introduces improved frost resistance, greater wear resistance and smaller creep and shrinkage.

117. In R.C.C., steel is used because it can provide good tensile strength.

118. The width of an RCC beam is limited to span/60.

119. The range of effective depth of a T-beam for heavy loads and light loads is taken as span/15 to span/20.

120. Slope of line joining the surface of road and corner is cross slope.

121. Average water depth (delta) required for sugarcane is 190 cm.

122. Gradient of road in hilly area is kept as less than 20% to 25% in comparison to ruling gradient.

123. Place of maximum traffic low most suitable for rotary.

124. Maximum range of super elevation for broad gauge is 16.76 cm.

125. Permissible compressive strength of M200 concrete grade is 200 kg/cm^2.

Q.1 If the end stations of a line are free from local attraction, then the difference between fore bearing and back bearing of that line should be

A. 120^0 **B.** 180^0 **C.** 360^0 **D.** 90^0

Q.2 The angle between the two plane mirrors of an optical square should be

A. 30^0 **B.** 45^0 **C.** 60^0 **D.** 90^0

Q.3 The whole circle bearing of line AB and AC are 18^0-15' and 335^0-45' respectively. What is the value of the included angle CAB?

A. 307^0 - 30'   **B.** 354^0 - 0'
C. 177^0 - 0'   **D.** 45^0 - 30'

Q.4 The two point problem or three point problem is method of

A. Orientation   **B.** Resection
C. Traversing   **D.** (A) and B)

Q.5 Working edge of an Alidate is known as

A. Ebonite edge   **B.** Fiducial edge
C. Straight edge   **D.** Graduated edge

Q.6 A correction for error due to refraction is {where d is horizontal distance in km.}

A. $0.01\ d^2$ m   **B.** $0.001\ d^2$ m
C. $0.01122\ d^2$ m   **D.** $0.078\ d^2$ m

Q.7 Length of long chord in a simple circular curve having central angle θ is?
{where R is radius of the curve}

A. $R \sin \frac{\theta}{2}$ **B.** $2R \sin \frac{\theta}{2}$
C. $R \cos \frac{\theta}{2}$ **D.** $2r \cos \frac{\theta}{2}$

Q.8 Planimeter is used for measuring

A. Volume   **B.** Area
C. Slope angle   **D.** Contour gradient

Q.9 The first reading from a level station is

A. Fore sight   **B.** Intermediate sight
C. Back sight   **D.** Straight sight

Q.10 Correction for pull or tension in a tape is given by

A. $C_P = \frac{(P-P_0)L}{AE}$ **B.** $C_P = \frac{(P-P_0)}{LAE}$
C. $C_P = \frac{(P-P_0)AE}{L}$ **D.** $C_P = \frac{L}{AE(P-P_0)}$

Q.11 Minimum pitch of rivets should not be less than

A. 3 d   **B.** 1.5 d1   **C.** 2.0 d   **D.** 2.5 d

Q.12 The effective throat thickness of a fillet weld is

A. equal to the size of the weld.
B. a function of the angle between the fusion sides.
C. length of the hypotenuse of the triangle formed.

D. 0.7 times the size of weld.

Q.13 For a steel member in tension, the permissible stress in axial tension is given by

A. 0.5 f_y **B.** 0.6 f_y **C.** 0.66 f_y **D.** 0.75 f_y

Q.14 For a steel column, the permissible stress in axial compression depends mainly on

A. effective length   **B.** sectional area
C. radius of gyration   **D.** slenderness ratio

Q.15 For simply supported steel beam, the maximum deflection should be

A. 1/300 of the span   **B.** 1/325 of the span
C. 1/350 of the span   **D.** 1/400 of the span

Q.16 The member of a roof truss which supports the purlins is known as

A. Principal rafter   **B.** Principal tie
C. Main strut   **D.** Sag tie

Q.17 Most economical section for a steel column is

A. Square section   **B.** Circular section
C. Tubular section   **D.** Hexagonal section

Q.18 The structural member in which the tensile force is acting parallel to its longitudinal axis is called

A. Tension member   **B.** Tie
C. (A) and (B) both   **D.** None of these

Q.19 The load on a lintel is assumed as uniformly distributed, if the height of the masonry above it is upto a height of

A. the effective span
B. 1.25 times the effective span
C. 1.50 times the effective span
D. 2.0 times the effective span

Q.20 The difference between gross diameter and nominal diameter for the rivets upto 25 mm diameter is

A. 1.0 mm   **B.** 1.5 mm   **C.** 2.0 mm   **D.** 2.5 mm

Q.21 The ratio of volume of voids (V_v)in the soil to its total volume (v) is defined as

A. Porosity   **B.** Void ratio
C. Degree of saturation   **D.** Mass density

Q.22 Density of the soil may be increased by

A. Compaction   **B.** Consolidation
C. (A) and (B) both   **D.** Stabilization

Q.23 Uniformity coefficient is the ratio of the following :

A. D_{10} and D_{20} **B.** D_{30} and D_{60}
C. D_{40} and D_{50} **D.** None of these

Q.24 The relation between void ratio (e) and degree of saturation (s) of soil is given by

A. $e = \dfrac{S}{WG}$ **B.** $e = \dfrac{WG}{S}$

C. $e = \dfrac{WS}{G}$ **D.** $e = \dfrac{G}{WS}$

Q.25 When C is cohesion, σ is the applied normal stress ϕ is angle of internal friction, the shear strength of the soil τ will be equal to.

A. $\tau = c - \sigma\tan\phi$ **B.** $\tau = c + \sigma\tan\phi$

C. $\tau = \sigma + c\tan\phi$ **D.** $\tau = \sigma - c\tan\phi$

Q.26 A soil sample has a porosity of 40%. If $G = 2.70$, the dry density of soil
will be

$(\gamma_w = 9.81 kN/m^3)$

A. 15.89 kN/m³   **B.** 31.78 kN/m³

C. 17.85 kN/m³   **D.** 19.81 kN/m³

Q.27 Load carrying capacity of the foundation on sand, mainly depends upon

A. length of the foundation

B. depth of foundation

C. breadth of foundation

D. size of foundation

Q.28 The dry unit weight of a soil sample is 1.9 gm/cc and the specific gravity is 2.65, what will be the porosity of the soil ?

A. 29.91%   **B.** 28.30%

C. 2.83%   **D.** None of these

Q.29 The liquid limit and plastic limit of a soil are 35% and 15% respectively. If the flow index is 10%, then toughness index is

A. 1.0   **B.** 1.5   **C.** 2.0   **D.** 2.5

Q.30 The liquid limit and plastic limit of a cohesive soil are determined in laboratory as 40% and 20% respectively. The plasticity index of the soil will be

A. 10%   **B.** 20%   **C.** 30%   **D.** 40%

Q.31 The maximum area of tension reinforcement in beams should not exceed

A. 0.15%   **B.** 1.5%   **C.** 4%   **D.** 1%

Q.32 If E_c and E_s are modulus of elasticity of concrete and steel respectively, then the modular ratio (m) will be

A. E_c / E_s **B.** E_s / E_c **C.** $\dfrac{E_c + E_s}{E_s - E_c}$ **D.** $\dfrac{4E_c}{E_c}$

Q.33 In case of a reinforced concrete beam, as the percentage of tension steel increases

A. depth of neutral axis decreases

B. depth of neutral axis increases

C. there is no effect on neutral axis

D. None of the above

Q.34 In a singly reinforced beam, if the stress in concrete reaches its permissible limit earlier than that in steel, the beam section is called

A. under-reinforced section

B. over-reinforced section

C. economic section

D. critical section

Q.35 Which of the following square slab will behave as one-way slab ?

A. Simply supported along two opposite edges

B. Simply supported along three edges

C. Simply supported along all the four edges

D. None of the above

Q.36 The shear reinforcement in a reinforced concrete beam is provided to resists

A. bending moment

B. compression force

C. diagonal compression

D. diagonal tension

Q.37 Equivalent area of a reinforced cement concrete column section is

A. m A_c + A_{sc} **B.** A_c + m A_{sc}

C. A_c + A_{sc} **D.** (A_c + m A_{sc}) σ_c

Q.38 The diameter of longitudinal bars in a column should not be less than

A. 8 mm   **B.** 10 mm   **C.** 12 mm   **D.** 16 mm

Q.39 The minimum number of longitudinal bars provided in RCC circular column is

A. 2   **B.** 4   **C.** 6   **D.** 8

Q.40 According to IS:456 – 2000, side face reinforcement is provided in RCC beams, when depth of beam exceeds

A. 450 mm   **B.** 750 mm

C. 1000 mm   **D.** 1250 mm

Q.41 The most reliable estimate is

A. Detailed estimate

B. Preliminary estimate

C. Plinth-area estimate

D. Cube rate estimate

Q.42 In a construction project, the time corresponding to minimum total project cost is

A. normal time

B. crash time

C. between normal and crash time

D. None of these

Q.43 Number of bricks needed for 1 cu.m. brick work will be

A. 1350   **B.** 650   **C.** 500   **D.** 550

Q.44 The water absorption capacity of first class bricks should not be more than _______ of its weight.

A. 30%   **B.** 25%   **C.** 20%   **D.** 50%

Q.45 Lime concrete is prepared by using aggregate and ________ as binding material.

A. slaked lime

B. quick lime

C. mixture of quick lime and cement

D. lime stone powder

Q.46 The age of a tree may be ascertained by the

A. radius of its stem
B. number of branches
C. circumference of its stem
D. number of annual rings

Q.47 Which of the following is not the constituent of a paint
A. Iron oxide
B. Sodium chloride
C. Turpentine oil
D. Linseed oil

Q.48 Soundness of cement is tested by
A. Vicat's apparatus
B. Le-Chatelier's apparatus
C. Compression testing machine
D. None of these

Q.49 The type of bond in which every course contains both header and stretcher is called
A. English bond
B. Flemish bond
C. Mixed bond
D. Russian bond

Q.50 The base material for distemper is
A. Lime putty
B. Lime
C. Cement wash
D. Chalk

Q.51 Per capita consumption of water per day for domestic purpose should be
A. 85 litres
B. 100 litres
C. 115 litres
D. 135 litres

Q.52 Fire demand of water according to Kuichling's formula, in litres/minute, is given by
{where P is population in thousands}
A. Q = 3182 P
B. Q = 3182 / P
C. $Q = 3182 \sqrt{P}$
D. $Q = \frac{3182}{\sqrt{P}}$

Q.53 Maximum permissible amount of fluoride for domestic consumption of water should be
A. 0.15 ppm
B. 1.5 ppm
C. 15 ppm
D. 150 ppm

Q.54 The velocity of flow of sewage in a combined sewer should not be less than
A. 0.3 m/s
B. 0.75 m/s
C. 1.0 m/s
D. 6.0 m/s

Q.55 The time interval of cleaning of septic tank should not be more than
A. 5 years
B. 1 years
C. 6 months
D. 2 years

Q.56 Alum is a
A. Coagulant
B. Flocculent
C. Catalyst
D. Disinfectant

Q.57 Turbidity in water is due to
A. Organic salts
B. Suspended and colloidal particles
C. Algae
D. Fungi

Q.58 The trap used for an Indian water closet is called

A. Gully trap
B. P-trap
C. Intercepting trap
D. Anti-syphon trap

Q.59 Sewage treatment units are generally designed for
A. maximum flow only
B. minimum flow only
C. average flow only
D. Both (A) and (B)

Q.60 Bleaching powder is
A. $Ca(OH)_2$
B. ClO_2
C. $CaCl_2$
D. $CaCl(OCl)$

Q.61 The number of independent equations to be satisfied for static equilibrium in a space structure is
A. 2
B. 3
C. 4
D. 6

Q.62 The relationship between Young's modulus of elasticity (E), Bulk modulus (K) and Poisson ratio μ is given by
A. $E = 2K(1 - 2\mu)$
B. $E = 3K(1 + \mu)$
C. $E = 3K(1 - 2\mu)$
D. $E = 2K(1 + \mu)$

Q.63 For a circular cross-section, the relationship between the maximum shear stress q_{max} and average shear stress q_{av} is gives as
A. $q_{max} = \frac{9}{8}q_{av}$
B. $q_{max} = \frac{4}{3}q_{av}$
C. $q_{max} = \frac{3}{2}q_{av}$
D. $q_{max} = \frac{8}{3}q_{av}$

Q.64 The number of points of contraflexure in a cantilever beam are
A. zero
B. one
C. two
D. None of these

Q.65 The maximum deflection of a cantilever beam of length (L) with a point load (W) at the free end is
A. WL³/8EI
B. WL³/3EI
C. WL³/16EI
D. WL³/48EI

Q.66 The load shared by the member BC of the structure shown in figure below is:

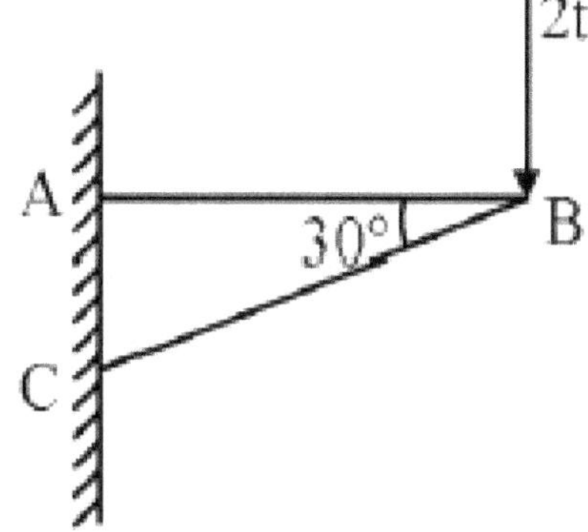

A. $2\sqrt{3}\, t$
B. $3\sqrt{2}\, t$
C. 4t
D. 3t

Q.67 Slenderness ratio of an RC column is the ratio of its length to its
A. shortest side of a column
B. long side of a column
C. area of cross section
D. None of these

Q.68 A steel rod of 2 cm² area and 1 metre in length is subjected to a pull of 40,000 N. If Young's modulus is $2 \times 10^5 \ N/mm^2$, the elongation of the rod will be

A. 10 mm   **B.** 100 mm   **C.** 1 mm   **D.** 0.1 mm

Q.69 A cantilever beam of span L is subjected to a u.d.l. of W per unit length intensity throughout its length. The maximum deflection in the beam will be

A. WL⁴/6EI

B. WL⁴/8EI

C. WL⁴/48EI

D. WL⁴/96EI

Q.70 If Poisson's ratio for a material is 0.5, then the elastic modulus for the material is

A. three times its shear modulus

B. four times its shear modulus

C. three times its bulk modulus

D. two times its bulk modulus

Q.71 The shear force diagram for a simply supported beam of span L is shown in figure. The maximum bending moment in the beam is

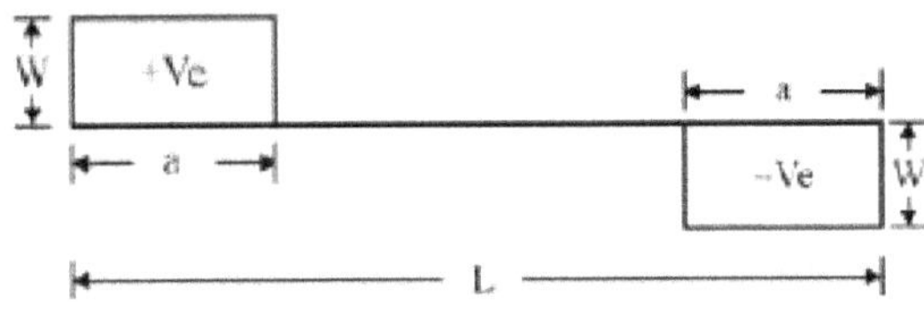

A. WL/2

B. $W\left(\frac{L}{2} - a\right)$

C. W . a

D. W(L-a)

Q.72 The ratio of the moment of inertia of a rectangular section about its base and an axis parallel to its base and passing through its centre of gravity is

A. 1.0   **B.** 2.0   **C.** 3.0   **D.** 4.0

Q.73 The maximum value of Poisson's ratio for an elastic material is

A. 0.25   **B.** 0.5   **C.** 0.75   **D.** 1.0

Q.74 If a material has identical properties at all locations, the material is assumed as

A. Isotropic

B. Elastic

C. Homogeneous

D. None of these

Q.75 When a solid shaft is subjected to torsion, the shear stress induced at its centre is

A. zero

B. maximum

C. minimum

D. average

Q.76 If the shear force at a section of a simply supported beam is zero, the bending moment at the section is

A. zero

B. maximum

C. minimum

D. average of maximum and minimum

Q.77 The simple bending equation is

A. $\frac{M}{I} = \frac{R}{E} = \frac{f}{y}$

B. $\frac{I}{M} = \frac{E}{R} = \frac{f}{y}$

C. $\frac{M}{I} = \frac{E}{R} = \frac{f}{y}$

D. $\frac{M}{I} = \frac{R}{E} = \frac{y}{f}$

Q.78 For a column of length L having one end fixed and other free, the effective length of the column is

A. 2L   **B.** L   **C.** L/2   **D.** $L/\sqrt{2}$

Q.79 The maximum bending moment, for a simply supported beam of span L and having a uniformly distributed load 'W' per unit length all over its length, is

A. WL²/2   **B.** WL²/4   **C.** WL²/8   **D.** WL²/12

Q.80 The ratio of lateral strain to longitudinal strain is called

A. Strain ratio

B. Modular ratio

C. Poisson's ratio

D. Young's modulus

Q.81 Reynold's number is defined as the ratio of

A. inertia force to gravity force

B. viscous force to gravity force

C. viscous force to elastic force

D. inertia force to viscous force

Q.82 The soil becomes practically infertile when its pH value is about

A. 0

B. 7

C. 11

D. None of these

Q.83 If the density of a fluid changes from point to point in a flow region, it is called

A. steady flow

B. unsteady flow

C. non-uniform flow

D. compressible flow

Q.84 The inlet length of a venturimeter is

A. equal to the outlet length

B. more than the outlet length

C. less than the outlet length

D. None of the above

Q.85 Manometer is used for measuring

A. velocity at a point in a fluid

B. pressure at a point in a fluid

C. difference of pressure between two points

D. both (B) and (C)

Q.86 When the pipes are connected in series, the total rate of flow is

A. equal to the sum of the rate of flow in each pipe

B. equal to the reciprocal of the sum of the rate of flow in each pipe

C. the same as flowing through each pipe

D. None of the above

Q.87 The range for coefficient of discharge (C_d) for a venturimeter is

A. 0.6 to 0.7

B. 0.7 to 0.8

C. 0.8 to 0.9

D. 0.95 to 0.99

Q.88 Pitot tube is used for the measurement of

A. pressure at a point

B. velocity at a point

C. discharge at a point

D. None of the above

Q.89 Flow in a pipe is laminar, if

A. Reynold's number is equal to 2000

B. Reynold's number is equal to 4000

C. Reynold's number is more than 4000

D. Reynold's number is less than 2000

Q.90 The necessary condition for the flow to be steady is that

A. the velocity does not change from place to place

B. the velocity is constant at a point with respect to time

C. the velocity changes at a point with respect to time

D. None of the above

Q.91 Sprinkler irrigation is preferred when

A. the ground is undulating

B. the crop has shallow roots

C. the irrigation water is scarce

D. All of the above

Q.92 If specific yield of a particular sand is 30% and its porosity is 50%, then the specific retention of the sand will be

A. 80 %   **B.** 55 %   **C.** 40 %   **D.** 20 %

Q.93 For the upstream face of an earthen dam, the most adverse condition for stability of slope is

A. sudden drawdown   **B.** steady seepage

C. during construction   **D.** sloughing of slope

Q.94 The major resisting force in a gravity dam is

A. water pressure   **B.** self weight of dam

C. wave pressure   **D.** uplift pressure

Q.95 When water content in a soil is reduced beyond the shrinkage limit

A. the total volume of soil will reduce.

B. the total volume of soil will remain constant.

C. the total volume of soil will increase.

D. None of these

Q.96 The permeability of cohesive soil is best determined by using

A. Falling-head permeameter

B. Constant-head permeameter

C. Oedometer

D. None of these

Q.97 The Darcy's law states as

A. $V \propto A$ **B.** $V \propto Q$ **C.** $V \propto h$ **D.** $V \propto i$

Q.98 Coefficient of consolidation is measured in

A. cm^2/g **B.** cm^2/sec

C. $g/cm^2/sec$ **D.** g-cm/sec

Q.99 Sheep foot roller is mostly used for the compaction of which type of soil?

A. Clays   **B.** Silt   **C.** Sand   **D.** Gravel

Q.100 Trapezoidal combined footings are required when

A. the space outside the exterior column is limited.

B. the exterior column is heavier.

C. Both (A) and (B)

D. None of the above

Q.101 As per IS : 456 – 2000, the minimum grade of concrete to be used in reinforced cement concrete is

A. M5   **B.** M10   **C.** M20   **D.** M25

Q.102 In pre-stressed concrete member, it is advised to use

A. low strength concrete only

B. high strength concrete only

C. low strength concrete but high strength steel

D. high strength concrete and high strength steel

Q.103 As per IS : 456-2000, the maximum spacing of shear reinforcement along the axis of the beam for vertical stirrups should be less than

A. 0.75 d   **B.** 0.80 d   **C.** 0.70 d   **D.** 0.75 D

Q.104 In limit state design method, the partial safety factor for steel as per IS : 456-2000 is

A. 1.5   **B.** 1.85   **C.** 1.15   **D.** 3.2

Q.105 The nominal shear stress (τ_v) in a reinforced concrete beam is given by

A. $\frac{bd}{V_u}$ **B.** $\frac{V_u}{bd}$ **C.** $V_u \cdot bd$ **D.** $\frac{V_u \cdot b}{d}$

Q.106 The formwork including the props can be removed from beams only after

A. 1 day   **B.** 3 days   **C.** 4 days   **D.** 14 days

Q.107 When shear stress exceeds the permissible limit in a slab, then it is reduced by

A. increasing the depth of slab

B. providing shear reinforcement

C. using high strength steel

D. using thinner bars but more in number

Q.108 The minimum grade of concrete for pre-tensioned member is

A. M30   **B.** M35   **C.** M40   **D.** M60

Q.109 High strength concrete possesses

A. higher modulus of elasticity

B. small creep strain

C. Both (A) and (B)

D. None of these

Q.110 Method used to make an estimate is

A. thin wall and thick wall method

B. centre line method

C. Both (A) and (B)

D. centre of gravity method

Q.111 The unit for measurement of damp proof course is

A. m   **B.** m^2

C. m^3 **D.** None of these

Q.112 While submitting a tender, the contractor is to deposit a certain amount of money of the estimated cost. It is called

A. Security money   **B.** Contract money

C. Earnest money   **D.** None of these

Q.113 The vertical member used in a door frame is called

A. Post   **B.** Sill   **C.** Rail   **D.** Bracing

Q.114 The sewerage system originates from

A. Main sewer   **B.** House sewer
C. Outfall sewer   **D.** Sub-main sewer

Q.115 In house plumbing system, the leakage of different pipes is tested by

A. Smoke test   **B.** Air test
C. Water test   **D.** All of these

Q.116 A simply supported beam carries two equal point loads 'W' at a distance of L/3 from either supports. The bending moment at mid span is

A. 5 WL/3   **B.** 2 WL/ 3   **C.** WL/3   **D.** zero

Q.117 The Euler's crippling load for a 2 m long slender steel rod of uniform cross-section hinged at both the ends is 1 kN. The Euler's crippling load for a 1 m long steel rod of the same cross-section and hinged at both the ends will be

A. 2 kN   **B.** 4 kN   **C.** 6 kN   **D.** 8 kN

Q.118 The force in the vertical member of the truss shown in figure will be

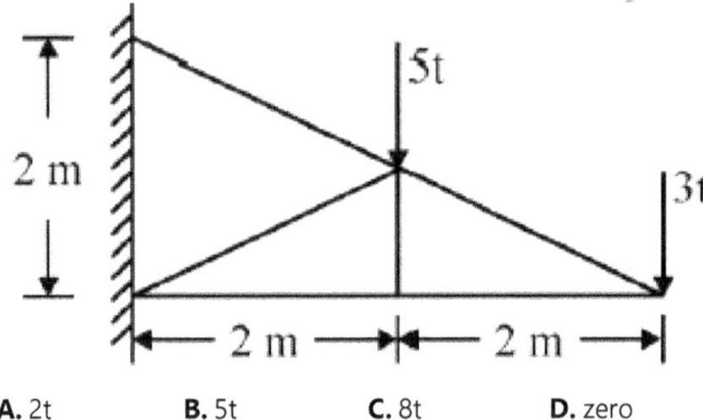

A. 2t   **B.** 5t   **C.** 8t   **D.** zero

Q.119 Moment of inertia of a solid sphere is
{Where M = mass of the solid sphere r = radius of the sphere}

A. Mr^2 **B.** $\frac{2}{3}Mr^2$ **C.** $\frac{2}{5}Mr^2$ **D.** $\frac{1}{2}Mr^2$

Q.120

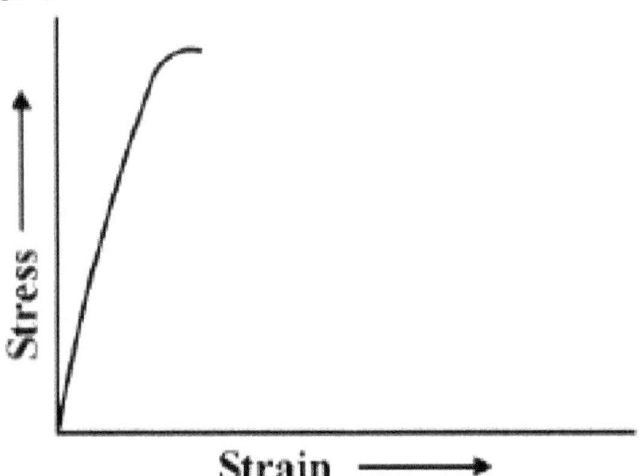

The above stress-strain diagram is for

A. Ductile material   **B.** Brittle material
C. Soft material   **D.** None of these

Q.121 The longitudinal joint of a boiler shell is always a

A. Lap joint   **B.** Butt joint
C. Lozenge joint   **D.** Diamond joint

Q.122 Strain is defined as the ratio of

A. change in volume to original volume.
B. change in length to original length.
C. change in lateral dimension to original lateral dimension.
D. All of the above

Q.123 Necking phenomenon in stress-strain is observed for

A. Brittle materials
B. Ductile materials
C. Both brittle as well as ductile materials
D. None of the above

Q.124 The bending moment on a section is maximum where shear force is

A. maximum   **B.** minimum
C. changing sign   **D.** zero

Q.125 When a wire is stretched to double its length, the longitudinal strain produced in it is

A. 0.5   **B.** 1.   **C.** 1.5   **D.** 2.

// Smart Answer Sheet //

Correct Percentage of students who answered correctly. **Skipped** Percentage of students who skipped.

Q.	Ans.	Correct / Skipped	Q.	Ans.	Correct / Skipped	Q.	Ans.	Correct / Skipped	Q.	Ans.	Correct / Skipped	Q.	Ans.	Correct / Skipped
1	B	75.0 % / 7.14 %	17	C	46.43 % / 25.0 %	33	B	57.14 % / 28.57 %	49	B	42.86 % / 28.57 %	65	B	32.14 % / 35.72 %
2	B	67.86 % / 25.0 %	18	C	57.14 % / 32.15 %	34	B	71.43 % / 17.86 %	50	D	57.14 % / 32.15 %	66	C	10.71 % / 39.29 %
3	D	25.0 % / 35.71 %	19	B	46.43 % / 32.14 %	35	A	39.29 % / 28.57 %	51	D	71.43 % / 28.57 %	67	A	46.43 % / 28.57 %
4	D	57.14 % / 21.43 %	20	B	75.0 % / 17.86 %	36	D	42.86 % / 28.57 %	52	C	78.57 % / 21.43 %	68	C	21.43 % / 46.43 %
5	B	35.71 % / 32.15 %	21	A	64.29 % / 21.42 %	37	B	42.86 % / 28.57 %	53	B	60.71 % / 21.43 %	69	B	53.57 % / 32.14 %
6	C	53.57 % / 35.72 %	22	C	60.71 % / 17.86 %	38	C	57.14 % / 35.72 %	54	B	39.29 % / 39.28 %	70	A	25.0 % / 39.29 %
7	B	53.57 % / 28.57 %	23	D	64.29 % / 28.57 %	39	C	64.29 % / 28.57 %	55	D	25.0 % / 28.57 %	71	C	21.43 % / 39.28 %
8	B	53.57 % / 35.72 %	24	B	75.0 % / 17.86 %	40	B	57.14 % / 35.72 %	56	A	60.71 % / 28.58 %	72	D	21.43 % / 17.86 %
9	C	71.43 % / 28.57 %	25	B	60.71 % / 28.58 %	41	A	64.29 % / 28.57 %	57	B	57.14 % / 32.15 %	73	B	71.43 % / 21.43 %
10	A	57.14 % / 35.72 %	26	A	21.43 % / 46.43 %	42	C	50.0 % / 21.43 %	58	B	42.86 % / 35.71 %	74	C	21.43 % / 35.71 %
11	D	64.29 % / 28.57 %	27	D	25.0 % / 32.14 %	43	C	71.43 % / 28.57 %	59	C	28.57 % / 32.14 %	75	A	50.0 % / 28.57 %
12	D	32.14 % / 28.57 %	28	B	17.86 % / 35.71 %	44	C	78.57 % / 21.43 %	60	D	46.43 % / 32.14 %	76	B	57.14 % / 35.72 %
13	B	42.86 % / 28.57 %	29	C	35.71 % / 35.72 %	45	A	25.0 % / 32.14 %	61	D	32.14 % / 25.0 %	77	C	64.29 % / 28.57 %
14	D	50.0 % / 21.43 %	30	B	67.86 % / 21.43 %	46	D	78.57 % / 21.43 %	62	C	46.43 % / 32.14 %	78	A	39.29 % / 35.71 %
15	B	53.57 % / 28.57 %	31	C	60.71 % / 28.58 %	47	B	50.0 % / 28.57 %	63	B	64.29 % / 28.57 %	79	C	60.71 % / 28.58 %
16	A	67.86 % / 28.57 %	32	B	64.29 % / 28.57 %	48	B	67.86 % / 28.57 %	64	A	46.43 % / 28.57 %	80	C	78.57 % / 17.86 %

Q.	Ans.	Correct	Skipped
81	D	57.14 %	21.43 %
82	C	67.86 %	21.43 %
83	D	25.0 %	28.57 %
84	C	28.57 %	46.43 %
85	D	28.57 %	35.72 %
86	C	42.86 %	39.28 %
87	D	46.43 %	32.14 %
88	B	53.57 %	35.72 %
89	D	60.71 %	28.58 %

Q.	Ans.	Correct	Skipped
90	B	32.14 %	42.86 %
91	D	57.14 %	28.57 %
92	D	28.57 %	46.43 %
93	A	10.71 %	46.43 %
94	B	46.43 %	21.43 %
95	B	42.86 %	28.57 %
96	A	39.29 %	28.57 %
97	D	57.14 %	28.57 %
98	A	3.57 %	35.72 %

Q.	Ans.	Correct	Skipped
99	A	53.57 %	28.57 %
100	C	60.71 %	28.58 %
101	C	64.29 %	25.0 %
102	D	46.43 %	39.28 %
103	A	53.57 %	32.14 %
104	C	57.14 %	35.72 %
105	B	67.86 %	28.57 %
106	D	32.14 %	39.29 %
107	A	32.14 %	28.57 %

Q.	Ans.	Correct	Skipped
108	C	25.0 %	21.43 %
109	C	64.29 %	32.14 %
110	B	35.71 %	21.43 %
111	B	71.43 %	28.57 %
112	C	35.71 %	21.43 %
113	A	46.43 %	35.71 %
114	B	67.86 %	25.0 %
115	D	67.86 %	28.57 %
116	C	32.14 %	35.72 %

Q.	Ans.	Correct	Skipped
117	B	28.57 %	42.86 %
118	D	28.57 %	25.0 %
119	A	14.29 %	35.71 %
120	C	14.29 %	21.42 %
121	D	25.0 %	32.14 %
122	A	0 %	100 %
123	D	0 %	100 %
124	B	10.71 %	21.43 %
125	C	14.29 %	39.28 %

//Hints and Solutions//

1. If the end stations of a line are free from local attraction, then the difference between fore bearing and back bearing of that line should be 180^0.

2. The angle between the two plane mirrors of an optical square should be 45^0.

3. Bearing of $AB = 18°15'$
Bearing of $AC = 335°45'$
Included angle $CAB = 335°45' - 18°15'$
$= 317°30'$
$= 360° - 317°30'$
$= 42°30'$

4. The two point problem or three point problem is method of Orientation and Resection.

5. Working edge of an Alidate is known as Fiducial edge.

6. A correction for error due to refraction is 0.01122 d^2 m.

7. Length of long chord in a simple circular curve having central angle is $2R\ \sin\dfrac{\theta}{2}$.

8. Planimeter is used for measuring area.

9. The first reading from a level station is back sight.

10. Correction for pull or tension in a tape is $C_P = \dfrac{(P-P_0)L}{AE}$

11. Minimum pitch of rivets should not be less than 2.5 d.

12. The effective throat thickness of a fillet weld is 0.7 times the size of weld.

13. For a steel member in tension, the permissible stress in axial tension is 0.6 f$_y$.

14. For a steel column, the permissible stress in axial compression depends mainly on slenderness ratio.

15. For simply supported steel beam, the maximum deflection should be 1/325 of the span.

16. The member of a roof truss which supports the purlins is known as principal rafter.

17. Most economical section for a steel column is tubular section.

18. The structural member in which the tensile force is acting parallel to its longitudinal axis is called Tension member and Tie.

19. The load on a lintel is assumed as uniformly distributed, if the height of the masonry above it is upto a height of 1.25 times the effective span.

20. The difference between gross diameter and nominal diameter for the rivets upto 25 mm diameter is 1.5 mm.

21. The ratio of volume of voids (Vv)in the soil to its total volume (v) is defined as porosity.

22. Density of the soil may be increased by compaction and consolidation.

23. There is no one option is correct.

Uniformity Coefficient (Cu) The uniformity coefficient (Cu) is defined as the ratio of D$_{60}$ to D$_{10}$.

24. The relation between void ratio (e) and degree of saturation (s) of soil is $e = \dfrac{WG}{S}$

25. When c is cohesion, σ is the applied normal stress ϕ is angle of internal friction, the shear strength of the soil τ will be equal to
$\tau = c + \sigma\tan\phi$

26. $n = 40\%, G = 2.70$
$e = \dfrac{n}{1-n} = \dfrac{.4}{.6} = 0.666$
$\gamma_a = \left(\dfrac{G}{1+e}\right)\gamma_w$
$= \left(\dfrac{2.7}{1.66}\right) \times 9.81 = 15.95 KN/m^3$

27. Load carrying capacity of the foundation on sand, mainly depends upon size of foundation.

28. $\gamma_a = 1.9gm/cc, \quad G = 2.65$
$\gamma_d = \left(\dfrac{G}{1+e}\right)\gamma_w$
$1.9 = \dfrac{2.65}{1+e} \times 1$
$1 + e = \dfrac{2.65}{1.9} = 1.39$
$e = 1.39 - 1 = 0.39$
$n = \dfrac{e}{1+e} = \dfrac{0.39}{1.39} \times 100 = 28.057\%$

29. $I_T = \dfrac{I_P}{I_F} = \dfrac{35-15}{10} = 2.0$

30. The liquid limit and plastic limit of a cohesive soil are determined in laboratory as 40% and 20% respectively. The plasticity index of the soil will be

I$_p$ = 40-20 =20%

31. The maximum area of tension reinforcement in beams should not exceed 4%.

32. If E$_c$ and E$_s$ are modulus of elasticity of concrete and steel respectively, then the modular ratio (m) will be E$_s$ / E$_c$.

33. In case of a reinforced concrete beam, as the percentage of tension steel increases depth of neutral axis increases.

34. In a singly reinforced beam, if the stress in concrete reaches its permissible limit earlier than that in steel, the beam section is called over-reinforced section.

35. Simply supported along two opposite edges square slab will behave as one-way slab.

36. The shear reinforcement in a reinforced concrete beam is provided to resists diagonal tension.

37. Equivalent area of a reinforced cement concrete column section is A$_c$ + m A$_{sc}$

38. The diameter of longitudinal bars in a column should not be less than 12 mm.

39. The minimum number of longitudinal bars provided in RCC circular column is 6.

40. According to IS:456 – 2000, side face reinforcement is provided in RCC beams, when depth of beam exceeds 750 mm.

41. The most reliable estimate is detailed estimate.

42. In a construction project, the time corresponding to minimum total project cost is between normal and crash time.

43. Number of bricks needed for 1 cu.m. brick work will be 500.

44. The water absorption capacity of first class bricks should not be more than 20% of its weight.

45. Lime concrete is prepared by using aggregate and slaked lime as binding material.

46. The age of a tree may be ascertained by the number of annual rings.

47. Sodium chloride is not the constituent of a paint.

48. Soundness of cement is tested by Le-Chatelier's apparatus.

49. The type of bond in which every course contains both header and stretcher is called flemish bond.

50. The base material for distemper is chalk.

51. Per capita consumption of water per day for domestic purpose should be 135 litres.

52. Fire demand of water according to Kuichling's formula, in litres/minute, is given by $Q = 3182\ \sqrt{P}$

53. Maximum permissible amount of fluoride for domestic consumption of water should be 1.5 ppm.

54. The velocity of flow of sewage in a combined sewer should not be less than 0.75 m/s.

55. The time interval of cleaning of septic tank should not be more than 2 years.

56. Alum is a coagulant. An alum is a type of chemical compound, usually a hydrated double sulfate salt of aluminium with the general formula XAl(SO. 4) 2·12H. 2O.

57. Turbidity in water is due to suspended and colloidal particles.

58. The trap used for an Indian water closet is called P-trap.

59. Sewage treatment units are generally designed for average flow only.

60. Bleaching powder is CaCl(OCl).Calcium hypochlorite is an inorganic compound with formula Ca(ClO)2. It is the main active ingredient of commercial products called bleaching powder, chlorine powder, or chlorinated lime, used for water treatment and as a bleaching agent.

61. The number of independent equations to be satisfied for static equilibrium in a space structure is 6.

62. The relationship between Young's modulus of elasticity (E), Bulk modulus (K) and Poisson ratio μ is given by $E = 3K(1 - 2\mu).$

63. For a circular cross-section, the relationship between the maximum shear stress qmax and average shear stress qav is gives as $q_{max} = \frac{4}{3} q_{av}$

64. The number of points of contraflexure in a cantilever beam are zero.

65. The maximum deflection of a cantilever beam of length (L) with a point load (W) at the free end is WL³/3EI.

66. $F_{BC}\sin 30° = 2t$
$F_{BC} = 4t$

67. Slenderness ratio of an RC column is the ratio of its length to its shortest side of a column.

68. $\delta = \frac{PL}{AE} = \frac{40000 \times 1000}{2 \times 10^5 \times 2 \times 10^2} = 1mm$

69. A cantilever beam of span L is subjected to a u.d.l. of W per unit length intensity throughout its length. The maximum deflection in the beam will be WL⁴/8EI.

70. If Poisson's ratio for a material is 0.5, then the elastic modulus for the material is three times its shear modulus.

71. The shear force diagram for a simply supported beam of span L is shown in figure. The maximum bending moment in the beam is W . a

72. The ratio of the moment of inertia of a rectangular section about its base and an axis parallel to its base and passing through its centre of gravity is 4.0.

73. The maximum value of Poisson's ratio for an elastic material is 0.5.

74. If a material has identical properties at all locations, the material is assumed as homogeneous.

75. When a solid shaft is subjected to torsion, the shear stress induced at its centre is zero.

76. If the shear force at a section of a simply supported beam is zero, the bending moment at the section is maximum.

77. The simple bending equation is $\frac{M}{I} = \frac{E}{R} = \frac{f}{y}.$

78. For a column of length L having one end fixed and other free, the effective length of the column is 2L.

79. The maximum bending moment, for a simply supported beam of span L and having a uniformly distributed load 'W' per unit length all over its length, is WL²/8.

80. The ratio of lateral strain to longitudinal strain is called poisson's ratio.

81. Reynold's number is defined as the ratio of inertia force to viscous force.

82. The soil becomes practically infertile when its pH value is about 11.

83. If the density of a fluid changes from point to point in a flow region, it is called compressible flow.

84. The inlet length of a venturimeter is less than the outlet length.

85. Manometer is used for measuring pressure at a point in a fluid and difference of pressure between two points.

86. When the pipes are connected in series, the total rate of flow is the same as flowing through each pipe.

87. The range for coefficient of discharge (C_d) for a venturimeter is 0.95 to 0.99.

88. Pitot tube is used for the measurement of velocity at a point.

89. Flow in a pipe is laminar, if Reynold's number is less than 2000.

90. The necessary condition for the flow to be steady is that the velocity is constant at a point with respect to time.

91. Sprinkler irrigation is preferred when the ground is undulating, the crop has shallow roots and the irrigation water is scarce.

92. If specific yield of a particular sand is 30% and its porosity is 50%, then the specific retention of the sand will be

Specific retention = 50 - 30 = 20%

93. For the upstream face of an earthen dam, the most adverse condition for stability of slope is sudden drawdown.

94. The major resisting force in a gravity dam is self weight of dam.

95. When water content in a soil is reduced beyond the shrinkage limit the total volume of soil will remain constant.

96. The permeability of cohesive soil is best determined by using falling-head permeameter.

97. The Darcy's law states as $V \propto i$

98. Coefficient of consolidation is measured in cm^2/g.

99. Sheep foot roller is mostly used for the compaction of clays type of soil.

100. Trapezoidal combined footings are required when the space outside the exterior column is limited and the exterior column is heavier.

101. As per IS : 456 – 2000, the minimum grade of concrete to be used in reinforced cement concrete is M20.

102. In pre-stressed concrete member, it is advised to use high strength concrete and high strength steel.

103. As per IS : 456-2000, the maximum spacing of shear reinforcement along the axis of the beam for vertical stirrups should be less than 0.75 d.

104. In limit state design method, the partial safety factor for steel as per IS : 456-2000 is 1.15.

105. The nominal shear stress $\left(\tau_v\right)$ in a reinforced concrete beam is given by $\dfrac{V_u}{bd}$

106. The formwork including the props can be removed from beams only after 14 days.

107. When shear stress exceeds the permissible limit in a slab, then it is reduced by increasing the depth of slab.

108. The minimum grade of concrete for pre-tensioned member is M40.

109. High strength concrete possesses higher modulus of elasticity and small creep strain.

110. Method used to make an estimate is centre line method.

111. The unit for measurement of damp proof course is m^2.

112. While submitting a tender, the contractor is to deposit a certain amount of money of the estimated cost. It is called earnest money.

113. The vertical member used in a door frame is called post.

114. The sewerage system originates from house sewer.

115. In house plumbing system, the leakage of different pipes is tested by smoke test, air test and water test.

116. A simply supported beam carries two equal point loads 'W' at a distance of L/3 from either supports. The bending moment at mid span is WL/3.

117. The Euler's crippling load for a 2 m long slender steel rod of uniform cross-section hinged at both the ends is 1 kN. The Euler's crippling load for a 1 m long steel rod of the same cross-section and hinged at both the ends will be 4 kN.

118. The force in the vertical member of the truss will be zero.

119. Moment of inertia of a solid sphere is Mr^2.

120. The stress-strain is soft material.

121. The longitudinal joint of a boiler shell is always a diamond joint.

122. Strain is defined as the ratio of change in volume to original volume.

123. There is no one option is correct.

Necking results from instability during tensile deformation when a material's cross-sectional area decreases by a greater proportion than the material strain hardens. Considère published the basic criterion for necking in 1885. Three concepts provide the framework for understanding neck formation.

1. Before deformation, all real materials have heterogeneities such as flaws or local variations in dimensions or composition that cause local fluctuations in stresses and strains. To determine the location of the incipient neck, these fluctuations need only be infinitesimal in magnitude.

2. During tensile deformation, the material decreases in cross-sectional area. (Poisson effect)

3. During tensile deformation, the material strain hardens. The amount of hardening varies with the extent of deformation.

124. The bending moment on a section is maximum where shear force is minimum.

125. When a wire is stretched to double its length, the longitudinal strain produced in it is 1.5.

Q.1 If the shear modulus of a material is half of its Young's modulus, then what will be the value of its Poisson's ratio?

A. –1.0   **B.** -0.5   **C.** 0   **D.** 0.5

Q.2 In a beam of circular cross-section with diameter d, the ratio of maximum shear stress to average shear stress will be

A. 3/4   **B.** 4/3   **C.** 3/2   **D.** 2/3

Q.3 The fatigue strength of a metallic material increases when

A. the temperature of the material increases
B. the surface of the material is scratched
C. the material is overstressed
D. the material is understressed

Q.4 The moment of inertia of a triangular section with base b and height h is

A. $b^3h/12$ **B.** $bh^3/36$ **C.** $bh^3/12$ **D.** $b^3h/36$

Q.5 If the shear force at a section of beam under bending is equal to zero, then the bending moment at the section is

A. zero   **B.** constant
C. maximum   **D.** minimum

Q.6 Every cross-section of a shaft which is subject to a twisting meoment, is under

A. compressive stress   **B.** shear stress
C. tensile stress   **D.** bending stress

Q.7 T-beam is generally constructed in

A. deck bridge   **B.** semi-through bridge
C. any of the above   **D.** none of the above

Q.8 Couple M is applied at C on a simply supported beam AB. What is the maximum shear force for the beam?

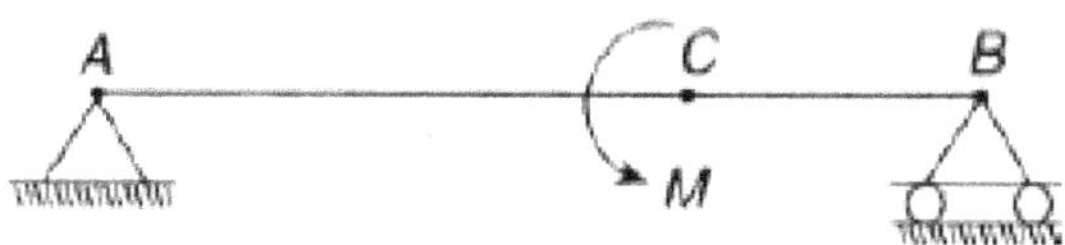

A. zero   **B.** M   **C.** 2M/3   **D.** M/3

Q.9 A king post truss is suitable for spans

A. less than 4m
B. less than 6m
C. between 12 m and 15 m
D. between 6 m and 9 m

Q.10 For a conjugate beam, the load diagram is

A. EI diagram
B. bending moment diagram
C. M/EI diagram
D. shear force diagram

Q.11 A perfect plane fram having n number of member and j number of joints should satisfy

A. n < (2j-3)   **B.** n = (2j-3)
C. n > (2j-3)   **D.** n = (3 - 2j)

Q.12 The minimum area of tension reinforcement in a beam should be greater than

A. $0.85\ bd/f_y$ **B.** $0.87\ f_y/bd$
C. 0.04bd   **D.** 0.4 bd.y

Q.13 A reinforced concrete structure has to be constructed along a sea coast. The minimum grade of concrete to be used as per IS: 456-2000 is

A. M15   **B.** M20   **C.** M25   **D.** M30

Q.14 The minimum diameter of bars for a slab is usually

A. 8 mm   **B.** 12 mm   **C.** 16 mm   **D.** 20 mm

Q.15 The effective depth of a beam in the RCC design has to be

A. $(D - \phi)^2$ **B.** $D - 3\phi$
C. D-Cover   **D.** 10ϕ

Q.16 General shrinkage of cement concrete is caused by

A. carbonation
B. stress due to external load
C. drying starting with a stiff consistency
D. drying starting with a wetter consistency

Q.17 Shear in a concrete beam is caused by

A. props only
B. variation of bending moment along the span
C. weak bond
D. all of the above

Q.18 The maximum cube strength of a prestressed concrete member is (in MPa)

A. 10   **B.** 15   **C.** 20   **D.** 35

Q.19 A column is considered as a long column if its slenderness ratio (effective length/least radius of gyration) exceeds

A. 12   **B.** 20   **C.** 24   **D.** 3

Q.20 For a two-way slab, main reinforcement is provided along

A. length of the slab   **B.** width of the slab
C. diagonal of the slab   **D.** all of the above

Q.21 In case of an under-reinforced section,

A. steel will yield first
B. concrete will yield first
C. steel is provided on the underside of the section
D. concrete cover is not provided for reinforcement

Q.22 The expression $p \times t \times \sigma_t$ in case of a riveted joint is called

A. tearing strength

B. bearing strength
C. crushing strength
D. strength of solid plate

Q.23 The buckling factor is defined as the ratio of

A. equivalent length of a column to the minimum radius of gyrations
B. length of the column to the minimum radius of gyrations
C. length of the column to the area of cross section of the column
D. None of the above

Q.24 Bearing stiffeners are provided to avoid

A. bending failure of the flange
B. local crippling of buckling of web
C. crushing of web
D. All the above

Q.25 Which one of the following is a compression member?

A. Purlin   **B.** Boom   **C.** Grit   **D.** Tie

Q.26 The slenderness ratio of lacing bars should not exceed:

A. 100   **B.** 200   **C.** 145   **D.** 180

Q.27 On which of the following concepts is the basic principle of structural design based?

A. Weak column strong beam
B. Strong column weak beam
C. Equally strong column-beam
D. Partially weak column-beam

Q.28 The number of rivets required in a joint is given by

A. Force/Tearing strength of rivet
B. Force/Shearing strength of rivet
C. Force/Bearing strength of rivet
D. Force/Rivet value

Q.29 The effective length of a fillet weld of length L and size s is given by

A. $L - \sqrt{2}s$ **B.** L-2s
C. $L - \frac{s}{\sqrt{2}}$ **D.** L

Q.30 In the roof trusses, the beams spanning between the two adjacent trusses are known as

A. connectors   **B.** jointers
C. rafters   **D.** purlins

Q.31 In a fillet weld, the weakest section is the

A. smaller side of the fillet
B. throat of the fillet
C. side perpendicular to force
D. side parallel to force

Q.32 Which one of the following relations is not correct?

A. $e = \frac{n}{1-n}$ **B.** $\gamma_{sat} = \left(\frac{G+e}{1+e}\right)\gamma_w$
C. $n = \frac{e}{1-e}$ **D.** $e = \frac{WG}{S}$

Q.33 A clay sample has a void ratio of 0.50 in dry state and specific gravity of solids is 2.70. Its shrinkage limit will be

A. 12%   **B.** 13.5%   **C.** 18.5%   **D.** 22%

Q.34 When the degree of consolidation is 50%, than time factor is about

A. 0.2   **B.** 0.5   **C.** 1.0   **D.** 2.0

Q.35 A sand deposit has a porosity of 0.375 and a specifc gravity of 2.6, the critical hydraulic gradient for the sand deposit is

A. 2.975   **B.** 2.225   **C.** 1   **D.** 0.75

Q.36 The critical gradient of a soil increases with

A. increase in void ratio
B. decrease in void ratio
C. decrease in specific gravity
D. none of the above

Q.37 The effective stress for soil is

A. actual contact stress   **B.** an abstract quantity
C. equal to total stress   **D.** none of above

Q.38 The coefficient of permeability of clay is generally

A. Between 10^{-4} and 10^{-2} mm/s
B. Between 10^{-5} and 10^{-4} mm/s
C. Between 10^{-5} and 10^{-8} mm/s
D. Less than 10^{-8} mm/s

Q.39 Stoke's law does not hold good if the size of particles is

A. greater than 0.2 mm   **B.** less than 0.2 μm
C. Neither (a) nor (b)   **D.** Both (a) and (b)

Q.40 The radius of the friction circle is equal to

A. $R \sin\phi$ **B.** $R \cos\phi$ **C.** $R \tan\phi$ **D.** $R\phi$

Q.41 Vane test is normally used to determine in-situ shear strength of:

A. Soft clays   **B.** Sand
C. Stiff clays   **D.** Gravels

Q.42 For an undisturbed soil sample, the area ratio for the samples should be

A. zero   **B.** 10% or less
C. 10% to 20%   **D.** more than 20%

Q.43 The liquid limit (LL), plastic limit (PL), adn shrinkage limit (SL) of a cohesive soil satisfy the relation.

A. LL>PL<SL   **B.** LL>PL>SL
C. LL<PL<SL   **D.** LL<PL>SL

Q.44 The specific energy E in a critical flow at depth y_c occurring in a traingular channel is given by

A. $E = 1.25y_c$ **B.** $E = 1.5y_c$
C. $E = 1.75y_c$ **D.** $E = 2y_c$

Q.45 The pressure gradient in the direction of flow is equal to the

A. shear gradient parallel to the direction of flow
B. shear gradient normal to the direction of flow
C. velocity gradient parallel to the direction of flow
D. velocity gradient normal to direction of flow

Q.46 The separation of boundary layer takes place when the pressure gradient is

A. negative   **B.** positive   **C.** zero   **D.** constant

Q.47 To pipe systems in series are said to be equivalent when

A. the average diameter in both the systems is same

B. the average friction factor in both the system is same

C. the total length of the pipes is same in both the systems

D. the discharge under the same head is same in both the systems

Q.48 Both Reynolds and Froude numbers assume significance in one following examples:

A. Motion of submarine at large depths

B. Motion of ship in deep sea

C. Cruising of missile in air

D. Flow over spillways

Q.49 Streamlines and equipotential lines

A. can be drawn graphically for viscous flow around any boundary

B. from meshes of perfect squares

C. are orthogonal wherever they meet

D. can be determined mathematically for all bounary conditions

Q.50 For turbulent flow in horizontal pipe, the pressure gradient

A. is zero

B. is constant

C. varies linearly with distance

D. varies exponentially with distance

Q.51 Given that g = acceleration due to gravity and R = hydraulic mean depth, the Darcy-Weisbach friction factor is related of Manning's rugosity coefficient n as

A. $\frac{8gn^2}{R^{1/3}}$ **B.** $\frac{gn^2}{8R^{1/3}}$ **C.** $\frac{64gn}{R^{1/3}}$ **D.** $\frac{R^{1/3}}{8gn^2}$

Q.52 The quantity of wood for the shutters of doors and windows is calculated in:

A. m   **B.** m^2

C. m^3 **D.** lump-sum

Q.53 The floor area includes the area of the balcony upto:

A. 75%   **B.** 50%   **C.** 25%   **D.** 85%

Q.54 The plan of a building is in the form of square with centreline dimensions of outer walls as 14.7 m × 14.7 m. If the thickness of the wall in superstructure is 0.30 m, then its plinth area is:

A. 216 m^2 **B.** 225 m^2 **C.** 234 m^2 **D.** 150 m^2

Q.55 Thickness of Plastering is usually:

A. 12 mm   **B.** 25 mm   **C.** 40 mm   **D.** 6 mm

Q.56 Using straight line method annual depreciation D is equal to:

A. $\frac{Original\ cost - life\ in\ year}{scrap\ value}$

B. $\frac{Original\ cost - scrap\ value}{life\ in\ year}$

C. $\frac{Life\ in\ year - scrap\ value}{Original\ cost}$

D. $\frac{Scrap\ value - life\ in\ year}{Original\ cost}$

Q.57 The following document contains detailed description of all items of work excluding their quantities, along with the current rates:

A. Abstractestimate   **B.** Schedule of rates

C. Analysis of rates   **D.** Tender document

Q.58 Estimate for electrical wiring is prepared on the basis of?

A. Voltage

B. Power

C. Number of points

D. Number of appliances

Q.59 Turbidity of water is expressed in terms of

A. silica scale

B. platimum cobalt scale

C. ph value

D. none of these

Q.60 Slow sand filter is more efficient for the removal of

A. bacteria   **B.** odour

C. turbidity   **D.** all of these

Q.61 A septic tank is a

A. sedimentation tank

B. digestion tank

C. combination of sedimentation and digestion tank

D. aeration tank

Q.62 A road connecting two towns is called a

A. country road   **B.** urban road

C. highway   **D.** none of these

Q.63 The thickness of base, in no case, should be more than

A. 10 cm   **B.** 15 cm   **C.** 20 cm   **D.** 30 cm

Q.64 The number of sleepers used for rail varies from

A. (n+1) to (n+4)   **B.** (n+4) to (n+7)

C. (n+2) to (n+7)   **D.** (n+4) to (n+8)

Q.65 The relation between the radius of curve (R) and its degree of curvature (D) is given by

A. $R = \frac{1245}{D}$ **B.** $R = \frac{1546.8}{D}$

C. $R = \frac{1746.5}{D}$ **D.** $R = \frac{1835.6}{D}$

Q.66 The soil transported by glaciers either by ice or water is called

A. talus   **B.** loess

C. drift   **D.** none of these

Q.67 Granite is mainly composed of

A. quartz and mica

B. felspar and mica

C. quartz and felspar

D. quartz, felspar and mica

Q.68 The dressing of stone is done

A. immediately after quarrying

B. after seasoning

C. after three months of quarrying

D. just before building

Q.69 Excess of alumina in the clay
A. makes the brick brittle and weak
B. makes the brick crack adn warp on drying
C. changes colour of the brick from red to yellow
D. improves impermeability and durability of the brick

Q.70 The compressive strength of paving bricks should not be less than
A. 20 MN/m^2
B. 30 MN/m^2
C. 40 MN/m^2
D. 50 MN/m^2

Q.71 Eminently hydraulic lime is one in which the percentage of silica, alumina and iron oxide is
A. 5 to 10%
B. 10 to 25%
C. 25 to 30%
D. 30 to 40%

Q.72 The ultimate strength of cement is provided by
A. silica
B. di-calcium silicate
C. tri-calcium silicate
D. tri-calcium aluminate

Q.73 The specific surface (in cm^2/g) of a good Portland cement should no be less than.
A. 500
B. 110
C. 2250
D. 3200

Q.74 The defect caused due to over-maturity and unventilated storage of the wood during its transit, is called
A. knot
B. rind gall
C. foxiness
D. heart shake

Q.75 The timber whose thickness is less than 5 cm and the width exceeds 12 cm, is called a
A. board
B. plank
C. batten
D. log

Q.76 Enamel paint is made by adding
A. white lead in varnish
B. bitumen is varnish
C. white lead in lacquer
D. zinc white in spirit

Q.77 The commonly used solvent in oil paints is
A. turpentine
B. naptha
C. either (A) or (B)
D. none of these

Q.78 The light-weight concrete is prepared by
A. mixing Portland cement with sawdust in specified proportion in the concrete
B. using coke-breeze, cinder or slag as aggregate in the concrete
C. mixing aluminium in the concrete
D. none of the abvoe

Q.79 The breaking up of cohesion in a mass of concrete is called
A. workability
B. bleeding
C. segreagation
D. creep

Q.80 Low percentage of tricalcium silicate and high percentage of dicalcium silicate in cement results in
A. rapid hardening
B. high early strength
C. high early strength
D. none of these

Q.81 "Colocrete" is the commercial term for
A. high alumina cement
B. coloured cement
C. low heat cement
D. rapid hardening cement

Q.82 If the slump of concrete mix is 70 mm, its workability is considered to be
A. very low
B. low
C. medium
D. high

Q.83 As per IS : 459 – 1978, the concrete mixes are designated into
A. 4 grades
B. 5 grades
C. 6 grades
D. 7 grades

Q.84 To prevent segregation, the concrete should not be thrown from a hight of more than
A. 1/2 m
B. 1 m
C. 1.5 m
D. 2 m

Q.85 The window usualy provided near the main roof of a room and opens above the adjoining verandah, is called
A. dormer window
B. corner window
C. bay window
D. clerestorey window

Q.86 The most commonly used bond for all wall thicknesses is
A. English bond
B. Flemish bond
C. stretching bond
D. heading bond

Q.87 A bat is the portion of a
A. wall not exposed to weather
B. brick cut across the width
C. wall between facing and backing
D. brick cut in such a manner that its one long face remains uncut

Q.88 The most commonly used material for damp proofing is
A. bitumen
B. paraffin wax
C. cement solution
D. cement concrete

Q.89 The curvature of the earth is taken into consideration if the limit of survey is
A. 50 to 100 km^2
B. 100 to 200 km^2
C. 200 to 250 km^2
D. more than 250 km^2

Q.90 The correction to be applied to each 30 m chain for a line measured along a slope of θ is
A. $30\,(1 - \sin\theta)$
B. $30\,(1 - \cos\theta)$
C. $30\,(1 - \tan\theta)$
D. $30\,(1 - \cot\theta)$

Q.91 The lines of earth's magnetic field run from
A. south to north
B. north of south
C. east to west
D. west to east

Q.92 The magnetic bearing of a line is S35^0 30'E and the magnetic declination is east. The true bearing of a line will be
A. $S\,31°\,30'E$
B. $S\,31°\,30'W$
C. $S\,39°\,50'E$
D. $S\,39°\,50'W$

Q.93 When the cross-hairs are not clearly visible
A. the cross-hairs should be adjusted
B. the eye-piece should be focussed
C. the objective should be focussed
D. the parallex should be removed

Q.94 The multiplying constant for the tacheometer is
A. f/i
B. i/f
C. f/d
D. f+d

Q.95 In route surveys, the most suitable method of contouring is
A. by squares
B. by radial lines
C. by cross-sections
D. by tacheometer

Q.96 The rise and fall method for obtaining the reduced levels of points provides a check on
A. fore sights only
B. back sights only
C. intermediate sights only
D. all of these

Q.97 Which of the following is the most correct estimate?
A. plinth area estimate
B. cube rate estimate
C. detailed estimate
D. building cost index estimate

Q.98 For electric wiring such as fan, light, plug etc., the estimate is made in terms of
A. type of point
B. number of points
C. total load at main in kW
D. total length of wiring in metres.

Q.99 The value of the property (without being dismantled) at the end of the useful life period is known as
A. scrap value
B. salvage value
C. junke value
D. book value

Q.100 Wood work for doors and windows is measured in
A. cubic metres
B. square metres
C. metres
D. lump-sum.

Q.101 For a circular section $I_{zz} = I_{xx} + I_{yy}$. Then zz-axis
A. coincides with xx-axis
B. coincides with yy-axis
C. will be tangential to the circle
D. will be passing through point of intersection of xx and yy-axes and perpendicular to the plane of cross-section.

Q.102 A simply supported beam is subjected to a central concentrated load. The slope at the two ends is given by
A. $\frac{WL^2}{6EI}$
B. $\frac{WL^3}{48EI}$
C. $\frac{WL^2}{48EI}$
D. $\frac{WL^2}{16EI}$

Q.103 A thin cylinder is the one in which
A. the variation is hoop stress along the thickness can be neglected
B. the hoop stress can be neglected
C. the thickness is less than 20 mm

D. only internal fluid pressure acts.

Q.104 The Euler crippling load for a column with one end fixed and the other hinged is
A. $\frac{\pi^2 EI}{L^2}$
B. $\frac{4\pi^2 EI}{L^2}$
C. $\frac{\pi^2 EI}{4L^2}$
D. $\frac{2\pi^2 EI}{L^2}$

Q.105 A cantilever beam of length l is subjected to a conentrated load of P newtons at its free end. The reaction at the fixed end will be
A. Anti-clockwise moment Pl and an upward vertical force P
B. Anti-clockwise moment Pl and an downward vertical force P
C. clockwise moment Pl and an upward vertical force P
D. clockwise moment Pl and an downwared vertical force P.

Q.106 The coefficient of permeability is proportional to void ratio as
A. e
B. $1/e^3$
C. $e^3/1+e$
D. $e/1+e^2$

Q.107 The expression for critical gradient is
A. $i_c = \frac{G-1}{1+e}$
B. $i_c = \frac{G+1}{1+e}$
C. $i_c = \frac{1-e}{G-1}$
D. $i_c = \frac{1+e}{G+1}$

Q.108 If k_x and k_z are the permeability values in x and z directions respectively in a two dimensional flow situation, the equivalent coefficient of permeability k^e is given by
A. $k_e = k_x + k_z$
B. $k_e = k_x + k_z$
C. $k_e = k_x/k_z$
D. $k_e = \sqrt{k_x . k_z}$

Q.109 A flownet may be used for the determination of
A. exit gradient
B. seepage flow rate
C. seepage pressure
D. all the above

Q.110 Two or more footings connected by a beam is called as
A. Strap footings
B. Cantilever footing
C. Fump-handle foundation
D. All the above

Q.111 Max amount of super elevation should not be greater than
A. 2%
B. 3%
C. 5%
D. 7%

Q.112 When the distance between the axles 'l' and radius of curve is R then mechanical widening width is
A. $\frac{l^2}{R}$
B. $\frac{l^2}{2R}$
C. $\frac{2l^2}{R}$
D. $\frac{l}{2R}$

Q.113 Skidding occurs on ______ pavement
A. dry
B. wet
C. smooth
D. soft

Q.114 An instrument used to measure Roughness index is
A. Enoscope
B. Deflectometer
C. Seismograph
D. Bump integrator

Q.115 Purpose of the seal coat is to provide
A. an even surface
B. required grade
C. camber
D. an impervious layer

Q.116 The safe speed on a highway is
A. 50th percentile speed

B. 75th percentile speed

C. 85th percentile speed

D. 98th percentile speed

Q.117 Quick setting cement is used

A. for the construction of structures under water

B. to obtain very high strength

C. where resistance to acidic water is required

D. none of the above

Q.118 The sand in mortar

A. increases the volume of mortar

B. reduces the shrinkage and cracking

C. helps the pure lime to set by allowing penetration of air which provides the needed carbon dioxide

D. all the above

Q.119 The tensile strength of concrete to be used in the design of reinforced concrete members is

A. $0.2\sqrt{f_{ck}}$ **B.** $0.1\sqrt{f_{ck}}$

C. $0.7\sqrt{f_{ck}}$ **D.** zero

Q.120 The depths to N.A. in a singly reinforced section is given by

A. $\dfrac{x_u}{d} = \dfrac{700}{1100+0.87f_y}$ **B.** $\dfrac{x_u}{d} = \dfrac{1100+0.87f_y}{700}$

C. $\dfrac{x_u}{d} = \dfrac{700}{1100-0.87f_y}$ **D.** $\dfrac{x_u}{d} = \dfrac{1100-0.87f_y}{700}$

Q.121 The effective width of flange in R.C.C. T-beams should be restricted to

A. $\dfrac{l_0}{6} + b_\omega + 6D_f$

B. $\dfrac{l_0}{12} + b_\omega + 3D_f$

C. $\dfrac{l_0}{3}$

D. centre to centre distance of the beams

Q.122 For cantilever beams and slabs, the basic value of span to effective depth ratio is

A. 7   **B.** 1   **C.** 20   **D.** 26

Q.123 A compression member is termed as column or strut if the ratio of its effective length to the least lateral dimension is more than

A. 1   **B.** 2   **C.** 3   **D.** no limit

Q.124 The minimum eccentricity that should be used in the design of any R.C.C. column is given by

A. 50 mm

B. $\dfrac{unsupported\ lenght}{500}$

C. $\dfrac{leteral\ dimension}{30}$

D. $\dfrac{unsupported\ lenght}{500} + \dfrac{leteral\ dimension}{30}$

Q.125 The maximum percentage of longitudinal reinforcement in R.C.C. columns is

A. 0.8   **B.** 2.0   **C.** 4.0   **D.** 6.0

// Smart Answer Sheet //

Correct Percentage of students who answered correctly.　　**Skipped** Percentage of students who skipped.

Q.	Ans.	Correct / Skipped
1	C	26.92 % / 11.54 %
2	B	50.0 % / 23.08 %
3	D	19.23 % / 26.92 %
4	C	34.62 % / 19.23 %
5	B	7.69 % / 19.23 %
6	B	53.85 % / 23.07 %
7	A	15.38 % / 19.24 %
8	D	19.23 % / 34.62 %
9	D	57.69 % / 23.08 %
10	C	53.85 % / 26.92 %
11	B	65.38 % / 19.24 %
12	A	50.0 % / 19.23 %
13	D	76.92 % / 19.23 %
14	A	65.38 % / 19.24 %
15	C	53.85 % / 26.92 %
16	D	38.46 % / 23.08 %

Q.	Ans.	Correct / Skipped
17	B	30.77 % / 19.23 %
18	D	50.0 % / 19.23 %
19	A	84.62 % / 7.69 %
20	B	34.62 % / 19.23 %
21	A	53.85 % / 19.23 %
22	D	46.15 % / 19.23 %
23	A	57.69 % / 15.39 %
24	D	61.54 % / 19.23 %
25	B	50.0 % / 19.23 %
26	C	69.23 % / 19.23 %
27	B	26.92 % / 26.93 %
28	D	73.08 % / 19.23 %
29	B	61.54 % / 19.23 %
30	D	65.38 % / 19.24 %
31	B	57.69 % / 23.08 %
32	C	65.38 % / 19.24 %

Q.	Ans.	Correct / Skipped
33	C	38.46 % / 30.77 %
34	A	42.31 % / 26.92 %
35	C	38.46 % / 30.77 %
36	B	65.38 % / 19.24 %
37	B	15.38 % / 34.62 %
38	C	34.62 % / 23.07 %
39	D	50.0 % / 19.23 %
40	A	34.62 % / 23.07 %
41	A	61.54 % / 19.23 %
42	B	30.77 % / 26.92 %
43	B	53.85 % / 23.07 %
44	A	38.46 % / 19.23 %
45	B	11.54 % / 34.61 %
46	B	34.62 % / 26.92 %
47	C	11.54 % / 23.08 %
48	D	23.08 % / 30.77 %

Q.	Ans.	Correct / Skipped
49	C	26.92 % / 34.62 %
50	C	19.23 % / 19.23 %
51	A	23.08 % / 30.77 %
52	B	76.92 % / 19.23 %
53	B	57.69 % / 23.08 %
54	B	50.0 % / 23.08 %
55	A	80.77 % / 19.23 %
56	B	73.08 % / 19.23 %
57	B	46.15 % / 26.93 %
58	C	73.08 % / 23.07 %
59	A	38.46 % / 19.23 %
60	A	23.08 % / 19.23 %
61	C	61.54 % / 19.23 %
62	A	26.92 % / 19.23 %
63	D	38.46 % / 26.92 %
64	B	42.31 % / 23.07 %

Q.	Ans.	Correct / Skipped
65	C	73.08 % / 19.23 %
66	C	42.31 % / 19.23 %
67	D	69.23 % / 19.23 %
68	A	61.54 % / 23.08 %
69	B	69.23 % / 19.23 %
70	C	46.15 % / 34.62 %
71	C	50.0 % / 23.08 %
72	B	80.77 % / 19.23 %
73	C	73.08 % / 19.23 %
74	C	65.38 % / 19.24 %
75	A	42.31 % / 23.07 %
76	A	57.69 % / 23.08 %
77	C	65.38 % / 19.24 %
78	B	46.15 % / 23.08 %
79	C	65.38 % / 19.24 %
80	D	50.0 % / 23.08 %

Q.	Ans.	Correct / Skipped	Q.	Ans.	Correct / Skipped	Q.	Ans.	Correct / Skipped	Q.	Ans.	Correct / Skipped	Q.	Ans.	Correct / Skipped
81	B	61.54 % / 19.23 %	90	B	76.92 % / 19.23 %	99	B	57.69 % / 19.23 %	108	D	46.15 % / 26.93 %	117	A	76.92 % / 15.39 %
82	C	69.23 % / 19.23 %	91	B	65.38 % / 19.24 %	100	B	69.23 % / 19.23 %	109	D	65.38 % / 19.24 %	118	D	73.08 % / 19.23 %
83	D	50.0 % / 19.23 %	92	A	15.38 % / 42.31 %	101	D	53.85 % / 26.92 %	110	A	50.0 % / 23.08 %	119	C	76.92 % / 15.39 %
84	B	53.85 % / 19.23 %	93	B	65.38 % / 23.08 %	102	D	50.0 % / 23.08 %	111	D	53.85 % / 15.38 %	120	A	65.38 % / 23.08 %
85	D	23.08 % / 26.92 %	94	A	65.38 % / 19.24 %	103	A	23.08 % / 34.61 %	112	B	69.23 % / 19.23 %	121	A	76.92 % / 19.23 %
86	A	57.69 % / 23.08 %	95	C	46.15 % / 19.23 %	104	D	73.08 % / 19.23 %	113	B	42.31 % / 23.07 %	122	A	69.23 % / 19.23 %
87	B	53.85 % / 19.23 %	96	D	76.92 % / 19.23 %	105	A	11.54 % / 34.61 %	114	D	42.31 % / 23.07 %	123	C	50.0 % / 23.08 %
88	A	38.46 % / 19.23 %	97	C	76.92 % / 19.23 %	106	C	50.0 % / 23.08 %	115	D	69.23 % / 19.23 %	124	D	61.54 % / 19.23 %
89	D	73.08 % / 19.23 %	98	A	7.69 % / 19.23 %	107	A	76.92 % / 19.23 %	116	C	38.46 % / 19.23 %	125	D	57.69 % / 19.23 %

//Hints and Solutions//

1. Shear modulus $= \dfrac{\text{Young's modulus}}{2}$

$E = 2G(1 + \mu)$
$1 = 1 + \mu$
$\mu = 1 - 1 = 0$

2. In a beam of circular cross-section with diameter d, the ratio of maximum shear stress to average shear stress will be 4/3.

3. The fatigue strength of a metallic material increases when the material is understressed.

4. The moment of inertia of a triangular section with base b and height h is bh³/12.

5. $\dfrac{dM}{dx} = \text{Shear force} = 0$
then B.M. will be constant

6. Every cross-section of a shaft which is subject to a twisting meoment, is under shear stress.

7. T-beam is generally constructed in deck bridge.

8. $R_a + R_b = 0$
taking moment about B
$R_a \times 3 - M = 0$
$R_a = \dfrac{M}{3}, R_b = -\dfrac{M}{3}$
So maximum shear force is $\dfrac{M}{3}$

9. A king post truss is suitable for spans between 6 m and 9 m.

10. For a conjugate beam, the load diagram is M/EI diagram.

11. A perfect plane fram having n number of member and j number of joints should satisfy n = (2j-3).

12. The minimum area of tension reinforcement in a beam should be greater than 0.85 bd/f$_y$.

13. A reinforced concrete structure has to be constructed along a sea coast. The minimum grade of concrete to be used as per IS: 456-2000 is M30.

14. The minimum diameter of bars for a slab is usually 8 mm.

15. The effective depth of a beam in the RCC design has to be D-Cover.

16. General shrinkage of cement concrete is caused by drying starting with a wetter consistency.

17. Shear in a concrete beam is caused by variation of bending moment along the span.

18. The maximum cube strength of a prestressed concrete member is (in MPa) 35.

19. A column is considered as a long column if its slenderness ratio (effective length/least radius of gyration) exceeds 12.

20. For a two-way slab, main reinforcement is provided along width of the slab.

21. In case of an under-reinforced section, steel will yield first.

22. The expression p×t×σt in case of a riveted joint is called strength of solid plate.

23. The buckling factor is defined as the ratio of equivalent length of a column to the minimum radius of gyrations.

24. Bearing stiffeners are provided to avoid bending failure of the flange, local crippling of buckling of web and crushing of web.

25. Boom is a compression member.

26. The slenderness ratio of lacing bars should not exceed 145.

27. Strong column weak beam concepts is the basic principle of structural design based.

28. The number of rivets required in a joint is given by Force/Rivet value.

29. The effective length of a fillet weld of length L and size s is given by L-2s.

30. In the roof trusses, the beams spanning between the two adjacent trusses are known as purlins.

31. In a fillet weld, the weakest section is the throat of the fillet.

32. $n = \dfrac{e}{1-e}$ relations is not correct.

33.
$$W_s = \dfrac{e}{G} \quad \text{note} \quad Gw = se \quad S = 1$$
$$W = \dfrac{e}{G}$$
$$= \dfrac{0.50}{2.70}$$
$$= 0.185$$
$$= 18.5\%$$

34. $T_V = \dfrac{\pi}{4}\left(\dfrac{V\%}{100}\right)^2$
$= \dfrac{\pi}{4}\left(\dfrac{50}{100}\right)^2, = \dfrac{\pi}{4} \times \dfrac{1}{4}, = \dfrac{\pi}{16}, = 0.2$
$h \qquad = 0.375$
$G \qquad = 2.6$
$e \qquad =?$

35. $l = \dfrac{G-1}{1+e}$ or $(G - 1)(1 - n)$
$= (2.6 - 1)(1. -0.375)$
$= 1.6 \times 0.625 = 1$

36. The critical gradient of a soil increases with decrease in void ratio.

37. The effective stress for soil is an abstract quantity.

38. The coefficient of permeability of clay is generally Between 10⁻⁵ and 10⁻⁸ mm/s.

39. Stoke's law does not hold good if the size of particles is greater than 0.2 mm and less than 0.2 μm.

40. The radius of the friction circle is equal to

$R \sin\phi$

41. Vane test is normally used to determine in-situ shear strength of soft clays.

42. For an undisturbed soil sample, the area ratio for the samples should be 10% or less.

43. The liquid limit (LL), plastic limit (PL), adn shrinkage limit (SL) of a cohesive soil satisfy the relation is "LL>PL>SL".

44. The specific energy E in a critical flow at depth yc occurring in a traingular channel is given by E = 1.25y$_c$.

45. The pressure gradient in the direction of flow is equal to the shear gradient normal to the direction of flow.

46. The separation of boundary layer takes place when the pressure gradient is positive.

47. To pipe systems in series are said to be equivalent when the total length of the pipes is same in both the systems.

48. Both Reynolds and Froude numbers assume significance in one examples is flow over spillways.

49. Streamlines and equipotential lines are orthogonal wherever they meet.

50. For turbulent flow in horizontal pipe, the pressure gradient varies linearly with distance.

51. Given that g = acceleration due to gravity and R = hydraulic mean depth, the Darcy-Weisbach friction factor is related of Manning's rugosity coefficient n as $\dfrac{8gn^2}{R^{1/3}}$.

52. The quantity of wood for the shutters of doors and windows is calculated in m^2.

53. The floor area includes the area of the balcony upto 50%.

54.
$$\text{Plinth area} = (14.7 + 0.3) \times (14.7 + 0.3)$$
$$= 225m^2$$

55. Thickness of Plastering is usually 12 mm.

56. Using straight line method annual depreciation D is equal to $\dfrac{Original\ cost - scrap\ value}{life\ in\ year}$

57. The following document contains detailed description of all items of work excluding their quantities, along with the current rates Schedule of rates.

58. Estimate for electrical wiring is prepared on the basis of number of points.

59. Turbidity of water is expressed in terms of silica scale.

60. Slow sand filter is more efficient for the removal of bacteria.

61. A septic tank is a combination of sedimentation and digestion tank.

62. A road connecting two towns is called a country road.

63. The thickness of base, in no case, should be more than 30 cm.

64. The number of sleepers used for rail varies from (n+4) to (n+7).

65. The relation between the radius of curve (R) and its degree of curvature (D) is given by $R = \dfrac{1746.5}{D}$.

66. The soil transported by glaciers either by ice or water is called drift.

67. Granite is mainly composed of quartz, felspar and mica.

68. The dressing of stone is done immediately after quarrying.

69. Excess of alumina in the clay makes the brick crack adn warp on drying.

70. The compressive strength of paving bricks should not be less than 40 MN/m^2.

71. Eminently hydraulic lime is one in which the percentage of silica, alumina and iron oxide is 25 to 30%.

72. The ultimate strength of cement is provided by di-calcium silicate.

73. The specific surface (in cm2/g) of a good Portland cement should no be less than 2250.

74. The defect caused due to over-maturity and unventilated storage of the wood during its transit, is called foxiness.

75. The timber whose thickness is less than 5 cm and the width exceeds 12 cm, is called a board.

76. Enamel paint is made by adding white lead in varnish.

77. The commonly used solvent in oil paints is turpentine/naptha.

78. The light-weight concrete is prepared by using coke-breeze, cinder or slag as aggregate in the concrete.

79. The breaking up of cohesion in a mass of concrete is called segreagation.

80. There is no one option is correct.

81. "Colocrete" is the commercial term for coloured cement.

82. If the slump of concrete mix is 70 mm, its workability is considered to be medium.

83. As per IS : 459 – 1978, the concrete mixes are designated into 7 grades.

84. To prevent segregation, the concrete should not be thrown from a hight of more than 1 m.

85. The window usualy provided near the main roof of a room and opens above the adjoining verandah, is called clerestorey window.

86. The most commonly used bond for all wall thicknesses is english bond.

87. A bat is the portion of a brick cut across the width.

88. The most commonly used material for damp proofing is bitumen.

89. The curvature of the earth is taken into consideration if the limit of survey is more than 250 km^2.

90. The correction to be applied to each 30 m chain for a line measured along a slope of θ is

$$30\,(1 - \cos\theta)$$

91. The lines of earth's magnetic field run from north of south.

92. Magnetic Bearing $= S35°30'E = 144°30'$

Magnetic Declination $= 4°$ East

True Bearing $= 144°30' + 4°$

$$= 148°30'$$
$$= S31°30'E$$

93. When the cross-hairs are not clearly visible the eye-piece should be focussed.

94. The multiplying constant for the tacheometer is f/i.

95. In route surveys, the most suitable method of contouring is by cross-sections.

96. The rise and fall method for obtaining the reduced levels of points provides a check on fore sights, back sights and intermediate sights.

97. Detailed estimate is the most correct estimate.

98. For electric wiring such as fan, light, plug etc., the estimate is made in terms of type of point.

99. The value of the property (without being dismantled) at the end of the useful life period is known as salvage value.

100. Wood work for doors and windows is measured in square metres.

101. For a circular section $I_{zz} = I_{xx} + I_{yy}$. Then zz-axis will be passing through point of intersection of xx and yy-axes and perpendicular to the plane of cross-section.

102. A simply supported beam is subjected to a central concentrated load. The slope at the two ends is given by

$$\frac{WL^2}{16EI}$$

103. A thin cylinder is the one in the variation is hoop stress along the thickness can be neglected.

104. The Euler crippling load for a column with one end fixed and the other hinged is

$$\frac{2\pi^2 EI}{L^2}$$

105. A cantilever beam of length l is subjected to a conentrated load of P newtons at its free end. The reaction at the fixed end will be Anti-clockwise moment Pl and an upward vertical force P.

106. The coefficient of permeability is proportional to void ratio as $e^3/1+e$.

107. The expression for critical gradient is $i_c = \dfrac{G-1}{1+e}$

108. If kx and kz are the permeability values in x and z directions respectively in a two dimensional flow situation, the equivalent coefficient of permeability ke is given by $k_e = \sqrt{k_x . k_z}$

109. A flownet may be used for the determination of exit gradient, seepage flow rate and seepage pressure.

110. Two or more footings connected by a beam is called as Strap footings.

111. Max amount of super elevation should not be greater than 7%.

112. When the distance between the axles 'l' and radius of curve is R then mechanical widening width is $\dfrac{l^2}{2R}$

113. Skidding occurs on wet pavement.

114. An instrument used to measure Roughness index is bump integrator.

115. Purpose of the seal coat is to provide an impervious layer.

116. The safe speed on a highway is 85th percentile speed.

117. Quick setting cement is used for the construction of structures under water.

118. The sand in mortar increases the volume of mortar, reduces the shrinkage and cracking and helps the pure lime to set by allowing penetration of air which provides the needed carbon dioxide.

119. The tensile strength of concrete to be used in the design of reinforced concrete members is

$$0.7\sqrt{f_{ck}}$$

120. The depths to N.A. in a singly reinforced section is given by

$$\frac{x_u}{d} = \frac{700}{1100 + 0.87f_y}$$

121. The effective width of flange in R.C.C. T-beams should be restricted to

$$\frac{l_0}{6} + b_\omega + 6D_f$$

122. For cantilever beams and slabs, the basic value of span to effective depth ratio is 7.

123. A compression member is termed as column or strut if the ratio of its effective length to the least lateral dimension is more than 3.

124. The minimum eccentricity that should be used in the design of any R.C.C. column is given by

$$\frac{unsupported\ lenght}{500} + \frac{leteral\ dimension}{30}$$

125. The maximum percentage of longitudinal reinforcement in R.C.C. columns is 6.0

Q.1 In linear measurement ,the correction for sag is :-
- **A.** Always additive
- **B.** Always subtractive
- **C.** Always zero
- **D.** Additive for "steel tape" and subtractive "metallic tape"

Q.2 If the quadrant bearing of a line is S 35⁰ then the whole circle bearing of the line is :-
- **A.** 325⁰ **B.** 145⁰ **C.** 215⁰ **D.** 125⁰

Q.3 In a simple curve if the angle of deflection is Δ degree then angle subtended by the long chord at the centre of the curve is :-
- **A.** $180° - \Delta$ **B.** Δ
- **C.** $\Delta/2$ **D.** 2Δ

Q.4 In plastic analysis of steel structures, at the location of plastic hinge:-
- **A.** Curvature is zero **B.** Curvature is infinite
- **C.** Moment is infinite **D.** Moment is zero

Q.5 The Indian Standard code used for Wind load analysis is:-
- **A.** Is 875 part-1 **B.** Is 875 part-2
- **C.** Is 875 part-3 **D.** IS875 part -4

Q.6 Effective length of a compression member of length L and Having both ends fixed, is :-
- **A.** 0.80 L **B.** L **C.** 0.65 L **D.** 2L

Q.7 SI unit of kinematic viscosity is :-
- **A.** N s/m² **B.** m²/s **C.** N/m **D.** N.s/m

Q.8 Surface tension of water :-
- **A.** Increases with increase in temperature
- **B.** Decreases with increase in temperature
- **C.** Independent of temperature
- **D.** None of the above is correct

Q.9 If f = friction coefficient for a pipe; Land D are length and diameter for the pipe respectively and V is velocity of flow through the pipe then according to Darcy-Weisbach equation the head loss due to friction resistance (h_f) is given by :-
- **A.** fLV^2/gD **B.** $2fLV^2/gD$
- **C.** $fLV^2/2gD$ **D.** $3fLV^2/4gD$

Q.10 If V = mean velocity; R = Hydraulic radius; S = bottom slop of channel and n = Manning's coefficient then Manning's formula for channel flow is given by :-
- **A.** $V = (R^{1/3} S^{1/2}) / n$ **B.** $V = (R^{1/2} S^{2/3}) / n$
- **C.** $V = (R^{2/3} S^{1/2}) / n$ **D.** $V = (R^{1/2} S^{1/3}) / n$

Q.11 A rectangular channel section will be most efficient when:-
- **A.** Hydraulic radius is equal to half the depth of flow
- **B.** Hydraulic radius is equal to the depth of flow
- **C.** Depth of flow is equal to the bottom width
- **D.** Depth of flow is equal to half the hydraulic radius

Q.12 The position of base course in a flexible pavement is :-
- **A.** Below the sub-base
- **B.** Over the sub-base
- **C.** Over the sub-grade but below sub-base
- **D.** Over the wearing course when renewal of surface is neede

Q.13 If a National Highway in plain terrain has a ruling design speed of 100 km per hour with super elevation (e) = 0.075 and friction coefficient =0.145 then the ruling minimum radius of such horizontal curve is close to :-
- **A.** 430 m **B.** 360 m **C.** 250 m **D.** 170 m

Q.14 For a vehicle with a speed of V m/s on a road surface with the coefficient of friction f and acceleration due to gravity g, the braking distance is given by :-
- **A.** V^2 / gf **B.** $V^2 / 2gf$ **C.** $2V^2 / gf$ **D.** $V^2 / 4gf$

Q.15 As per IRC recommendations the ruling gradient for plain terrain is :-
- **A.** 1 in 15 **B.** 1 in 20 **C.** 1 in 40 **D.** 1 in 30

Q.16 'CPM' stands for :-
- **A.** Critical Project Management
- **B.** Critical Project Monitoring
- **C.** Critical Path Method
- **D.** Creative Project Management

Q.17 In a construction project, "Parallel Activities" are those activities which can be performed:-
- **A.** One after the other and are dependent on each other
- **B.** One after the other and are independent of each other
- **C.** Simultaneously and are dependent on each other
- **D.** Simultaneously and are independent of each other

Q.18 On highways the sign of "Dead Slow" is a :-
- **A.** Regulatory sign **B.** Warning sign
- **C.** Information sign **D.** None of these

Q.19 Alligator or map cracking is the common type of failure in :-
- **A.** Bituminous surfacing
- **B.** Water Bound Macadam {WBM}
- **C.** Concrete pavements
- **D.** Gravel Roads

Q.20 If the soil sample has water content = 20%; specific gravity = 2.70; and void ratio = 0.75 then degree of saturation of the given sample is :-
- **A.** 68% **B.** 13.8%
- **C.** 54% **D.** None of these

Q.21 If the ratio (e) of a given soil sample is 0.77 then its porosity (n) is :-

A. 0.435%

B. 43.50%

C. 23.3%

D. Data given are insufficient to calculate porosity

Q.22 If V = mean velocity; R = Hydraulic radius; S = bottom slop of channel and n = Manning's coefficient then Manning's formula for channel flow is given by :-

A. $\frac{p}{\omega}\left(\frac{1+\sin\phi}{1-\sin\phi}\right)^2$ **B.** $\frac{p}{\omega}\left(\frac{1+\sin\phi}{1-\sin\phi}\right)$

C. $\frac{p}{\omega}\left(\frac{1-\sin\phi}{1+\sin\phi}\right)$ **D.** $\frac{p}{\omega}\left(\frac{1-\sin\phi}{1+\sin\phi}\right)^2$

Q.23 The particle size distribution curve with steep slope indicates that the type of soil is:-

A. Well graded soil   **B.** Gap graded soil

C. Uniform size soil   **D.** None of the above

Q.24 If the plasticity index of a soil mass is zero, the type of soil is :-

A. Sand   **B.** Clay

C. Silt   **D.** Clayey silt

Q.25 Lime stabilization is very effective in treating

A. Sandy soils   **B.** Silty soils

C. Non-plastic soils   **D.** Plastic Clayey soils

Q.26 The lime produced by slaking burnt lime stone with just sufficient quantity of water required to complete the chemical reaction and which is available in the form of dry powder is :-

A. Fat lime   **B.** Hydrated lime

C. Lime putyd   **D.** Hydraulic lime

Q.27 In Portland cement the compound first to set after adding water is :-

A. Tetra-calcium alumino-ferrite

B. Di-calcium silicate

C. Tri-calcium silicate

D. Tri-calcium aluminate

Q.28 For testing of compressive strength of cement, the size of cube mould is:-

A. 10 cm   **B.** 7.06 cm   **C.** 50 cm   **D.** 15 cm

Q.29 The vertical distance between the springing line and the highest point of the inner curve of an arch is known as :-

A. Intrados   **B.** Rise

C. Span   **D.** Thickness

Q.30 Minimum thickness of wall where single Flemish bond can be used is :-

A. Half brick thick

B. One brick thick

C. One and Half brick thick

D. Two brick thick

Q.31 If P is standard consistency of the given cement sample, then quantity of water to be added to prepare a cement paste for determining the initial setting time is :-

A. (P/4 + 3)% of weight of cement

B. 0.85 P% of weight of cement

C. P% of weight of cement

D. 0.78 P% of weight of cement

Q.32 Le-Chatelier test detects the unsoundness of cement due to :-

A. Excess magnesia only

B. Free lime only

C. Both excess magnesia and free lime

D. None of the above

Q.33 Aluminium powder in concrete is used as:-

A. Retarder   **B.** Air-entraining agent

C. Accelerator   **D.** Super plasticizer

Q.34 The height of the mould (cone) used for slump test is :-

A. 450 mm   **B.** 300 mm   **C.** 200 mm   **D.** 100 mm

Q.35 To control the deflection limit state, the basic values of span to effective depth ratio (As per IS 456-2000) for simply supported and continuous beams are kept as :-

A. 20 and 26 respectively

B. 7 and 20 respectively

C. 26 and 20 respectively

D. 20 and 7 respectively

Q.36 In limit state design of reinforced concrete structures the partial safety factors for strength of concrete and steel taken as :-

A. 1.50 and 1.20 respectively

B. 3.00 and 1.50 respectively

C. 1.50 and 1.15 respectively

D. 2.50 and 1.50 respectively

Q.37 A helically reinforced column of 300 mm diameter has 6 bars of 24 mm diameter as longitudinal reinforcement provided at an effective cover of 60 mm and spiral of 8 mm diameter provided at clear cover of 40 mm. The core diameter of the this column is :-

A. 212 mm   **B.** 220 mm   **C.** 180 mm   **D.** 204 mm

Q.38 In limit state design of reinforced concrete structures the value of limiting neutral axis depth factor X_{umax} depends upon :-

A. Grade of concrete only

B. Grade of steel only

C. Grade of concrete and steel both

D. None of the these

Q.39 A septic tank is :-

A. Aerobic method of on-site sewage treatment

B. Anaerobic method of on-site sewage treatment

C. Physical method of water treatment

D. Physico-chemical method of water treatment

Q.40 The probability P and the recurrence interval T_r are related as :

A. $P = T_r$ **B.** $P = 2T_r$ **C.** $p^2 = T_r$ **D.** $P = 1/T_r$

Q.41 If the line of action of the resultant forces on the dam lies outside the middle third of the base, then the dam is susceptible to :-

A. Crushing failure   **B.** Tension failure

C. Sliding failure   **D.** Overturning failure

Q.42 Khosala's formula for the long range run off assumes that the losses are function of :-

A. Temperature   **B.** Wind velocity

C. Relative Humidity   **D.** Evaporation

Q.43 The temporary hardness of water is caused by :-

A. Bi-carbonates of calcium and magnesium

B. Sulphates of calcium and magnesium

C. Chlorides of calcium and magnesium

D. Nitrates of calcium and magnesium

Q.44 The removal of dissolved organic matter occurs in :-

A. Slow sand filters   **B.** Trickling filters

C. Rapid sand filters   **D.** Dual media filter

Q.45 An isochrone is a line on the basin map :-

A. Joining points of having equal reduced levels {R.L.}

B. Joining points having equal time of travel of surface-runoff to the catchment outlet

C. Joining points having equal rainfall depth in a given time internal

D. Joining points which are at equal from the catchment outlet

Q.46 A rectangular bar having cross section A, length L, modulus of elasticity E and Poisson's ratio 1/m, is subjected to axial pull of P. The volumetric strain will be given by :-

A. $\frac{PL}{AE}\left(1-\frac{2}{m}\right)$ **B.** $\frac{P}{AE}\left(1-\frac{2}{m}\right)$

C. $\frac{PL}{AE}\left(1-\frac{1}{m}\right)$ **D.** $\frac{P}{AE}\left(1-\frac{1}{m}\right)$

Q.47 In a thin cylindrical shell, the ratio of longitudinal stress to hoop stress is:-

A. 0.5   **B.** 1   **C.** 2   **D.** 4

Q.48 The greatest amount of strain energy per unit volume that a material can absorb up to its elastic limit is :-

A. Toughness Index   **B.** Proof resilience

C. Resilience   **D.** Potential energy

Q.49 Ratio of the maximum shear stress intensity to average shear stress intensity for a rectangular section as:-

A. 3/2   **B.** 4/3   **C.** 5/2   **D.** 2/1

Q.50 Shape to the Force Diagram for a simply supported beam (AB) subjected to point load W at the centre of span shall be :-

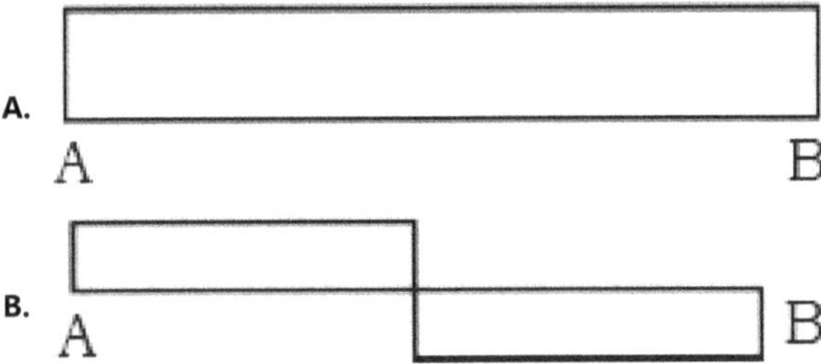

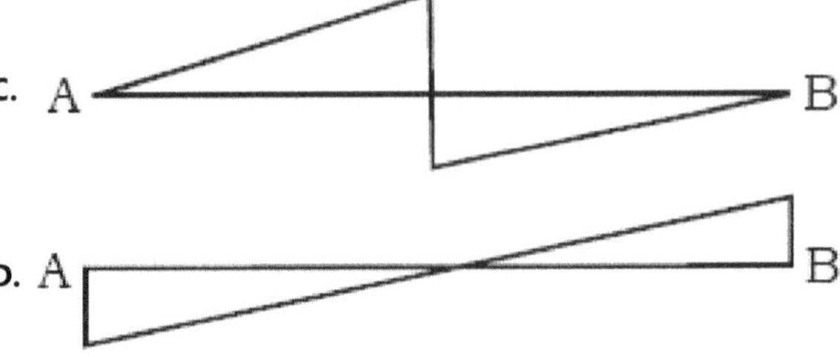

Q.51 The degree of indeterminacy of the following beam for general case of loading is :

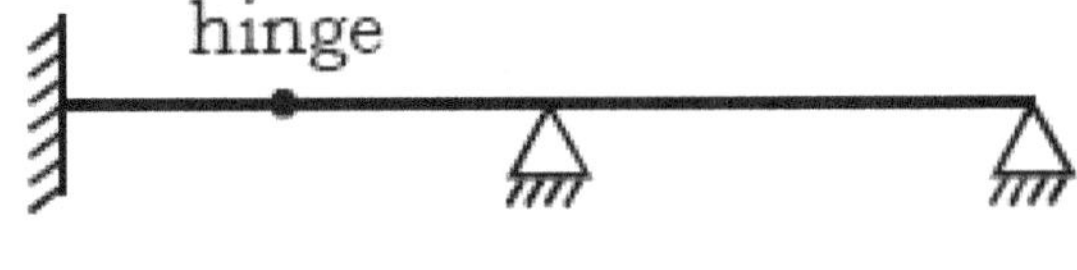

A. 01   **B.** 02   **C.** 03   **D.** 04

Q.52 The moment k required to rotate the near end of a prismatic beam through unit angle without translation, the far end being fixed, is given by :-

A. EI/L   **B.** 2EI/L   **C.** 3EI/L   **D.** 4EI/L

Q.53 If an element of a stressed body is in the state of pure shear with magnitude of shear stress as 80 N/mm² then the principal stress at that element is :-

A. 40 N/mm²   **B.** 120 N/mm²

C. 148 N/mm²   **D.** 80 N/mm²

Q.54 A cantilever beam of span 3 m is subjected to uniformly distributed load of 80 kN/m throughout the span. Determine the value of point load that can be applied in upward direction at free end in order to gave the resulting deflection at free end as zero:-

A. 30 kN   **B.** 90 kN   **C.** 60 kN   **D.** 80 kN

Q.55 Which one of the following statements is incorrect when lintels are compared with arches :-

A. Lintels are simpler in construction

B. Arches does not require strong abutments (walls) to withstand the arch thrust

C. Arches require more head room to span the openings.

D. Lintels transfer the loads vertically to the walls.

Q.56 In case of a framed RCC Construction, the form work to be removed first are :-

A. Bottom of beams

B. Bottom of roof slab

C. Sides of beams

D. Any of Bottom of beams or Bottom of roof slab

Q.57 A fluid, which satisfies the relation $\tau' = \mu(du/dv)$, where $\{\beta\}$ is shear stress, μ constant of proportionality and (du/dy) is the rate of deformation, is known as :-

A. Newtonian fluid

B. Non-Newtonian fluid

C. Thixotropic fluid/substance

D. Plastic

Q.58 What shall be pressure head of a liquid of specific gravity 0.8 for a pressure head of 100 m of water :-

A. 80 m   **B.** 125 m   **C.** 160 m   **D.** 64 m

Q.59 Hydraulic radius is equal to the :-
A. Area divided by the square of wetted perimeter
B. Area divided by the wetted perimeter
C. Wetted perimeter divided by the Area
D. Square root of the area

Q.60 A list of air pollutants is given below : a) Sulphur dioxide b) Carbon monoxide c) Radioactive substances d) Sulphuric acid Which of these are 'primary' pollutants :-
A. 'a' and 'b' only   **B.** 'a', 'b' and 'c' only
C. 'a' and 'd' only   **D.** 'c' and 'd' only

Q.61 A 30 -m steel tape was standardized at 20^0C. The tape was used when the ambient temperature was 40^0. A 30 -m length measured with the tape will actually be (take coefficient of expansion of tape material as 15×16^{-6})
A. 30.09 m   **B.** 30.009 m
C. 29.991 m   **D.** 29.91 m

Q.62 Two consecutive readings in the levelling data are 1.445 m and 1.955 m. The first is a foresight and the second is a backsight. Then,
A. the rise from the first point to second point is 0.51 m.
B. the fall from the first point to second point is 0.51 m.
C. the two readings are taken to the same point from two instrument stations.
D. the level difference between the two points is 3.410 m.

Q.63 When the contour lines having the same colour interval are farther apart, it shows a :-
A. plane surface   **B.** very steep slope
C. gentle slope   **D.** A valley

Q.64 The distance formula for finding distances using a theodolite, for a horizontal line of sight, is (K is multiplying constant, s is intercept and C is additive constant):-
A. K + Cs   **B.** Ks + C   **C.** K/s + C   **D.** K + C/s

Q.65 A total station can measure :-
A. Only distances electronically
B. Only horizontal angles accurately
C. Horizontal and vertical angles and distances
D. Vertical angles and distance only

Q.66 The damp proof course (D.P.C.) is measured is :-
A. Meters   **B.** Sqm.
C. Cubic meters   **D.** Litres

Q.67 The water treatment required for water obtained from a deep tube well is :-
A. Co agulation and flocculation only
B. Filtration only
C. Disinfection only
D. Co agulation, flocculation and filtration

Q.68 In a rapid gravity filter :-

A. Raw water from a river reservoir is supplied as input
B. Disinfected water is the input
C. Water passed through co agulation tank is the input
D. Water after settling only is the usual input

Q.69 Drinking water is to have a MAXIMUM content/value of some substances/characteristics. Which of the following does have a limit on its MINIMUM value as well :-
A. Total hardness   **B.** Dissolved solids
C. Turbidity   **D.** pH

Q.70 As per IS:1172-1963, water required per head per day for average domestic purposes is approximately equal to :-
A. 25 litters   **B.** 75 litters
C. 135 litters   **D.** 350 litters

Q.71 Which one of the following pairs is not correctly matched for bitumen properties :-
A. Softening point - Between 35⁰C to 70⁰C
B. Specific gravity of pure bitumen - 0.97 to 1.02
C. Pure Bitumen - Completely soluble in carbon tetrachloride
D. Pensky Marten Flash Point - Minimum specified is 50⁰C

Q.72 If the velocity, pressure, density etc. do not change at a point with respect to time, the flow is called :-
A. Uniform   **B.** Non uniform
C. Incompressible   **D.** Steady

Q.73 Flow in a circular pipe will be laminar if Reynold's number is :
A. Less than 2000
B. More than 4000
C. Between 2000 - 4000
D. None of these

Q.74 Condition favouring the adoption of sprinkler irrigation method is/are :-
A. When the water is available with difficulty and is scarce.
B. When the water table is low.
C. When the land soil is excessively permeable or when the soil is 'highly impermeable.'
D. When the water is available with difficulty and is scarce And When the land soil is excessively permeable or when the soil is 'highly impermeable.'

Q.75 The critical shear stress, at which incipient motion of sediment takes place is proportional to :-
A. $\sqrt{particle\ size}$ **B.** (Particle size)²
C. Particle size   **D.** (Particle size)¹ᐟ³

Q.76 A lined alluvial canal is best designed on the basis of :-
A. Lacey's formula   **B.** Kennedy's formula
C. Continuity equation   **D.** Manning's formula

Q.77 If two canals are taken off from both the flanks of a river at the site of a diversion headwork, then the number of undersluices and divide walls, will respectively be ;
A. 2 and 2   **B.** 1 and 1   **C.** 1 and 2   **D.** 2 and 1

Q.78 The 'useful storage' in a dam reservoir is the volume of water stored between :-

A. Normal and maximum reservoir levels
B. Minimum and normal reservoir levels
C. Minimum and maximum reservoir levels
D. Up to normal reservoir level including dead storage

Q.79 The bottom portion of a concrete or a masonry gravity dam is usually stepped, in order to :-
A. Increase the shear strength at the base of the dam
B. Decrease the shear strength at the base of the dam
C. Increase the overturning resistance of the dam
D. Increase the weight of the dam only.

Q.80 If 'p' the precipitation, 'a' is the area represented by a raingauge, and 'n' is the number of raingauges in the catchment area, then the weighted mean rainfall is :-
A. $\sum ap/n$
B. $\sum ap^2/\sum a^2$
C. $\sum ap/\sum a$
D. $\sum ap^3/\sum a^2$

Q.81 Bhakra dam of our country is located in the state of :-
A. Punjab
B. Uttar Pradesh
C. Madhya Pradesh
D. Himachal Pradesh

Q.82 The value of Poisson's ration of the materials lie between :-
A. 1 and 2
B. 0 and 1/2
C. 0 and 1
D. 2 and 3

Q.83 The value of stress up to which a member regains its original shape or size after load removal is called :-
A. Elastic limit
B. Proportional limit
C. Yield stress
D. Plastic limit

Q.84 The slope of the bending moment diagram of any section of a loaded beam is :-
A. Torsion at the section.
B. Maximum shear force of the beam.
C. Shear force at that section.
D. Maximum bending moment of the beam.

Q.85 In conjugate beam, the loading is equal to :-
A. Shear force diagram of actual beam
B. Bending moment diagram of actual beam
C. Loading of actual beam
D. M/EI diagram of actual beam

Q.86 What kind of bending moments, (if any) are developed at the intermediate support of a continuous beam loaded by vertical loads :-
A. Hogging
B. Sagging
C. No moment
D. Mostly sagging, but sometimes zero.

Q.87 Written below are same types of structures :- a) Beams b) Frames c) Trusses Miller - Breslau's principle is applicable to which types of strictures, select correct answer from the following :-
A. (a) only
B. (b) only
C. (a) and (b) only
D. (a), (b) and (c)

Q.88 Silt particle size as per unified soil classification system is :-
A. > 4.75 mm
B. 0.075 to 4.75 mm
C. 0.002 to 0.075 mm
D. < 0.002 mm

Q.89 A sand sample of 25 cm length was subjected to a constant head permeability in a permeameter having an area of $30 cm^2$. A discharge of $120 cm^2$ was obtained in a period of 1 minute under a head of 40 cm. The coefficient of permeability is equal to :-
A. (1/240) cm/sec
B. 2.4 cm/sec
C. (1/24) cm/sec
D. 24 cm/sec

Q.90 Which one of the following statements is incorrect is respect to shear strength of granular soils :-
A. It is affected largely by the initial void ratio.
B. It is not affected by the effective stresses.
C. The cohesion value of uncemented granular soil is approximately zero.
D. Undrained strength is insignificant except during the earthquake.

Q.91 Which of the following statements is incorrect in respect to capillarity in soils :-
A. Gravitational water may be removed from soils by drainage.
B. At the water table, the pore water pressure is greater than zero.
C. Capillary water is held above the water table by 'surface tension'.
D. Capillary rise is controlled by pore size and not the grain size, and that the same soil mass with the same D10 can have different pore size distributions depending upon soil structure and fabric, geological history etc.

Q.92 Which one of the following pairs is not correctly matched in context of IS456 provisions for reinforced concrete :-
A. Footing Design - Punching shear generally considered.
B. Concrete Cover - Essential for durability.
C. Beams are mostly - without shear reinforcement.
D. Roof slab design may be - Without shear reinforcement.

Q.93 Side face reinforcement is required when the depth of beam is :-
A. Greater than 750 mm
B. Greater then 1000 mm
C. Greater then 300 mm
D. Greater then 500 mm

Q.94 For design of slabs, IS456 specifies effective span to overall depth ratios, this is to safeguard mainly :-
A. Strength Criterion
B. Deflection Criterion
C. Crack widths
D. Temperature stresses

Q.95 Specify the percentage increase in load carrying capacity (specified in IS456) for a column having longitudinal reinforcement tied with spirals as compared to the allowable load for it with lateral ties :-
A. 10%
B. 20%
C. 25%
D. 5%

Q.96 Which of the following types of losses of prestressing occurs only in pretensioning and not in post-tensioning case :-
A. Friction
B. Creep of concrete
C. Relaxation of stress in steel
D. Elastic shortening (deformation) of concrete

Q.97 The effective length of the fillet weld is :-
A. 0.7 × total length
B. total length − $\sqrt{2}$× weld size
C. total length − 2 × throat size
D. total length − 2 × weld size

Q.98 For same load, unsupported length and end conditions a laced column as compared to a battened column :-
A. is stronger
B. is weaker
C. is equally strong
D. cannot be compared

Q.99 Consider the following statements :- Bearing stiffeners are provided in a plate girder (a) to avoid local bending failure of flange (b) to prevent buckling of web (c) to strengthen the web (d) under uniformly distributed loads. Which of these statements are correct ?
A. (a), (b) and (c)
B. (b) and (c)
C. (a), (c) and (d)
D. (a), (b) and (d)

Q.100 The design wind speed depends upon (a) risk coefficient (b) topography of the area (c) size of the structure of the above,
A. (a), (b) are correct
B. (b), (c) are correct
C. (c), (a) are correct
D. (a), (b) and (c) are correct

Q.101 Fly ash is residue generated from :
A. Chemical Industries
B. Hydel Power Plant
C. Nuclear Power Plants
D. Thermal Power Plants

Q.102 Marble is a :
A. Igneous Rock
B. Sedimentry Rock
C. Metamorphic Rock
D. Granite Rock

Q.103 The two main compounds of ordinary Portland cement are :
A. Tricalcium silicate and dicalcium silicate
B. Dicalcium Silicate and alkali oxide
C. Tricalcium aluminates and alkali oxide
D. Tricalcium silicate and alkali oxide

Q.104 The strength of concrete is directly proportional :
A. Water Cement Ratio
B. Cement water ratio
C. Sand Cement Ratio
D. Water aggregate Ratio

Q.105 Cross staff is an instrument used for :
A. Measuring approximate horizontal angles
B. Setting out right angles
C. Measuring bearings of the line
D. None of These

Q.106 The variation of the bending moment in the segment of a beam where the load is uniformly distributed is :
A. Zero
B. Linear
C. Parabolic
D. Cubic

Q.107 The radius of Mohr's circle gives the value of :
A. minimum normal stress
B. minimum shear stress
C. maximum normal stress
D. maximum shear stress

Q.108 The diameter of lateral ties in a column is taken as :
A. 1/4 diameter of the largest longitudinal bar
B. 6 mm
C. Greater of 1/4 diameter of the largest longitudinal bar or 6 mm
D. None of These

Q.109 Concrete in sea water shall be at least .... grade in case of reinforced concete.
A. M20   **B.** M25   **C.** M30   **D.** M40

Q.110 A beam shall be deemed to be a deep beam when the ratio of effective span to overall depth is less than ...... for a continuous beam.
A. 2.5   **B.** 3   **C.** 3.5   **D.** 4

Q.111 Number of phases in soil mass is :
A. 1   **B.** 2   **C.** 3   **D.** 4

Q.112 Surface tension of water
A. Increase with decrease in temperature
B. Decrease with decrease in temperature
C. Is independent of temperature
D. None of these

Q.113 For a fully submerged body of homogeneous composition, the centre of buoyancy always
A. Coincides with the centre of gravity
B. Coincides with the centroid of the volume of fluid displaced
C. Remains above the centre of gravity
D. Remains below the centre of gravity

Q.114 Which notch is preferable for low flow rates
A. rectangular
B. triangular
C. Both Rectangular and Triangular
D. None of these

Q.115 An artesian aquifer is the one where
A. Water surface under the ground is at atmospheric pressure
B. Water is under pressure between two impervious strata
C. Water table serves as upper surface of zone of saturation
D. None of these

Q.116 The alum when added as a coagulant in water
A. Does not require alkalinity in water for flocculation

B. Does not affect pH value of water

C. Increase pH value of water

D. Decrease pH value of water

Q.117 MPN index is a measure of which one of the following

A. B.O.D.   **B.** Hardness

C. D.O.   **D.** Coliform Bacteria

Q.118 The type of valve which allows water to flow in one direction but prevents its flow in the reverse direction is

A. Reflux valve   **B.** Sluice valve

C. Air relief valve   **D.** Pressure relief valve

Q.119 Distance between the centres of two adjacent fastners in a line, lying in the direction of stress in tension members should be :

A.   < 16 t or 200 mm whichever is less

B.   < 32 t or 300 mm whichever is less

C.   > 16 t or 200 mm whichever is more

D.   > 32 or 300 mm whichever is more

Q.120 The shoulder provided along the road edge should be

A.   Rougher than the traffic lanes

B.   Smoother than the traffic lanes

C.   Of same colour as that of the pavement

D.   Of very low load bearing capacity

Q.121 Width of carriage way for a single lane is recommended to be

A. 7.5 m   **B.** 7.0 m   **C.** 3.75 m   **D.** 5.5 m

Q.122 The most suitable equipment for compacting clayey soils is a

A.   smooth wheeled roller

B.   pneumatic tyred roller

C.   sheep foot roller

D.   vibrator

Q.123 The shape of the camber, best suited for cement concrete pavements, is

A.   straight line

B.   parabolic

C.   elliptical

D.   combination of straight and parabolic

Q.124 Which one is the correct sequence of various operations of preparation of BrickEarth

I. Blending

II. Digging

III. Weathering

IV. Unsoiling

V. Tempering

A. IV, II, III, V, I   **B.** IV, II, III, I, V

C. II, IV, V, III, I   **D.** II, III, IV, V, I

Q.125 Normally the Mastic Asphalt is used for

A. fire proofing   **B.** sound insulation

C. water proofing   **D.** None of these

// Smart Answer Sheet //

Correct Percentage of students who answered correctly. **Skipped** Percentage of students who skipped.

Q.	Ans.	Correct / Skipped	Q.	Ans.	Correct / Skipped	Q.	Ans.	Correct / Skipped	Q.	Ans.	Correct / Skipped	Q.	Ans.	Correct / Skipped
1	B	58.33 % / 4.17 %	17	D	8.33 % / 37.5 %	33	B	25.0 % / 20.83 %	49	A	58.33 % / 29.17 %	65	C	33.33 % / 29.17 %
2	C	29.17 % / 33.33 %	18	A	20.83 % / 29.17 %	34	B	66.67 % / 25.0 %	50	B	62.5 % / 25.0 %	66	B	75.0 % / 25.0 %
3	B	8.33 % / 25.0 %	19	A	25.0 % / 16.67 %	35	A	58.33 % / 25.0 %	51	C	16.67 % / 33.33 %	67	C	20.83 % / 33.34 %
4	B	29.17 % / 45.83 %	20	D	41.67 % / 33.33 %	36	C	75.0 % / 20.83 %	52	D	25.0 % / 33.33 %	68	C	20.83 % / 37.5 %
5	C	29.17 % / 33.33 %	21	B	45.83 % / 37.5 %	37	B	8.33 % / 45.84 %	53	D	12.5 % / 45.83 %	69	D	0 % / 100 %
6	C	62.5 % / 25.0 %	22	D	50.0 % / 29.17 %	38	B	25.0 % / 29.17 %	54	B	16.67 % / 45.83 %	70	C	66.67 % / 29.16 %
7	B	50.0 % / 29.17 %	23	C	37.5 % / 16.67 %	39	B	50.0 % / 33.33 %	55	B	37.5 % / 25.0 %	71	D	33.33 % / 20.84 %
8	B	58.33 % / 25.0 %	24	A	58.33 % / 25.0 %	40	D	29.17 % / 37.5 %	56	C	45.83 % / 29.17 %	72	D	41.67 % / 20.83 %
9	C	33.33 % / 29.17 %	25	D	45.83 % / 33.34 %	41	B	12.5 % / 33.33 %	57	A	29.17 % / 37.5 %	73	A	62.5 % / 29.17 %
10	C	37.5 % / 29.17 %	26	B	29.17 % / 29.16 %	42	A	0 % / 100 %	58	B	29.17 % / 29.16 %	74	D	50.0 % / 25.0 %
11	A	54.17 % / 25.0 %	27	D	50.0 % / 20.83 %	43	A	62.5 % / 20.83 %	59	B	54.17 % / 25.0 %	75	C	8.33 % / 41.67 %
12	B	25.0 % / 25.0 %	28	B	62.5 % / 29.17 %	44	B	33.33 % / 25.0 %	60	B	25.0 % / 20.83 %	76	D	12.5 % / 29.17 %
13	B	25.0 % / 37.5 %	29	B	58.33 % / 20.84 %	45	B	25.0 % / 33.33 %	61	B	12.5 % / 45.83 %	77	A	12.5 % / 45.83 %
14	B	45.83 % / 29.17 %	30	C	37.5 % / 25.0 %	46	B	8.33 % / 33.34 %	62	C	12.5 % / 33.33 %	78	B	25.0 % / 41.67 %
15	D	25.0 % / 29.17 %	31	B	62.5 % / 25.0 %	47	A	50.0 % / 25.0 %	63	C	8.33 % / 33.34 %	79	A	8.33 % / 25.0 %
16	C	58.33 % / 20.84 %	32	B	50.0 % / 20.83 %	48	B	41.67 % / 25.0 %	64	B	58.33 % / 33.34 %	80	C	29.17 % / 37.5 %

Q.	Ans.	Correct / Skipped	Q.	Ans.	Correct / Skipped	Q.	Ans.	Correct / Skipped	Q.	Ans.	Correct / Skipped	Q.	Ans.	Correct / Skipped
81	D	37.5 % / 20.83 %	90	B	8.33 % / 45.84 %	99	B	12.5 % / 29.17 %	108	C	50.0 % / 29.17 %	117	D	41.67 % / 25.0 %
82	B	62.5 % / 25.0 %	91	B	12.5 % / 41.67 %	100	D	45.83 % / 25.0 %	109	C	75.0 % / 20.83 %	118	A	62.5 % / 25.0 %
83	A	50.0 % / 33.33 %	92	C	12.5 % / 41.67 %	101	D	33.33 % / 29.17 %	110	A	41.67 % / 29.16 %	119	A	45.83 % / 25.0 %
84	C	12.5 % / 29.17 %	93	A	70.83 % / 20.84 %	102	C	75.0 % / 25.0 %	111	C	58.33 % / 20.84 %	120	A	54.17 % / 25.0 %
85	D	20.83 % / 41.67 %	94	B	58.33 % / 33.34 %	103	A	70.83 % / 29.17 %	112	A	50.0 % / 29.17 %	121	C	70.83 % / 20.84 %
86	A	20.83 % / 45.84 %	95	D	37.5 % / 33.33 %	104	B	20.83 % / 25.0 %	113	B	25.0 % / 20.83 %	122	C	62.5 % / 25.0 %
87	D	20.83 % / 50.0 %	96	D	25.0 % / 37.5 %	105	B	66.67 % / 29.16 %	114	B	25.0 % / 33.33 %	123	A	62.5 % / 20.83 %
88	C	54.17 % / 25.0 %	97	D	54.17 % / 29.16 %	106	C	45.83 % / 25.0 %	115	B	33.33 % / 29.17 %	124	B	29.17 % / 33.33 %
89	C	8.33 % / 41.67 %	98	A	25.0 % / 25.0 %	107	D	29.17 % / 20.83 %	116	D	25.0 % / 25.0 %	125	B	16.67 % / 33.33 %

//Hints and Solutions//

1. In linear measurement ,the correction for sag is always subtractive.

2. $R.B = 535°W$
$W.C.B = 180° + 35°$
$= 215°$

3.
$$e + f = \frac{V^2}{127R}$$
$$0.075 + 0.145 = \frac{(100)^2}{127R}$$
$$R = \frac{100\times100}{22\times127} \times 100$$
$$R = 360$$

4. In plastic analysis of steel structures, at the location of plastic hinge curvature is infinite.

5. The Indian Standard code used for Wind load analysis is Is 875 part-3.

6. Effective length of a compression member of length L and Having both ends fixed, is 0.65 L.

7. SI unit of kinematic viscosity is m^2/s .

8. Surface tension of water decreases with increase in temperature.

9. If f = friction coefficient for a pipe; Land D are length and diameter for the pipe respectively and V is velocity of flow through the pipe then according to Darcy-Weisbach equation the head loss due to friction resistance (hf) is given by fLV²/2gD .

10. If V = mean velocity; R = Hydraulic radius; S = bottom slop of channel and n = Manning's coefficient then Manning's formula for channel flow is given by V = (R²/³ S¹/²) / n

11. A rectangular channel section will be most efficient when hydraulic radius is equal to half the depth of flow.

12. The position of base course in a flexible pavement is over the sub-base.

13. If a National Highway in plain terrain has a ruling design speed of 100 km per hour with super elevation (e) = 0.075 and friction coefficient =0.145 then the ruling minimum radius of such horizontal curve is close to 360 m.

14. For a vehicle with a speed of V m/s on a road surface with the coefficient of friction f and acceleration due to gravity g, the braking distance is given by V² / 2gf.

15. As per IRC recommendations the ruling gradient for plain terrain is 1 in 30.

16. 'CPM' stands for Critical Path Method.

17. In a construction project, "Parallel Activities" are those activities which can be performed simultaneously and are independent of each other.

18. On highways the sign of "Dead Slow" is a regulatory sign.

19. Alligator or map cracking is the common type of failure in bituminous surfacing.

20. $Se = GW$
$$S = \frac{2.7\times0.2}{0.75}$$
$$= 72 \%$$

21. $n = \frac{e}{1+e}$
$$= \frac{0.77}{1.77}$$
$$= 43.5\%$$

22. If V = mean velocity; R = Hydraulic radius; S = bottom slop of channel and n = Manning's coefficient then Manning's formula for channel flow is given by :-

$$\frac{p}{\omega} \left(\frac{1-\sin\phi}{1+\sin\phi}\right)^2$$

23. The particle size distribution curve with steep slope indicates that the type of soil is uniform size soil.

24. If the plasticity index of a soil mass is zero, the type of soil is sand.

25. Lime stabilization is very effective in treating plastic Clayey soils.

26. The lime produced by slaking burnt lime stone with just sufficient quantity of water required to complete the chemical reaction and which is available in the form of dry powder is hydrated lime.

27. In Portland cement the compound first to set after adding water is tri-calcium aluminate.

28. For testing of compressive strength of cement, the size of cube mould is 7.06 cm.

29. The vertical distance between the springing line and the highest point of the inner curve of an arch is known as rise.

30. Minimum thickness of wall where single Flemish bond can be used is one and Half brick thick.

31. If P is standard consistency of the given cement sample, then quantity of water to be added to prepare a cement paste for determining the initial setting time is 0.85 P% of weight of cement.

32. Le-Chatelier test detects the unsoundness of cement due to free lime only.

33. Aluminium powder in concrete is used as air-entraining agent.

34. The height of the mould (cone) used for slump test is 300 mm.

35. To control the deflection limit state, the basic values of span to effective depth ratio (As per IS 456-2000) for simply supported and continuous beams are kept as 20 and 26 respectively.

36. In limit state design of reinforced concrete structures the partial safety factors for strength of concrete and steel taken as 1.50 and 1.15 respectively.

37. $Core\ dia = Total\ dia - 2 \times clear\ cover\ of\ helical\ bar$

$= 300 - 2 \times 40$

$= 220$

38. $X_{ulim} = \dfrac{700}{1100 + 0.87 f_y} \times d$

In limit state design of reinforced concrete structures the value of limiting neutral axis depth factor Xumax depends upon - Grade of steel only

39. A septic tank is anaerobic method of on-site sewage treatment.

40. The probability P and the recurrence interval T_r are related as-

P = 1/T_r

41. If the line of action of the resultant forces on the dam lies outside the middle third of the base, then the dam is susceptible to tension failure.

42. Khosala's formula for the long range run off assumes that the losses are function of temperature.

43. The temporary hardness of water is caused by bi-carbonates of calcium and magnesium.

44. The removal of dissolved organic matter occurs in trickling filters.

45. An isochrone is a line on the basin map joining points having equal time of travel of surface-runoff to the catchment outlet.

46. A rectangular bar having cross section A, length L, modulus of elasticity E and Poisson's ratio 1/m, is subjected to axial pull of P. The volumetric strain will be given by $\dfrac{P}{AE}\left(1 - \dfrac{2}{m}\right)$

47. $\sigma_l = \dfrac{pd}{4t}$

$\sigma_h = \dfrac{pd}{2t}$

$\dfrac{\sigma_l}{\sigma_h} = \dfrac{1}{2} = 0.5$

48. The greatest amount of strain energy per unit volume that a material can absorb up to its elastic limit is proof resilience.

49. Ratio of the maximum shear stress intensity to average shear stress intensity for a rectangular section as 3/2.

50. Shape to the Force Diagram for a simply supported beam (AB) subjected to point load W at the centre of span shall be

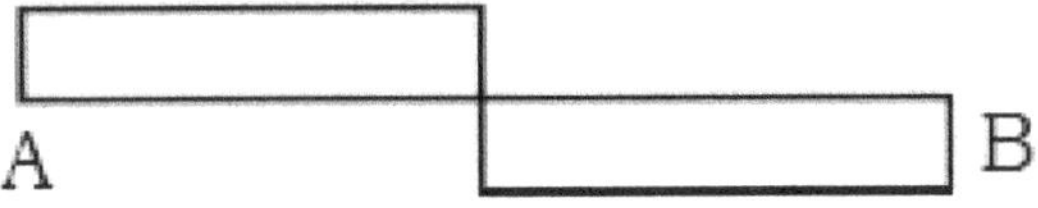

51. The degree of indeterminacy of the following beam for general case of loading is 03.

52. The moment k required to rotate the near end of a prismatic beam through unit angle without translation, the far end being fixed, is given by 4EI/L.

53. If an element of a stressed body is in the state of pure shear with magnitude of shear stress as 80 N/mm2 then the principal stress at that element is 80 N/mm².

54. $\dfrac{\omega_1 l^4}{8EI} - \dfrac{\omega_2 l^3}{3EI} = 0$

$\dfrac{\omega_1 l}{8} = \dfrac{\omega_2}{3}$

$\omega_2 = \dfrac{80 \times 3}{8} \times 3$

$= 90\ kN$

55. Arches does not require strong abutments (walls) to withstand the arch thrust statements is incorrect when lintels are compared with arches.

56. In case of a framed RCC Construction, the form work to be removed first are sides of beams.

57. A fluid, which satisfies the relation

$=\mu$ (du/dv), where {{}} is shear stress, μ constant of proportionality and (du/dy) is the rate of deformation, is known as Newtonian fluid.

58. $S_1 h_1 = S_2 h_2$

$0.8\ h_1 = 1 \times 100$

$h_2 = 125\ m$

59. Hydraulic radius is equal to the area divided by the wetted perimeter.

60. A list of air pollutants is given below : a) Sulphur dioxide b) Carbon monoxide c) Radioactive substances d) Sulphuric acid 'a', 'b' and 'c' are 'primary' pollutants.

61. $C_t = l \propto (t_m - t_s)$

$= 30 \times 15 \times 10^{-6} \times 20$

$C_t = 0.009m$

Correctly length measured $= 30 + 0.009$

$= 30.009m$

62. Two consecutive readings in the levelling data are 1.445 m and 1.955 m. The first is a foresight and the second is a backsight. Then the two readings are taken to the same point from two instrument stations.

63. When the contour lines having the same colour interval are farther apart, it shows a gentle slope.

64. The distance formula for finding distances using a theodolite, for a horizontal line of sight, is (K is multiplying constant, s is intercept and C is additive constant) Ks + C.

65. A total station can measure horizontal and vertical angles and distances.

66. The damp proof course (D.P.C.) is measured is sqm.

67. The water treatment required for water obtained from a deep tube well is disinfection.

68. In a rapid gravity filter water passed through co agulation tank is the input.

69. Drinking water is to have a MAXIMUM content/value of some substances/characteristics. Which of the following does have a limit on its MINIMUM value as well pH.

70. As per IS:1172-1963, water required per head per day for average domestic purposes is approximately equal to 135 litters.

71. Pensky Marten Flash Point - Minimum specified is 50^0C pairs is not correctly matched for bitumen properties.

72. If the velocity, pressure, density etc. do not change at a point with respect to time, the flow is called steady.

73. Flow in a circular pipe will be laminar if Reynold's number is less than 2000.

74. Condition favouring the adoption of sprinkler irrigation method is when the water is available with difficulty and is scarce And When the land soil is excessively permeable or when the soil is 'highly impermeable.'

75. The critical shear stress, at which incipient motion of sediment takes place is proportional to particle size.

76. A lined alluvial canal is best designed on the basis of Manning's formula.

77. If two canals are taken off from both the flanks of a river at the site of a diversion headwork, then the number of undersluices and divide walls, will respectively be 2 and 2.

78. The 'useful storage' in a dam reservoir is the volume of water stored between minimum and normal reservoir levels.

79. The bottom portion of a concrete or a masonry gravity dam is usually stepped, in order to increase the shear strength at the base of the dam.

80. If 'p' the precipitation, 'a' is the area represented by a raingauge, and 'n' is the number of raingauges in the catchment area, then the weighted mean rainfall is $\sum ap / \sum a$.

81. Bhakra dam of our country is located in the state of Himachal Pradesh.

82. The value of Poisson's ration of the materials lie between 0 and 1/2.

83. The value of stress up to which a member regains its original shape or size after load removal is called elastic limit.

84. The slope of the bending moment diagram of any section of a loaded beam is shear force at that section.

85. In conjugate beam, the loading is equal to M/EI diagram of actual beam.

86. Hogging bending moments, (if any) are developed at the intermediate support of a continuous beam loaded by vertical loads.

87. The correct answer is (a), (b) and (c)

Beams,Frames and Trusses Miller.

88. Silt particle size as per unified soil classification system is 0.002 to 0.075 mm.

89.
$$A = 30m^2$$
$$Q = 120cm^3$$
$$t = 1 \text{ minute} = 60sec$$
$$h = 40cm$$
$$L = 25cm$$
$$\frac{Q}{t} = KiA \quad \left(i = \frac{h}{l}\right)$$
$$k = \frac{Q \times l}{h \times A \times t}$$
$$= \frac{120 \times 25}{40 \times 30 \times 60}$$
$$= \frac{50}{1200}$$
$$= \frac{1}{24}$$

90. It is not affected by the effective stresses.

91. At the water table, the pore water pressure is greater than zero.

92. Beams are mostly - without shear reinforcement pairs is not correctly matched in context of IS456 provisions for reinforced concrete.

93. Side face reinforcement is required when the depth of beam is greater than 750 mm.

94. For design of slabs, IS456 specifies effective span to overall depth ratios, this is to safeguard mainly Deflection Criterion.

95. Specify the percentage increase in load carrying capacity (specified in IS456) for a column having longitudinal reinforcement tied with spirals as compared to the allowable load for it with lateral ties 5%

96. Elastic shortening (deformation) of concrete losses of prestressing occurs only in pretensioning and not in post-tensioning case.

97. The effective length of the fillet weld is total length – 2 × weld size.

98. For same load, unsupported length and end conditions a laced column as compared to a battened column is stronger.

99. The correct answer is (b)and (c).

To prevent buckling of web and To strengthen the web

100. The correct answer is a, b and c

(a) risk coefficient (b) topography of the area (c) size of the structure

101. Fly ash is residue generated from Thermal Power Plants.

102. Marble is a Metamorphic Rock.

103. The two main compounds of ordinary Portland cement are tricalcium silicate and dicalcium silicate.

104. The strength of concrete is directly proportional cement water ratio.

105. Cross staff is an instrument used for setting out right angles.

106. The variation of the bending moment in the segment of a beam where the load is uniformly distributed is parabolic.

107. The radius of Mohr's circle gives the value of maximum shear stress.

108. The diameter of lateral ties in a column is taken as greater of 1/4 diameter of the largest longitudinal bar or 6 mm.

109. Concrete in sea water shall be at least M30 grade in case of reinforced concete.

110. A beam shall be deemed to be a deep beam when the ratio of effective span to overall depth is less than 2.5 for a continuous beam.

111. Number of phases in soil mass is 3.

112. Surface tension of water increase with decrease in temperature.

113. For a fully submerged body of homogeneous composition, the centre of buoyancy always coincides with the centroid of the volume of fluid displaced.

114. Triangular notch is preferable for low flow rates.

115. An artesian aquifer is the one where water is under pressure between two impervious strata.

116. The alum when added as a coagulant in water decrease pH value of water.

117. MPN index is a measure of Coliform Bacteria.

118. The type of valve which allows water to flow in one direction but prevents its flow in the reverse direction is reflux valve.

119. Distance between the centres of two adjacent fastners in a line, lying in the direction of stress in tension members should be < 16 t or 200 mm whichever is less.

120. The shoulder provided along the road edge should be rougher than the traffic lanes.

121. Width of carriage way for a single lane is recommended to be 3.75 m.

122. The most suitable equipment for compacting clayey soils is a sheep foot roller.

123. The shape of the camber, best suited for cement concrete pavements, is straight line.

124. The correct answer is IV, II, III, I, V

IV. Unsoiling

II. Digging

III. Weathering

I. Blending

V. Tempering

125. Normally the Mastic Asphalt is used for sound insulation.

Q.1 A thin-walled cylindraical pressure vessel having a radius of 0.5 m and wall thickness of 25 mm is subjected to an internal pressure of 700 kPa. The hoop stress developed is

A. 14 MPa
B. 1.4 MPa
C. 0.14 MPa
D. 0.014 MPa

Q.2 What are relations between discharge velocity and seepage velocity through the soil sample?

A. $v = v_s n$
B. $v_s v n = 1$
C. $v_s = vn$
D. $n = v_s/v$

Q.3 A soil has liquid limit of 60%, plastic limit of 35%, and shrinkage limit of 20%. It has a natural moisture content of 50%. The liquidity index of soil is

A. 1.5   **B.** 1.25   **C.** 0.6   **D.** 0.4

Q.4 A dry soil has a mass specific gravity of 1.35. If the specific gravity of soilids is 2.7, then the void ratio will be

A. 0.5   **B.** 1.0   **C.** 1.5   **D.** 2.0

Q.5 In a laminar flow between two static parallel plates the velocity at midpoint is found to be 2.0 m/s. If the space between the plates is 10 cm, then the discharge per unit width (in m3/sm) will be

A. 0.01   **B.** 0.02   **C.** 010   **D.** 0.20

Q.6 Surface tension of water when in contact with air is 0.0737 N/m. The difference of pressure between inside and outside of a droplet of rain water 1 mm in diameter is nearly equal to

A. 0.15 kN/m^2
B. 0.20 kN/m^2
C. 0.25 kN/m^2
D. 0.30 kN/m^2

Q.7 The plan of a map was photocopied to a reduced size such that a line originally 100 mm, measures 90 mm. The original scale of the plan was 1 : 1000. The revised scale is

A. 1 : 900   **B.** 1 : 1111   **C.** 1 : 1121   **D.** 1 : 1221

Q.8 For a curve with degree of curve 5° 30' and deflection angle 60° , what will be the radius?

A. 343.8 m
B. 429.75 m
C. 312.54 m
D. 286.5 m

Q.9 Kaolin is chemically classified as

A. metamorphic rock
B. argillaceous rock
C. calcareous rock
D. silicious rock

Q.10 The kiln which may work throughout the year, is

A. Clamp
B. Bull's kiln
C. Hoffman's kiln
D. None of these

Q.11 Lime concrete is generally used for

A. Wall foundations
B. Flooring at ground level
C. Both {A} and {B}
D. Neither {A} nor {B}

Q.12 The minimum percentage of silica, alumina and derric oxide in lime for white washing is

A. 20   **B.** 15   **C.** 10   **D.** 0

Q.13 Due to attack of dry rot, the timber

A. Cracks
B. shrinks
C. Feduces to powder
D. None of these

Q.14 The most fire resistant paints are

A. enamel paints
B. aluminium paints
C. asbestos paints
D. cement paints

Q.15 Which one of the following is an air binding material

A. Gypsum
B. Acid resistant cement
C. Quick lime
D. All of these

Q.16 Name the type of cement from the following for canal linings

A. sulphate resisting cement
B. rapid hardening cement
C. quick setting cement
D. pozzuolana cement

Q.17 Bitumen completely dissolves in

A. Carbon bisulphide
B. Chloroform
C. Benzol
D. All of these

Q.18 The maximum permissible differential settlement, in case of foundations in clayey soil is usually limited to

A. 10 mm   **B.** 20 mm   **C.** 30 mm   **D.** 40 mm

Q.19 The process of working a flat for the finishing coat, is known

A. dubbing out
B. floating
C. knetting
D. blistering

Q.20 According to National Building Code the hydrants in water mains is provided at minimum interval of

A. 50 m   **B.** 60 m   **C.** 75 m   **D.** 90 m

Q.21 The limiting length of an offset does not depend upon

A. accuracy of the work
B. method of setting out perpendiculars
C. scale of plotting
D. indefinite features to be surveyed

Q.22 For the construction of highway (or railway)

A. longitudinal sections are required
B. cross sections are required
C. both longitudinal and cross sections are required
D. none of these

Q.23 The direction of steepest slope on a contour is

A. along the contour

B. at an angle of 45^0 to the contour
C. at right angles to the contour
D. None of these

Q.24 Magnetic declination at any place
A. remains constant
B. does'n remain constant
C. fluctuates
D. changes abruptly

Q.25 With usual notations, the expression V^2/gR represents
A. Centrifugal force
B. Centrifugal ratio
C. Super elevation
D. radial acceleration

Q.26 For indirect ranging, number of ranging rods required, is
A. 1   **B.** 2   **C.** 3   **D.** 4

Q.27 Bergchrund is a topograhical feature in
A. plains
B. water bodies
C. hills
D. glaciated region

Q.28 The distance between the point of intersection of an upgrade + g_1% and downgrade g_2% and the highest point of the vertical curve of length L, is
A. $\frac{L(g_1-g_2)}{400}$ **B.** $\frac{L(g_1+g_2)}{400}$ **C.** $\frac{L(g_1+g_2)}{800}$ **D.** $\frac{L(g_1-g_2)}{800}$

Q.29 The Huygen's telescope eye piece
A. is aplanatic
B. achromatic
C. Both (A) and (B)
D. Neither (A) non (B)

Q.30 The probable error of the adjusted bearing at the middle is
A. $\frac{1}{2}r\sqrt{n}$ **B.** $\frac{1}{3}r\sqrt{n}$ **C.** $\frac{1}{4}r\sqrt{n}$ **D.** $\frac{1}{5}r\sqrt{n}$

Q.31 A retarding force on a body does not
A. change the motion of the body
B. retard the motion of the body
C. introduce the motion of the body
D. None of these

Q.32 The C.G. of a hemisphere from its base measured along the vertical radius is at a distance of
A. $4R/3\pi$ **B.** 3R / 8   **C.** $3\pi R/4$ **D.** 8R/3

Q.33 Power developed by a torque is
A. $2\pi NT$ kg m/min   **B.** $\frac{2\pi NT}{4500}$ $h.p.$
C. $\frac{2\pi NT}{600}$ watts   **D.** All of the above

Q.34 The weakest section of a diamond riveting is the section which passes through
A. first row
B. second row
C. central raw
D. on rivet hole of end row

Q.35 The maximum resistance against rotation is offered by the weld at a point
A. most distant
B. least distant
C. at either end
D. centrally located

Q.36 Hooke's law states that stress and strain are
A. directly proportional
B. Inversely proportional
C. curvilinearly related
D. None of these

Q.37 An arch may be subjected to
A. shear and axial force
B. bending moment and shear force
C. bending moment and axial force
D. thrust, shear force and bending moment

Q.38 The resistance offered by a loaded section of a bar per unit area is called
A. stress
B. strain
C. intensity of stress
D. load

Q.39 Mercury is generally used in barometers because
A. its vaour pressure is practically zero
B. the height of the barometer will be less
C. it is a best liquid
D. both (A) and (B) above

Q.40 Hydraulic grade line
A. remains above the centre line of conduit
B. remains below the centre line of conduit
C. remains parallel the centre line of conduit
D. may be above or below the centre line of conduit

Q.41 Chezy's constant $C = \dfrac{157.6}{1.81+\frac{K}{\sqrt{M}}}$ is suggested by
A. Bazin   **B.** Kutter   **C.** Manning   **D.** Powell

Q.42 Flow of water in pipes of diameter more than 3 metres can be measured by
A. pitot tube
B. venturi meter
C. orifice plate
D. rotameter

Q.43 Non-over flow double curvature concrete arch, is provided in
A. Bhakra dam
B. Hirakund dam
C. Nagarajuna Sagar dam
D. Iddiki dam

Q.44 The value closure is said to be sudden if
A. t < L/C   **B.** t < 2L/C   **C.** t < 3L/C   **D.** t < 5L/C

Q.45 for critical depth of flow of water in open channels, f_c the specific energy must be
A. minimum
B. maximum
C. average of maximum and minimum
D. None of these

Q.46 Specific energy of a flowing fluid per unit weight is
A. $\frac{P}{W}+\frac{V^2}{2g}$ **B.** $\frac{P}{W}+\frac{V}{2g}$
C. $\frac{V^2}{2g}+h$ **D.** $\frac{P}{W}+\frac{V^2}{2g}+h$

Q.47 The run off a drainage basin is

A. Initial recharge + ground water accretion + precipitation

B. Precipitation + ground water accretion + Initial recharge

C. Precipitation – ground water accretion + Initial recharge

D. Precipitation – ground water accretion – Initial recharge

Q.48 The drop man holes are generally provided in sewers for

A. Industrial areas

B. large town ships

C. hilly town ships

D. cities in plains

Q.49 Primary treatment of sewage consists of removal of

A. large suspended organic solids

B. oil and grease

C. sand and grit

D. floating materials

Q.50 Which one of the following gases is most significant as air pollutant

A. Carbondioxde

B. Oxygen

C. Nitrogen

D. Sulphurdioxide

Q.51 The most efficient method of BOD removal, is

A. oxidation ditch

B. trickling filter

C. oxidation pond

D. aerated lagoon

Q.52 The inventor of the term soil mechanics, was

A. Kray

B. Dr. Karl Terzaghi

C. Leygue

D. Fellenius

Q.53 A pycnometer is used to determine

A. voids ratio

B. dry density

C. water content

D. density index

Q.54 The plasticity index is the numerical difference between

A. liquid limit and plastic limit

B. plastic limit and shrinkage limit

C. liquid limit and shrinkage limit

D. none of these

Q.55 The change of moisture content of soils, changes the

A. value of the angle of repose

B. amount of compaction required

C. cohesive strength of soil

D. all the above

Q.56 The capillary rise of water

A. depends upon the force responsible

B. increase as the size of the soil particles increase

C. decrease as the size of the soil particles decrease

D. is less in wet soil than in dry soil

Q.57 A failure wedge develops if a retaining wall

A. moves away from the backfill

B. moves towards the backfill

C. sinks downwards

D. stresses equally be vertical and horizontal forces

Q.58 To hydrate 500 kg cement fully, water needed is

A. 100 kg

B. 110 kg

C. 120 kg

D. 130 kg

Q.59 The commercial name of white and coloured cement in India is

A. Colocrete

B. Rainbow cement

C. Silvicrete

D. All the above

Q.60 The datum temperature for maturity by Plowman is

A. 23^0 C

B. 0^0 C

C. -5.6^0 C

D. -11.7^0 C

Q.61 If X, Y and Z are the fineness modulli of coarse, fine and combined aggregates, the percentage (P) of fine aggregates to combined aggregates, is

A. $P = \frac{Z-X}{Z+X} \times 100$

B. $P = \frac{X-Z}{Z-Y} \times 100$

C. $P = \frac{X-Z}{Z+Y} \times 100$

D. None of these

Q.62 While compacting the concrete by a mechanical vibrator, the slump should not exceed

A. 2.5 cm

B. 5.0 cm

C. 7.5 cm

D. 10 cm

Q.63 Common sugar can be suitably used

A. to delay the setting time of concrete

B. to accelerate the setting time of concrete

C. to increase the strength of concrete

D. None of these

Q.64 No shrinkage occurs if the concrete is placed in a relative humidity of

A. 100 percent

B. 85 percent

C. 70 percent

D. 50 percent

Q.65 Match List I with List II and select correct answer using the codes given below the lists:

List I (Bogue's compound)
(Tornebohm ompound)

List II

(A) C_3 S   1. Celite

(B) C_2 S   2. Fehte

(C) C_3 A   3. Belite

(D) C_4 AF   4. Alite

Code:

	A	B	C	D
A.	1	2	4	3
B.	4	3	2	1
C.	4	3	1	2
D.	3	2	1	4

Q.66 The maximum shear stress (q) in concrete of a reinforced cement concrete beam is

A. Shear force / Lever arm × Width

B. Lever arm / Shear force × Width

C. Width / Lever arm × Shear force

D. Shear force × Width / Lever arm

Q.67 The radius of a bar bend to form a hook, should not be less than

A. twice the diameter

B. thrice the diameter

C. four times the diameter

D. five times the diameter

Q.68 For initial estimate for a beam design the width is assumed

A. 1/15th of span

B. 1/20th of span

C. 1/25th of span   **D.** 1/30th of span

Q.69 The maximum diameter of a bar used in a ribbed slab, is

A. 12 mm   **B.** 6 mm   **C.** 20 mm   **D.** 22 mm

Q.70 A per IS : 1343, total shrinkage for a pretensioned beam is

A. 3.0×10^{-2} **B.** 3.0×10^{-3}

C. 3.0×10^{-4} **D.** 3.0×10^{-5}

Q.71 An RCC roof slab is designed as a two way slab if

A. It supports live loads in both directions

B. the ratio of spans in two directions is less than 2

C. the slab is continuous over two supports

D. the slab is discontinuous at edges

Q.72 Steel beam theory is used for

A. design of simple steel beams

B. steel beams encased in concrete

C. doubly reinforced beams ignoring compressive stress in concrete

D. beams if shear exceeds 4 times allowable shear stress.

Q.73 Design of RCC cantilever beams is based on the resultant force at

A. fixed end

B. free end

C. mid span

D. mid span and fixed support

Q.74 Failure of a reinforced concrete beam occurs as soon as the concrete strain in compression reaches:

A. 0.0025   **B.** 0.0030   **C.** 0.0035   **D.** 0.0040

Q.75 Yielding of steel in singly reinforced beam occurs in

A. balanced reinforced beam

B. under reinforced beam

C. over reinforced beam

D. none of these

Q.76 Rolled steel beams are designated by Indian standard series and its

A. weight per metre and depth of its section

B. depth of section and weight per metre

C. width of flange and weight per metre

D. weight per meter and flange width

Q.77 Maximum permissible slenderness ratio of compression members which carry dead and superimposed load, is

A. 350   **B.** 250   **C.** 180   **D.** 80

Q.78 The net area of round bars to resist the tension is the area of cross section at

A. mid-section

B. root of the thread

C. difference of {A} and {B}

D. None of these

Q.79 For a cantilever beam of length L built in at the support and restrained against torsion at the free end the effective projecting length l is

A. l = 0.7L   **B.** l = 0.75L

C. l = 0.85L   **D.** l = 0.5L

Q.80 The greatest gauge of long rivets should not exceed

A. 2d   **B.** 4d   **C.** 6d   **D.** 8d

Q.81 The effective length of a compression member of length L, held in position and restrained in direction at both ends is

A. L   **B.** 0.67L   **C.** 0.85L   **D.** 1.5L

Q.82 The Indian standard code which deals with steel structures is

A. IS : 875   **B.** IS : 800   **C.** IS : 456   **D.** IS : 1893

Q.83 Stiffeners are used in a plate girder

A. to reduce the compressive stress

B. to reduce the shear stress

C. to take the bearing stress

D. to avoid bulking of web plate

Q.84 Maximum permissible slenderness ratio of a member normally acting as a tie in a roof truss is

A. 180   **B.** 20   **C.** 250   **D.** 350

Q.85 The state of the soil when plants fail to extract, sufficint water for their requirements is

A. maximum saturated point

B. permanent wilting point

C. ultimate utilisation point

D. None of these

Q.86 For standing crops in undulating sandy fields, the best method of irrigation is

A. sprinkler irrigation   **B.** free flooding

C. check method   **D.** furrow method

Q.87 Annual rent is generally fixed at

A. 1% to 2% of value of building

B. 2% to 5% of value of building

C. 5% to 10% of value of building

D. 10% to 25% of value of building

Q.88 Annual financial statement of the anticipated receipts and expenditures is called

A. balance sheet

B. financial statement

C. budget

D. expenditure receipt statement

Q.89 The estimated quantity of cement required in cement mortar (1 : 6) per cubic metre will be

A. 5.6 bags   **B.** 4.8 bags   **C.** 8 bags   **D.** 3 bags

Q.90 The full width of land acquired before finalizing a highway, alignment is known

A. width of formation   **B.** right of way

C. carriage way   **D.** roadway

Q.91 If C is basic capacity per lane, V is velocity in km/hour, S is stopping distance plus length of the vehicles in metres, the formula is applicable to

A. district roads

B. two lane roads

C. 2 lane roads in 1 direction

D. None of these

Q.92 Along high ways confirmatory route markers are generally fixed

A. before the crossing on the left side

B. after the crossing on the left side

C. before the crossing on the right side

D. after the crossing on the right side

Q.93 The weaving length of a roadway is the distance

A. between the channelizing islands

B. equal to half circumference

C. equal to total width of adjoining radial roads

D. equal to diameter of rotary

Q.94 The minimum cross fall of shoulders is kept

A. 0.5 %　　**B.** 1.0 %　　**C.** 1.5 %　　**D.** 3 %

Q.95 At yield point of a test piece, the material

A. obeys Hooke's law

B. behaves in an elastic manner

C. regains its original shape on removal of the load

D. undergoes plastic deformation

Q.96 Pick up the item of work not included in the plinth area estimate

A. Wall thickness　　　　**B.** Room area

C. Verandah area　　　　**D.** Courtyard area

Q.97 The floor area includes the area of the balcony up to

A. 100 %　　**B.** 75 %　　**C.** 50 %　　**D.** 25 %

Q.98 While estimating the qualities for the construction of a building the correct metric unit is

A. Metre for length

B. Cubic metre for area

C. square metres for volume

D. litre for capacity

Q.99 If B is the width of formation d is the height of the embankment, side slope S : 1, for a highway with no transverse slope, the area of cross-section is

A. B ÷ d + Sd　　　　**B.** Bd + Sd^2

C. B × d - Sd$^{1/2}$　　**D.** 1/2 (Bd + Sd^2)

Q.100 The correct prismoidal formula for volume is

A. $\dfrac{D}{3}\left[first\ area\ +\ last\ area\ +\ \Sigma Even\ area\ +\ 2\Sigma odd\ areas\right]$

B. $\dfrac{D}{3}\left[first\ area\ +\ last\ area\ +\ 4\ \Sigma Even\ area\ +\ 2\Sigma odd\ areas\right]$

C. $\dfrac{D}{3}\left[first\ area\ +\ last\ area\ +\ 2\ \Sigma Even\ area\ +\ 4\ \Sigma odd\ areas\right]$

D. $\dfrac{D}{6}\left[first\ area\ +\ last\ area\ +\ 2\ \Sigma Even\ area\ +\ 4\ \Sigma odd\ areas\right]$

Q.101 The radius of Mohr's circle for two unlike principal stresses of magnitude p is

A. p　　　　　　**B.** p/2

C. p/4　　　　　**D.** none of these

Q.102 The modulus of resilience is

A. the maximum energy stored at elastic limit

B. the maximum strain energy stored at elastic limit per unit volume

C. strain energy per unit area

D. None of these

Q.103 Euler's formula is not valid for mild steel column when slenderness ratio is

A. more than 80　　　**B.** more than 120

C. less than 80　　　**D.** more than 30

Q.104 A short column of external diameter D and internal diameter d, is subjected to load W, with an eccentricity 'e' causing zero stress at an extreme fibre. Then the value of 'e' must be

A. $\dfrac{D^2+ d^2}{8\pi D}$　　**B.** $\dfrac{D^2+ d^2}{8D}$　　**C.** $\dfrac{D^2- d^2}{8D}$　　**D.** $\dfrac{D^3- d^3}{8D^2}$

Q.105 List I
(Loaded member)

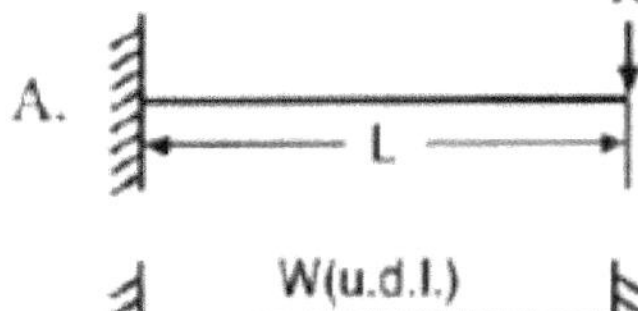

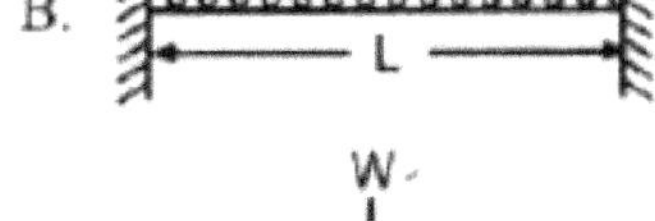

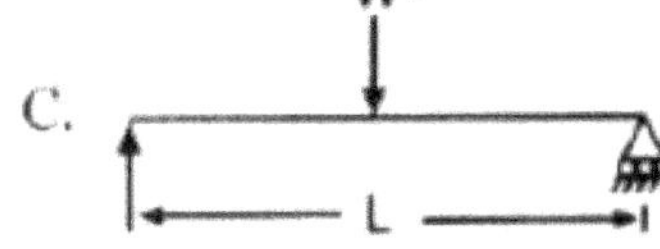

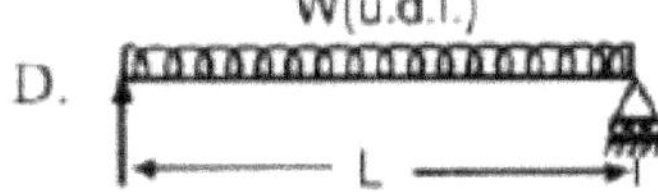

List II
(Maximum deflection)

1. $\dfrac{WL^3}{8EI}$

2. $\dfrac{WL^3}{48EI}$

3. $\dfrac{WL^3}{3EI}$

4. $\dfrac{5WL^3}{384EI}$

A. 3   1   2   4   **B.** 1   2   3   4

C. 2   3   4   1   **D.** 4   2   3   1

Q.106 In a saturated soil deposit having a density 22 kN/m³ the effective normal stress on a horizontal plane at 5m depth will be

A. 22 kN/m³   **B.** 50 kN/m³

C. 60 kN/m³   **D.** 110 kN/m³

Q.107 Permeability of soil varies

A. Inversely as square of grain size

B. Inversely as grain size

C. as grain size

D. Square of grain size

Q.108 The type of foundation suitable for under water structures is

A. Cast in situ concrete piles

B. Continuous footing

C. Pier foundation

D. Stepped foundation

Q.109 It is essential to known in machine foundation design

A. Natural frequency

B. Forced frequency

C. Damped frequency

D. Undamped frequency

Q.110 The ultimate bearing capacity of a surface strip footing on clay, according to Terzaghi's theory is

A. 5.7c   **B.** 5.14c   **C.** $q_u B$ **D.** 9c

Q.111 The longitudinal shearing stresses acting on the surface between the steel and concrete are called

A. compressive stresses

B. tensile stresses

C. bond stresses

D. none of the above

Q.112 In the limit state design of concrete structure, the strain distribution is assumed to be

A. linear

B. non linear

C. Parabolic

D. Parabolic and rectangular

Q.113 The purpose of lateral ties in short RC columns is to

A. avoid buckling of longitudinal bars

B. facilitate construction

C. facilitate compaction of concrete

D. Increase the load carrying capacity of the columns

Q.114 In a doubly reinforced beam the maximum shear stress occurs

A. along the centroid

B. along the neutral axis

C. on planes between neutral axis and the compressive reinforcement

D. on planes between neutral axis and the tensile reinforcement

Q.115 The ratio, width of rib to depth of rib, for T-beam is generally kept as

A. 1/4 to 1/3   **B.** 1/3 to 2/3

C. 1/2 to 3/4   **D.** 2/3 to 7/8

Q.116 For a given grade of steel, the limiting renforcement index for a singly reinforced beam is proprtional to

A. f_{ck} **B.** f_y **C.** f_y/f_{ck} **D.** f_{ck}/f_y

Q.117 Minimum percentage area of HYSD reinforcement in a 150 mm thick water tank wall is

A. 0.16   **B.** 0.16   **C.** 0.23   **D.** 0.24

Q.118 Deflection's can be controlled by using the appropriate

A. aspect ratio   **B.** modular ratio

C. span/depth ratio   **D.** water cement ratio

Q.119 As per the assumption made in moment distribution method, all the joints of a frame are

A. hinged   **B.** rigidly clamped

C. rigidly fixed   **D.** flexible

Q.120 Generally for tendons, the high tensile steel reinforcement used are of diameter

A. 3 mm to 5 mm   **B.** 5 mm to 8 mm

C. 5 to 10 mm   **D.** 10 mm to 20 mm

Q.121 Anticreep bearing plates are provided on

A. Bridges

B. Joints

C. Both sides of sleepers

D. All of the above

Q.122 Parking lanes are provided on

A. Urban roads   **B.** National highways

C. Major district road   **D.** State highway

Q.123 The width of bay on a concrete road is generally taken as

A. $> 4.52\ m$ **B.** $< 4.5\ m$

C. 3 to 4 m   **D.** 2 to 3 m

Q.124 In a parabolic vertical curve the rising grade g_1 = + 0.8% and the falling grade g_2 = 0.7%. The rate of change of grade is 0.05 per chain. The length of the vertical curve is

A. 30 chains   **B.** 40 chains

C. 50 chains   **D.** 60 chains

Q.125 Which of the following causes travelling in bituminous

A. Use of soft bitumen

B. excessive bitumen content

C. Low bitumen content

D. Use of open graded aggregates

// Smart Answer Sheet //

Correct Percentage of students who answered correctly.　**Skipped** Percentage of students who skipped.

Q.	Ans.	Correct / Skipped
1	A	80.06 % / 11.87 %
2	A	86.46 % / 11.61 %
3	C	78.2 % / 12.88 %
4	B	82.5 % / 16.85 %
5	C	85.28 % / 11.18 %
6	D	82.03 % / 14.95 %
7	B	79.6 % / 20.34 %
8	C	77.7 % / 10.39 %
9	B	83.52 % / 12.7 %
10	C	84.51 % / 13.64 %
11	B	80.55 % / 18.85 %
12	D	81.64 % / 14.72 %
13	C	81.13 % / 10.02 %
14	C	83.86 % / 15.48 %
15	D	85.22 % / 12.36 %
16	A	79.48 % / 16.52 %
17	D	81.67 % / 14.38 %
18	D	80.54 % / 17.24 %
19	B	79.04 % / 10.11 %
20	C	89.37 % / 10.5 %
21	D	85.47 % / 10.71 %
22	C	89.82 % / 10.05 %
23	C	88.57 % / 11.15 %
24	B	76.08 % / 22.94 %
25	B	76.63 % / 14.95 %
26	D	85.38 % / 14.48 %
27	B	89.33 % / 10.05 %
28	D	80.39 % / 12.3 %
29	C	85.07 % / 12.22 %
30	A	78.99 % / 16.3 %
31	B	82.23 % / 15.88 %
32	B	84.58 % / 11.31 %
33	D	83.31 % / 15.04 %
34	A	88.29 % / 11.16 %
35	A	79.66 % / 16.46 %
36	A	89.83 % / 10.11 %
37	D	84.61 % / 13.42 %
38	B	79.85 % / 18.48 %
39	D	83.22 % / 12.26 %
40	D	81.35 % / 11.64 %
41	A	77.17 % / 11.15 %
42	D	81.57 % / 18.0 %
43	D	88.95 % / 10.67 %
44	B	87.77 % / 11.45 %
45	A	83.1 % / 11.94 %
46	C	82.28 % / 10.41 %
47	D	85.2 % / 12.0 %
48	C	76.44 % / 17.74 %
49	A	87.62 % / 10.16 %
50	D	87.34 % / 12.5 %
51	D	85.87 % / 12.95 %
52	B	81.43 % / 15.58 %
53	C	88.07 % / 11.48 %
54	A	82.53 % / 10.27 %
55	D	84.09 % / 15.13 %
56	A	89.55 % / 10.07 %
57	A	89.62 % / 10.1 %
58	D	86.32 % / 11.76 %
59	D	77.98 % / 21.61 %
60	D	78.12 % / 13.08 %
61	B	83.82 % / 10.73 %
62	B	76.98 % / 18.47 %
63	A	76.34 % / 10.46 %
64	A	88.07 % / 11.42 %
65	C	89.77 % / 10.11 %
66	A	86.76 % / 12.62 %
67	A	78.94 % / 15.58 %
68	D	79.58 % / 15.92 %
69	D	87.75 % / 12.08 %
70	C	88.23 % / 10.22 %
71	B	78.62 % / 15.63 %
72	C	77.64 % / 13.38 %
73	A	78.62 % / 16.04 %
74	C	79.8 % / 19.97 %
75	B	79.24 % / 18.15 %
76	B	84.61 % / 11.45 %
77	B	87.31 % / 10.16 %
78	B	79.33 % / 12.09 %
79	B	88.44 % / 10.76 %
80	D	79.45 % / 18.58 %

Q.	Ans.	Correct / Skipped	Q.	Ans.	Correct / Skipped	Q.	Ans.	Correct / Skipped	Q.	Ans.	Correct / Skipped	Q.	Ans.	Correct / Skipped
81	B	88.08 % / 10.64 %	90	B	84.67 % / 15.18 %	99	B	85.13 % / 13.71 %	108	C	86.66 % / 11.53 %	117	C	82.77 % / 16.88 %
82	B	79.31 % / 11.96 %	91	C	87.27 % / 12.72 %	100	B	81.78 % / 17.36 %	109	A	83.96 % / 13.46 %	118	C	80.66 % / 11.7 %
83	D	76.43 % / 13.14 %	92	B	77.68 % / 12.31 %	101	A	89.21 % / 10.54 %	110	A	88.21 % / 10.82 %	119	B	78.59 % / 15.05 %
84	D	79.15 % / 12.39 %	93	A	81.76 % / 15.79 %	102	B	83.32 % / 12.89 %	111	C	84.27 % / 11.15 %	120	B	82.83 % / 12.49 %
85	D	89.14 % / 10.71 %	94	D	89.04 % / 10.78 %	103	C	77.26 % / 18.6 %	112	D	76.56 % / 13.46 %	121	C	78.38 % / 18.68 %
86	A	82.22 % / 12.33 %	95	D	80.89 % / 13.16 %	104	B	79.23 % / 14.03 %	113	A	82.48 % / 13.87 %	122	A	80.51 % / 13.11 %
87	C	81.32 % / 17.38 %	96	D	78.1 % / 10.27 %	105	A	89.25 % / 10.74 %	114	D	81.22 % / 11.29 %	123	B	85.33 % / 12.42 %
88	D	76.63 % / 20.18 %	97	C	79.33 % / 12.82 %	106	C	84.63 % / 10.56 %	115	B	86.94 % / 11.41 %	124	A	88.53 % / 10.43 %
89	A	79.26 % / 19.4 %	98	D	87.15 % / 11.47 %	107	D	85.56 % / 12.57 %	116	D	83.99 % / 15.22 %	125	D	84.85 % / 13.78 %

//Hints and Solutions//

1. Hoop stress $= \dfrac{pd}{2t} = \dfrac{700 \times 10^3 \times 2 \times 0.5}{2 \times 25 \times 10^{-3}}$

$= 14$ MPa

2. $v = v_s\, n$ is the relations between discharge velocity and seepage velocity through the soil sample.

3. $I_P = W_L - W_P = 0.6 - 0.35 = 0.25$

$$I_L = \frac{\omega - \omega_P}{I_P} = \frac{0.5 - 0.35}{0.25} = 0.6$$

4. $G_M = G_S(1-n) = G_S/(1+e)$

$e = G_S/G_M - 1$

$= 2.7/1.5 - 1 = 1$

5. Average Velocity $= \dfrac{2}{3} \times 2 = \dfrac{4}{3}\ m/s$

Discharge per unit width

$$= \frac{4}{3} \times 0.1 = 0.13\ m^3/sm$$

6. $P = \dfrac{4\sigma}{d}$

Here $\sigma = 0.0737$ N/m

$d = 0.0001$ m

$$P = \frac{4 \times 0.0737}{0.001} = 0.3\ KN/m^2$$

7. Shrinkage factor $= \dfrac{90}{100} = 0.9$

Revised side = Original scale $\times$ reduction factor/ Shrinkage

factor $= \dfrac{1}{1000} \times 0.9 = \dfrac{1}{1111.11}$

8. Radius = 1719 / Degree of Curve

$= 1719 / 5^0\ 30'$

$= 312.54$ m

9. Kaolin is chemically classified as argillaceous rock.

10. The kiln which may work throughout the year, is Hoffman's kiln.

11. Lime concrete is generally used for flooring at ground level.

12. The minimum percentage of silica, alumina and derric oxide in lime for white washing is zero.

13. Due to attack of dry rot, the timber feduces to powder.

14. The most fire resistant paints are asbestos paints.

15. Gypsum, Acid resistant cement and Quick lime are an air binding material.

16. Sulphate resisting cement.

17. Bitumen completely dissolves in Carbon bisulphide, Chloroform and Benzol.

18. The maximum permissible differential settlement, in case of foundations in clayey soil is usually limited to 40 mm.

19. The process of working a flat for the finishing coat, is known floating.

20. According to National Building Code the hydrants in water mains is provided at minimum interval of 75 m.

21. The limiting length of an offset does not depend upon indefinite features to be surveyed.

22. For the construction of highway (or railway) longitudinal sections and cross sections are required.

23. The direction of steepest slope on a contour is at right angles to the contour.

24. Magnetic declination at any place does'n remain constant.

25. With usual notations, the expression V_2/gR represents centrifugal ratio.

26. For indirect ranging, number of ranging rods required, is 4.

27. Bergchrund is a topograhical feature in water bodies.

28. The distance between the point of intersection of an upgrade + $g_1\%$ and downgrade $g_2\%$ and the highest point of the vertical curve of length L, is $\dfrac{L(g_1 - g_2)}{800}$

29. The Huygen's telescope eye piece is aplanatic and achromatic.

30. The probable error of the adjusted bearing at the middle is $\dfrac{1}{2} r\sqrt{n}$

31. A retarding force on a body does not retard the motion of the body.

32. The C.G. of a hemisphere from its base measured along the vertical radius is at a distance of 3R / 8.

33. Power developed by a torque are $2\pi NT$ kg m/min , $2\pi NT/4500$ h.p. and $2\pi NT/600$ watts.

34. The weakest section of a diamond riveting is the section first row passes through.

35. The maximum resistance against rotation is offered by the weld at a point most distant.

36. Hooke's law states that stress and strain are directly proportional.

37. An arch may be subjected to thrust, shear force and bending moment.

38. The resistance offered by a loaded section of a bar per unit area is called strain.

39. Mercury is generally used in barometers because its vaour pressure is practically zero and the height of the barometer will be less.

40. Hydraulic grade line may be above or below the centre line of conduit.

41. Chezy's constant $C = \dfrac{157.6}{1.81+\frac{K}{\sqrt{M}}}$ is suggested by Bazin.

42. Flow of water in pipes of diameter more than 3 metres can be measured by rotameter.

43. Non-over flow double curvature concrete arch, is provided in Iddiki dam.

44. The value closure is said to be sudden if $t < 2L/C$.

45. for critical depth of flow of water in open channels, f_c the specific energy must be minimum.

46. Specific energy of a flowing fluid per unit weight is $\dfrac{V^2}{2g} + h$.

47. The run off a drainage basin is Precipitation – ground water accretion – Initial recharge.

48. The drop man holes are generally provided in sewers for hilly town ships.

49. Primary treatment of sewage consists of removal of large suspended organic solids.

50. Sulphurdioxide gas is most significant as air pollutant.

51. The most efficient method of BOD removal, is aerated lagoon.

52. The inventor of the term soil mechanics, was Dr. Karl Terzaghi.

53. A pycnometer is used to determine water content.

54. The plasticity index is the numerical difference between liquid limit and plastic limit.

55. The change of moisture content of soils, changes the value of the angle of repose, amount of compaction required and cohesive strength of soil.

56. The capillary rise of water depends upon the force responsible.

57. A failure wedge develops if a retaining wall moves away from the backfill.

58. To hydrate 500 kg cement fully, water needed is 130 kg.

59. The commercial name of white and coloured cement in India is Colocrete, Rainbow cement and Silvicrete.

60. The datum temperature for maturity by Plowman is -11.7^0 C.

61. If X, Y and Z are the fineness modulli of coarse, fine and combined aggregates, the percentage (P) of fine aggregates to combined aggregates, is $P = \dfrac{X-Z}{Z-Y} \times 100$

62. While compacting the concrete by a mechanical vibrator, the slump should not exceed 5.0 cm.

63. Common sugar can be suitably used to delay the setting time of concrete.

64. No shrinkage occurs if the concrete is placed in a relative humidity of 100 percent.

65. (A) C₃ S 　　　　　　4. Alite

(B) C₂ S 　　　　　　3. Belite

(C) C₃ A 　　　　　　1. Celite

(D) C₄ AF 　　　　　　2. Fehte

66. The maximum shear stress (q) in concrete of a reinforced cement concrete beam is Shear force / Lever arm × Width.

67. The radius of a bar bend to form a hook, should not be less than twice the diameter.

68. For initial estimate for a beam design the width is assumed 1/30th of span.

69. The maximum diameter of a bar used in a ribbed slab, is 22 mm.

70. A per IS : 1343, total shrinkage for a pretensioned beam is 3.0×10^{-4}.

71. An RCC roof slab is designed as a two way slab if the ratio of spans in two directions is less than 2.

72. Steel beam theory is used for doubly reinforced beams ignoring compressive stress in concrete.

73. Design of RCC cantilever beams is based on the resultant force at fixed end.

74. Failure of a reinforced concrete beam occurs as soon as the concrete strain in compression reaches 0.0035.

75. Yielding of steel in singly reinforced beam occurs in under reinforced beam.

76. Rolled steel beams are designated by Indian standard series and its depth of section and weight per metre.

77. Maximum permissible slenderness ratio of compression members which carry dead and superimposed load, is 250.

78. The net area of round bars to resist the tension is the area of cross section at root of the thread.

79. For a cantilever beam of length L built in at the support and restrained against torsion at the free end the effective projecting length l is l = 0.75L .

80. The greatest gauge of long rivets should not exceed 8d.

81. The effective length of a compression member of length L, held in position and restrained in direction at both ends is 0.67L.

82. The Indian standard code which deals with steel structures is IS : 800 .

83. Stiffeners are used in a plate girder to avoid bulking of web plate.

84. Maximum permissible slenderness ratio of a member normally acting as a tie in a roof truss is 350.

85. The state of the soil when plants fail to extract, sufficint water for their requirements is maximum saturated point, permanent wilting point and ultimate utilisation point.

86. For standing crops in undulating sandy fields, the best method of irrigation is sprinkler irrigation.

87. Annual rent is generally fixed at 5% to 10% of value of building.

88. Annual financial statement of the anticipated receipts and expenditures is called expenditure receipt statement.

89. The estimated quantity of cement required in cement mortar (1 : 6) per cubic metre will be 5.6 bags.

90. The full width of land acquired before finalizing a highway, alignment is known right of way.

91. If C is basic capacity per lane, V is velocity in km/hour, S is stopping distance plus length of the vehicles in metres, the formula is applicable to 2 lane roads in 1 direction.

92. Along high ways confirmatory route markers are generally fixed after the crossing on the left side.

93. The weaving length of a roadway is the distance between the channelizing islands .

94. The minimum cross fall of shoulders is kept 3 % .

95. At yield point of a test piece, the material undergoes plastic deformation .

96. Pick up the item of work not included in the plinth area estimate courtyard area .

97. The floor area includes the area of the balcony up to 50 % .

98. While estimating the qualities for the construction of a building the correct metric unit is litre for capacity .

99. If B is the width of formation d is the height of the embankment, side slope S : 1, for a highway with no transverse slope, the area of cross-section is Bd + Sd^2 .

100. The correct prismoidal formula for volume

$$\frac{D/3}{\left[first\ area\ +\ last\ area\ +\ 4\ \Sigma Even\ area\ +\ 2\Sigma od d\ areas\right]}$$

is

101. The radius of Mohr's circle for two unlike principal stresses of magnitude p is p

102. The modulus of resilience is the maximum strain energy stored at elastic limit per unit volume.

103. Euler's formula is not valid for mild steel column when slenderness ratio is less than 80.

104. A short column of external diameter D and internal diameter d, is subjected to load W, with an eccentricity 'e' causing zero stress at an extreme fibre. Then the value of 'e' must be $\dfrac{D^2 + d^2}{8D}$

105. option a is right option.

106. In a saturated soil deposit having a density 22 kN/m^3 the effective normal stress on a horizontal plane at 5m depth will be 60 kN/m^3

107. Permeability of soil varies Square of grain size.

108. The type of foundation suitable for under water structures is Pier foundation.

109. It is essential to known in machine foundation design Natural frequency.

110. The ultimate bearing capacity of a surface strip footing on clay, according to Terzaghi's theory is 5.7c.

111. The longitudinal shearing stresses acting on the surface between the steel and concrete are called bond stresses.

112. In the limit state design of concrete structure, the strain distribution is assumed to be Parabolic and rectangular.

113. The purpose of lateral ties in short RC columns is to avoid buckling of longitudinal bars.

114. In a doubly reinforced beam the maximum shear stress occurs on planes between neutral axis and the tensile reinforcement.

115. The ratio, width of rib to depth of rib, for T-beam is generally kept as 1/3 to 2/3

116. For a given grade of steel, the limiting renforcement index for a singly reinforced beam is proprtional to f_{ck}/f_y

117. Minimum percentage area of HYSD reinforcement in a 150 mm thick water tank wall is 0.23.

118. Deflection's can be controlled by using the appropriate span/depth ratio.

119. As per the assumption made in moment distribution method, all the joints of a frame are rigidly clamped.

120. Generally for tendons, the high tensile steel reinforcement used are of diameter 5 mm to 8 mm.

121. Anticreep bearing plates are provided on Both sides of sleepers.

122. Parking lanes are provided on Urban roads.

123. The width of bay on a concrete road is generally taken as $< 4.5\ m$

124.
$$L = \frac{(g_1 - g_2)\%}{r\%}$$
$$= \frac{(0.8 + 0.7)}{0.05}$$
$$= \frac{1.5}{0.05}$$
$$= \frac{150}{5} = 30$$

125. Use of open graded aggregates ceses travelling in bituminous.

// Notes //

// Notes //